MOSCOW AND CHINESE COMMUNISTS

Moscow and Chinese Communists

SECOND EDITION

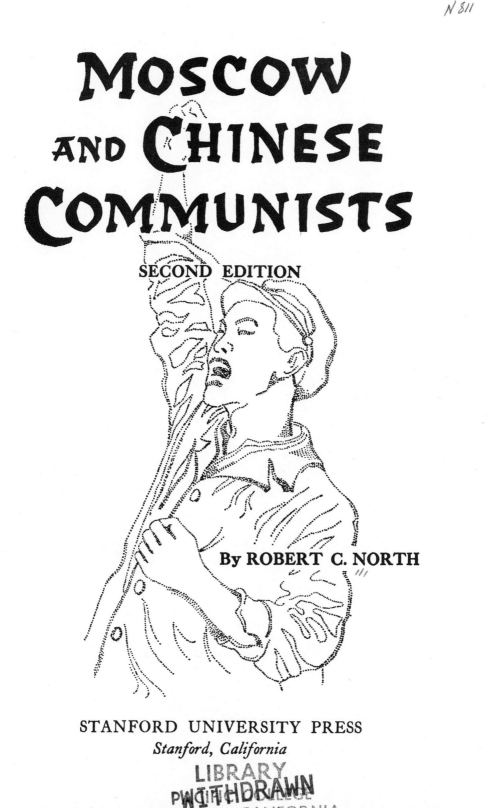

By ROBERT C. NORTH

STANFORD UNIVERSITY PRESS

Stanford, California

PREFACE TO THE SECOND EDITION

This book seeks to outline the beginnings of the Chinese Communist movement, its relations with Moscow, the rise of Mao Tse-tung, the establishment of the People's Republic of China, and the course of Sino-Soviet relations over the succeeding decade.

When the first edition of the book was published in 1953, there were serious gaps in our knowledge about Chinese Communist Party origins, the Kiangsi and Yenan periods of development, and the details of Mao Tse-tung's rise to power within the movement. As this revised edition goes to press nearly a decade later, it is discouraging to note that most of these gaps are as wide as ever.

It is frequently overlooked that the political institutions of the People's Republic had a long and important history before the establishment of Chinese Communist sovereignty over the Mainland in 1949. In Kiangsi, during the early 1930's, and in Yenan later on, the Chinese Communist regime governed territory and populations as large as many European states. It was in those early years that the institutional theory and practice of the People's Republic sank their roots.

Yet over the last decade incredibly little research or writing has been done on the history and politics of the Kiangsi and Yenan periods of the Chinese Communist movement. For some years Professor Hsiao Tso-liang has undertaken basic, pioneering work in the collection and analysis of primary documents from the Kiangsi period, but at no point have his labors received the attention or the support they deserve. Meanwhile, to this date, we do not have a single standard monograph devoted to the Kiangsi period, nor is there much on the Yenan period.

A persistent myth has it that basic documents on the development of the Chinese Communist movement are not available. In fact, of course, there resides in the Hoover Institution at Stanford University a vast store of primary documentation almost untouched, and there are other important repositories elsewhere. In the late 1940's and early 1950's Western scholars wrote a number of general monographs about the course of Chinese Communist development, and in recent years several books have appeared on the Chinese People's Republic. In general, however, one is hard put to account for the inhibition—psychological or other—which seems to have blocked penetrating research into Chinese Communist institutions and history during several of the most formative and crucial years. The failure of Western scholarship to undertake, encourage, and support dispassionate and disciplined studies of Chinese communism on a wider scale and more sustained basis is in itself a phenomenon worthy of sober investigation.

This revised edition makes no attempt to fill these gaps. A number of errors in the original text have been corrected, and footnotes have been added here and there to cite research or points of view which seem pertinent but which were not available at the time of the first writing. Beyond this, the revised edition presents an account of broad developments during the first decade or so of the People's Republic and a discussion of differences in policy, doctrine, and interest between the Moscow and Peking regimes.

The writing of the first edition was made possible by funds granted by the Ford Foundation. That foundation is not, however, the author, owner, publisher, or proprietor of this publication and is not to be understood as approving by virtue of its grant any of the statements made or views expressed.

In the preparation of the revised edition the author is particularly indebted to Mrs. Helen Grace for secretarial and research assistance well beyond the bounds of duty.

R.C.N.

Department of Political Science
Stanford University
September 15, 1962

PREFACE TO THE FIRST EDITION

This book seeks to outline the beginnings of the Chinese Communist movement, the course of its relations with Moscow, the rise of Mao Tse-tung, and the implications of the People's Republic. The author has aimed to be accurate and objective, but he remains fully aware that much of his data is incomplete and many of his interpretations and conclusions wholly tentative. Gathering material about Moscow and the Chinese Communists is something like probing about in a black and seemingly bottomless pit, and whatever evidence is drawn out and put together now will be subject to new weighing and fresh analysis for years to come. Documents seized in various raids on Soviet diplomatic premises, though bearing every earmark of Communist origin, await systematic appraisal. Men like M. N. Roy and Chang Kuo-t'ao have provided many important links, but, lacking precise records, they would be among the first to caution that their memories are not infallible.

Bit by bit, however, the story emerges, and a growing number of scholars are devoting themselves to problems that still remain. An incomplete listing of these specialists and their work in progress appears in the Bibliography. During the next few years their findings will fill many gaps and support or modify hypotheses so far put forward.

In preparing this work, the author has made constant referrals to the materials, research, and critical advice of persons in the same or related fields, and in this respect he owes special debts of gratitude to Harold H. Fisher, Xenia Joukoff Eudin, John K. Fairbank, Benjamin Schwartz, K. C. Chao, Conrad Brandt, Harold Isaacs, Charles McLane, Allen S. Whiting, Richard Sorich, Howard Boorman, Olga Gankin, Mary Wright, Arthur Wright, and C. Martin Wilbur. He is also deeply grateful to Carl Spaeth, Wen-shun Chi, P. F. Tao, George Schueller, Philip McLean, Ruth Perry, Charlotte Cole, Arline Paul, Hannah Green, and numerous others. To Harold H. Fisher and C. Easton Rothwell he is indebted for long years of unwavering support, and to Woesha C. North for encouragement and inspiration. For all errors of omission and commission, however, the author himself is solely responsible.

The writing of the book was made possible by funds granted by the Ford Foundation. That foundation is not, however, the author, owner, publisher, or proprietor of this publication and is not to be understood as approving by virtue of its grant any of the statements made or views expressed therein. But as the book goes to press, the author wishes to record his appreciation for this assistance and for the friendly interest which the foundation has taken in his work.

ROBERT C. NORTH

Hoover Institute and Library
Stanford, California
September 15, 1953

CONTENTS

CHAPTER I

PROGRAM FOR REVOLT

A NEW GOVERNMENT PROCLAIMED

Nearly two hundred thousand men, women, and children of Peking jammed their way into a great city square on October 1, 1949, to hear the new government proclaimed and to see the marching soldiers. Before the gate of the former imperial palace there stood a reviewing stand with a huge picture of Mao Tse-tung fastened to the side. There was a stir among the people, excitement after all the waiting, and the Communist leader himself appeared upon the reviewing stand. "The people throughout China have been plunged into bitter sufferings and tribulations . . . ," he declared. "However, our People's Liberation Army . . . has eliminated the reactionary troops and overthrown the reactionary rule of the Nationalist Government . . . The Central People's Government Council of the People's Republic of China took office today in this capital . . ."

Following the proclamation Chu Teh, head of the Chinese Communist armed forces, took his place at the side of Mao, and column after column of civilian groups and soldiers began their march past the reviewing stand—infantry units, many of them armed with American weapons, an armored division, artillery, units of the new navy—all these and a student drum corps, dramatic troupes, dance teams performing the traditional *yanko*—three hundred thousand disciplined human beings celebrating the establishment of a government new in the history of Asia.

Already, on the previous day, Mao Tse-tung had been elected chairman of the central government of the People's Republic of China which, according to an official declaration, would "unite with all peace- and freedom-loving countries, nations and peoples, first of all the Soviet Union . . ."[1]

In a Common Program the new government pledged fundamental freedoms to the Chinese people—freedom of thought, speech, publication, assembly, correspondence, domicile, religion; the right to hold processions and demonstrations. In many quarters there was great rejoicing, but close observers knew from earlier official statements that the People's Republic, like its ally the Soviet Union, intended

---

[1] "Declaration of the People's Political Consultative Conference," *China Digest* (Hong Kong), Supplement, VII, No. 1, 2.

to deny these rights and freedoms to certain classes of people to which it was bitterly antagonistic.

With the proclamation of the new government, cities in Communist-controlled China took up a celebration scheduled to last until October 10, the Double Tenth, or anniversary of the Chinese revolution of 1911. Red stars and red bunting graced the house fronts; red banners and red flags of the new government flowed from their staffs. City streets echoed with the ruffle and clatter of drums and gongs and cymbals. Schoolgirls in snood raincoats marched through the downpour, singing revolutionary songs. Radios blared the "March of the Volunteers," selected as the new national anthem.

On October 2, 1949, the USSR announced its decision to establish diplomatic relations with the People's Republic of China; within the next few days Bulgaria, Romania, the Communist government in North Korea, Czechoslovakia, Hungary, Poland, and Mongolia recognized the new Chinese government. In Peking it was announced that slogans for celebrating the formation of the People's Republic would include: "Unite with the Nations of the World Treating Us on a Footing of Equality!" "Support Sino-Soviet Co-operation!" And newspapers in Moscow exulted over the fact that Communist victories in China had fulfilled long-standing Leninist and Stalinist prophecies of Bolshevik success in leading the Chinese revolution.[2]

Thoughtful Western observers dared not underestimate the critical nature of Communist successes in China. The expulsion of Chiang Kai-shek from the mainland and the founding of the Chinese People's Republic had placed Mao Tse-tung and his followers in a position that was unique within the world Communist movement. Their sovereignty included an area more than seven times greater than all the satellites taken together and a population nearly two and a half times that of the Soviet Union itself.[3] With more than 3 million members in 1949, the Chinese Communist party was second in size only to that of the Soviet Union,[4] and its generals controlled a victorious army of a reported 4 million regulars.[5] This army had driven out of China proper a government with recognized great power standing, and Communist leaders claimed a like status for the Chinese People's Republic.

What concerned Westerners even more than the emergence of a

[2] Editorial, *Pravda*, October 5, 1949. For an English translation, see *Soviet Press Translations*, November 15, 1949, p. 612.

[3] These conclusions are based upon statistics provided by the *World Almanac and Book of Facts for 1951*.

[4] By 1951 the Chinese Communist party reported a membership of 5,800,000.

[5] *Jen-min shou-ts'e, 1950* (People's Handbook of 1950) (Shanghai, 1950), Section F, p. 1.

powerful Communist China was the seemingly inevitable development of a Sino-Soviet bloc. If Mao Tse-tung's protestations of unity with the USSR are founded on a sound relationship, the Western world will have to take into account a Communist empire of frightening dimensions. Considered together, Soviet Russia and its satellites and China with its outlying territories cover roughly one-fifth of the earth's land surface and embrace nearly a third of its peoples.[6] This represents a notable change since the Bolshevik seizure of power in Russia, when the world Communist movement consisted of only scattered and previously ineffective forces. In April 1917 the Russian party had a total of a few thousand members;[7] scarcely one Russian in two hundred was a member.[8] But today, after the passage of a little more than thirty years, the Communist movement, with an estimated membership of more than 20 million,[9] is in control of two great powers which dominate important satellites and keep the West alerted along a vast perimeter from Japan and Korea, through Southeast Asia, India, and the Middle East, and straight across Europe from Greece to Scandinavia.

RESULT OF CODIFIED ACTION

How has this come about? There are many factors involved, most of them complex and interrelated, but among them there is one that is especially important precisely because non-Communists find it difficult to analyze and comprehend. This is the tactical code developed by early Bolsheviks and designed to guide their actions toward other governments and peoples.

These tactics are not like the diplomatic rules and patterns of behavior sanctioned through the years by Western states, although the Communists have adapted even such established procedures to their special needs. These tactics are keen, double-edged, revolutionary principles, worked out largely by men who overthrew the old order in Russia. Once formulated and tested by use, the whole tactical code was written down and incorporated into volumes where it may be studied today.

In the beginning the central aim of those who built the Soviet Union was to bring about an international working-class revolution designed to accomplish the overthrow of capitalism throughout the world and create a new socialist order. It was for this purpose that

---

[6] These estimates are based on figures from S. H. Steinberg (ed.), *The Statesman's Year-Book, 1951* (New York, 1951).

[7] *Pervyi Kongress Kominterna, Mart 1919* (Moscow, 1933), p. 19.

[8] *Ibid.*

[9] *New York Herald Tribune*, May 27, 1947.

Communists from various countries, under Lenin's leadership, organized in 1919 the Third International, or Comintern, which was, in effect, an international general staff for world revolution.

Basing themselves on Marxist theory, Communist leaders expected revolution to break out in economically advanced nations first, and post–World War I Europe exhibited precisely the unrest and confusion which the Bolsheviks hoped to transform into a decisive struggle. But when Communist-led revolts collapsed in Germany and Hungary and failed to materialize elsewhere, Bolshevik leaders found themselves saddled with the problem of ruling Russia, a single Communist state, in a world of capitalist nations largely hostile to it. The problem was more complex than simply that of running a state of the traditional sort, for Soviet Russia was not only a new kind of government and social order; it was also the headquarters and territorial base of the international Communist movement. The Russian Bolsheviks thus found themselves trying to double as legitimate heads of states and as international conspirators seeking to subvert the citizenry of other states and turn them against their respective governments.

While securing their territorial base and making their government function, Russian Communists found it necessary from time to time to make important concessions, both internally and in their foreign policy, in order to survive at all. Early attempts at extreme socialism were temporarily softened in favor of the New Economic Policy of the 'twenties, which in many respects prepared the way for more radical Five-Year Plans of a later day. So, too, the belligerence and scorn which Lenin and his followers exhibited toward the leaders of capitalist states in early days of the Soviet were gradually replaced by a willingness to establish formal relations and even, under certain circumstances, to conclude close alliances.

The Soviet Union joined the League of Nations, which its leaders had despised and scorned, while the conspiratorial Third International withered in importance and finally, in 1943, was officially dissolved. During World War II Soviet representatives in Berlin and London and Washington made deals and pacts with governments which they had once openly threatened to overthrow. Generals, resplendent in epaulets and braid, found themselves ordering Red Army troops into what they had formerly castigated as an "imperialist" war, allying themselves with one set of capitalist nations against another set. This seeming transformation in Soviet attitudes was nowhere more striking than in China, where between 1937 and 1940 the Kremlin granted more than 200 million American dollars' worth of aid—not to the Chinese Communists but to the bitter anti-Communist, Chiang Kai-shek.[10] For a number of years it looked as though the Russian Communists had turned their backs upon their Chinese comrades, and at Yalta in February 1945 the Stalinist government strengthened this impression by guaranteeing continued support of the Chiang regime.[11]

Many Westerners concluded that since Stalin was behaving more and more like a capitalist, he must be growing into one, and their hopes in this direction were reinforced by shrill cries from the followers of Trotsky, who insisted that those holding power in the Kremlin had betrayed communism and its revolutionary program for Russia and the rest of the world. Yet post–World War II developments indicated conclusively that hopes for Stalin turning capitalist or fostering a live-and-let-live policy were utterly without foundation. Stalinist policies in Europe—the enfolding of Romania and Hungary under Russian domination, the part played by Russian and Russian-trained agents in the Czechoslovakian coup, the struggle leading to Tito's breakaway, and similar evidences of belligerence, subversion, and the exercise of untempered power—tended to convince all but disciplined Communists and their most thoroughly indocrinated fellow travelers that the Kremlin not only was dedicated to communizing the West but, even more reprehensible, was determined to do it the Russian way and, wherever necessary, by deception and brute force. Yet, with the death of Stalin, many of the old doubts and bewilderments and hopes for reconciliation came bubbling to the surface again.

Westerners have been even less clear about Communist developments in China. In the early 'twenties few observers knew who the real Communists were; Sun Yat-sen was frequently identified as one, and so, somewhat later, was Chiang Kai-shek. Many Westerners wondered whether the Chinese comrades were really "red," or whether they were indigenous and relatively harmless. For a time while Borodin was in China, the connection with Moscow became more obvious, but then, as Soviet Russians disappeared and as Chinese Communists took refuge underground or in the Hunan and Kiangsi mountains, the old uncertainties were raised again. During World War II Mao Tse-tung and his colleagues were often mistaken for "agrarian reformers" or Jeffersonian democrats of an Oriental cast, and the Kremlin was careful to nurture this misconception.

Events toward the end of World War II and increasingly after V–J Day lifted the Chinese Communists to a level of world-wide controversy. Whether Mao Tse-tung and his colleagues were "real Com-

[10] *China Handbook, 1937–1945* (New York, 1947), p. 167.
[11] "Yalta Agreement on the Kuriles," in *Department of State Bulletin*, XIV (1946), 282.

munists" or not became important to the West in terms of national interests—and perhaps in terms of democratic survival. Between the apologists and those who condemned the whole Chinese revolution as a Soviet Russian plot there developed a spectrum of viewpoints.

The Great Debate over United States Far Eastern policy arose largely from this confusion and controversy. To what degree was the Kremlin dictating Chinese Communist policy? Did Mao Tse-tung's regime enjoy support of the Chinese people, or was it simply propped into place by Moscow? Had Americans in high places "sold Nationalist China down the river" to the Communists? Was China the most effective front on which to strike a crippling blow at world communism? Would an American attack on Chinese soil win the support or enmity of the Chinese people, and would it provoke Russia into an all-out war? Would indigenous elements in the Chinese movement tend to overwhelm Russian influences, or were Mao Tse-tung and his colleagues too deeply committed? Were there possibilities for a Chinese Tito? There were many views, heatedly expressed, but when the excitement had subsided, many Americans felt as bewildered as ever.

There are good reasons why Westerners find it difficult to analyze what has happened in China. The country is far away, on the other side of the world from us; the culture and historical background of the Chinese people are utterly different from our own; economically and technically China, despite generations of cultural development, has existed on a level far below that of the United States; the masses of the Chinese people have grown up in poverty, as contrasted to American plenty. These are all critical factors contributing to American bewilderment, but equally mystifying, perhaps, is the seemingly paradoxical nature of Communist policies, both Russian and Chinese.

Popular misconceptions about communism have tended to change as Bolshevik leaders have shifted their policies. When the hierarchy conducts purges, we like to think that the population is about to rise up. When policy controls are relaxed, the Kremlin has been forced into retreat. When Moscow aids Chiang Kai-shek, the Soviet Union has turned its back on the Chinese Communists. When the Russians denounce Chiang, the Chinese Communists become mere puppets utterly dependent on the Kremlin, and so it goes. What many Westerners fail to comprehend is, first, that within its rigid, dogmatic framework, Communist theory and practice allow considerable, sometimes almost paradoxical, fluidity of action; second, that Communist activities are undertaken on many different planes, some visible, some partially obscured, some revealed only to the innermost core of party faithful, some appearing to obstruct one another; and third, that the

Communist system, contrary to the claims of its proponents, is as fallible as any other bureaucracy, with high-level leaders making crucial errors and with low-level functionaries misinterpreting policy and committing all manner of unforeseeable blunders.

In practical terms Communist fluidity means that Bolshevik leaders are, under proper circumstances, quite capable of resorting to procedures that are inconsistent with Communist principles. Formal and informal alliances have been made with capitalist and even fascist groups; capitalist incentives and capitalist institutions have been used in struggles for the final destruction of capitalism; in Asia today the Communists are championing nationalist movements in order, eventually, to destroy nationalism. To Communists, and equally to those who would oppose communism, the important truth is that the central purpose does not change.

ON VARIOUS LEVELS OF PROCEDURE

All these various kinds and levels of action are difficult to keep track of—even, sometimes, among the Communists themselves. But the picture is still more complicated: Communists see all development, including their own activities, moving through a series of stages, each different from its predecessor and each requiring a separate kind of action. What is good for one stage, therefore, may be utterly wrong for its successor. According to Communist theory, for example, Russia and China are passing through altogether different stages. Hence, there is no simple approach to communism; there is no counteraction that is both simple and effective.

The question arises, then, how can Western leaders—how can citizens of Western nations—analyze Communist actions, especially in countries as complicated as China, and devise democratic programs to meet this totalitarian challenge?

There are many possible approaches, and they should all be investigated. One aspect of Communist theory and practice, much talked about but seldom properly understood, offers a peculiarly direct road into the heart of Communist intentions and Communist political and economic procedures. This is the Bolshevik code of strategy and tactics.

What is meant by Bolshevik strategy and tactics? The terms do not denote military strategy and tactics, but something much broader, something so fundamental that military strategy and tactics take shape as limited aspects of this larger phenomenon. Bolshevik strategy and tactics have been best defined, perhaps, by Stalin himself: *the science of leadership in the class struggle of the working class.*[12]

[12] J. Stalin, *Problems of Leninism* (Foreign Languages Publishing House edition; Moscow, 1940), p. 58.

Enlarging upon his definition, Stalin described strategy as the determination of the direction of the proletariat's main blow against the capitalists at any given stage of the revolution; the elaboration of a corresponding plan for the disposition of revolutionary forces; and the fight to carry out this plan—again, for a given stage of the revolution.[13] Strategy, then, deals with the main forces of the revolution—not just the military forces, but the total of revolutionary peoples—and their reserves. Strategy remains essentially unaltered throughout a given revolutionary stage but changes with the passage of the revolution from one stage to another.[14]

Tactics, on the other hand, are more consistently fluid, being the determination of proletarian lines of conduct for each ebb and flow, each rise or decline of the revolutionary flood. Tactics are concerned, too, with implementing lines of proletarian conduct by replacing action suitable to the ebb with action suitable to the flow; by substituting outdated slogans with new; by constantly adjusting Bolshevik methods of struggle to suit shifting revolutionary conditions.[15]

Once the premises of this operational system have been grasped, once this manual of Bolshevik strategy and tactics has been delineated and digested, the Western observer will be in a better position to judge not only what the Communists want, but how they intend to get it. Many popular Western misconceptions will then be recognized for what they are, and Western governments and their citizens will perhaps be less inclined to behave precisely as the Bolshevik strategists and tacticians expect—and, for Communist purposes—want them to behave.

No single volume could satisfactorily analyze the whole of Bolshevik theory and practice; the subject is too vast. This book seizes upon a single aspect—an exceedingly controversial aspect—of the problem, namely, the strategy and tactics of Soviet relationships with China, and traces it through a series of phases: the early post–World War I years of Russian diplomacy in Asia; the Kuomintang-Communist alliance; the development of mountain soviets; the rise to power of Mao Tse-tung; the emergence of the Chinese Communist movement as a major element in international relations and cold-war diplomacy; and the proclaiming of the Chinese People's Republic as a model for Communist-led revolutions over much of Asia and thence, by logical extension, into Africa.

By the end of the book we shall see in rough outline the program—as Russian and Chinese Communists have projected it—for drawing

13 *Ibid.*, p. 59.
14 *Ibid.*, pp. 60–61.
15 *Ibid.*, p. 61.

the millions of these two continents into a struggle for world Bolshevism and the destruction of Western civilization as we know it. But to understand present-day Communist plans we must first see how modern Bolshevik leaders have depended on the ideas of their forerunners, Karl Marx and V. I. Lenin.

FROM THE THEORY OF TWO CAMPS

Communist plans for China and the rest of Asia are only a part—though an extremely important part—of Communist plans for the world as a whole. But to masters of Bolshevik reasoning, these preparations for earth-wide revolution are not simply the result of secret plotting. On the contrary, Communist leaders see their program as a course of action determined by historical necessity. Irresistible material forces have shaped the world into its present state. The duty of Bolshevik leaders, themselves a part of this development, is to make a "scientific" Marxist-Leninist analysis of the situation and then, through the use of "scientific" Marxist-Leninist dialectical reasoning, to arrive at a scientifically correct plan of action.

One of the clearest Bolshevik analyses published in recent years was presented in 1947 by the late Andrei Zhdanov to the newly established Cominform. It will be remembered that in 1943 the Communist International had been "dissolved"—partly as a Soviet concession to Western allies in World War II, but largely because that particular organizational structure no longer served Kremlin purposes. Shortly after the war, on October 5, 1947, the announcement was made that a Communist Information Bureau had been established by nine of the European Communist parties, including that of the Soviet Union, and that under new conditions this organization was taking over many of the functions previously handled by the Communist International.[16]

In the course of deliberations held "somewhere in Poland," Andrei Zhdanov, then a leading member of the Russian Politburo, made it clear that Kremlin leaders had not altered in any fundamental fashion their concepts of class struggle, their identification of Western foreign policies with an imperialism that is actually all but dead, their faith in the inevitable conflict between capitalist and proletarian worlds, nor their expectations of a Soviet victory.[17]

As World War II receded into the past, Zhdanov described two

---

[16] The text of the official communiqué appears in *The Strategy and Tactics of World Communism* (House Committee on Foreign Affairs, U.S. Congress), Report, Subcommittee No. 5, Supplement I (Washington, 1948), pp. 207–8, hereinafter cited as *Strategy and Tactics*.

[17] The Russian text of this speech is in A. A. Zhdanov, *O Mezhdunarodnom Polozhenii* (Moscow, 1947).

major trends in international policy corresponding to what he called the division of international forces into two major camps: an imperialist (and anti-"democratic") camp, on the one hand, and a "democratic" (and anti-imperialist) camp, on the other.[18]

The principal driving force of the imperialist camp, according to Zhdanov, is the United States, with Great Britain and France in close alliance with it, while the "democratic" camp is based upon the USSR and the "new democracies," and includes countries "that have broken with imperialism and have firmly set foot on the path of democratic development, such as Rumania, Hungary and Finland." In true Communist fashion, Zhdanov saw the imperialist camp enjoying support from all colony-owning countries and from countries politically and economically dependent upon the United States, such as Middle Eastern and South American nations and Nationalist China. The "anti-imperialist" camp, according to Zhdanov, enjoys the sympathy of countries like India, Egypt, and Syria, and is backed by labor and democratic movements throughout the world, by *the fighters for national liberation in the colonies and dependencies,* and by "progressive and democratic" forces in all nations.[19]

The chief purposes of the imperialist camp, according to Zhdanov, are to strengthen imperialism, destroy "democracy," and hatch a new "imperialist" war. The aims of the Soviet Union, on the other hand, are to oppose national, racial, and colonial exploitation, to defend the "liberty and independence" of all nations, and to struggle for "external" peace.

Zhdanov saw American policy toward Europe pressing along the following lines of action: strategic military measures, including the building of bases; economic expansion through the Marshall Plan and other devices; and an anti-"democratic" ideological struggle based on anti-Sovietism. In Asia he saw the policy of the United States as one designed to keep colonial and semicolonial countries "under the sway of imperialism and in continued political and economic bondage."[20]

The chief task of the Communist camp, Zhdanov said, was "to lead the resistance to the American plan for the enthrallment of Europe and of boldly denouncing all coadjutors of American imperialism," each Communist party taking the initiative in its own country.[21]

Zhdanov was a Russian speaking to Communist delegates from European countries, and his analysis of the world situation, while taking Asia into serious account, developed European phases in greater

---

[18] For an English translation of Zhdanov's speech, see *Strategy and Tactics,* pp. 211–30.

[19] *Ibid.,* pp. 216–17.

[20] *Ibid.,* pp. 220–21.

[21] *Ibid.,* p. 229.

detail. Somewhat less than two years later a Chinese Communist leader made clear the allegiance of his movement within the two-camp world. As Chinese Communist armies pushed southward across the face of China, Mao Tse-tung told his followers on July 1, 1949: "Internationally, we belong to the anti-imperialist front headed by the Soviet Union, and we must rely on the friendly help of this group and not on the imperialists."[22]

Mao saw only two choices for the Chinese people: they must take either the side of the Soviet camp or that of the "imperialists." It is impossible to remain between the two, he said; there is no third way. Moreover, if the Soviet Union had not come into existence, according to Mao, the "Chinese people" could not have won their victories, for the pressure of international "reactionary forces" would have been far stronger.[23]

A PRODUCT OF MARX, LENIN, AND THE "SCIENCE" OF BOLSHEVISM

There is nothing essentially new in the Zhdanov and Mao analyses. Both men have merely restated fundamental Marxist and Leninist theories in terms applicable to the post–World War II international situation. Being loyal Communists, both men have seen all historical and political developments motivated by economic and related material factors and moving forward according to predetermined patterns. Both men regarded these human processes as fundamental and universal in their application and in no way dependent upon human recognition for their existence and operation. Both men looked upon these processes of human development, not as inventions of Communist theoreticians, but as laws discovered and evolved from nature itself in the same sense that any scientific law is observed and systematized by pragmatic investigators.[24] Thus, when Zhdanov told Cominform founders in September 1947 that the United States was then threatened by an economic crisis which the Marshall Plan was designed to postpone,[25] he was not indulging in idle bombast, but interpreting a Marxist "law" which declares economic crises to be inevitable in capitalist nations and only a forerunner of the eventual, unavoidable collapse. So, too, when Mao Tse-tung stated in 1949 that the only path for

[22] Mao Tse-tung, "On the Dictatorship of the People's Democracy." The Chinese text of this article appears in *The China Weekly* (San Francisco), July 9, 1949; a Russian translation was published in *Pravda*, July 6, 1949; and an English translation of the Russian version appeared in *Current Digest of the Soviet Press*, August 9, 1949, pp. 3–8.

[23] *Ibid.*

[24] For an explanation of how Marx and Engels saw their universal laws applying to human behavior, see Friedrich Engels, *Herr Eugen Dühring's Revolution in Science (Anti-Dühring)* (New York, 1935).

[25] *Strategy and Tactics*, p. 228.

eliminating classes and establishing world communism lay through the People's Republic under the leadership of the working class,[26] he was not speculating, but speaking with "scientific" accuracy. "Bolshevism has been victorious because it is a correct science," a Chinese Communist official, Ch'en Po-ta, wrote on the thirty-second anniversary of the Communist seizure of power in Russia, "and because it represents the aspirations of mankind. It has been victorious in Russia, in the countries of East Europe, and in China. It will continue to be victorious in one country after another through the world because no reactionary force [recognizes] this revolutionary truth."[27]

This Bolshevism, which Ch'en Po-ta calls a "correct science," represents the doctrine of Karl Marx as modified, extended, and applied by Lenin, Stalin, Mao Tse-tung, and other Communist leaders. It is not a simple concept; rather, it is a vast body of theory and practice developed from a few fundamental premises into a behavior pattern embracing every possible phase of human life. Marx, writing in the mid-nineteenth century, saw the affairs of mankind developing in accordance with what he considered to be universal laws of conflict and change. All entities, both human and purely physical, are divided, he believed, into double, antagonistic parts, engaging in a conflict which tends to transform each into its opposite. This process produces, then, an entirely new category consisting likewise of mutually antagonistic parts.[28]

In obedience to these fundamental laws of the universe, Marx maintained, human society has developed through a series of bitter class conflicts. Historically, the antagonists have included freeman and slave, patrician and plebeian, baron and serf, guild burgess and journeyman, bourgeoisie and proletariat. Historically, and into the present, these contending classes have carried on perpetual warfare, sometimes masked, sometimes open and acknowledged, which has ended invariably either in a revolutionary change in the whole structure of society, or in the common ruin of the contending classes.[29] Modern society—bourgeois society—has arisen from the ruins of feudal society, thus setting up new, and in this case simplified, antagonisms. For the bourgeoisie, in developing modern industry, not only has forged the weapons that will slay it, but has engendered the

[26] Mao, "On the Dictatorship of the People's Democracy," loc. cit.

[27] Ch'en Po-ta, "The October Socialist Revolution and the Chinese Revolution," transmitted in English Morse to North America by the New China News Agency, November 7, 1949.

[28] Engels, op. cit., p. 17.

[29] The Communist Manifesto of Karl Marx and Friedrich Engels (International Publishers' Edition), with an introduction and explanatory notes by D. Ryazanoff (New York, 1930), pp. 25–26. Cited hereinafter as The Manifesto.

men who will use these weapons—the modern workers or proletarians.[30] "More and more," Marx said in words that Zhdanov was to use a hundred years later, "society is splitting into two hostile camps, into two great and directly contraposed classes: the bourgeoisie and the proletariat."[31] Marx went on to say that this struggle could end only with the mutual destruction of the two elements and the eventual emergence of a classless state in which there would be no further need for force.

Lenin extended these theories to account for the development of capitalism into stages which Marx had not lived to observe. In a book called *Imperialism, the Highest Stage of Capitalism*, written in 1916, Lenin maintained that Marx—unlike his contemporaries, who were accepting free competition as a natural law—had seen free competition actually giving rise to monopoly.[32] "Big capitalist tends to expropriate small capitalist," Marx had said, "and capital grows in one place to a huge mass in a single hand."[33]

Lenin described monopolist combines — cartels, syndicates, and trusts—dividing among themselves the whole internal market of a given capitalist country and thus imposing control upon the whole national industry.[34] Through this process, he said, there accumulates in advanced capitalist countries an enormous superabundance of capital, much more than can be invested profitably at home. This concentration would never be used for the purpose of raising mass working conditions locally, Lenin thought, for this would mean a decline in profits for the capitalists. On the contrary, he saw this superabundance of capital being exported to economically retarded areas where capital was usually scarce, the value of land relatively depressed, wages low, raw materials cheap, and profits high.[35] In this contingency, therefore, finance capital, "almost literally, one might say, spreads its net over all countries of the world."[36]

The rate of expansion among industrialist nations, Lenin pointed out, was markedly uneven. "If, for instance, we compare France, Germany and Japan, which do not differ much in area and population, we shall see that the first has annexed almost three times as much colonial territory as the other two combined."[37] Thus, even though the

[30] *Ibid.*, p. 34.

[31] *Ibid.*, p. 26.

[32] V. I. Lenin, *Imperialism, the Highest Stage of Capitalism* (Moscow: Foreign Languages Publishing House, 1947), p. 26. Cited hereinafter as *Imperialism*.

[33] Karl Marx, *Capital*, translated from the third German edition by Samuel Moore and Edward Aveling (London, 1889), p. 639.

[34] *Imperialism*, p. 83.

[35] *Ibid.*, p. 77.

[36] *Ibid.*, p. 81.

[37] *Ibid.*, p. 99.

world was now too small for adequate subdivision, the "younger" capitalist powers found themselves impelled toward further expansion. Under these circumstances, he maintained, the characteristic feature becomes the final partition of the globe, "not in the sense that a new partition is impossible—on the contrary, new partitions are possible and inevitable—but in the sense that the colonial policy of capitalist countries has *completed* the seizure of unoccupied territories on our planet."[38]   In short, the point had been reached, according to Lenin, where only redistribution was possible, and it was this struggle for the colonies which he held responsible for antagonisms among the great powers and for "imperialist" cataclysms such as World War I.[39]

These were the doctrines—the Marxist concept of two camps engaged in an inevitable conflict and the Leninist theory of an imperialist struggle for the division of the world—from which Zhdanov in 1947 derived his analysis of the world situation. In due course we shall discover that these convictions were fundamental also to Mao Tse-tung's development of the Chinese People's Republic and to Ch'en Po-ta's confidence in Bolshevism as a "correct science." The next few pages will show us how a disagreement between Lenin and a young Indian revolutionist shaped fundamental Communist policies toward China.

THE COMMUNIST GENERAL STAFF LOOKS EAST

It was the summer of 1920, and revolutionaries from all over the world were beating their way toward Moscow. Many carried false passports, and others had no identification at all, but they pushed forward somehow, stowing away on ships, slipping across borders during moonless nights, riding freight car buffers. From France and England and America they came, and from China and India, converging toward Moscow, the center of all their hopes. For Russia, with the victory of Bolshevism there, had become more than simply a Soviet state; it had become the general headquarters and supply base for the world Communist movement.

For many of these foreign revolutionists the Russian air seemed to crackle with excitement. "At last our slow-moving train reached Leningrad," an Englishman wrote years later when, disillusioned, he had left the Communist movement. "And what did I see? Drabness? Yes, drabness. Ruined buildings and shops closed? Yes, ruined buildings, shops closed, streets torn up and the famous Nevsky Prospect in the shabbiest raiments it had ever worn. Yes, I saw all that and more. I saw battalions of the new Red Army marching down that famous highway. Some had German uniforms, some had British,

---

[38] *Ibid.*, p. 94.   [39] *Ibid.*, pp. 94, 101, 105.

some had French, some American; some had fur hats, some caps, a few had boots. Most had their feet wrapped up in rags and tied up in straw matting. Never had I seen such a shabbily clothed army. But also I saw then a light in their eyes such as I had never seen in the eyes of soldiers on the march. Perhaps I, too, had that light in my eyes for I saw in this marching ragged army a new force rising from the ruins of the old order, a new creation which cradled the future in its hands."[40]

These foreign revolutionaries had come to Soviet Russia for a purpose. Already Lenin and his followers had recognized a twofold task: to govern Russia, i.e., to make their Soviet system work; and to facilitate the spread of Communist revolution across the rest of the earth.[41] But in seeking to carry out these purposes, the Bolsheviks were beginning to see the need for action on dual planes. Through the Treaty of Brest Litovsk, Russian Communists had secured the "breathing space" from conflict that they deemed necessary if they were going to preserve and strengthen their new Soviet state.[42] Yet the same treaty which brought them a respite at the same time restrained them from carrying on revolutionary propaganda in Germany,[43] a nation which the Communists considered on the verge of revolt. "But this does not mean we intend to give up in the least that propaganda," a Bolshevik leader told the Seventh Congress of the Russian Communist party in March 1918. "What we shall have to do is to carry on propaganda in the name, not of the Sovnarkom, but of the Central Committee of our party."[44] Thus, from the very beginning, Soviet leaders took up the practice of wearing one hat for government affairs, to which they wanted to lend an impression of respectability, and another for carrying out essentially revolutionary, and hence often subversive, tasks.

In 1919 the Russian Communist party took the lead in organizing the various Communist movements of the world into a single tightly knit and highly disciplined body, the Third International, or Communist International (Comintern), and it was for the Second Congress of this body that Communist leaders from various parts of the world

[40] J. T. Murphy, *New Horizons* (London, 1941), p. 107.

[41] James Bunyan and H. H. Fisher, *The Bolshevik Revolution, 1917–1918*, Hoover Library Publications, No. 3 (Stanford University, Calif., 1934), pp. 277–79, 280, 285.

[42] Jane Degras (ed.), *Soviet Documents on Foreign Policy, 1917–1924*, issued under the auspices of the Royal Institute of International Affairs (London, 1951), I, 57–61. Cited hereinafter as *Soviet Documents*.

[43] *Ibid.*, pp. 50–55.

[44] Y. M. Sverdlov, "The Aims of the Party," a partial translation of which appears in James Bunyan and H. H. Fisher, *The Bolshevik Revolution, 1917–1918*, pp. 550–51.

were meeting in 1920. Throughout 1918 and 1919 Russian Communist leaders had expected postwar revolts in central Europe to materialize into a general revolution, but in Germany, Hungary, and Austria, newly formed workers' and soldiers' soviets one after another met rapid defeat. By the time of the Second Congress, Lenin and his followers were looking hopefully toward revolutionary unrest in other quarters.

The number of delegates from Eastern lands offered a clue to what this new orientation was. In Petrograd (Leningrad) the famous old Smolny Institute, formerly a school for daughters of the nobility, now held offices of various commissars, and it was there that the Russian Bolshevik Zinoviev welcomed the various delegates. When this ceremony was over, a great crowd marched in procession to the Uritsky Theater. Only delegates and spectators with special tickets could gain admittance, but shortly the place was packed with people sitting on the floor and jammed in every corner and passageway.[45] There near the front sat an American, and not far from him a brown-skinned delegate, M. N. Roy, from India. Represented also were Turkey, Persia, the Dutch East Indies, Korea, China, and more than thirty other states and dependencies. In his convocation the Russian leader Zinoviev said, "Comrades, we are here at a truly World Congress of the Communist International. The fighting advance-guard of the workers of the world are represented."[46]

Lenin now took his place on the rostrum to analyze the international situation, which, he said, could be interpreted almost wholly in terms of imperialism and its economic relations. In restating his theories of monopoly and colonialism, he charged that by the era of World War I more than 600 million people had fallen subject to colonial rule and that another 400 million in Persia, Turkey, and China had been reduced to a semicolonial status. "The Imperialist war of 1914–1918," he said, "grew inevitably from this division of the whole world, from this domination of capitalist monopoly, from this unlimited power of a mere handful of the biggest banks, say, two to five in each country. This war was waged over the question of the division of the whole world. It was waged over the question as to which of the two groups of the biggest states—the British or the German—should secure the opportunity and the right of robbing, crushing and exploiting the entire world. And you know that the war settled this question in favor of the British group."[47]

[45] Murphy, op. cit., pp. 109–10.
[46] The Second Congress of the Communist International, Proceedings of the Petrograd Session of July 17th and of the Moscow Sessions of July 19th–August 7th, 1920 (Moscow, 1920), p. 12. Cited hereinafter as The Second Congress, Proceedings.
[47] Ibid., p. 19.

In Lenin's opinion the war — and the Versailles Treaty — had placed Russia, Austria-Hungary, Germany, and Bulgaria — a total of another 250 million people—under bondage to the victorious capitalist powers, all to the benefit of three nations—Japan, Great Britain, and the United States. But crucial contradictions were fast developing within this capitalist world: Europe, saddled with war debts, was approaching bankruptcy; prices were rising all out of proportion to wages; currency was depreciating; America, the richest country, could neither buy raw materials nor sell its finished products; and finally, the workers in capitalist nations were faced with living conditions that were all but unbearable. "These economic roots of the crisis," Lenin said, "are the prime causes of the splendid successes achieved by the Communist International."[48]

Under these circumstances the task of the revolutionary parties, Lenin said, was to prove by actual deed that they possessed sufficient class consciousness and sufficient power of organization, and were sufficiently in touch with the "exploited masses" to take advantage of the crisis for a successful, victorious revolution. "A union between the revolutionary proletariat of the advanced capitalist countries and the revolutionary masses of those countries where there is a very small or almost no proletariat," he said, "this union with the oppressed masses of the colonial countries of the East has been brought about by this Congress. It is up to us now to make this union a strong one, and I have no doubt we are going to do it."

The greatest obstacle to Bolshevik success, in Lenin's analysis, was the ability of capitalist leaders, using profits from colonial areas, to "bribe" their own working classes by raising cultural levels and by turning them into defenders of the bourgeoisie through other means. "The bourgeoisie could not have maintained itself," Lenin stated, "except for the work of these [labor] leaders." Here was Bolshevism's most dangerous enemy, he said; winning over labor forces loyal to capitalism presented the Communist International's greatest problem.[49]

After this, "when the revolutionary onslaught of the exploited and oppressed workers within each country, having overcome the resistance of an insignificant number of the philistines of their labor aristocracy, will combine with the revolutionary onslaught of hundreds of millions of humanity which have hitherto been beyond the pale of history, which have been regarded as mere objects of exploitation, then imperialism will have to fall."

Lenin maintained that the imperialist war had furthered the in-

48 *Ibid.*, p. 28.
49 *Ibid.*, p. 32.

terests of this latent revolution. "Out of the colonies, out of the backward countries, out of isolation, the bourgeoisie has recruited her soldiers for the imperialist war. The English bourgeoisie tried to make the Hindu soldiers believe that it is the business of the Hindu peasant to protect Great Britain against Germany; the French bourgeoisie tried to make soldiers from the French colonies believe that it was the business of the coloured peoples to defend France. They have taught them the art of war. This is an extremely useful accomplishment, for which we might be very grateful to the bourgeoisie—grateful in the name of all the Russian workers and peasants and particularly in the name of the Russian Red Army." As time went on, he concluded, the Communists were becoming more and more the representatives and protectors of 70 percent of the population of the earth, of the masses of those who toil and are oppressed.[50]

DISAGREEMENT BETWEEN LENIN AND ROY

During subsequent sessions of the Second Congress, held in Alexander Palace of the Kremlin in Moscow, Lenin's analysis and proposals were subjected to challenge, especially by the Indian revolutionist M. N. Roy. In meetings of the Commission on National and Colonial Questions, which deliberated in separate sittings, Lenin insisted that the Communist International and the various Communist parties were bound to support "bourgeois democratic" movements in the backward countries.[51] His reasoning was that the Bolsheviks could strengthen their initial position in the colonies and semicolonies by allying themselves with local groups opposed to foreign imperialism. M. N. Roy argued, on the other hand, that the appeal of nationalists, particularly in India, had found no response in the masses of the population, who were interested exclusively in questions of "a socioeconomic character." The broad revolutionary movement in India, in so far as it concerned the popular masses, he said, had nothing in common with the nationalist liberation movement. Consequently, the Communist International should assist exclusively the institution and development of the Communist movement in India, and the Communist party of India should devote itself exclusively to the organization of the broad popular masses in the struggle for the class interests of the latter.[52]

Roy further contended that the revolutionary movement in Europe

[50] *Ibid.*, p. 33.

[51] "Preliminary Draft of Some Theses on the National and Colonial Questions," *The Second Congress, Proceedings,* p. 478. Also M. N. Roy, in an interview with the author, Dehra Dun, India, October 15, 1951.

[52] *Petrogradskaia Pravda,* July 29, 1920.

was absolutely dependent on the course of revolution in Asia, that world capitalism was drawing its main resources and incomes from the colonies, principally in Asia. In an emergency, he said, European capitalists might give their workmen the entire surplus value, the full fruits of colonial exploitation, in order to distract revolutionary tendencies and win the proletariat to the capitalist side. Therefore, it was necessary to direct all efforts toward developing mass revolutionary movements, rather than nationalist revolutionary groups, in India and other parts of Asia.

Lenin took exception to parts of Roy's argument. He recalled how Russian Bolsheviks had supported liberal-liberation movements in the struggle against tsarism and insisted that the Indian Communists were "duty bound" to support "bourgeois-liberation movements" without, however, merging with them. Roy, he said, had gone too far in declaring that the destiny of the West would depend exclusively upon the strength of the mass revolutionary movement in Asia. The Bolsheviks, in short, by exploiting nationalist unrest, could further world revolution without waiting for class antagonisms to mature in economically retarded areas.[53] Maring (whose real name was Sneevliet), a Dutchman claiming to represent revolutionary movements in the Netherlands Indies, put it this way: "The difficulty lies only in finding the precise formula for the relationship between the revolutionary national and the Socialist movements in the backward countries."[54]

After considerable debate, the Second Congress tried to resolve the contradiction between Roy's emphasis on class conflict and Lenin's concept of co-operation with nationalist revolutionaries by approving both: *While extending support to middle-class nationalists, Communist leaders were expected to make every effort to arouse and organize the working masses and to penetrate and gain leadership over existing revolutionary movements.*[55]

It was agreed that action of this kind would hasten the downfall of capitalism. "One of the main sources from which European Capitalism draws its chief strength," according to the "Theses" which the Congress adopted, "is to be found in the colonial possessions and dependencies. Without the control of the extensive markets and vast

[53] This interpretation of the Lenin-Roy dispute is based upon evidence in *The Second Congress, Proceedings,* pp. 108–10, 112, 114–18, 153–57; and upon statements made by M. N. Roy in the author's interview with him at Dehra Dun, India, October 15, 1951.

[54] *The Second Congress, Proceedings,* p. 145.

[55] Paraphrased from "Preliminary Draft of Some Theses on the National and Colonial Questions," *The Second Congress, Proceedings,* pp. 570–79. The italics are mine.

fields of exploitation in the colonies, the capitalist powers of Europe cannot maintain their existence even for a short time."[56] Revolutionary masses in economically backward areas, moreover, with proletarian leadership from advanced capitalist countries, could move toward communism without passing through all the various phases of capitalist development.[57] "It is impossible," Lenin said, "to indicate beforehand the means to be used for this purpose; practical experience will show the way, but it is firmly established that all working masses, including those of the remotest nationalities, are susceptible to the soviet idea, and that these soviet organizations must be adapted to precapitalist relationships, and that the work of the Communist Parties all over the world must start at once in this direction."[58]

Despite these boldly stated theses the leaders of world communism were not yet in agreement concerning interpretations and practical applications of the principles they had adopted. Turning their attention to China, Russian Communist leaders in the 'twenties promoted peasant and working-class unrest while seeking at the same time to preserve an alliance with "bourgeois-nationalists" of the Kuomintang. The results were confusion, distrust, and finally the near annihilation of the Chinese Communist movement. On a more theoretical level, Stalin and Trotsky, struggling for power in Russia, fell into a dispute over whether the time had come for establishing soviets in China.

Yet the concepts approved by the Second Congress survived to provide a framework, three decades later, for the Chinese People's Republic. In those thirty years there were shifts in leadership and adjustments in procedure. It was a Chinese, Mao Tse-tung, and not a Russian, who achieved a working balance between the policy of promoting class conflict and that of effecting nationalist alliances. So, too, the Chinese peasant—rather than the urban workingman—turned out to be the main force of the revolution. Even the term "soviet" was abandoned. But throughout this thirty-year tangle of events and ideas the concepts of Lenin and Roy, enunciated at the Second Congress, interweave like two scarlet threads.

Before tracing them, however, we should isolate and examine some of the tactical theories and techniques which are likely to confront us during the unfolding of Chinese Communist history.

THEORIES AND TECHNIQUES OF ACTION

On the basis of their concept of a world divided into two irreconcilable camps, Bolshevik leaders have developed their strategy and

---

[56] *Ibid.*, p. 576.
[57] *Ibid.*, p. 578.
[58] *Ibid.*, p. 111.

tactics for a Soviet-led victory over the "imperialist-dominated" part of the world. "As long as capitalism and [Bolshevik] socialism exist," Lenin declared, "we cannot live in peace of mind; in the end one or the other will triumph—a funeral dirge will be sung either over the Soviet Republic or over world capitalism."[59] Looking outward from Moscow, Lenin, and later Stalin, saw his own camp as relatively weak and entirely encircled by the capitalist enemy. All-out war might well prove disastrous for the new Soviet state.

Communists from Marx on down had seen the capitalist world implanted with the seeds of its own destruction—labor unrest, depressions, runaway inflation, international wars, and so on. But Lenin was not prepared to stand by and wait for capitalism to destroy itself. The whole concept of the Communist party and the Communist International was to train a disciplined revolutionary elite for hastening the downfall of capitalism. The problem for the Bolsheviks was to devise effective methods, short of actual warfare, for waging this struggle.

On a strategic level the Communists set forth three primary objectives: *to develop and organize discontent and subversion within the various capitalist-dominated countries through local Communist parties; to exploit existing antagonisms among the "imperialist" powers and to foment new conflicts, setting one nation against another; and to drive a wedge, so to speak, between "imperialist" nations and the "colonies and semi-colonies," drawing the latter into the Communist camp.*[60]

It was Lenin, of course, who developed the fundamentals of Communist tactics (as well as most of the strategy), but Stalin, more than any other man, was responsible for using them first in China. In our examination of the record we shall discover that the Georgian was generally not successful. On the contrary, historical documents show him committing one error after another—usually at the expense of Chinese lives—and then holding his subordinates responsible. At a later date Mao Tse-tung took Stalinist principles, gave them a Chinese twist, and thus won victories which even Moscow may not have expected.

Under the tsarist regime Lenin had accumulated nearly a lifetime of experience in revolutionary tactics and subversion, and it was from this experience that he drew techniques for application to the world-wide struggle. One rule was fundamental: *Bolsheviks must master all means of warfare and train themselves to pass from one form to*

[59] Speech delivered at a meeting of nuclei secretaries of the Moscow Organization of the Russian Communist party, V. I. Lenin, *Selected Works*, III, 279–98.

[60] Paraphrased from "Preliminary Draft of Some Theses on the National and Colonial Questions," *The Second Congress, Proceedings*, pp. 570–79. The italics are mine.

another in the quickest and most unexpected manner. "Everyone will agree," he wrote, "that an army which does not train itself to wield all arms, all the means and weapons of warfare that the enemy possesses or may possess, behaves in an unwise and even in a criminal fashion."[61] Lenin believed that this fundamental rule applied even more to politics than to actual warfare, the chief difference being that in political conflict leaders find it more difficult to foresee what methods and tactics will be applicable and effective under future conditions. Unless Bolshevik leaders mastered all the means of warfare, Lenin warned, the capitalists might use ones in which Communist forces were particularly weak and thus inflict a decisive defeat on the revolutionists. But if Bolshevik leadership perfected techniques and an ability to feint and shift, Lenin foresaw that the Communist revolution would inevitably be victorious simply because it represented "the interests of the really foremost and really revolutionary class," the proletariat.[62]

In following the course of Communist strategy and tactics in China from 1920 until the present time, we shall observe Bolshevik leaders—both Russian and Chinese—applying a variety of techniques and weapons of political warfare. Lenin, differentiating among the many methods in the Communist manual, isolated three which, in his opinion, young revolutionists found most difficult to master: *the tactical retreat; the tactical compromise; and the exploitation of existing antagonisms within the enemy's ranks.*

Communists, in Lenin's opinion, had long since learned to attack, but a true Bolshevik victory would be impossible until they learned how to retreat properly. For a Bolshevik to accept battle when it was advantageous to the enemy was not "revolutionary,"[63] Lenin believed, but stupid and even criminal. "It is just as if 10,000 soldiers were to fling themselves into battle against 50,000 enemy soldiers," Lenin wrote, "when it would have been wiser to 'stop,' to 'turn,' or even to effect a 'compromise' pending the arrival of the 100,000 reinforcements which were on their way but which could not go into action immediately."

Lenin considered the ability to compromise vitally important; to stand on "principle" was utterly childish. He was careful to distinguish, however, between "compromises and compromises." A good Bolshevik must be able to analyze each situation and the concrete conditions for compromise. Imagine, he reasoned, that your automobile

[61] V. I. Lenin, *"Left-Wing" Communism, an Infantile Disorder* (Moscow: Foreign Languages Publishing House, 1947), p. 100. Hereinafter cited as *Left-Wing Communism.*

[62] *Ibid.*

[63] *Ibid.,* pp. 86–87.

is held up by armed bandits. You hand over your money, passport, revolver, and automobile. In return you are relieved of the unpleasant company of the bandits. ". . . it would be difficult to find a sane man," Lenin declared, "who would declare such a compromise to be 'inadmissible on principle,' or who would proclaim the compromiser an accomplice of the bandits (even though the bandits might use the automobile and the firearms for further robberies)." The Soviet signing of the Brest Litovsk treaty with Germany, he maintained, was this kind of compromise; and so, in Bolshevik terms, were all subsequent united front and other alliances effected by Communists with non-Communist groups.

What the Bolshevik must learn, Lenin felt, was to distinguish between those who give the bandits money and firearms in order to lessen the evil resulting to the victim and those, on the other hand, who give bandits money and firearms in order to share in the loot. One need only substitute "capitalist" for "bandit" and the philosophy of all Communist agreements and alliances with non-Communist groups is made clear.

With his emphasis upon tactical retreats and compromises, Lenin insisted that Communists must win their victories through technique and maneuver rather than by the application of sheer mass force. It was for this reason that he urged his followers to recognize weak points in the class structure of their opponents. "As long as we have not conquered the whole world," he said, "as long as, from the economic and military standpoint, we are weaker than the capitalist world, we must adhere to the rule that we must know how to take advantage of the antagonisms and contradictions existing among the imperialists."[64] Those who had not proved by *deeds* their ability to apply this technique were not yet ready to lead the proletariat. "The more powerful enemy," he warned, "can be conquered only by exerting the utmost effort and by *necessarily,* thoroughly, carefully, attentively and skilfully taking advantage of every, even the smallest, 'rift' among the enemies, of every antagonism of interest among the bourgeoisie of the various countries, and also by taking advantage of every, even the smallest, opportunity of gaining a mass ally, even though this ally be temporary, vacillating, unstable, unreliable and conditional."[65]

The historical record reveals Bolshevik leaders employing this technique on many levels: touching the edge of their chisel between American and British interests in the Far East; trying to split off the Peking war-lord government from its dependence on the West; supporting Chiang Kai-shek against that same Peking government; ally-

[64] To the nuclei secretaries, Lenin, *Selected Works,* p. 280.
[65] *Left-Wing Communism,* p. 70. The italics are in the original.

ing with the Chinese businessman against the Western "imperialist";
setting the laborer against his employer, the poor peasant against the
rich peasant, and all the peasants against the landlords.

Lenin suggested that the exploitation of antagonisms was something more than the mere driving of wedges and fracturing off of
isolated groups. Communists, he thought, must learn to turn the
enemy against himself. Ever since the Bolshevik Revolution in Russia,
he observed, the whole world—and especially the bourgeoisie—had
changed. Capitalists were now terrified of Bolshevism, "incensed with
it almost to the point of frenzy," a fact which supposedly accelerated
events to the Communist advantage. The capitalist world, by concentrating its energies on the suppression of Bolshevism by force, was
thereby weakening its position in a number of other vital fields and
at the same time drawing mass attention to the very ideology it wished
to suppress. ". . . when the American bourgeoisie, having completely
lost its head, seizes thousands and thousands of people on suspicion
of Bolshevism, creates an atmosphere of panic, and broadcasts stories
of Bolshevik plots; when the British bourgeoisie—the most 'solid' in
the world—despite all its wisdom and experience, commits incredible
follies, founds richly-endowed 'anti-Bolshevik societies,' creates a
special literature on Bolshevism, and hires an extra number of scientists, agitators and parsons to combat it—we must bow and thank
the capitalist gentry. They are working for us."[66]

Thus it was not sufficient for the Communists to win over the
working class. *Bolshevik leaders must also goad their non-Communist
opponents into weakening and even destroying themselves.* Bolshevik
strategists and tacticians must recognize not only whether they had
won sufficient proletarian support for a telling blow, but also "whether
the historically effective forces of *all* classes—positively all classes of
the given society without exception—are aligned in such a way that
everything is ripe for the decisive battle; in such a way that (1) all
the class forces hostile to us have become sufficiently entangled, are
sufficiently at loggerheads with each other, have sufficiently weakened
themselves in a struggle which is beyond their strength; that (2) all the
vacillating, wavering, unstable intermediate elements—the petty bourgeoisie and the petty bourgeois democrats as distinct from the
bourgeoisie—have sufficiently exposed themselves in the eyes of the
people, have sufficiently disgraced themselves through their partial
bankruptcy; and that (3) among the proletariat a mass sentiment in
favor of supporting the most determined, supremely bold, revolutionary action against the bourgeoisie has arisen and begun vigorously

66 *Ibid.,* pp. 104–5.

to grow. Then, indeed, revolution is ripe; then, indeed, if we have gauged all the conditions indicated and briefly outlined above, and if we have chosen the moment rightly, our victory is assured."[67]

Lenin also used other words to put the same concept across; e.g., that *successful revolution is impossible without a nation-wide crisis:* ". . . it is not enough for revolution," he said, "that the exploited and the oppressed masses should understand the impossibility of living in the old way and demand changes. It is essential for revolution that the exploiters should not be able to live and rule in the old way. Only when the *'lower classes' do not want* the old way, and when the upper classes *cannot carry on in the old way*—only then can revolution triumph . . . It follows that for revolution it is essential, first, that a majority of the workers (or at least a majority of the class-conscious, thinking, politically active workers) should fully understand that revolution is necessary and be ready to sacrifice their lives for it; secondly, that the ruling classes should be passing through a governmental crisis, which draws even the most backward masses into politics (a symptom of every real revolution is a rapid, tenfold, and even hundred-fold increase in the number of members of the toiling masses—hitherto apathetic—who are capable of waging the political struggle), weakens the government and makes it possible for the revolutionaries to overthrow it rapidly."[68]

Looking at China in late 1920, Lenin was of the opinion that these conditions either prevailed or were on the point of emerging, and it was therefore with considerable optimism that he and other leaders of the Third International took initial steps toward aggravating the Chinese revolution, splitting apart the existing class structure, and gathering the parts under Bolshevik control.

For the implementation of their tactics, Bolshevik leaders depended upon the Communist International, the Soviet Russian government, and the various Communist parties throughout the world, but in a more fundamental sense the basic organizational units were the *nucleus,* or *cell,* and the *fraction.*

The cells of individual party members—whether in factory, store, farm, city neighborhood, aboard ship, or elsewhere—were (and still are) the foundation of all Communist superstructure. In urban areas all cells were united into subsections which, in turn, were united into sections. All the sections of a given city constituted a local party organization, and thus the various party organs were designed to pyramid upward through national to international levels. In each stratum the membership was charged with electing the next higher

[67] *Ibid.,* p. 98.
[68] *Ibid.,* p. 87. The italics are from the original.

organ—except when the Communist party was illegal, in which case the whole system was streamlined for security purposes.

The Comintern was specific in outlining tasks for the cell. Its members were charged with the conduct of Communist agitation and propaganda among the workers (or local residents, in case of a neighborhood) ; with discussing factory, store, farm, or shipboard problems; with publishing a factory paper; with participating in all demonstrations and strikes; with pointing out to fellow workers the political consequences of any given labor struggle; with carrying on an obstinate fight against other parties and antagonistic groups; and with assuming responsibility for party organization and discipline on the lowest level.

The fraction was assigned a much more specialized—and, in a sense, more insidious—function. For this was essentially conceived as a parasitic organism, an outpost of the Communist party within some non-Communist grouping. Communist members of a non-Communist labor union (political party, factory committee, parliamentary body, church board, learned society, athletic association, university faculty, and so forth) were charged with organizing themselves and—through caucuses, block voting, and other maneuvers—with increasing Communist influence and introducing Communist policy into non-Communist masses. The strength of the fraction depended on two cardinal rules: first, *every question subject to decision of a nonparty body or institution must be discussed and decided upon during an earlier meeting of the parasite fraction;* second, *all fraction members must act and vote as a unit on all questions within meetings of the non-Communist body or institution.*[69] By following these two rules, Chinese Communist members were to achieve within the Kuomintang, the Nationalist armies, non-Communist labor unions, and a host of other organizations an influence far out of proportion to their relatively limited numbers.

The Communist program for China was scarcely under way when Lenin fell ill, and so it was not he, but Stalin, who was largely responsible for its implementation—and its many early failures. The Georgian—and later Mao Tse-tung, the Chinese—accepted Lenin's premises and relied almost wholly on his techniques. But Stalin's character was altogether different from that of Lenin, the Georgian being more personally ambitious and exercising power under different circumstances. Consequently Bolshevik strategy and tactics were altered in the shift from Leninist theory to Stalinist practice, just as—at a later date—Stalinist policy was transformed by Maoist implementation.

[69] "Organization of Factory Nuclei and Fractions," *International Press Correspondence,* February 27, 1924, pp. 111–13.

TRENDS UNDER STALIN

Communist strategy and tactics under Lenin, who subordinated personal ambition, were directed almost exclusively toward achievement of over-all Bolshevik victories. Stalin preserved this objective, but at the same time he used political techniques and party apparatus for achieving and guarding his personal power as well. A victory for communism in China often doubled as a personal victory for Stalin, but—and it was here that the system revealed one of the inherent weaknesses of dictatorship—Stalin managed quite as frequently to serve his personal designs with a party defeat.

In years immediately preceding Stalin's death, world Communist leaders tried to present the Georgian as a master strategist and tactician with a political insight that was infallible. One disciple claimed to have discovered repeated proof of Stalin's ability to foresee history—an ability so rare that it was inherent in him alone. He "senses the new coming into being," wrote the Hungarian Mátyás Rákosi, "and can foresee from the way the seed sprouts where the shadow of the grown tree will fall."[70] Because of this "uncanny insight," Stalin, "the greatest scientist and organizer known to the modern world,"[71] was credited by his followers with always foreseeing events correctly and adopting the precisely correct course.[72] We shall see from the record of events in China how accurate such claims really were. It is worth noting at the moment that these statements about a single political leader were issued by members of a movement which had considered itself to be scientific and strictly materialistic, rather than mystical or idealistic in habits of thought.

Marx had long maintained, of course, that by observing the dialectical laws allegedly inherent in all of human history a skilled theoretician could predict the general course of future events much after the fashion in which a meteorologist predicts the weather. Lenin was to declare later that the art of Marxist statesmanship and the correct understanding by a Communist of his task lay in a precise gauging of revolutionary conditions and in an instant recognition of the moment when a revolutionary vanguard could successfully seize power and maintain it.[73] But neither Marx nor Lenin claimed omniscience, nor did they expect it from others.

Throughout this account we shall be confronted with other basic—

[70] For a Lasting Peace, for a People's Democracy (a Cominform newspaper published in Bucharest), December 21, 1949.

[71] Boleslaw Bierut, chairman of the Central Committee, the United Workers' party of Poland, in For a Lasting Peace, for a People's Democracy.

[72] K. Gottwald, chairman, Communist party of Czechoslovakia, in For a Lasting Peace, for a People's Democracy.

[73] Left-Wing Communism, p. 35.

and often perplexing—Communist techniques which Bolshevik leaders regularly used but were disinclined to formulate. Since these practices are largely foreign to the Westerner, it may be helpful to consider at this point a brief outline pattern of certain stratagems which later pages will document.

While aiming to win over the working class and the peasantry, for example, *Bolshevik agents in China went first to the intellectuals and brought numbers of them into the Communist camp as leaders.* This was accomplished through the formation of Marxist study groups, especially in the universities, the publication of Communist newspapers and journals, the founding of Communist educational institutions, the translation and distribution of Marxist books, proselyting among Chinese students in French or German universities, and the sending of qualified Chinese students to the Soviet Union for the completion of their studies.

With an elite corps of Bolshevik-trained intellectuals, the Communist movement could speak to Chinese professional men, businessmen, shopkeepers, soldiers, students, and peasants, not through suspicious-looking foreigners, but through local Chinese. Bolshevik leaders, though aiming at the lower strata of Chinese society, recruited from an upper level first and relied on these converts to work among the masses.

In carrying out Communist policy, Bolshevik leaders faced always a threefold task: to keep their own membership alerted and informed regarding the party line for carrying on agitation, propaganda, organizational activities, and so forth; to win the greatest possible non-Communist support for any given Communist program; and to neutralize any unavoidable opposition. To keep party members alert, the leadership depended upon constant indoctrination and discipline, but the manipulation of non-Communist groups required techniques of a subtler sort. *Bolshevik leaders put the Communist party forward as the champion of what was most wanted by the groups they sought to influence.* Before peasants the Communist party pressed for agrarian reform; in approaching feminine groups they demanded protection for working children, equal rights for women, and special protection for working women; before labor unions they advocated the eight-hour day and a long list of other benefits; addressing the Chinese people as a whole, they denounced the foreign exploiter.

Whatever the program advocated, *Bolshevik leaders sought, by narrowing choices, to polarize opinion and thus destroy democratic middle groups and similar opposition.* There are only two paths, they held, and you must take one or the other. Follow us, and you will be working for freedom, democracy, peace, child welfare, an eight-hour day. Oppose us, and you have joined the camp of the enemy. There were times, of course, when the Communists seemed to speak differently. Join the Kuomintang, they might have told a middle-class businessman in 1926. But the Kuomintang, at that time, was to a considerable degree under Communist control, and so the effect was the same.

Polarization has been a world-wide Communist technique, but in countries like China—largely illiterate, lacking a strong middle class, with a population almost wholly unschooled in democratic processes, and without a long tradition of middle-of-the-road political parties—the maneuver has proved especially effective.

The record in China will show how *Bolshevik leaders often won support by equating—under appropriate circumstances—non-Communist principles with concepts that are strictly Communist.* During World War II, for example, the Bolsheviks used the term "democracy" in referring to their own governmental system, and down to the present time they have spoken of Asian "nationalism" as though it meant the same thing to them as it did to a non-Communist Chinese or Indian or Burmese. And again, during the wartime alliance with non-Communist groups, Chinese Communists often equated Mao Tse-tung's "new democracy" with the Three Principles of Sun Yat-sen—although in their party councils Communist theoreticians made clear that the differences between the two were far more crucial than the similarities.

The course of events in China demonstrates that *the Communist alliance with non-Communist groups has been intended to be wholly tactical and Machiavellian.* Their numbers being relatively small, Communists knew that in order to succeed in China they had to win temporary support at critical moments in history from millions who were not Communists. Temporarily they were obliged to persuade their potential enemies to support them, or at least not to resist them. Thus, they formed alliances, whenever feasible, with the widest possible variety of classes—the national bourgeoisie (capitalist groups unsympathetic to the West), petty bourgeoisie (shopkeepers, tradesmen, small professional groups), non-Communist intellectuals, and peasants, both poor and well-to-do. From the very beginning, the Communists have preserved the intention—once in power—to squeeze out one after another of these allies in the measure that their support was no longer needed. The pity has been that so many non-Communist sympathizers have been so slow to perceive the strictly tactical nature of these alliances.

But Communists have not exerted their influence in non-Communist groups and organizations entirely by persuasion or by what might be called "open subterfuge." The planting of fractions in non-Communist organizations has given handfuls of Communists extraordinary power over otherwise legitimate bodies, and with this advantage *the Communist party has used the facilities of innocent labor unions, scholarly institutions, political parties, and like groups for spreading its propaganda and influence.* But this maneuver, by itself, has not been considered sufficient, for concurrently *the Communist party has also established its own corresponding "front" organizations*—its own labor unions, its own scholarly bodies, and so forth.

The precise pattern of Communist maneuvers has always depended to a considerable degree upon the legal status of the party itself. Once outlawed, the organization is streamlined and the discipline severely tightened. It is axiomatic, of course, that *Bolshevik leaders demand freedoms for their own party which, once in power, they fully intend to deny to their opposition.* There are two reasons for this stand. To begin with, the Communists are quite ready to use their civil rights for the destruction of the society guaranteeing them. But equally important, *by fighting for democratic freedoms (which his own system will not guarantee) the Communist poses as a champion of the very liberties for which many non-Communist peoples are striving.*

Finally, we shall observe from Communist sources how *Mao Tse-tung's "new democratic" government, theoretically a coalition of various class interests, is actually a weapon for neutralizing or destroying opposition and seizing control of or squeezing out all non-Communist elements within the country.* The record will show that Communist leaders invoke democratic slogans to destroy the last semblances of democracy; they use certain capitalist incentives and institutions in order to move toward the eventual destruction of all capitalist incentives and institutions.

These are some of the major theories, techniques, and revolutionary behavior patterns which the Bolsheviks followed. Succeeding pages will indicate how a whole series of ambitious and ruthless men—but especially Stalin and later Mao Tse-tung—have used them for the achievement of Communist supremacy in China and, even more diabolically, as weapons in personal drives for power. Through the years their effectiveness, as the Communists themselves admit, has depended to an important degree upon the nature and condition of Chinese political, economic, social, and cultural institutions.

CHAPTER II

CHINA UNDER WESTERN IMPACT

By 1920 China presented an open target for Communist weapons. The factors responsible for this vulnerability are multiple and complex, but the Westerner can achieve some perspective from a hasty consideration of the overturn which the country and its people had suffered over the previous century.

For generations prior to the Opium War of 1839 China had lived in splendid isolation, the focal point of what the Chinese people viewed as the only world order that really counted. With its century-deep culture, its highly developed value system, and its self-contained economic, political, and social structures, China and its people saw no reason for dealing with other parts of the earth except with the condescension which great empires traditionally have displayed toward fringe "barbarians."

During the Ming dynasty (A.D. 1368–1644) China's relations with other states had developed into an institutionalized pattern, and it was essentially this system, with minor modifications, which the Ch'ing, or Manchu, dynasty (1644–1912) adopted. Fundamental to Ming and Manchu diplomacy was the imperial tributary system, which had emerged, in turn, from an age-old tradition of Chinese superiority over foreign barbarians. When within the course of a few decades Western penetration and influence had destroyed the pattern, it was inevitable that Chinese pride and self-assurance should suffer acutely.

In essence, the Chinese perceived their superiority as emerging less from China's political or military power than from the cultural richness and prestige of the Chinese way of life. From this it followed, according to John Fairbank and S. Y. Teng,[1]

. . . that those barbarians who wished to "come and be transformed" [*lai-hua*], and so participate in the benefits of [Chinese] civilization, must recognize the supreme position of the Emperor; for the Son of Heaven represented all mankind, both Chinese and barbarian, in his ritual sacrifices before the forces of nature. Adherence to the Chinese way of life automatically entailed the Emperor's mandate to rule all men. This supremacy of the Emperor as mediator between Heaven and Earth was most obviously acknowledged in the performance of the kowtow, the three

[1] J. K. Fairbank and S. Y. Teng, "On the Ch'ing Tributary System," *Harvard Journal of Asiatic Studies*, VI, No. 4 (June 1941), 138–39.

kneelings and nine prostrations to which European envoys later objected. It was also acknowledged by the bringing of tribute, by the formal bestowal of a seal, comparable to the investiture of a vassal in medieval Europe, and in other ways. Thus the tributary system, as the sum total of these formalities, was the mechanism by which barbarous non-Chinese regions were given their place in the all-embracing Chinese political, and therefore ethical, scheme of things.

Thus we see that precisely as the West was developing its nation-state and international treaty system, the Chinese, geographically insulated from much of the world, were practicing a diplomacy which not only placed their empire in a position of monolithic prestige, but also failed to evolve the concept of international dealings on an equal basis. As early as the days of Kublai Khan (1260–94) envoys were sent from Annam, Laos, northern Burma, and other localities in order to pay tribute. Intermittently over the centuries tribute embassies were dispatched not only from these regions, but also from Tibet (invaded by Chinese forces in 1751), Nepal, Bhutan, Siam, the Sulu Islands, the Ryukyus, and particularly Korea.

It is doubtful whether, in all cases, the tributary states interpreted their relations with China as did the Chinese, who took their own suzerainty largely for granted. Certainly, a double standard of evaluation emerged in later years when Holland and other European states established tributary relations as a bothersome formality prerequisite to the profits of Chinese trade. Undoubtedly, too, there was a wide variation in the nature of tributary ties, those between China and Korea, for example, being generally closer and of longer and more continuous duration than those between China and Burma. But the Chinese—even the Communist Chinese—tend to take these historical relationships with what appears to us as unwarranted seriousness.

With the Opium War of 1839 and with the subsequent acceleration of Western penetrations—economic, political, and cultural—of long-isolated China, the traditional pattern broke up rapidly. In the course of a few decades a "barbaric" (from the Chinese viewpoint) but technologically superior West brought about a reversal of the old relationship: China, wide open to Western economic exploitation, became, in effect, a tributary to the West.

The most telling blows were not necessarily political or economic. A century of exposure to the West left gaping holes in the Chinese cultural and ethical fabric. The Western merchant, the Western missionary, and finally the Western intellectual chipped and hacked and battered at foundations of the age-old Confucian "world order." It came to be doubted whether the Son of Heaven (for several centuries, now, a Manchu "foreigner") really represented the people of

China, let alone the whole of mankind, or was in any way competent to mediate between Heaven and the Earth of nineteenth- and twentieth-century technology and science.

Western influences served increasingly as a catalyst, intensifying indigenous weaknesses of the political, economic, and social structure and transforming them into a dry rot. In the midst of doubt and uncertainty the Ch'ing dynasty crumbled, and a large part of the Confucian value system fell into doubt and disrepute. What replaced the old empire and the beliefs pervading it was something akin to chaos, with one war-lord group replacing another as the successor to the rejected Emperor and with thousands of thoughtful Chinese groping for something to believe in.

This political, social, economic, cultural, intellectual, and—perhaps above all—psychological and spiritual upheaval pushed many Chinese Westward in search of salvation. They studied in Europe and America, hoping to employ for the uplifting and transforming of China the same knowledge and techniques which had so suddenly overturned it. To an uprooted twentieth-century Chinese intellectual the ideas of Western political scientists, economists, philosophers, and statesmen—particularly John Dewey, Bertrand Russell, and Woodrow Wilson—offered a powerful stimulation but not, unfortunately, a tangible program. The thought system of two other Western intellectuals, Karl Marx and V. I. Lenin, comprised not only an ideology offering answers to every conceivable question, but a plan of action, an ethical structure, and a pseudoreligious faith, replete with earthly salvation.

Under these circumstances, it is not altogether surprising that many Chinese should have looked toward Moscow—especially after the revolutionist Sun Yat-sen had turned to the West for help in building a republic and had been refused or ignored. The question which arises today is whether these Chinese, and their sons and daughters, having embraced Marx's Russian disciples, are likely to be willing or able to break away.

In order to function in the twentieth-century world, China and other countries of the East need the machines and skills of modern communications, agriculture, transportation, industry, finance, administration, and public sanitation. The Communists—both Russian and Chinese—offer class warfare and totalitarian formulas for the acquisition of these elements. They promise—at high cost to individual freedom and dignity—a rapid transformation of technologically retarded and, in several cases, seriously overpopulated regions into industrialized states. For Western democracies and for the free nations of Asia and similar areas, therefore, one of the prime challenges of our time is the development of vehicles for conveying twentieth-century methods into technologically medieval cultures with a minimum of disruption and bloodshed and a maximum of good will and orderliness.

Unhappily, the historical record shows that the behavior of European powers in their pre–World War I relations with the East was sufficient to predispose many Asians toward acceptance of Lenin's doctrinaire charges against the West. Indeed, it can be said with considerable justice that policies of the United States and other Western powers in the mid-twentieth century suffer grievously from the sins of earlier and now all but extinct generations of true imperialists.

THE PATTERN OF WESTERN ENCROACHMENTS

Foreign encroachments on China took a variety of forms. In the mid-nineteenth century Western nations secured "settlements" or "concessions" in certain Chinese cities (e.g., Shanghai, Tientsin, Canton, Hankow) over which the government of China had no administrative jurisdiction. In these areas, as in China generally, resident aliens and corporations enjoyed extraterritorial status exempting them from Chinese law and authority.[2] Other areas in China were later leased outright: Port Arthur and Dairen to Imperial Russia for twenty-five years;[3] Kiaochow to Germany for ninety-nine years;[4] Weihaiwei, Deep Bay, and Mirs Bay to Great Britain;[5] and Kwangchowan to France for ninety-nine years.[6] The growth of these foreign encroachment patterns led to the marking out of the country into "spheres of special interest." It was said that Manchuria belonged to Imperial Russia's sphere of interest, Shantung province to that of Germany, and so forth, with possession of a coastal leasehold tending to provide presumptive claims to areas of the Chinese hinterland.[7] In many cases the positions of foreign syndicates were strengthened through rights of exploiting mineral and other natural wealth of the region, and foreign loans were often secured by payments from the likin or other internal revenues collected in Chinese provinces, or on maritime customs revenue or the salt tax.[8]

The Ch'ing dynasty in China found itself helpless against this onslaught of Western technology and economic and political pene-

[2] W. W. Willoughby and C. G. Fenwick, *Types of Restricted Sovereignty and of Colonial Autonomy* (Washington: Government Printing Office, 1919), pp. 99, 105, 110.

[3] William Woodville Rockhill, *Treaties and Conventions with or Concerning China and Korea, 1894–1904* (Washington: Government Printing Office, 1904), p. 50.

[4] *Ibid.*, p. 46.

[5] *Ibid.*, pp. 59, 60.   [6] *Ibid.*, p. 55.

[7] P. H. Kent, *Railway Enterprizes in China* (London: E. Arnold Co., 1907), p. 95, as quoted in T. W. Overlach, *Foreign Financial Control in China* (New York, 1919), p. 58.

[8] Overlach, *op. cit.*, pp. 220–25; *The China Year Book, 1913*, p. 333.

tration. The dilemma was nearly inescapable, for if China was to build its economic defenses it needed both money and railroads. Yet each new acquisition of this sort brought a deeper entrenchment of foreign influence, with further Chinese indebtedness and unfavorable balances of trade. Under the empire, China's leadership remained unable to agree upon proper measures. Especially toward the end of the nineteenth century, sincere and able efforts were made to adjust the governmental structure for coping not only with the direct foreign impact, but also with the internal dislocations that were resulting from the invasion of an alien culture. Yet the framework and machinery and functions of the empire proved inadequate. The Ch'ing dynasty crumbled in 1911, to be followed by a declared republic which soon degenerated into a cabal of war-lord cliques.

There were many reasons for Chinese inadequacy. This most recent foreign "invasion" — in contrast to earlier ones — depended upon a more complex system of commercial and mechanical techniques than Chinese culture had so far produced. Its transportation system was more highly developed than those of previous invasions and of China itself. Its warfare was more highly mechanized and mobilized. Its trade lines, its communications, its whole cultural pattern had spread over continents and seas and had, in a sense, nearly surrounded China before the penetration began.

Individual leaders under the empire tended to range themselves according to their attitudes toward the foreign impact. Some hoped to resist through rigid preservation of the structure as it was; others wanted to modify the structure, machinery, and functions to cope with foreign influences and new conditions; still others saw no solution short of tearing down the old framework and rebuilding according to Western models; a few, rejecting the past of China and of the West, dreamed of something totally new.

Throughout later phases of the nineteenth century and until the outbreak of World War I European powers pressed for economic and political advantages in China and other parts of Asia and competed among themselves for a lion's share. In this conflict Great Britain, France, Germany, and other nations, communicating with China by sea, moved from treaty ports on into the interior. Imperial Russia, advancing overland, sought to check British expansion along the Russian frontiers from Turkey to Korea, to protect its Far Eastern flank against Japan, and to secure warm-water ports on the Pacific coast.[9] After World War II Western powers have steadily withdrawn

[9] Prince A. Lobanov-Rostovsky, *Russia and Asia* (New York, 1933), pp. 113, 147, 193, 226–27; Abraham Yarmolinsky (trans. and ed.), *The Memoirs of Count Witte* (New York, 1921), pp. 82–84, 90, 97–110—cited hereinafter as *Witte*; E. J. Dillon, *The Eclipse of Russia* (New York, 1918), pp. 224–52, 260–69, 279–311.

from Asia, but Soviet Russia, adapting tsarist practices to Communist theory, pursues an aggressively imperialist course.

With the seventeenth century Tsarist Russia had begun expanding slowly eastward across Siberia, but it was not until the time of the Crimean War that imperial interest in Asia became acute. Thereafter, in the words of Prince Lobanov-Rostovsky, "it becomes a law of Russian history that every time Russia finds herself checked in Europe she intensifies her drive in Asia."[10]

In 1854 Count Muraviev seized the Amur Valley and laid the foundations for the city of Khabarovsk, strengthening Russian Far Eastern defenses as conflicts inspired by the Crimean War spread into the Pacific.[11] Then, during the Anglo-French occupation of Peking in 1860 the Russian, acting as intermediary, promised to "secure" for China a withdrawal which he knew the British had already decided upon, and as a result Russia, through the Convention of Peking, obtained title to the whole coast of Manchuria east of the Ussuri River and south to the Korean border.[12] With this new sphere and with a Pacific outlet through Vladivostok, the Russians in 1895 completed construction of a first link in the Trans-Siberian Railway. But since a line restricted to Russian territory would necessarily loop northward around Manchuria, the imperial government negotiated for a right of way cutting across Chinese territory.[13] Peking authorities had made surveys for extending a Chinese line into Manchuria, but tsarist representatives in China opposed this, pressing for the development of a Russian system.[14] China had recently been defeated in the Sino-Japanese War, and Nipponese forces still remained in Port Arthur and Korea. The tsarist government prevailed upon Germany and France to join Russia in demanding Japanese withdrawal, and this action increased Russia's prestige in Peking.[15] Tsarist diplomats succeeded in convincing the Manchu government that for Russia to uphold effectively the principle of Chinese integrity (a cause which St. Petersburg claimed to champion), it would be necessary to improve communications between China, on the one hand, and both European Russia and Vladivostok, on the other.[16] The result of these negotiations was a series of agreements pointing toward the construction

10 Lobanov-Rostovsky, *op. cit.*, p. 147.

11 *Ibid.*, pp. 141–42.

12 *Ibid.*, p. 144; see also Hosea Ballou Morse, *The International Relations of the Chinese Empire* (London, New York: Longmans, Green and Co., Inc., 1910–18), I, 613–14.

13 *Witte*, p. 86.

14 Morse, III, 80–81.

15 *Ibid.*, p. 47; Lobanov-Rostovsky, *op. cit.*, pp. 221–23; *Witte*, pp. 81–85.

16 *Witte*, p. 89.

across Manchuria of the Chinese Eastern Railway, a line which was to become an exceedingly important factor in Far Eastern diplomacy. A Russo-Chinese bank was chartered,[17] and on September 8, 1896, the two nations signed a contract for construction of the railroad.[18] It was agreed that the bank was to organize a company to build the line and to issue shares for sale to Russian and Chinese citizens.[19] The railway was to be jointly operated with exclusive rights during the period of construction and for eighty years thereafter; after thirty-six years the Chinese government would have the right to buy back the line. Provisions were made for the use of natural resources needful for construction and maintenance.[20] Eighteen months later the tsarist government obtained from China a twenty-five-year lease of the Port Arthur and Dairen areas for use as a naval base; and an extension of the Chinese Eastern Railway concessions was secured for the purpose of building a spur system (the Chan Chung, or South Manchurian Railway) to connect Dairen with the main line.[21]

Tsarist influence spread in other directions. In 1911 Outer Mongolia proclaimed its independence of China, but during World War I the Kiakhta Agreement of 1915, while labeling the area a Chinese vassal state, actually transformed it into a protectorate of Imperial Russia. In sum, Tsarist Russia was establishing far-flung spheres which Bolshevik Russia of a later date would struggle many years to recover.

Great Britain and Japan provided the chief obstacles to this Russian expansion of influence. The British, competing with a Belgian syndicate, obtained concessions for 2,800 miles of line over ten provinces, as compared with 1,530 for Russia in Manchuria.[22] But in spite of these successes, British interests remained apprehensive of Russian intentions and began negotiations, therefore, with the Tokyo government, which had its own reasons for opposing the Tsar.

The Japanese feeling was that, except for Russo-German-French interference, their recent victory over China in the Sino-Japanese War would have left them in full control of the Liaotung Peninsula.[23]

---

[17] Rockhill, op. cit., "Charter of the Russo-Chinese Bank," pp. 207-11.

[18] Rockhill, op. cit., "Agreement Between the Chinese Government and the Russo-Chinese Bank," pp. 212-14.

[19] Rockhill, op. cit., "Statutes of the Chinese Eastern Railway Company," pp. 215-24.

[20] Rockhill, op. cit., "Agreement Between the Chinese Government and the Russo-Chinese Bank," p. 214.

[21] Rockhill, op. cit., "Convention Between Russia and China for Lease to Russia of Port Arthur, Talienwan, and the Adjacent Waters," pp. 50-52.

[22] Rockhill, op. cit., "Peking-Hankow (Lu Han) Railway Contracts," pp. 225-48.

[23] A. M. Pooley (ed.), The Secret Memoirs of Count Tadasu Hayashi (New York, 1915), pp. 109-10.

Tokyo joined readily with London, therefore, in negotiating the Anglo-Japanese Offensive and Defensive Alliance of January 30, 1902.[24] This agreement served temporarily to check tsarist expansion, while three years later a Japanese victory in the Russo-Japanese War substituted Nipponese—for Russian—economic and political penetration on the Asian mainland.

The Treaty of Portsmouth (September 5, 1905), which concluded hostilities between the Russians and the Japanese, provided for Russian recognition of Japan's political, economic, and military interests in Korea. The tsarist government further renounced to Tokyo all territorial advantages and other concessions in southern Manchuria, together with Russia's Port Arthur and Dairen leases, the South Manchurian Railway with all rights and privileges pertaining to it, and the southern half of Sakhalin Island.[25]

These losses left Russia seriously weakened, while Japan appeared as the dominant power. In the course of German expansion in China proper, however, St. Petersburg and Tokyo found themselves forced to recognize a stalemate in their own rivalries by negotiating a series of secret agreements (1907, 1910, 1912) which reserved northern Manchuria for Russian and southern Manchuria for Japanese exploitation. During World War I Russia secretly recognized Japanese spheres of interest in Shantung, Manchuria, and eastern Inner Mongolia, while in return Tokyo sanctioned a number of minor Russian advances in Outer Mongolia.[26] But these were small concessions to an imperial government which had once been a dominant power in Asia. It was Bolshevik, not tsarist, diplomacy that was destined to win back for Russia in 1945 what had been lost at Portsmouth forty years earlier.

THE RISE OF JAPANESE IMPERIALISM

During latter phases of World War I Russian spheres of influence remaining in the Far East suffered near-extinction. On the Western front Imperial Russian armies were collapsing, and in the spring of 1917 antitsarist forces overthrew the old order. By autumn Lenin and his Bolsheviks had toppled the middle-of-the-road Kerensky government. During months that followed, various counterrevolutionary leaders — including Lieutenant General Dmitrii Horvath, general

[24] Amos S. Hershey and Susanne W. Hershey, *Modern Japan* (Indianapolis, 1919), p. 259. The text appears in *Accounts and Papers, State Papers*, CXXX (1902). Dispatch to His Majesty's Minister at Tokyo, January 30, 1902.

[25] J. V. A. MacMurray (ed.), *Treaties and Agreements with and Concerning China* (New York, 1921), I, 522–28.

[26] Ernest Batson Price, *The Russo-Japanese Treaties of 1907–1916 Concerning Manchuria and Mongolia* (Baltimore, 1933), pp. 35–38, 107–8.

manager of the Chinese Eastern Railway, and Admiral Aleksandr Kolchak—tried to mobilize counterrevolution in the Far East.[27] The allies—especially the Japanese—intervened by landing troops in Siberia.

Developments in Russian Asia during this period have been described and analyzed elsewhere and need no elaboration here.[28] Important is the fact that by the war's end the Russian-built Chinese Eastern Railway was lost to the Bolshevik government's jurisdiction, and Japanese troops controlled large sectors of eastern Siberia; Russia as an Asian power had almost ceased to exist.

Japan, meanwhile, had been moving in still another direction. Throughout the whole of World War I the Tokyo government had been exploiting various circumstances in order to extend its interests. When the question first arose as to whether or not Japan would adhere to the Allied cause, Great Britain, more than any of the other powers, found itself in a dilemma. Generally, the British would have preferred to keep Japan out of the war, but it was believed that Japanese naval assistance was needed in order to aid in the destruction of German naval strength in the Pacific.[29] In the course of negotiations, Great Britain agreed that Japan, in return for its participation in the war, could count upon British support for Japanese claims in regard to the disposal of Germany's rights in Shantung and Pacific island possessions north of the equator.[30] In due course France and Russia reached similar understandings with the Tokyo government, and in November 1917 the United States, through the Lansing-Ishii Agreement (which was recognized until April 14, 1923, when it was superseded by the Washington treaties), was to concede that Japan, because of her geographical propinquity, had special interests in China.[31]

In the meantime, once Japan had sent Germany an ultimatum and had received Berlin's rejection, Japanese forces moved swiftly into the German possessions in the Far East, going so far as to violate neutral Chinese territory (as did the Germans) during the occupation of Kiaochow. Great Britain condoned the Japanese action,[32] where-

[27] See Elena Varneck and H. H. Fisher (eds.), *The Testimony of Kolchak and Other Siberian Materials* (Stanford, Calif., 1935).

[28] John Albert White, *The Siberian Intervention* (Princeton, 1950). See also Benjamin Bock, "The Origins of the Inter-Allied Intervention in Eastern Asia 1918–1920," an unpublished doctoral dissertation in the Hoover Library, Stanford University, 1940. Pertinent diplomatic correspondence appears in publications of the Department of State, *Papers Relating to the Foreign Policy of the United States* (cited hereinafter as *Foreign Relations*), *Russia* (1918), Vol. II.

[29] G. P. Gooch and H. W. V. Temperley (eds.), *British Documents on the Origins of the World War, 1898–1914* (London, 1926–38), Vol. XI, Grey to Green, August 4, 1914.   [30] MacMurray, *op. cit.*, II, 1167–68.

[31] *Foreign Relations* (1922), II, 595.

[32] *Foreign Relations* (1914), Reinsch to Bryan, September 30, p. 182.

upon China appealed to the United States for support. From Acting Secretary Lansing came the reply that "it would be quixotic in the extreme to allow the question of China's integrity to entangle the United States in international difficulties."[33] By the end of the year Japan enjoyed control of the entire province of Shantung as well as most of the German islands north of the equator. Then, on January 18, 1915, the Tokyo government sent Peking the now notorious Twenty-one Demands.[34]

In their original form, the Twenty-one Demands were arranged in five groups. The first required China's "full assent" to whatever disposition of German rights in Shantung the Tokyo government chose to make at the end of the war; a Chinese promise not to lease or cede any part of Shantung to any third power; and the granting to Japan of sweeping commercial and railway privileges in the province. The second group sought to strengthen the Japanese special position in Manchuria and eastern Inner Mongolia. The third group insisted on special industrial and mining privileges in the Yangtze Valley. The fourth demanded from China a pledge not to lease or cede "to any power any harbor or bay or any island" along the China coast. And the fifth group, designated as "desires" rather than demands, requested vital political rights in China proper.

In China the knowledge of these demands gave rise to violent anti-Japanese sentiments, and there were outspoken expressions of indignation in the West as well. But official Western protests were relatively mild. During negotiations the Japanese somewhat modified the original Demands to a point where China finally agreed to accept them. As this news reached Washington, the United States issued a warning that no agreement entered into by Japan and China "impairing the treaty rights of the United States and its citizens in China or the territorial integrity of China, or the international policy relative to China commonly known as the Open Door Policy" could be recognized in Washington.[35]

In the final agreements embodied in the Sino-Japanese treaties of May 25, 1915, the "desires" of Group Five were set aside, but not given up. In part, these instruments granted special rights in Manchuria and extended the lease of Port Arthur and Dairen and the provisions of the railway agreements to ninety-nine years; they granted special mining and commercial rights to Japanese citizens in China and extraterritorial trials of Japanese offenders against Chinese law; and they provided that China should give "full assent to all matters upon

[33] *Foreign Relations* (1914), Lansing to Reinsch, November 4, pp. 189–90.
[34] Text in MacMurray, *op. cit.*, II, 1231–34.
[35] *Foreign Relations* (1915), Bryan to Guthrie and Reinsch, May 11, p. 146.

which the Japanese government may hereafter agree with the German government" relative to Shantung.[36]

In the face of these developments, the Chinese still hoped to regain sovereignty and integrity for their country during the peace treaty negotiations at Versailles, but once again there was disappointment in store. At the Peace Conference the Chinese delegation advanced claims for the abrogation of the offending Sino-Japanese treaties and agreements and for the transfer of German rights in Shantung to China. But the Council of Four declined to consider this proposal and suggested that China call "these important matters" to the attention of the new League of Nations.[37] According to the Treaty of Versailles, German rights, titles, and privileges in Shantung were renounced—not to China, but to Japan.[38]

In China the disappointment among intellectuals and especially among students was acute. ". . . when the news of the Paris Peace Conference finally reached us we were greatly shocked," a Peking University student recalled. "We at once awoke to the fact that foreign nations were still selfish and militaristic and that they were all great liars . . . We came to the conclusion that a greater world war would be coming sooner or later and that this great war would be fought in the East. We had nothing to do with our government, that we knew very well, and at the same time we could no longer depend upon any so-called great leader like Woodrow Wilson, for example. Looking at our people and at the pitiful ignorant masses, we couldn't help but feel that we must struggle."[39]

It was dissatisfaction and bitterness arising from all these many complex developments—from dissolution of the traditional Chinese order, from the Western record of political and economic penetration, from Western attitudes at Versailles, from the inadequacies of the Washington Conference agreements of 1922, from inequality of treatment which China continued to suffer within the family of nations—it was this dissatisfaction and unrest which a disrupted, but increasingly Bolshevik-controlled Russia sought to exploit in its first diplomatic overtures toward the Peking government.

[36] MacMurray, *op. cit.*, II, 1215–30.

[37] Thomas Edward La Fargue, *China and the World War,* Hoover War Library Publications, No. 12 (Stanford, Calif., 1937), pp. 173–232.

[38] *The Treaties of Peace, 1919–1923* (New York: Carnegie Endowment for International Peace, 1924), I, 93–94.

[39] The quotation is from an interview with a student of Peking University as it appears in Wen-Han Kiang, *The Chinese Student Movement* (New York, 1948), p. 37. The original is in Tsi C. Wang, *The Youth Movement in China* (New York, 1928), pp. 161–62.

CHAPTER III

CHINA AND THE FIRST SOVIET OVERTURES

Between 1919 and 1927 Russian Bolshevik leaders developed a China policy that was multifold: the Soviet Union made overtures and finally sent an ambassador to the legal Chinese government in Peking; this representative acted concurrently as an agent for the Third International, which was aiding Sun Yat-sen's Kuomintang in an effort to overthrow the government in Peking; and while the Third International was supporting the Kuomintang, Chinese Communists began joining that party in order to win contact with the masses and eventually to capture it or oust it from leadership of the Chinese revolution.

Communist leaders had not taken their eyes from the primary goal. "We wish to put an end to the power of capital all over the world," Grigorii Zinoviev told the Congress of Eastern People, called by the Executive Committee of the Communist International (ECCI) and held in Baku September 1–8, 1920. "This will be possible only when we have set off the conflagration of revolution all over the world— and not only in Europe and America—and when all toiling mankind which inhabits Asia and Africa shall follow us."[1]

China was a primary target, and no one knew better than Bolshevik leaders that the Peking regime was little else than a façade propped up by various foreign powers. Behind this front, moreover, there moved a bewildering succession of war lords who assembled, unseated one another, and reassembled, as in a game of musical chairs. Under such circumstances it is not to be wondered at that the Peking government was proving less capable of ruling China than the imperial rulers had been—or that the Russians should decide to take double advantage of it.

SUN YAT-SEN GROPES FOR A PROGRAM

The fall of the Ch'ing dynasty in 1912 had marked the beginning of a prolonged struggle between Yuan Shih-k'ai, who preferred the retention of monarchical forms, and Sun Yat-sen, who demanded a republic. Immediately after the Manchu overthrow, Sun was elected to a provisional presidency, but he retired somewhat later in favor of Yuan who, he hoped, could unite the nation. Yuan proceeded, how-

---

[1] *Pervyi S'ezd Narodov Vostoka, Baku,* Stenograficheskie otchety (Petrograd, 1920). A manuscript translation by Xenia Eudin is available in the Hoover Institute and Library, Stanford, California.

ever, to strengthen his personal position while plotting to restore the monarchy with himself as emperor. Members of the new Chinese parliament sent out a punitive expedition to deter Yuan, but the venture failed, and Sun fled to Japan. The republican leader scorned Yuan as a creature of foreign interests. Writing to his American friend, James Deitrick, in August 1914, Sun begged him to block any loan which Yuan Shih-k'ai might seek to raise in the United States:[2]

At present he [Yuan] cannot get any more loan [sic] from Europe, and I am told that he intends to give great inducements to American capitalists to secure money which is his only power . . . during the Revolution panic is sure to follow and all trades will be at a stand-still for lack of money, and more so in China, for the medium of exchange in the commercial centre of the country is controlled by foreign bankers. So foreign banks, such as the Hongkong-Shanghai Banking Corporation, really hold the balance of power in an internal struggle. If we cannot get rid of that money control we can never be independent and Yuan Shi Kai is but a mere tool of those foreign bankers.

Sun proposed a program of state controls to eliminate foreign financial interference:[3]

My way of getting rid of this curse is that the Revolutionary Government must prepare to control the trade so that we can use any kind of money we please and thus we can do away with foreign bankers and be our own master. In order to do that the government must (1) organize department stores to conduct distribution; (2) control both the land and water traffic, i.e., to conduct transportation; and last but not least by manufacturing some of the most important goods which have been, hitherto, dependent upon foreign supply, i.e., to conduct production. Thus China can be independent both politically and economically . . .

But Sun, in proposing state control and planning, immediately found himself facing an old dilemma: Chinese leaders could not resist Western encroachments without the aid of Western techniques and Western finance. His plea to Deitrick continued:[4]

. . . I want you to look [in the United States] for expert men in different lines for me . . . I think it will not be difficult for you to pick out such experts, but they must be men of honesty, great courage and ability.

It would be splendid if you can make arrangements with some of the most influential department store trust [sic] and get them to cooperate with this scheme of ours. In that case we should like them to advance us a sum of at least ten million dollars as initiative war fund, for the franchise given.

[2] *10 Letters of Sun Yat-sen, 1914–1916* (Stanford University Libraries, 1942), pp. 1, 3, 4.   [3] *Ibid.*, pp. 4–5.   [4] *Ibid.*, pp. 7–8.

Granting Deitrick power of attorney, Sun proposed more and more sweeping inducements for American-operated "department stores" and other joint enterprises :[5]

Provided that you can arrange it you will dispose of the entire privileges granted therein [in the power of attorney] for a joint undertaking with the Government of China to establish a system of department stores, upon an advance of ten million dollars to me and my party. This money is to be used for the promotion of affairs of the party and country and within the boundary of China. If, owing to the disturbed financial conditions, you find it inconvenient to secure said sum, then you will use your own judgment as to disposal of districts to various persons and for such sums as may be deemed prudent and fair. For example, say the district around Hankow or Nanking or Shanghai, etc. . . .

In case you cannot find such a party willing to undertake this department store, you are authorized to close a deal with said party to undertake work in such industrial lines as Mining, Iron and Steel Works, Transportation, Grain Elevators, Manufactures, and Arsenal for the Navy and A Army [sic] of China, etc., under the same agreements, and with the same understanding that half of its shares must be owned by the Government.

It was Sun's intention that such joint arrangements should be transitional :[6]

For a certain period of time this system will be under the foreign management entirely, later the natives gradually train up to take its place.

Yet the fact remains that he was begging American capitalists to put him into essentially the same position he had condemned Yuan Shih-k'ai for occupying.

Awaiting European and American aid that was not forthcoming, Sun achieved slight success in organizing revolt against the Peking government. He and his Kuomintang, or Nationalist party,[7] made a number of abortive attempts, but they had few funds and no reliable troops. In 1916, upon the death of Yuan Shih-k'ai, there began in Peking a prolonged struggle between two main factions of northern military leaders. One of these groups organized itself into the so-called Anfu Club, which found access to financial sources in Japan and, on achieving power, obtained for the Peking government a series of substantial loans. In due course the Anfu clique became known to the people of China as pro-Japanese, and popular dissatisfaction gave rise to the May Fourth Movement of 1919, an outburst of student

[5] *Ibid.*, p. 14.
[6] *Ibid.*, p. 16.
[7] Sun's party underwent a number of reorganizations; in these pages it will be referred to as the Kuomintang, or as the Nationalist party.

demonstrations which rallied revolutionary sentiments among many classes of Chinese.[8]

SOVIET RUSSIA DISCLAIMS SPECIAL PRIVILEGE

It was against this background that Soviet Russian leaders sought to establish relations with Peking and to influence both the domestic and foreign policies of China. On July 4, 1918, G. V. Chicherin, People's Commissar of Foreign Affairs in Moscow, told the Fifth Congress of Soviets that China had been notified of a new Russian policy: Moscow repudiated encroachments of the tsarist government in Manchuria; relinquished rights of extraterritoriality in China and Mongolia; waived tsarist levies which, "under various pretexts, had been imposed on the peoples of China"; and withdrew all military guards stationed by the tsarist government in its consulates in China. "Moreover, we believe that if China could refund the sum of money that had been invested in the construction of the [Chinese Eastern] railway by the Russian people," he declared, "China would be able to redeem the [Russian share of the indemnity] irrespective of the date which was stipulated in the contract [between China and Tsarist Russia], a contract which had been forced upon China."[9]

The Declaration of 1919, which appeared over the signature of L. M. Karakhan on July 15 of that year and which the Soviets communicated from Irkutsk, offered China a startling elaboration of Chicherin's statement. In this document the Deputy Commissar for Foreign Affairs announced a Soviet campaign to "free the people from the yoke of the military force of foreign money which is crushing the people of the East, and principally the people of China." Precisely how much the Russians promised China depends upon which of several texts the critic reads.

All versions of the manifesto gave the impression that Soviet Russia had given up those conquests made by the tsars in Manchuria and other Asiatic areas; that the Soviet government considered null and void all secret treaties concluded between Imperial Russia on the one hand and Japan, China, and the ex-Allies on the other; and that the Soviet government was renouncing indemnities payable by China for the insurrection of the Boxers in 1900. Subsequent Sino-Soviet disputes arose over the French text, which was communicated to the Peking government only after many months' delay:[10]

The Soviet government returns to the Chinese people without demanding any kind of compensation, the Chinese Eastern Railway, as well as all the

[8] For an analysis of the student movement see Wen-han Kiang, *op. cit.*

[9] *Izvestia*, July 5, 1918.

[10] This English translation of the French text appears in *The China Year Book, 1924–1925*, pp. 868–972.

mining concessions, forestry, gold mines, and all the other things which were seized from them by the government of the Tsars, that of Kerensky, and the Brigands, Horvat, Semenoff, Koltchak, the Russian Ex-generals, Merchants, and capitalists.

Soviet spokesmen denounced this text and denied that their government had offered to return the railway without compensation. But Allen S. Whiting recently located a Soviet Russian pamphlet which contains a text of the Karakhan manifesto with the disputed passage intact. The Russian Communists, then, *did* offer to return the Chinese Eastern Railway without compensation.[11]

Official communications between Moscow and Peking were slow, and it was a long time before the Russians received from the Chinese any comments concerning the Declaration of 1919. Chinese officials maintained later that the statement, cabled from Irkutsk, had not reached Peking until the following March.[12] In any case, the Peking government had so far cast its lot with the Allied powers, co-operating in the blockade of Bolshevik areas in Manchuria, supporting the intervention in Siberia, and concluding an agreement with White Russian elements for control of the Chinese Eastern Railway under General Horvath.

Yet Soviet promises found wide circulation in China and exerted a powerful impact, especially upon students and adult intellectuals. In contrast to the Western powers who, at Versailles, had supported Japan in the Shantung demands, here was Soviet Russia renouncing all privileges and asking China to enter into official relations on an equal basis.

OBSTACLES TO AN UNDERSTANDING

On an official level the Peking regime found the Russians somewhat less altruistic. Actual negotiations showed the two governments at variance over four primary issues—the Chinese Eastern Railway, the status of Mongolia, the disposition of Russian shares in the Boxer indemnities, and procedures for establishing Sino-Soviet relations. Prolonged discussions showed that Karakhan sitting across the table in Peking was not ready to give away as much as Karakhan in Moscow had seemed to promise.

Meanwhile, China was suffering the sort of domestic disturbances which Western diplomats had come to take almost for granted. In

---

[11] Vl. Vilenskii (Siberiakov), *Kitai i Sovetskaia Rossiia* (Moscow, 1919), p. 15. A translation appears in J. Degras, *Soviet Documents on Foreign Policy* (London, 1951), pp. 158–61. For an investigation of surrounding circumstances, see Allen S. Whiting, "The Soviet Offer to China of 1919," *The Far Eastern Quarterly*, X, No. 4 (August 1951), 355–64.

[12] *Peking Daily News*, November 24, 1923.

1920 the combined forces of the Manchurian war lord, Chang Tso-lin, and of Tsao K'un overthrew the Anfu government and assumed power. In the late summer a military-diplomatic mission proceeded to Moscow and began negotiations with a view to establishing official relations between the two governments.[13] On September 27 the People's Commissar of Foreign Affairs, Chicherin, handed to the mission for transmission to the Ministry of Foreign Affairs of the Chinese Republic a second declaration which somewhat amplified the 1919 statement, but, in place of renouncing Russian claims to the Chinese Eastern Railway, proposed the drawing up of a special treaty regarding this line "with due regard to the needs" of Soviet Russia.[14]

By December 1920 the Moscow viewpoint was being pressed in Peking by Ignatius Yurin, who officially represented, not the Soviets, but an entity known as the Far Eastern Republic. This government had come into being the previous April when a number of local Siberian leaders, with the blessing of Moscow, formed the republic as a "buffer state" which, for the next two years, was to serve not only as a base against Japanese intervention forces in Siberia, but also, by sending observers to the Washington Conference, as a channel of communication into circles where Soviet diplomats were not yet welcome.[15]

Yurin, while representing the Far Eastern Republic in Peking, was responsible for persuading the Chinese government to terminate relations with the Russian ambassador accredited by previous regimes.[16] Yurin also exerted his influence toward the termination of extra-territoriality, but failed to establish treaty relations between China and the Far Eastern Republic. In Moscow the signing of a commercial treaty between the military commander of Sinkiang and the Tashkent Soviet was hailed as an important step toward Soviet-Chinese rapprochement,[17] but in retrospect, this development appears as perhaps the first of many Russian moves toward direct penetration of Sinkiang, rather than as part of Russian diplomatic relations with China.

An important factor in Chinese unwillingness to press for closer relations with Moscow was undoubtedly the negative pressure which Western powers brought to bear in Peking. China was still looking

---

[13] Ya. Yanson, "Nashi predlozheniia Kitaiu," *Izvestia*, November 4, 1920.

[14] "Declaration of 1920," *The China Year Book, 1924–1925*, p. 870.

[15] The Special Delegation of the Far Eastern Republic to the United States was responsible for the publication of *A Short Outline History of the Far Eastern Republic* (Washington, 1922). The Special Delegation also released the *Memorandum of the Special Delegation of the Far Eastern Republic* (Washington, 1921) and *To the Washington Conference on the Limitation of Armaments* (Washington, 1922).

[16] *The China Year Book, 1921–1922*, p. 625.

[17] *Izvestia*, October 9, 1920.

to the capitalist West for support, and consequently, it was not until after the results of the Washington Conference had been appraised that Chinese diplomats began to look with fleeting favor toward Moscow.

Chinese reactions to the accomplishments of the Washington Conference were mixed.[18] The Nine-Power Treaty guaranteed the sovereignty, independence, and administrative integrity of China and also reaffirmed the Open Door principle.[19] Through a special conference, moreover, Japan restored the Shantung lease to China and agreed to withdraw its troops from that territory.[20] On the other hand, the powers made no move toward renouncing their extraterritorial rights, curtailing their vested interests, or restoring tariff autonomy to the Chinese people. Many Chinese were disappointed, and further irritation rose through delays in the ratification of various treaties inspired by the conference. The Peking government, moreover, was in no position to exert influence. In 1922 Wu P'ei-fu, who as a division commander under Tsao K'un had driven the Anfu-ites out of Peking, combined with his own subordinate ally, General Feng Yü-hsiang, to drive Chang Tso-lin back into Manchuria. Thereupon Chang, with encouragement from the Japanese, declared the "independence" of Manchuria while he awaited some opportunity for reasserting his authority in Peking.

During the autumn of 1922 Moscow began pressing Soviet negotiations with new vigor, sending Adolf Joffe to carry forward the work begun by Yurin. The new Soviet representative achieved little, and it was not until the following year, with Karakhan's appearance in Peking, that negotiations began to move forward.

Joffe, in the course of his representations, pressed the same four issues: the status of the Chinese Eastern Railway, the use of Russian shares of the Boxer indemnities, Soviet relations with Mongolia, and the possible establishment of formal Sino-Soviet relations. In his negotiations the Russian assertedly based himself upon the Karakhan Declarations of 1919 and 1920, but he declared categorically—and seemingly in contradiction to the 1919 Declaration—that Soviet Russia had not surrendered its interests in China, but had merely denounced the tsarist policy of force. "In particular," he declared, "even if Russia surrenders to the Chinese people her rights over the Chinese Eastern Railway, this fact will not annul Russia's interests in the Chinese Eastern Railway, which comprises a part of the great Siberian Railway and connects one part of Russia with another."[21]

18 Cf. *North China Herald*, February 18, 1922.
19 *International Conciliation*, No. 172, March 1922, "Washington Conference on the Limitation of Armaments," Part II, pp. 43–49.
20 *Ibid.*, pp. 87–136.   21 *Izvestia*, November 11, 1922.

In regard to Russian shares in the Boxer indemnity, Joffe insisted that, although the Soviet government, through the Declarations of 1919 and 1920, had renounced its claims, this action had been taken under the supposition that the Chinese government would in no case remunerate former Russian organizations and diplomatic officers for their losses. Moreover, the Declarations, he charged, had never been answered by the Chinese government. Under these circumstances, Joffe felt it necessary to protest any disposition of Russian shares in the Boxer fund until a Sino-Soviet conference had been called.[22]

On the Mongolian question Joffe admitted the presence of Soviet troops in Urga, but insisted that in terms of Russian and Chinese interests alike; their removal at that time was impossible. "The new Russia," he said, "has never forced its will on other peoples, and in spite of economic and political disadvantages, did not interfere with the establishment of new republics on Russian territory. Other countries, as, for example, China, should relinquish likewise their imperialist policies in regard to other countries as, for example, Mongolia."[23] Anyway, according to Joffe, the Mongolian people had requested that Russian troops remain in their country.

KARAKHAN PROCEEDS TO PEKING

Joffe had managed to arrange one Sino-Soviet conference, which convened September 2, 1922, but failed to achieve concrete results. During the proceedings it was clear that the Chinese negotiator, V. K. Wellington Koo, felt that Joffe's proposals fell far short of Karakhan's 1919 and 1920 pledges.[24]

Karakhan, on his way to China, stopped off in Manchuria, where he was received by Chang Tso-lin.[25] Reaching Peking September 2, 1923, he and his staff of ten assistants were accorded a warm and vociferous welcome both by student groups and by many government officials.[26] It was not customary for Western powers to dispatch top diplomats to China, and Karakhan himself made the most of this circumstance. "It is inadmissible," he told the People's Diplomatic Association in Peking, "that a great State like China, which should play a great role in the world, should, for some reason or other, have no Ambassadors, but only Ministers, thus appearing in the position of a second rate Power. Today, as you know, Russia has ambassadors

---

[22] *Pravda*, September 24, 1922.

[23] *Izvestia*, November 11, 1922.

[24] See the *Times* (London), September 21, 1922, and *Izvestia*, September 16, 1922.

[25] *North China Star* (Tientsin), September 6, 1923.

[26] From J. C. Huston, Consul, American Consulate General, Tientsin, China, File No. 800, "The Chinese Renaissance and Its Relation to Soviet Policy in the Far East," October 8, 1923. (From the Huston Collection in the Hoover Library.)

in Turkey, Persia, and other Asiatic countries, and I must express my hope that China will dare to say that in this country there must be a Russian Ambassador and that China herself must send an Ambassador to Russia."[27] The new envoy voiced solemn assurances, moreover, that Soviet diplomacy was open diplomacy. "Nothing is concealed from the Russian people of what is being done by Russian diplomats," he declared. "Under such circumstances the people cannot, as under the old form of diplomacy, be suddenly confronted with already concluded agreements, selling the people's own fate without their having had any previous knowledge of what was going on behind the scenes."[28]

Karakhan's assurances were not without initial effect. It was noted that Karakhan, if accredited as ambassador, would rank forthwith as dean of the diplomatic corps in Peking, and the *North China Star* used citations from diplomatic history texts to document the claim that Soviet diplomacy was "open."

But the tactful and often enthusiastic give-and-take of reception line and banquet hall soon gave way to stubborn diplomatic controversy. There was conflict over wording of the Declarations of 1919 and 1920, especially as they pertained to the Chinese Eastern Railway. Beyond this, the negotiations were obstructed by controversy over the timing of Chinese recognition of the Soviet Union and by the presence of Red troops in Outer Mongolia, which, from this point forward, the Russians systematically alienated from China.

While premising his negotiations squarely on the Declarations, Karakhan was now cautiously qualifying: ". . . not in any measure do we renounce our interests in China," he said, "so far as these do not infringe upon the sovereignty and interests of the Chinese people."[29] He pointed out that the Chinese Eastern Railway was of commercial interest to the Russians, and whereas there had been an unjust infringement by the tsarist government in alienating Chinese land adjacent to the line—a policy to which the Soviets were opposed—there was no doubt whatsoever that the road had been built by the money of the Russian people.[30] "Never and nowhere could I have said that all the rights of the CER belong to China," he wrote to C. T. Wang, the Chinese negotiator. "Neither do you say this yourself, nor, for that matter, has it yet been said by anyone else in China."[31]

In regard to Outer Mongolia, Karakhan insisted that difficulties

---

[27] *The Far Eastern Times* (Peking), September 13, 1923.
[28] *Ibid.*
[29] *The Far Eastern Times*, September 6, 1923.
[30] *The Far Eastern Times*, September 18, 1923.
[31] Karakhan to Wang, November 30, 1923, *The China Year Book, 1923–1924*, p. 875.

there were the fault not of Soviet Russia but of the Chinese, who, in supporting Allied interventions, had aided White Russian forces in the establishment of Mongolian bases.[32] "If there are in Mongolia, as some people like to express it, Russian troops, that is the 100 Red Army men who are there to prevent the formation of White bands," Karakhan declared. "Their presence there presents no obstacle to the restoration of relations between China and Mongolia. When we reach this point, we will show how justly New Russia is capable of solving questions."[33]

But China wanted a settlement of railway and Mongolian issues prior to recognition of the Moscow government.

Negotiations proceeded into the winter months, when a preliminary agreement was initialed. The terms of this document aroused so much further opposition in China that Wang withdrew in favor of V. K. Wellington Koo, and it was not until May 24, 1924, that a treaty was finally signed.

The new agreement established normal diplomatic relations between China and the Soviet Union, extinguished "all conventions, treaties, agreements, protocols, contracts, etc.,"[34] which had been concluded between China and Imperial Russia, and predicated future intercourse "on the basis of equality, reciprocity, and justice, as well as the spirit of the declarations of the Soviet government of the years 1919 and 1920."[35] The Soviet Union agreed that all tsarist treaties with third parties affecting China should be invalidated, and each state renounced the right to conclude agreements contrary to the rights and interests of the other.

Moreover, each party undertook to prohibit within its borders either organizations or activities subversive to the other party and pledged itself not to engage in propaganda against the social and political systems of the other. The Soviet Union recognized Outer Mongolia as an integral part of China—under Chinese sovereignty— and renounced all Russian concessions in China, together with extraterritorial rights and the Russian share of the Boxer indemnity.

Provisions were made for a new delimitation of frontiers, a renunciation of all tsarist concessionary rights, an end to consular jurisdiction, the negotiation of a commercial treaty "in accordance with the principles of equality and reciprocity," and the mutual settlement of financial claims.

[32] Karakhan to Wang, November 30, 1923, *The China Year Book, 1923–1924*, pp. 873–76.
[33] *The Far Eastern Times*, September 17, 1923.
[34] *The China Year Book, 1924–1925*, pp. 1192–1200.
[35] *Ibid.*

Annexed to the treaty was an agreement for provisional management, until a final settlement could be made, of the Chinese Eastern
Railway. Since the line lay under the control of neither the Soviets
nor the Peking government, but of Marshal Chang Tso-lin, no further
action could be taken until a separate instrument had been drawn up
between the Soviet Union and the Three Eastern Provinces. Once
completed, this latter treaty had the effect of recognizing Marshal
Chang's government on a footing almost equal to Peking, and consequently considerable resentment was aroused in China proper by its
conclusion.[36] Moreover, the Chinese Eastern Railway remained a
potential trouble spot. For Karakhan and Koo managed to agree only
that the line, having been built by Russian capital and constructed
entirely on Chinese territory, was a "purely commercial enterprise";
that, except for problems of business operation, all matters affecting
the rights of Chinese authorities should be administered by them;
and that in all other respects the enterprise was to be run under joint
Russo-Chinese management until such time as a final settlement could
be reached.

Clearly, China did not gain all that Moscow had promised a few
years earlier. Within less than a year, moreover, the Soviet Union
concluded with Japan an agreement which recognized the Treaty of
Portsmouth as a basis for Russo-Japanese relations and thus preju-
diced Chinese rights and interests in Manchuria.[37] Yet at the time of
its signature, the Sino-Russian Agreement of 1924, taken as a whole
and compared with conventional treaties involving China, did not
seem unfavorable to the interests of the Peking government.

In Soviet Russia, meanwhile, the treaty was presented as a triumph of Bolshevik diplomacy, with Chicherin himself hailing its
signature as "a big stride on the road to the liberation of colonial and
semi-colonial peoples from subordination to the Great Powers."[38] It
was true, he admitted, that China had been guilty, hitherto, of blockade, intervention, and nonrecognition, but all that unpleasantness had
passed. Now at last the Chinese people had recognized the Soviet
Republic as their only consistent and disinterested friend. "The significance of this expression of the independence of Chinese policy
extends beyond the frontiers of China," he concluded. "It is an historical event in the sphere of movement of the emancipation of Eastern
Peoples."[39]

[36] Ibid.
[37] League of Nations Treaty Series, XXXIV (Lausanne, 1925), p. 32.
[38] Pravda, June 1, 1924.
[39] Ibid.

CHAPTER IV

THE FOUNDING OF THE CHINESE COMMUNIST PARTY

~~~~~~

EARLY ORGANIZING ACTIVITIES

While Karakhan was mending Sino-Soviet relations on a diplomatic level, Russian Communists working through the Third International were aiding the development of the Chinese Communist party, negotiating toward the support of Sun Yat-sen in an effort to overthrow the legal Chinese government in Peking, using Kuomintang organizations in order to establish contact with and influence over labor and peasant masses, and preparing in the long run either to capture Sun Yat-sen's party or to oust it from leadership of the revolution.

In the spring of 1918, only a few months after the Bolshevik revolution, a small group of Chinese intellectuals at Peking University, inspired by Communist literature but as yet without demonstrable contact with Moscow, founded a Society for the Study of Marxism.[1] Instrumental in organizing the group was Li Ta-chao, professor of history and chief librarian at the University of Peking, and closely associated with him was another prominent scholar, Ch'en Tu-hsiu, who was dean of the Department of Literature at the same institution. As founder of *Hsin Ch'ing-nien* (New Youth)—a review demanding the introduction into China of Western ideas, opposition to traditional Chinese concepts, and the elimination of Confucianism— Ch'en wielded considerable influence in Chinese intellectual circles.[2]

In Peking Ch'en began publishing *Mei-chou p'ing-lun* (Weekly Review), which was devoted to labor problems. Arrested, he spent several months in jail. After his release, finding it impossible to work in the capital, he went to Shanghai, where he took part in a Marxist study group organized by Tai Chi-t'ao, former secretary of Sun Yat-sen in Japan, who subsequently supported Chiang Kai-shek against the Communists.

[1] Ken'ichi Hatano, *Saikin Shina Nenkan* (New China Yearbook) (Tokyo, 1935), p. 1597. Conflicting sources, such as Hua Ying-shen, *Chung-kuo kung-ch'an-tang lieh-shih chuan* (Biographies of the Martyrs of the CCP) (Shantung, 1947), p. 2, date of the founding of the Society somewhat earlier. Cf. Chow Ts'e-tsung, *The May Fourth Movement* (Cambridge: Harvard University Press, 1960), pp. 244 note k, 246–49; also C. Martin Wilbur (ed.), *The Communist Movement in China* (East Asian Institute of Columbia University, 1960), pp. 14–28.

[2] For an analysis of Ch'en Tu-hsiu's influence and of his relationship to Li Ta-chao, see Benjamin Schwartz, *Chinese Communism and the Rise of Mao* (Cambridge, 1951), pp. 7–27, and "Biographical Sketch, Ch'en Tu-hsiu, Pre-Communist Phase," *Papers on China* (Harvard University, 1948), Vol. II.

During the spring of 1919 Chinese students and intellectuals were caught up in the May Fourth Movement, from which the revolution of the 'twenties is often dated. Outwardly, these disturbances appeared as manifestations of resentment against Japanese encroachments in Shantung and against the pro-Japanese Anfu government in Peking. As the movement spread across the face of China, however, it became also an outlet for accumulated bitterness against those nations of the West which, flying in the face of Woodrow Wilson's promises of self-determination and justice, had surrendered to Japanese demands at Versailles. And finally, as factory workers went out on strike, the movement served as an expression of social discontent and rebellion.[3] Even as Karakhan dispatched his notorious Declaration of 1919, Chinese students, intellectuals, and workers were growing restless and impatient for action against their own status quo and against Japan and the West.

It was shortly after this, in the spring of 1920, that the Comintern dispatched two agents, Grigorii Voitinsky and an overseas Chinese named Yang Ming-chai, to help organize the Chinese Communist movement.[4] On reaching Peking, Voitinsky made contact with Li Ta-chao, who then introduced him to the Shanghai group to which Ch'en Tu-hsiu belonged. In that city he set up his headquarters and began organizational work. Unable to gather together a group of true Communists, he assembled leftists of varying shades and founded the nucleus of the Chinese Communist party.[5] This and subsequent organizational work was done with such secrecy that even the British Intelligence Service is said to have been unaware of the presence of Russian agents in China until nearly two years later.[6]

By September a similar group was functioning in Peking, while

[3] Wen-han Kiang, *op. cit.*, pp. 37–40.

[4] *Chung-kuo hsien-tai ko-ming yün-tung shih* (A History of the Contemporary Revolutionary Movement in China) (4th ed., n.p., 1938), I, 87.

[5] Sources disagree as to when various early groups were formed, and by whom. The following analysis leans heavily on "A Brief History of the Chinese Communist Party," translated by the East Asia Institute, Columbia University, from *Su-lien yin-mou wen-cheng hui-pien* (Collections of Documents on the Soviet Conspiracy) (Peking, 1928), and cited hereinafter as "Brief History"; and from another version of the same original source, "A Brief Sketch of the History of the Chinese Communist Party," *The China Weekly Review*, which is identified as a true copy and certified by one Kisseleff, under whose name the document will be cited hereinafter. Soviet sources condemn these accounts, which were captured during raids on the office of the Soviet military attaché in Peking, April 6, 1927, as forgeries. In general, the data found in them appear to be in harmony with related documentation, but their complete authenticity has yet to be firmly established.

[6] Jay Calvin Huston, "Sun Yat-sen, the Kuomintang and the Chinese-Russian Political Economic Alliance," an unpublished manuscript now on file in the Hoover Institute and Library, which was prepared by an American consular official in China at the time.

Mao Tse-tung started one in Hunan, and Tung Pi-wu formed one in Hupeh.[7] At about the same time four Chinese students established a cell in Japan, while others, including Chou En-lai and Li Li-san, founded one in Paris.[8]

In September 1920 the Shanghai group, meeting at Ch'en Tu-hsiu's house in the French concession, laid plans for establishing a foreign language school (Wai-kuo yü-yen hsüeh-hsiao), composed of the "best revolutionaries," who were to be trained, not only for work in China, but also for study at the University of the Toilers of the Far East in Moscow. The group undertook the establishment of vocational federations in Shanghai. The first of these was the Mechanics' Union, followed by the Printers' Union and the Federation of Labor.[9] The decision was made to establish a secretariat of the China Labor Union in Shanghai, with Chang Kuo-t'ao at its head, and a Russian language school with Yang Ming-chai as its principal.[10] The only source of income for these activities was profit from the magazine *New Youth*.[11] About the same time an evening class for workers was founded in Ch'ang-hsin-tien, a Peking-Hankow Railway station not far from Peking. "The workers there," according to one source, "were even more backward than the Shanghai proletariat, and hence the work was more difficult."

Early in 1921 a war lord named Ch'en Ch'iung-ming, having seized control of Kwangtung province, invited Sun Yat-sen to be responsible for political direction in Canton. Somewhat previously, moreover, Ch'en Tu-hsiu had attracted the attention of Ch'en Ch'iung-ming, who now asked the Communist organizer to serve as chief of the Education Board in Canton. Ch'en Tu-hsiu accepted with alacrity,[12] explaining to Voitinsky that he would take the position and use it for purposes of Communist propaganda. Once installed in Canton, Ch'en Tu-hsiu formed a party cell,[13] set up a training school, and started drafting a party platform.

During this first year of organized activity, a number of splits

---

[7] *Chung-kuo hsien-tai ko-ming yün-tung shih*, I, 2.

[8] *Ibid.* Chou Fo-hai, under the inspiration of Shih Ts'un-t'ung, is said to have organized the Japanese cell, while Lo Mai, Li Fu-ch'un, and Wang I-fei were among the early members in Paris.

[9] "Brief History," p. 11.

[10] Reizo Otsuka, "Red Influence in China," Institute of Pacific Relations, Japanese Council Papers, No. 17 (Tokyo: Nihon Kokusai Kyokai, 1936), p. 14.

[11] "Brief History," p. 11.

[12] Three sources—"Brief History," p. 13; *Chung-kuo hsien-tai ko-ming yün-tung shih*, I, 2; and "Communism in China," a document allegedly by Chang Kuo-t'ao, seized in a raid on the Soviet Consulate in Canton, December 1927, and published in the *South China Morning Post*, February 4, 1928—offer slightly varying accounts of this episode.

[13] "Brief History," p. 13.

occurred in the new Communist movement. For the most part these difficulties arose from disagreements between the anarchists and those who thought of themselves as protégés of the Bolshevik revolution. The first schism took place within the Peking cell while a provisional party statute was under discussion. One paragraph dealt with the dictatorship of the proletariat, a concept which the anarchists refused to accept, and many of them, therefore, left the movement.[14]

From available evidence it is not precisely clear how these developments in China were integrated with Communist activities in other parts of Asia. However, on February 10, 1921, the Soviet newspaper *Izvestia* carried the following brief statement:

Japanese newspapers issued in Tokyo have been aroused by news of a joint conference of Socialists of the Eastern countries held in one of the Chinese towns in the middle of December, 1920. The Conference was attended by 18 representatives from Japan, three from Korea, forty from China, and one from the Island of Formosa. All participants at the Conference were representatives of the extreme revolutionary trend. With a view to initiating activities by the enumerated socialist organizations the Conference decided to set up a Central Bureau in China which would act in contact with the world proletariat. A representative from India will shortly joint the membership of this Bureau.

THE FIRST CONGRESS OF THE CHINESE COMMUNIST PARTY

Certainly Moscow was keeping a watchful eye on developments in China, for midway during 1921 the Comintern dispatched the Hollander, Maring (or Sneevliet), to attend the formal organization meeting and First Congress of the Chinese Communist party.[15]

For purposes of subterfuge, the delegates to this meeting gathered first in a girls' private school on Pubalu Street in the French concession of Shanghai "where Chinese law did not reach."[16] This was during the summer vacation, and the school was empty; so the men made their homes there, settling on the top floor of the building.

On instructions from a go-between, the school watchman served meals for unexpected visitors while they consulted with one another. The Congress lasted for days and dealt with party rules and foremost tasks, with questions of organization, and with the political situation

[14] *Chung-kuo hsien-tai ko-ming yün-tung shih*, I, 4.

[15] According to Ken'ichi Hatano, "History of the Chinese Communist Party," *Ajia Mondai Koza* (Tokyo, 1939), those present were: Chang Kuo-t'ao (Peking), Ch'en Kung-po (Kwangtung), Ch'en T'an-ch'iu (Wuhan), Chou Fo-hai (Japan), Ho Shu-heng (Changsha), Li Han-chün (Shanghai), Li Ta (Shanghai), Liu Jen-ch'ing (Peking), Mao Tse-tung (Changsha), Pao Hui-seng (Kwangtung), T'ien En-min (Tsinan), Tung Pi-wu (Wuhan), Wang Ch'iu-meng (Tsinan). Maring is listed as present by *Chung-kuo hsien-tai ko-ming yün-tung shih*, I, 6.

[16] "Brief History," p. 15; also Wilbur, *The Communist Movement in China*, pp. 15–16.

in China. The final endorsement of the party platform was delayed, however, until the last day of the conference when, unluckily, the proceedings were cut short. Ch'en T'an-ch'iu wrote a decade and a half later:[17]

On this day after supper, when the delegates gathered together at eight o'clock in the evening in Li Han-tsin's [Li Han-chün] apartment, and the chairman announced the continuation of the work of the Congress, a suspicious person in a long coat appeared in a neighboring room. Li Han-tsin went along to find out who was this unknown. This person replied that he was seeking for the chairman of the Association of Social Organizations, Wan, by name, and then said he was mistaken and speedily left. It is true that the Association of Social Organizations was three houses away from Li Han-tsin's apartment, but everybody knew that it had no chairman, and least of all one named Wan. The appearance of the person seemed suspicious to us, and so we gathered together our documents and disappeared. Only Li Han-tsin and Chen Chun-bo [Ch'en Kung-po] stayed behind, and it was a fact that before ten minutes had passed after our departure, nine spies and policemen turned up at Li Han-tsin's apartment to institute a search. Apart from legal Marxist literature, they found nothing there, and were therefore unable to arrest anybody.

Unable to find any other safe place for continuing deliberations, the delegates retired to Niehpu Lake in Chekiang province, some hundred miles from Shanghai, where they hired a boat, bought food and wine, and carried through the work of the Congress under the pretense of having a quiet and respectable outing. "The weather that day was dull," according to Ch'en T'an-ch'iu. "However, many holiday-makers appeared after eight o'clock, and this, of course, made our work more difficult. At half past nine a light rain began. The holiday-makers departed, and this made it easier for us to continue our work in peace."[18]

During their discussion in the girls' school, the various delegates, who included followers of "biblical socialism, of social democracy, of anarchism, and of communism," found themselves in serious disagreement.[19] Ch'en Tu-hsiu, in drawing up a draft program, had emphasized the necessity of giving education to the members of the party, the guidance of this party in a "democratic" spirit, the development of party discipline, and the advisability of approaching the masses very cautiously in order to bring them into the Communist fold. In his proposed program, Ch'en is said to have insisted that the party was not yet facing the question of taking power into its own

[17] Chen Pan-tsu (Ch'en T'an-ch'iu), "Reminiscences of the First Congress of the Communist Party of China," *Communist International*, October 1936, pp. 1361, 1363; also Wilbur, *The Communist Movement in China*, p. 16.

[18] *Ibid.*, p. 1364.

[19] Kisseleff, *The China Illustrated Review*, III, No. 369 (January 21, 1928), 16.

hands, an undertaking that belonged among problems of the future, but rather the carrying out of vital preparatory work.[20] There were delegates to the First Congress, however, who considered these proposals too radical, while others felt that it was not necessary to accept any precise program. Li Han-chün offered the following opinion:[21]

We have at present a revolution in Germany and a revolution in Russia. Both these revolutions take different roads. We see in Russia the power in the hands of the communists and the dictatorship of the proletariat, and in Germany the democratic regime. We do not know which of these countries is right, because our connection with them is very weak. We must first make a thorough study of these two revolutions, before we are able to decide the question which has been brought up by Ch'en Tu-hsiu, i.e. the question relating to the program, and consequently to party tactics. And for that purpose some of our comrades must go to these countries and make there a study of these questions.

In regard to party organization, Li Han-chün argued that anyone accepting and spreading the principles of Marx should be admitted into the party without being obligated to participate in practical work. Joining him in this viewpoint were Li Ta and Ch'en Kung-po.[22]

Liu Jen-ch'ing voiced an opposite extreme. He considered the establishment of a proletarian dictatorship to be the immediate goal and was therefore opposed to all work of a legal nature. Pao Hui-seng agreed, but the majority of the delegates of the Congress opposed both "incorrect" points of view.

In defining the tactics of the struggle in the transition period, it was pointed out that the Party not only cannot reject, but, on the contrary, must actively call on the proletariat to take part in and to lead the bourgeois democratic movement as well. The line was adopted demanding the organization of a militant and disciplined Party of the proletariat. The development of the trade union movement was put forward as a central task of the work of the Communist Party. In relation to legal forms of work it was stated that the Party should make use of them under definite circumstances beneficial to the proletariat. As regards the organizational principles and conditions of acceptance of membership to the Party, it was decided to make use of the experience of the Russian Bolshevik Party.[23]

During the last day of the conference, while they were afloat on Niehpu Lake, the delegates discussed the question of their attitudes toward Sun Yat-sen and the problem of establishing a central party organization.

[20] Ibid.
[21] Ibid.
[22] Chen Pan-tsu, loc. cit., pp. 1362–63.
[23] Ibid., p. 1363.

Pao Hui-seng considered that the Communist Party and Sun Yat-sen represented two diametrically opposed classes, between which there could be no compromises, and therefore the attitude toward Sun Yat-sen must be the same as toward the Beiyan [Peiyang] militarists, and even still more negative, since he confused the masses by his demagogy. This conception was rejected by the delegates of the Congress. The following line was adopted toward this question: In general a critical attitude must be adopted toward the teachings of Sun Yat-sen, but his various practical and progressive actions should be supported, by adopting forms of non-Party collaboration. The adoption of this principle laid the basis for further collaboration between the Communist Party and the Kuomintang and for the development of the anti-militarist and anti-imperialist movement.[24]

The Congress decided that all members of the organization who were harboring non-Communist tendencies or views "would *eo ipso* place themselves outside the ranks of the party."[25] Elections were held, and the absent Ch'en Tu-hsiu was chosen secretary general of the party. Because the total membership of the Chinese Communist party was still so small, the Congress decided against organizing an official Central Committee, but to establish a Central Bureau to maintain contacts with the nuclei in the various parts of China.[26]

After his election as secretary general, Ch'en Tu-hsiu left Canton for Shanghai, but was arrested upon his arrival[27] and imprisoned by authorities in the International Settlement. "Fortunately," according to Chang Kuo-t'ao's account, "during the police raid at the house of Ch'en the former party failed to seize any of the Communist literature and consequently they were not in a position to prosecute Ch'en and the latter's wife with legitimate evidence. Both culprits were released by the police."[28]

One of Ch'en Tu-hsiu's first moves was to intensify work among the unions, and for this purpose a special bureau was set up, with Chang Kuo-t'ao at its head.[29] Working conditions in China left much to be desired, and the labor movement was already developing militancy. The Bolshevik problem was to win control away from non-Communist leaders. In the beginning it was not easy for Ch'en Tu-hsiu and his fellow intellectuals to establish contact. During 1921 and 1922 Communist agitators took an active part in railway and

[24] *Ibid.*, p. 1364.
[25] Kisseleff, *loc. cit.*, p. 16.
[26] Chen Pan-tsu, *loc. cit.*, p. 1364. According to this source, the Bureau consisted of Ch'en Tu-hsiu, Chang Kuo-t'ao, and Li Ta, with Chou Fo-hai, Li Han-chün, and Liu Jen-ch'ing as reserves.
[27] Chang Kuo-t'ao, "Communism in China," *loc. cit.* In this document Chang Kuo-t'ao states that Ch'en was imprisoned by *German* authorities.
[28] *Ibid.*
[29] Kisseleff, *loc. cit.*, p. 16.

seamen's strikes. "Even then," according to a Communist organizer, "we were nothing more than onlookers or assistants of the labor leaders in the latter's propaganda work, and not once during the many strikes then had we become their principal directors."[30] This was a weakness which the Communists worked hard to rectify. Private clubs were formed to further Bolshevik interests among the workers, labor schools were established, and a publications program inaugurated. Among the books translated and published were *The Communist Manifesto*, by Karl Marx, *The Program of the Russian Communist Party*, and similar works. Yet even this venture was not an immediate success.[31]

Persons in whose hands the direction of this work had been placed were under the impression that the literature was to be distributed gratis, because it would hardly find a ready sale. This proposal was carried into effect and as a result the publishing organization failed. . . . This episode is characteristic enough because it shows that even such stalwart communists as Ch'en Tu-hsiu and others were not quite sure of their own forces and entertained doubts as to whether their literature would find a ready sale on the book market . . .[32]

Despite these false starts, the Communists achieved a powerful influence over the Chinese labor movement during immediately succeeding years.

CONGRESS OF THE TOILERS OF THE FAR EAST

In January and February 1922 the Russian Communists organized in Moscow and Petrograd a Congress (not to be confused with the Baku Conference two years earlier) which was intended to acquaint the peoples of the Far East with Bolshevik views and at the same time to oppose the Washington Conference. To these gatherings, known as the Congress of the Toilers of the Far East, there went a Chinese delegation of about thirty members with representatives from both the Kuomintang and the Chinese Communist party. Opening the Congress on behalf of the Communist International, Zinoviev asserted, "Our international brotherhood, since the first day of its existence, takes clear account of the fact that the complete victory of the proletariat over the bourgeoisie under the circumstances, is possible only on a world wide scale."[33] The decisive victory, he insisted,

[30] Tang Chung-hsa (Teng Chung-hsia), "The Communist Labourers' Movement in China," a document seized by authorities in a raid on the Soviet Consulate in Canton, December 1927, and translated for the *South China Morning Post*, February 6, 1928. [31] Kisseleff, *loc. cit.*, p. 16. [32] *Ibid.*, p. 16.
[33] *The First Congress of the Toilers of the Far East*, published by the Communist International (Petrograd, 1922), p. 1. Both M. N. Roy and Chang Kuo-t'ao attended. Delegates represented China, Japan, Mongolia, Java, India, Korea (with fifty-two representatives, the largest delegation), and various peoples of Asian Russia.

could be assured only when the "hundreds of thousands, the hundreds of millions of the toiling and oppressed masses in the East" could be aroused and brought into the struggle. This meant that the struggle for emancipation among the various Asian peoples must be combined with the labor movement in Japan and America. Zinoviev warned, as he urged the Asian delegates to give up any faith they may have had in the Versailles and Washington conferences :[34]

Remember that the process of history has placed the question thus: you either win your independence side by side with the proletariat, or you do not win it at all. Either you receive your emancipation at the hands of the proletariat, in cooperation with it, under its guidance, or you are doomed to remain the slaves of an English, American and Japanese camarilla. Either the hundreds and millions of toilers of China, Korea, Mongolia and other countries understand that their ally and leader is the world proletariat and, once and for all, give up all hope in any kind of bourgeois and imperialist intrigue, or their national movement must be doomed to failure, and some imperialists will always ride on their backs, sow civil war and crush and carve out their country.

The Washington treaties had been concluded, Zinoviev charged, for the purpose of further exploiting the oppressed nations. But, fortunately, it was inevitable that the imperialist nations struggle among themselves and eventually break with one another.[35] These were tendencies which the oppressed peoples, in alliance with the proletariat, must exploit.

During the proceedings, a representative from Soviet Turkestan took issue with a Kuomintang delegate who had been so naïve as to maintain that the principles of the Soviet system were not dissimilar to those which Sun Yat-sen's party had been propagating for the preceding twenty years. Savarov declared :[36]

We are convinced that this Party [the Kuomintang] has done great revolutionary work which was absolutely necessary in China, and we hope to fight side by side with this Party in the future. But, on the other hand, we are not so naïve as to imagine that this Party is a revolutionary Communist Party. We say: In the colonial and semi-colonial countries the first phase of the revolutionary movement must inevitably be a national democratic movement. We give our support to this movement, as such, to the extent that it is directed against imperialism. We are supporting it, we have always supported it, and will do in the future, but, on the other hand, we cannot recognize this struggle as the struggle for the proletarian revolution.

The Communist movement must touch upon the vital interests of the masses, according to Savarov, so that they, in turn, would be

[34] *Ibid.*, Second Session, pp. 21–39.
[35] *Ibid.*   [36] *Ibid.*, Tenth Session, pp. 192–99.

willing to die for the Bolshevik cause. As for non-Communist revolutionaries, Savarov declared: ". . . we definitely demand from these bourgeois-democratic, these radical-democratic elements that they make no attempt to dominate over the young labor movement of China and Korea and that they make no attempt to divert it from its true path and substitute its ideas by radical democratic ideals painted in Soviet colors. We will more easily come to an understanding if we tell each other what we really are."[37]

Non-Communist members of the Chinese delegation tended to be disillusioned by their experiences in the Soviet Union. "A Brief Sketch of the History of the Chinese Communist Party" records:[38]

It is a generally known fact that there was a famine in Russia at that time. The food that the Chinese delegates were provided at Moscow, though not quite good, still was considerably better than that which was usually doled out to the Russian workers and to the population generally. It was not a question of principle or a political question, and for the politically conscious man not even a question at all; however, it played to a certain extent its role. Famine, disorder and other defects which were the result of the internecine war and which were striking sharply the eyes of everybody, produced a very oppressive impression on some of the delegates, particularly on the Kuomintang men.

According to this account the Communist delegates, being for the most part young and inexperienced, failed to explain "the causes of disorder, of famine and of other defects in Russia," but simply demanded that their companions accept the Communist viewpoint as correct. "They formulated their thesis in the following words, 'All is well, but to you all seems bad.' Besides, these words were usually accompanied by insults on the part of the Communists. Many members of the delegation, especially the Kuomintang men, on their return to China, declared that, during their journey together with the Communists and during their stay in Russia generally, they had come to the conviction that the Communists would hardly be able to do any good. They based this conclusion on the actual conditions prevailing at that time in Russia."[39]

THE SECOND CONGRESS OF THE CHINESE COMMUNIST PARTY

In June and July the Second Congress of the Chinese Communist party, held at West Lake, Hangchow, called for closer relations with the Kuomintang. In a manifesto dated June 10 the Chinese Communists had urged the calling of a joint conference with the Kuomin-

---

[37] *Ibid.*
[38] Kisseleff, *loc. cit.*, p. 18.
[39] *Ibid.*

tang for the purpose of creating a united front "against war lords of the feudal type and against all relics of feudalism" as a part of the war for the "liberation" of the Chinese people from the "dual yoke" of local militarists and foreign exploiters.[40]

In stating their aims to the Kuomintang, the Chinese Communists called for the revision of tariff systems imposed on China by foreign nations, the overthrow of war-lord regimes, the establishment of universal suffrage, the promulgation of freedoms of assembly, speech, and press, the initiation of compulsory education, the introduction of a progressive income tax, the reorganization of existing tax systems, the regulation of child and woman labor, and the recognition of the equality of the sexes.[41]

In a party manifesto the Second Congress made clear that support for the Kuomintang was temporary and did not imply surrender to the capitalists. "The CCP is the party of the proletariat. Its aims are to organize the proletariat and to struggle for [the establishment of] the dictatorship of the workers and peasants, the abolition of private property, and the gradual attainment of a Communist society."[42] A successful democratic revolution would develop Chinese capitalism, which remained so far in its infancy, with capitalist opposition to the proletariat being left to the future. "When that stage is reached," declared the Manifesto of the Second Congress, "the proletariat must launch the struggle of the second phase: [the struggle] for the dictatorship of the proletariat allied to the poor peasants against the bourgeoisie."

The Second Congress decided definitely that the Chinese Communist party belonged to the world Communist movement, and final steps were taken for joining the Communist International. The Manifesto reiterated the principal objectives described in the statement of June 10[43] and called upon the workers to develop the strength of their

[40] "Declaration of the Chinese Communist Party and the Present Political Situation in China," *Novyi Vostok*, No. 2, 1922, pp. 606–12. This declaration was translated from Chinese into Russian by A. E. Khodorov. From the Russian version Olga Gankin has made an English translation, which is on file in the Hoover Institute and Library. The Chinese text is not available.

[41] *Ibid.*

[42]"Ti erh-tz'ü ch'üan-kuo tai-piao ta-hui hsüan-yen" (Manifesto of the Second Congress), quoted in Chu Hsin-fan, *Chung-kuo ko-ming yü Chung-kuo she-hui ko chieh-chi* (The Chinese Revolution and China's Social Classes) (Shanghai, 1930), p. 260, as translated by the Russian Research Center, Harvard University.

[43] The "Manifesto of the Second Congress" called also for the unification of China proper and Manchuria into a "genuine democratic republic"; the establishment of a Chinese federated republic by the unification of China proper, Mongolia, Tibet, and Sinkiang; the abolition of contract labor; initiation of the eight-hour working day; and provision of employee clinics and sanitary installations in factories. Cf. Wilbur, *The Communist Movement in China*, pp. 29–38.

fighting organization in order to prepare, in conjunction with the poor peasants, for the establishment of soviets.

When the Communists approached Sun Yat-sen with their proposal for an alliance, the Kuomintang leader rejected it, maintaining that he might allow Communists to join his party, but that he could not approve of a close relationship. On August 22 the Hollander, Maring, who had recently returned to China and had already been in touch with Sun Yat-sen, called a Special Plenum of the Central Committee of the Chinese Communist party at West Lake, Hangchow.[44] According to Harold R. Isaacs, who interviewed Maring many years later in Amsterdam, the Comintern representative proposed that Chinese Communists "simply enter the Kuomintang and use its organizational structure as a means for developing their own propaganda and contacts among the masses."[45] In his conversations with Isaacs, Maring stated that a majority of the Central Committee, including Ch'en Tu-hsiu, accepted his views. "Those who opposed his plan did so on the grounds that they doubted the weight of the Kuomintang as a political force and did not believe it would or could develop into a mass movement."[46]

In an account written several years later, when he was seeking to justify his past policies and actions against criticism of the Li Li-san leadership, Ch'en Tu-hsiu told a different story. Maring, he wrote, urged that Chinese Communists join the Kuomintang on the premise that the Kuomintang "was not a bourgeois party but a coalition party of all classes" and could therefore be transformed, under proletarian leadership, into the driving force of the revolution. "Myself and other CC members, namely Li Ta-chao, Chang Kuo-t'ao, Ts'ai Ho-shen and Kao Yü [Kao Yü-han], were absolutely opposed because the conglomeration of forces within the Kuomintang blurred the class distinctions, thus checking our independent policy. Malin [Maring] countered by asking if we wanted to disobey a Comintern decision, so that the Central Committee gave in for the sake of party discipline and voted to join the Kuomintang."[47]

[44] Ken'ichi Hatano, "History of the Chinese Communist Party," *Ajia Mondai Koza* (Tokyo, 1939), Vol. II.

[45] Harold R. Isaacs, *The Tragedy of the Chinese Revolution* (rev. ed.; Stanford, Calif., 1951), p. 58.

[46] *Ibid.*, p. 59. Cf. *The Communist Movement in China*, pp. 38–47.

[47] Hatano, "History of the Chinese Communist Party," *loc. cit.* In his conversations with Isaacs, Maring denied invoking Comintern authority and pointed out that the Chinese Communists could have appealed to higher organs of the International. The Hollander insisted, too, that he had no specific instructions at the time. Isaacs, *op. cit.*, p. 59 n. A member of the Far Eastern Bureau of the Comintern, Pavel Mif, wrote that the first instructions "to coordinate the activities of the Kuomintang and the young Communist Party of China" were issued by the Executive Committee

However it came about, the Central Committee followed Maring's advice, and members of the Chinese Communist party soon began joining the Kuomintang.[48]

of the Communist International in a special communication dated January 12, 1923. Cf. P. Mif, *Heroic China* (New York, 1937), pp. 21–22. As Isaacs points out, however, the Communists by that time had already begun joining the Kuomintang as individuals, although the formal decision was not made until the Third Congress of the Chinese Communist party in June 1923.

[48] For a well-reasoned argument suggesting the authenticity of Ch'en Tu-hsiu's later account, see Schwartz, *op. cit.*, pp. 41–45.

CHAPTER V

THE COMMUNIST PARTY AND THE KUOMINTANG

Bolshevik leaders decided almost from the beginning to use the Kuomintang as a Trojan horse for gaining control of China, and so, in characteristic fashion, Russian and Chinese Communists approached Sun Yat-sen's party on two levels, making open overtures and agreements on one plane and secretly infiltrating and manipulating Nationalist groups on another. Joffe, Karakhan, and other Russian agents played roles in this attempt at subversion and control, but for more than three years the outstanding Comintern figure in China was a colorful agent named Mikhail Borodin, who consummated the entente between the Communists and the Kuomintang.

By 1920 the Kuomintang had already developed a considerable history. Its roots went back earlier than the Sino-Japanese war when, in 1894, Sun Yat-sen had organized a handful of relatives and followers into the Hsingchunghui (Society for the Regeneration of China), which, with financial support from overseas Chinese merchants, sought to overthrow the Manchu government.[1] When this undertaking failed, Sun went to the United States and to England, where he was kidnapped by the Chinese Legation and rescued only through intervention from the British Foreign Office. Until 1898 Sun remained in Europe investigating political and economic conditions and drawing conclusions which he later embodied in the fundamental principles of the Kuomintang.

During the Boxer Rebellion of 1900 Sun's followers, seeking again to overthrow the Manchu empire, launched an unsuccessful attack on Waichow, east of Canton.[2] In 1905 Sun made another trip to Europe, where in leading cities he organized meetings of Chinese students and merchants and explained his gradually developing theories of racial unity, popular sovereignty, and social economy. During the same year he held in Tokyo a conference of considerable size, which marked the reorganization of the Hsingchunghui into the T'ungmenghui (Alliance Society).[3] The membership of this new

[1] T. C. Woo, *The Kuomintang and the Future of the Chinese Revolution* (London, 1928), pp. 23–24.

[2] Leonard Shihlien Hsü, *Sun Yat-sen, His Political and Social Ideals* (Los Angeles, 1933), p. 58.

[3] Ch'ien Tuan-sheng, *The Government and Politics of China* (Cambridge, 1950), p. 56.

group was composed largely of scholars and students, including many young men who were in Tokyo studying military science. Numbers of the latter soon returned to China and worked for influential positions in order, at the proper time, to win control of the army.[4]

When the Revolution of 1911 broke out, however, Sun Yat-sen was in America, and although the T'ungmenghui claimed a large share of the credit for organizing the revolt, it was not until two months later that the party's leader finally reached China.[5] By that time negotiations were taking place between Yuan Shih-k'ai, representing the empire, and Li Yuan-hung, who had been in command of the revolutionary forces. During the course of these exchanges, delegations from the various rebellious provinces, many of them self-elected, met at Nanking and assumed control of the revolution.[6]

This Nanking group soon elected Sun Yat-sen Provisional President of a new government which continued peace negotiations with Yuan Shih-k'ai. In mid-January Sun, seemingly on his own initiative, offered Yuan the presidency if the latter would accept a Manchu abdication and the permanence of the republic.[7] In February 1912 the final terms of peace were agreed upon, and the Manchus, in consideration of a financial settlement, the promise of security for members of their nation and the imperial household, and the guaranty of upkeep for the imperial tombs, abdicated with the understanding that power would be transferred to Yuan Shih-k'ai. Then Sun Yat-sen resigned from the presidency, and the Nanking Assembly, upon his advice, elected Yuan Shih-k'ai in his place.[8]

Antagonisms developed almost immediately between Yuan and the followers of Sun Yat-sen, who, in order to strengthen their position, reorganized the T'ungmenghui into the Kuomintang, or Nationalist party.[9] Yuan, for his part, sought almost from the beginning to develop his own term of office into some form of permanent rule,[10] while Sun's followers were largely in favor of a republic modeled after the government of the United States. For a time the tensions between Yuan and Sun remained beneath the surface, with the former using every possible inconspicuous means to thwart his opponents, while the Kuomintang tried to increase its prestige in conservative circles by bringing former empire officials into its membership. Toward the end of 1912, however, these antagonisms broke into open opposition, which led to the "second revolution" of 1913.

[4] Woo, op. cit., p. 27.
[5] Hsü, op. cit., pp. 74–82.
[6] Ch'ien, op. cit., pp. 59–60.
[7] H. F. MacNair, China in Revolution (Chicago, 1931), pp. 32–33.
[8] Ch'ien, op. cit., p. 61.
[9] Ibid., p. 62.　　　　[10] MacNair, op. cit., pp. 34–36.

Yuan quickly suppressed this revolt, unseated all Kuomintang members of China's parliament, and sought to have himself enthroned as emperor. This latter intrigue led to a third revolution, which began in December 1915. Yuan died the following June, and during the uncertainty and unrest that followed, Chang Hsün, a powerful general of conservative leanings, seized Peking and restored the Manchu Emperor to the throne. This regime was short-lived, however, and the Anfu group (see page 44) gained control in Peking.

In June 1917 Sun Yat-sen, as well as members of the Peking parliament, withdrew to Canton, where the revolutionary leader became Generalissimo of the rebellious southern provinces. Because of opposition from southern military leaders, the government of Sun as Generalissimo came to an early end, and in January 1918 there was established in Canton a directorate of seven members which was supposed to head a constitutional government over most of the area south of the Yangtze and some territory to the north.[11] Sun did not attend directorate meetings, and in August 1919 he sent in his resignation.

The position of Sun Yat-sen and his Kuomintang parliamentarians was not enviable. Since they had no army of their own, few funds, and limited popular support, they found themselves unable to effect a stable government or even to maintain their position in Canton, whence they were expelled, on occasion, at the whim of local war lords. In October 1920 Ch'en Ch'iung-ming (see page 55), a local war lord sympathetic to the Kuomintang, succeeded in capturing the city. During the next spring Sun had himself elected president by a rump parliament and began drafting plans for a military expedition against the Peking government.[12]

A rift soon developed, however, between Sun Yat-sen and Ch'en Ch'iung-ming, who disapproved of Sun's election and of the proposal for a northern expedition against the Peking militarists. There was a seesawing of power between the two men, with Sun deposing Ch'en, and Ch'en banishing Sun.[13] More than ever determined to consolidate his revolutionary base in Canton, Sun Yat-sen sought support in diverse directions.[14] Among Chinese circles, he negotiated with the Manchurian war lord, Chang Tso-lin, and with members of Tuan Ch'i-jui's Anfu faction, while, on an international level, he appealed in one way or another to Canada, Great Britain, the United States, Germany, and Soviet Russia.

[11] MacNair, *op. cit.*, pp. 65–66.
[12] Ch'ien, *op. cit.*, pp. 87–88.
[13] MacNair, *op. cit.*, pp. 69–70.
[14] Ch'ien, *op. cit.*, p. 88.

MOSCOW APPROACHES SUN YAT-SEN

Lenin had been watching Sun Yat-sen and his revolutionary movement for a long time. As early as 1912 the Russian, taking note of an article written by Sun and published in the Brussels Socialist newspaper *Le Peuple*, compared the Chinese leader's program with that of the Russian Narodniks. In Asia, he said, the bourgeois democrats, with support from the peasantry, were still capable of performing historically progressive deeds.[15]

Did this mean that the materialist West, with its "decadent" bourgeoisie, was utterly decayed, that light shone only from the mystic, mysterious East? Lenin declared that it was just the opposite:

It means that the East has finally struck the path of the West, that new *hundreds and hundreds of millions of people* will henceforth take part in the struggle for the ideals which the West has worked out. The Western bourgeoisie has decayed and is already being confronted by its gravediggers —the proletariat. But in Asia there still exists a bourgeoisie capable of representing sincere, militant, consistent democracy, a worthy companion of the great preachers and great public men of the end of the eighteenth century in France.[16]

Soon after the Bolshevik Revolution, relations between Sun Yat-sen and the Russians began to develop. On August 1, 1918, Chicherin, replying for the Council of People's Commissars to a greeting which the South Chinese Assembly had dispatched to the Soviet government, drew parallels between the Russian Revolution and its "friends, the proletariat of South China."[17] Then, in the autumn of 1920 Voitinsky, head of the Eastern Department of the Communist International, called upon Sun, who was living at that time in the French concession of Shanghai. Comrade Ch. (presumably Ch'en Tu-hsiu) introduced the two men. According to Voitinsky,

Sun Yat-sen received us in his library, a huge room filled with bookcases. He gave the impression of a man 45–47 (actually he was over 54). He was well-built and erect, had soft manners, and very distinct gesticulations. The modesty and cleanliness of his attire at once attracted our attention . . .[18]

Sun interrogated the Comintern representative about Russia and the Bolshevik Revolution. Voitinsky's account continues:

"The geographical position of Canton does not permit us to establish con-

[15] V. I. Lenin, "Democracy and Narodism in China," *Selected Works*, International Publishers Edition, IV, 305–11.

[16] *Ibid.*, p. 307. Lenin's italics.

[17] *Soviet Documents*, pp. 92–93.

[18] *Pravda*, March 15, 1925. A translation of this document by Mrs. Xenia Eudin is available at the Hoover Institute and Library, Stanford.

tact with Russia," he [Sun] complained. He kept on asking whether it were not possible to place a very powerful radio station in Vladivostok or in Manchuria so that we [the Russians] could communicate with Canton.

The Chinese leader explained how he hoped to make use of a military victory in southern China in order to develop a revolutionary movement in the central and northern provinces. He wanted to make Kwangtung an example, he said, for other parts of China to follow.

Maring (or Sneevliet), who represented the Comintern in Shanghai during 1921, also talked with Sun,[19] but unfortunately no account of their conversations is available. In July 1922 Ch'en Ch'iung-ming expelled the Kuomintang from Canton, whereupon the Chinese Communist party, which was holding its Second Congress, sent representatives to confer with Sun. The Nationalist leader's attitude was described as "favorable," and in August the Communist Central Committee decided upon an alliance with the Kuomintang.[20]

The rationale for this move was stated by Liu Jen-ch'ing for the Fourth Congress of the Communist International in Moscow:

Starting from the premise that in order to exterminate imperialism in China an anti-imperialistic unity front will have to be forged, our party has decided to form a united front with the national revolutionary party Kuomintang. The form of this unity front consists of our joining this party in our name and as individuals. There are two reasons for this. In the first place, we want to propagandize the many organized workers in the national-revolutionary party and win them over for us. In the second place, we can only fight imperialism if we combine our forces, the forces of the petty bourgeoisie and the proletariat. We have the intention to go into competition with this party in regard to the organization and propagandizing of the masses. If we do not join this party we shall remain isolated and we shall preach a communism which consists of a great and noble ideal, but one which the masses do not follow. The masses certainly would follow the bourgeois party, and this party would use the masses for its purpose. If we join the party, we shall be able to show the masses that we too are for a revolutionary democracy, but that for us revolutionary democracy is only a means to an end. Furthermore, we shall be able to point out that although we are for this distant goal, we nevertheless do not forget the daily needs of the masses. We shall be able to gather the masses around us and split the Kuomintang party.[21]

The first Communist to take membership in the Kuomintang was Li Ta-chao, who joined with the understanding that he would retain

19 Chang Kuo-t'ao, a founder of the Chinese Communist party who left the movement in 1938, in an interview with the author November 3, 1950.

20 "Brief History," pp. 28–29.

21 *Protokoll des IV Kongresses der Kommunistischen Internationale* (Hamburg, 1923), p. 615.

his Bolshevik allegiance.[22] The new relationship between the two parties was not formalized until the issuance of the Sun-Joffe Declaration of January 1923. In that month the Soviet envoy quitted his Peking negotiations and set out for Japan (see page 48). En route he stopped off in Shanghai to hold a series of meetings with Sun Yat-sen, who had remained in that city after his expulsion from Canton. These conversations resulted in the formulation of a joint statement in which the Bolshevik representative agreed with Sun that conditions in China were not suitable for a Soviet system, but that the primary problem was one of national unification and independence. Joffe reaffirmed the Karakhan Declarations and emphasized a Soviet willingness "to enter into negotiations with China on a basis of the renunciation by Russia of all treaties and exactions which Tsardom imposed on China, including the treaty or agreements relating to the Chinese Eastern Railway." Through the Declaration Sun recognized, however, that the railway question in its entirety could be settled only at a competent Russo-Chinese conference and agreed with Joffe that the existing CER management should be temporarily reorganized by agreement between "the Chinese and Russian governments without prejudice, however, in the true rights and special interests of either party."[23] The Bolshevik representative concluded by assuring Sun that the Soviet Union had no imperialistic designs whatsoever.

Upon the conclusion of this exchange of views, Joffe proceeded to Japan, where he held further conversations with one of Sun's close associates, Liao Chung-k'ai, who was known for his pro-Communist sympathies.[24] According to a member of the Kuomintang Left Wing (the group which, under Wang Ching-wei, collaborated with the Communists for several months in 1927 after Chiang Kai-shek had broken his alliance), Joffe instructed Liao in methods used by the Russians for carrying on both domestic and foreign revolutionary work. "Equipped with the information that he was able to gather from his month of contact with Joffe, Mr. Liao was able to support Dr. Sun from the very beginning in the work of Russian policy, although there were many doubting Thomases among the members of the Kuomintang regarding that policy."[25]

[22] Ken'ichi Hatano, "History of the Chinese Communist Party," *Ajia Mondai Koza* (Tokyo, 1939), Vol. II.

[23] *The China Year Book, 1928*, p. 1318.

[24] Liao Chung-k'ai, who was assassinated August 20, 1925, was the father of Liao Ch'eng-chih of the present-day Chinese Communist party Central Committee and Liao Meng-hsing (Cynthia Liao), for some time a secretary to Mme Sun Yat-sen.

[25] T. C. Woo, *The Kuomintang and the Future of the Chinese Revolution* (London, 1928), p. 132.

In Moscow the Executive Committee of the Communist International defined the limits of Bolshevik participation in the Kuomintang. Co-ordinated action between the two parties was necessary, but the Chinese comrades were warned that membership in the Kuomintang should not be purchased "at the price of the effacement of the special political characteristics of the Chinese Communist Party." The organization and education of the working masses and the creation of trade unions for the purpose of preparing the basis for a strong Communist party must represent specific and important tasks for the Chinese Communists. In its collaboration with the Kuomintang, moreover, the Communist party must retain its own organization with its strictly centralized apparatus. In the realm of foreign policy, the Chinese Communists were instructed to oppose every Kuomintang attempt to "court the capitalist powers and their agents, i.e., the Chinese military governors who are hostile to proletarian Russia," and at the same time to make every effort in influencing the Kuomintang toward unifying its efforts with the policies and undertakings of Soviet Russia in the struggle against "European, American, and Japanese imperialism." Finally, the Comintern warned the Chinese Communist party not to merge with the Kuomintang or "fold up its own banner."[26]

THE COMMUNIST-KUOMINTANG ENTENTE

In the summer of 1923 Sun Yat-sen sent a young Kuomintang military officer, Chiang Kai-shek, to the Soviet Union for a few months in order to study the Russian Red Army. Shortly after this, Karakhan, on reaching Peking to replace Joffe, telegraphed his greetings to Sun, who not only replied in friendly terms, but asked that a Comintern representative be sent to Canton for advisory and organizational purposes.[27]

Chosen for this job was Mikhail Markovich Borodin (or Gruzenberg), a veteran revolutionist who had recently been released from a six months' prison sentence in Glasgow. Born in Russia, Borodin had been brought up and educated in Latvia. After a brief sojourn in Russia, in the course of which he was arrested by tsarist police for revolutionary activities, he emigrated to the United States, where in 1908 he organized the "Progressive Preparatory School" for émigrés in Chicago. Upon returning to Russia in July 1918, he became engaged in party work and was sent first to Mexico and later to England.[28]

[26] G. Kara-Murza (comp.) and P. Mif (ed.), *Strategiia i taktika Kominterna v natsional'no-Kolonial'noi Revoliutsii na Primere Kitaia* (Moscow, 1934), p. 112.
[27] *The China Year Book, 1928*, p. 1321.
[28] *Bolshaia Sovetskaia Entsiklopediia*, VII (Moscow, 1927), 162.

In Canton he appeared first as an agent of the ROSTA news service. According to M. N. Roy, the Soviet government did not in the first place dispatch Borodin in an official capacity. Roy now recalls:

Previously he was in some trouble in Moscow, being suspected of some irregularity in the mission of smuggling jewels to the New World. As I happened to be in Mexico at that time and Borodin contacted me there, on my evidence he was exonerated. But even then he was not given any important work in Moscow which would satisfy him. Meanwhile, Karakhan had been sent to Peking as Soviet Ambassador.[29] He was Borodin's old friend. Knowing that Borodin was in an unenviable position in Moscow, Karakhan suggested that he should come to Peking to help him in his work, which he was doing in behalf of the Communist International. Borodin was given an official assignment only when he had contacted Sun Yat-sen in 1924 and acquired influence in the Kuomintang.[30]

The precise circumstances of Borodin's attachment to the Kuomintang and his relationship with Moscow have long been controversial. Both the Kuomintang and the Soviets claimed that he was serving only in a private capacity, but three documents discovered by British police during a search of Soviet premises in London in 1927 throw grave doubts upon this assertion. The first document, a telegram dated November 12, 1926, and dispatched by the Commissariat of Foreign Affairs, Moscow, to a Soviet representative in Peking, presented the following instructions:[31]

I HEREWITH COMMUNICATE DEPARTMENT'S DECISION FOR YOUR EXECUTION:

1. UNTIL A SOVIET REPRESENTATIVE IS APPOINTED TO PEKING, COMRADE BORODIN IS TO TAKE HIS ORDERS DIRECT FROM MOSCOW.

2. THE FAR EASTERN BUREAU TO BE INFORMED THAT ALL ITS DECISIONS AND MEASURES REGARDING QUESTIONS OF THE GENERAL POLICY OF THE KUOMINTANG IN CHINA AND OF MILITARY POLITICAL WORK MUST BE AGREED ON WITH COMRADE BORODIN. IN THE EVENT OF DIFFERENCES OF OPINION ARISING ON THESE QUESTIONS THEY MUST BE REFERRED TO MOSCOW FOR INVESTIGATION. BORODIN AND THE FAR EASTERN BUREAU MUST KEEP MOSCOW'S

[29] Karakhan was not accredited as ambassador until 1924. As this book goes to press, Allen Whiting informs the author of having seen evidence that Borodin first went to China on a definite Soviet government assignment.

[30] M. N. Roy in a letter to the author written in Dehra Dun, India, January 29, 1953.

[31] Great Britain, Foreign Office, *Documents Illustrating the Hostile Activities of the Soviet Government and the Third International Against Great Britain* (London, 1927), p. 29. The Russian Communists have persistently maintained that these documents are forgeries.

REPRESENTATIVES IN PEKING INFORMED OF ALL THEIR DECISIONS
AND MOVES IN REGARD TO THESE QUESTIONS.
3. COMRADE BORODIN'S APPOINTMENT AS OFFICIAL SOVIET REPRE-
SENTATIVE IN CANTON IS CONSIDERED INADVISABLE. BORODIN
IS TO REMAIN [? IN CHARGE] OF THE WORK IN THE PROVINCES
UNDER CANTON RULE, AND AN OFFICIAL REPRESENTATIVE TO THE
CANTON GOVERNMENT IS TO BE APPOINTED.

A second telegram from the Soviet chargé d'affaires in London
to the Commissariat of Foreign Affairs in Moscow, dated February 1, 1927, stated:

IT IS ESSENTIAL TO GIVE A SHORT EXPLANATION TO THE PRESS ON TUES-
DAY SAYING THAT BORODIN IS NOT A SOVIET REPRESENTATIVE AND IS
NOT EVEN IN OUR SERVICE, BUT IS A PRIVATE CITIZEN IN THE SERVICE
OF THE CHINESE GOVERNMENT AND IS NOT ANSWERABLE FOR HIS AC-
TIONS.[32]

And a third telegram on February 4, 1927, also from the chargé
d'affaires to the Foreign Commissariat, gave the following instructions:

AN ANNOUNCEMENT OF BORODIN'S RECENT VISIT TO MOSCOW, WHERE
HE RECEIVED INSTRUCTIONS, HAD BEEN PREVIOUSLY PUBLISHED. IF
POSSIBLE, IT WOULD BE DESIRABLE TO CONTRADICT THIS.[33]

Among controversial documents seized during the 1927 raid on
the USSR Embassy in Peking there was one which gave the following account of Borodin's arrival in Canton:[34]

In order to avoid a stop at Hongkong, I left Shanghai on a small ship
straight for Canton. On the way I experienced a typhoon and had we not
found a shelter among the islands of Formosa, the writer of these lines
might have shared the fate of 200 sheep we had on board, all of which
perished.

I arrived at Canton on the 6th of October . . . Sun Yat-sen welcomed me
very warmly, made me sit with him and looked at me fixedly for several
seconds. I conveyed to him the greetings of Moscow, and of the Political
Representative, Comrade Karakhan, adding that the latter looks forward
to an interview with him on the first favorable occasion. Then I shortly

[32] *Ibid.*   [33] *Ibid.*, p. 30.
[34] N. Mitarevsky, *World Wide Soviet Plots* (Tientsin, n.d.), pp. 130–31. These
documents were denounced as forgeries by the Russian Communists. Mitarevsky was
associated with the Commission appointed by the Chinese government to examine and
translate the documents seized. The great mass of this material displays every indication of Soviet origin. For a detailed discussion of the problem of authenticity see C.
Martin Wilbur and Julie Lien-ying How, *Documents on Communism, Nationalism,
and Soviet Advisers in China, 1918–1927* (New York: Columbia University Press,
1956), pp. 8–37.

explained to him the aim of my coming to Canton and asked him several questions about the situation in the country and particularly in Kwang-tung . . .

In Canton Borodin found the Kuomintang disorganized, the workers divided, and Sun Yat-sen engaged in a military struggle with Ch'en Ch'iung-ming. In reporting these conditions, Borodin advised the strengthening of Sun's army. "The direct steamer route from Vladivostok to Canton, not calling at Hongkong," he wrote, "may be used to this effect. But the establishment of such a direct communication between Vladivostok and Canton must in some way be explained, and this could be easily done, because Canton needs timber, fish, beans, etc., which could be imported in exchange for local products. This line would at once create what he most needs, viz. a direct connection with Russia [the USSR]. Military supplies which are indispensable and which, owing to the blockade, cannot be received, could be brought from Vladivostok."[35]

Borodin and a staff of Russian colleagues began immediately to reorganize the Kuomintang and Sun Yat-sen's armies after Soviet patterns. The party structure was shaped into a series of organizational units pyramiding upward through subdistrict, district, and provincial levels to an annual National Congress, designed as the final authority on both party and governmental policy, and a Central Executive Committee to direct party affairs between meetings of the Congress. The system was tied together, like the Communist parties, by democratic centralism. The usual interpretation of the latter principle is that free discussion must be allowed within all party organs until the moment a decision has been reached, at which point unconditional obedience is required of all members regardless of private disagreement. In other terms, the party membership elected authorities to higher echelons, either directly or through intervening congresses, whereupon such authorities were endowed with powers of command and the right to be obeyed. Theoretically, then, the mandate of power flowed upward through the party pyramid, while control fanned downward. In practice it has usually come about under democratic centralism that whatever authorities control the central organization of a party actually control the party. In this respect the Kuomintang, even after separating itself from the Communists, was not to prove itself an exception.

Under Borodin's influence, the First Congress of the Kuomintang, held in late January 1924, passed a Declaration which, more than a decade later, Mao Tse-tung was to identify as the basis for Communist-Kuomintang co-operation with the Anti-Japanese Na-

[35] Mitarevsky, *op. cit.*, p. 131.

tional United Front. Reinterpreting the Three People's Principles, this document set forth a program calling for strict party discipline, an intense propaganda offensive, extensive social legislation, the "equalization" (but not the nationalization) of land, the state control of capital and of monopolistic industries, and the forging of an army to attack both domestic and foreign "imperialism."[36]

The Kuomintang Constitution,[37] written in English by Borodin, checked by Sun, and translated into Chinese by Liao Chung-k'ai,[38] placed supreme sovereignty in the National Congress; designated Sun Yat-sen president of the party throughout his lifetime (Article 21); and stated that "the members should follow the direction of the president and work for the advancement of the Party" (Article 22); that the president should have the power to disapprove resolutions of the National Congress (Article 25); and that his voice should be the decisive one in the Central Executive Committee (Article 26), which constituted the highest authority between congressional sessions.

In May 1924 the Kuomintang, under the supervision of Borodin and General Galen (Vassily Blücher), founded the Whampoa Military Academy. Chiang Kai-shek, who had spent the previous summer in Moscow, became commandant, and Chou En-lai, a founder of the French branch of the Chinese Communist party, was appointed head of the academy's political department.

Although Sun, later in the year, admitted reservations concerning Communist theory, he seems at this time to have foreseen no serious incompatibilities between his own program and that of the Communists. The Chinese revolution had so far failed, he maintained, because Kuomintang members, unlike the Russian Communists, still did not understand the Three People's Principles. "Essentially there is no real difference," he wrote, "between the Principle of People's Livelihood (Min-sheng chu-i) and Communism."[39] In its opening stage, the Russian Revolution had only carried out the Principles of People's Rights and People's Livelihood, but after six years of fight-

[36] An English translation of the Declaration is available in Leonard Shihlien Hsü, *Sun Yat-sen, His Political and Social Ideals*, pp. 119–41.

[37] An English translation of the Kuomintang Constitution is available in Arthur N. Holcombe, *The Chinese Revolution* (Cambridge, 1930), Appendix C, pp. 356–70.

[38] "Sun Yat-sen's Comments on an Accusation Against the CP." A partial translation of Sun's comments appears in Conrad Brandt, Benjamin Schwartz, and John K. Fairbank, *A Documentary History of Chinese Communism* (Cambridge, 1952), pp. 72–73, cited hereinafter as *A Documentary History*. The original comments are reproduced in photographic facsimile in *T'an-ho Kung-ch'an-tang liang ta yao-an* (Two Proposals for the Impeachment of the CP), published by the Kuo-min-tang chung-yang chien-ch'a wei-yuan-hui (The Central Control Committee of the Kuomintang) (Nanking, September 1927).

[39] *A Documentary History*, pp. 72–73.

ing with foreign powers, the Soviets had discovered that the Principle of Nationalism required "the utmost effort and attention."[40]

Like many other Chinese leaders, Sun Yat-sen not only refused to forget how much of China proper foreign nations had alienated, but recalled also the far-flung states from which China had once exacted tribute. ". . . we lost Korea, Formosa and Peng Fu to Japan after the Sino-Japanese War," he declared, "Annam to France, and Burma to Britain . . . In addition, the Riu Kiu [*sic*] Islands, Siam, Borneo, Sarawak, Java, Ceylon, Nepal and Bhutan, were once tributary states to China."[41] Thus a once proud nation had become a "sub-colony" of all the powers. The new China, according to Sun, must help other weak or minor states against the foreign oppressors.

Kuomintang policies toward the Chinese Communist party were formalized during the Second Plenum of the Central Executive Committee in August 1924. Several months earlier Sun, in answering attacks by young Chinese revolutionists on the Three People's Principles, had charged them with seeking to curry favor with the Russians and competing with the Kuomintang. He noted:

But the Russian revolutionary party are learned and experienced people, who were not fooled by these youngsters, but saw through their tactics. Consequently they [the Russian revolutionaries] disagreed with them, corrected them in our behalf, and ordered them to join the KMT for the purpose of acting in unison with us. In case of non-compliance [the youngsters] would be disavowed. [The Russian revolutionaries] also explained [to the Chinese Communists] that the Principle of Nationalism is a timely remedy [for the ills of China] and not an obsolete relic of the past. Thus many of them were enlightened and joined our Party. If Russia wants to cooperate with China, she must cooperate with our Party, and not with Ch'en Tu-hsiu. If Ch'en disobeys our Party, he will be ousted.[42]

The Kuomintang Constitution opened membership to anyone who displayed willingness to accept the principles of the party, to execute its decisions, and to pay required fees. Consequently, the Second Plenum decided, there was no necessity for interfering in cases where members had not violated the Constitution. "The Chinese Communist Party," the Plenum declared, "is neither the result of speculation on the part of any individual nor of artificial transplantation from abroad to China. The Chinese Communist Party is a political organization which is crystallized out of the natural class struggle of the industrial proletariat that is just developing in China."[43] Even if it were pos-

---

[40] *Ibid.*
[41] Hsü, *op. cit.*, pp. 182–83.
[42] *Ibid.*
[43] Quoted from T. C. Woo, *The Kuomintang and the Future of the Chinese Revolution*, pp. 165–66.

sible to destroy the Chinese Communist party by force, rationalized the Plenum, the proletariat could not be destroyed, but would most certainly organize again. "So the attitude of the Kuomintang toward Communists is to ask whether their conduct is in harmony with its principles and its platforms and nothing else, because everywhere and at all times the Kuomintang ought to govern all its members in accordance with its platform and regulations. Since the Communists have accepted the principles of the Kuomintang and are admitted to its membership, they ought to be governed as such."[44]

On these unsophisticated premises Kuomintang leaders formalized the entente which Maring, Joffe, Karakhan, Borodin, and other Comintern agents had so carefully fostered.

[44] *Ibid.*

CHAPTER VI

THE STRUGGLE FOR CHINESE POWER

Under Bolshevik supervision at least a part of Asia's "hundreds of millions of oppressed peoples" had been put into motion by the end of 1924, and portents suggested the beginnings of what might easily become a world revolt. In China the Bolsheviks seemed to have all possibilities covered: they had established relations with Peking; they had conceived an alliance with Sun Yat-sen; and the Communist party was growing. Somewhat later—just to be safe—they would dicker with a northwestern militarist, the so-called Christian General Feng Yü-hsiang, and equip his forces.

Yet within less than three years Borodin and his assistants were expelled from the Kuomintang, the tottering Peking government had severed its newly established relations with Soviet Russia, the Chinese Communist party was underground, and even the "Christian General" had turned against the Bolsheviks. It looked as though the Third International's plans were doomed to fail—with top Communist leaders in disagreement over the causes.

To some degree this unexpected failure was brought about by the deaths of two men—Lenin and Sun. To some degree, also, it was the result of the fundamental conflict between Lenin's emphasis on co-operation with revolutionary nationalists and M. N. Roy's insistence upon peasant and proletarian revolt.

The death of Lenin left Russia in a situation where two leaders, Stalin and Trotsky, were vying for power. In large part theirs was a personal struggle, but it was also a conflict between opposing concepts of revolutionary strategy and tactics. Stalin believed that a universal conflagration was unlikely in the immediate future and that Russian Bolsheviks should build the Soviet Union as a general headquarters and powerful base for world revolutionary activity. Trotsky demanded an immediate overthrow of capitalism. As the struggle developed, each antagonist used events in China as ammunition against the other: Trotsky demanded Communist withdrawal from the Kuomintang; Stalin preserved the alliance to the point of near-catastrophe; Trotsky demanded the formation of soviets; Stalin seized on this fact to prove his opponent's heresy.

Stalin and his supporters correlated the Chinese revolution with "imperialist contradictions" in the Pacific area "where the paths of three continents—America, Asia, and Europe—cross one another."[1] In late 1926 Dmitrii Manuilsky, a Stalinist spokesman, elaborated on a theory which Lenin had presented to the Second Congress in 1920. "Three imperialist powers stand face to face in the Pacific," he said, "the United States, Japan and Great Britain . . . The armed clash which may break out there in the near future will be of unimaginable violence and serious consequences."[2] Manuilsky, and presumably Stalin, expected two probable phases of this conflict: a struggle between the United States and Great Britain on one side and Japan on the other; and a postwar phase during which the British and American victors would divide up the spoils by parceling out Asia among themselves.

Only two developments could prevent this course of events, namely, a victorious Chinese revolution or a decisive proletarian revolt in Britain or the United States. Otherwise, according to Manuilsky, history would record a Pacific conflict that would "put the great imperialist war of 1914–1918 in the shade."[3]

Japan, tightly crowded, was pressing naturally toward the Philippines, the Malay Archipelago, and the islands of the Pacific, Manuilsky maintained; Britain was installing bigger guns in Singapore; and American economic penetration was stirring resentment among the Japanese, who, nevertheless, sorely needed American markets and American credits.

But China was the real battleground, for there American advances were threatening Japanese imperialism. It could not be otherwise, in Manuilsky's view, since China was a vast reservoir of raw materials for Japan and a major field for Japanese exports. "For Japan," he said, "it is a matter of—to be or not to be."[4]

Yet all these struggles for raw materials and markets depended, in the Communist view, upon one condition—a weak and disunited China. If the great Pacific conflict broke out before China could be unified, Japan, waging a preventive war against the United States and Great Britain, could advance through Manchuria to occupy China in order to master vital arteries for its defenses and its industry.

Hence Stalinists thought it vital to build a strong alliance between the Chinese revolutionists (both Communist and Kuomintang) and the world proletariat. Once this had been accomplished, there were two further tasks: the exclusion from China of foreign capital and the building of a peasant army. The order of these two tasks is important. Stalin, by relying on Chiang Kai-shek, sought to banish

---

[1] Cf. Manuilsky in *International Press Correspondence*, December 30, 1926, pp. 1592–97.
[2] *Ibid.*
[3] *Ibid.*   [4] *Ibid.*

foreign influence first—and failed. In later years Mao Tse-tung successfully reversed the two procedures.

In Stalin's view, the Peking war lords were Chinese arms of imperialist power. He told the Comintern in November 1926:

. . . we might imagine that there is at present in China no actual imperialist intervention, that there is nothing but a struggle between North and South, or of one group of generals against another group of generals. We are apt to understand under intervention a condition in which foreign troops march into Chinese territory, and if this does not take place, there is no intervention. This is a serious error, comrades . . . In the present circumstances, imperialism prefers to intervene against the revolution by organizing civil war within a dependent country, by financing the counter-revolutionary forces against the revolution, by moral and financial support of its Chinese agents . . . The fight of Wu P'ei-fu and Sun Ch'uan-fang against the revolution in China would be quite impossible were it not that the imperialists of all countries had inspired these counter-revolutionary generals and had supplied them with money, arms, instructors, "advisers," and so forth . . . Intervention by using other people—that is the kernel of imperialist intervention at present.[5]

On the basis of this analysis, Stalin looked upon Kuomintang forces as a major weapon against the Peking war lords and refused to believe that these same troops could be turned against him. "How is the power of the Canton troops to be explained?" he asked. "By their having an ideal, a passionate enthusiasm, by their being inspired in their fight for liberation from imperialism, by their wanting to give China her freedom."[6]

This is not to say that Stalin, in his dependence on Kuomintang armed force, overlooked the organization of labor and peasant unions and the development of class warfare. On the contrary, Bolshevik organizers as early as 1922 and 1923 were quick to take advantage of unrest among seamen, dockers, railway men, textile workers, and similar groups, and to play an important part in the strikes that gripped large sectors of the country at that time.

In mid-1925 there were two shootings—the May 30 and Shakee Shameen incidents—which the Communists exploited with particular success. During the spring of that year Chinese textile workers had begun to strike against working conditions in Japanese-owned cotton mills. In Tsingtao several strikers were shot down, and in Shanghai a Japanese foreman killed a Chinese worker. On May 30, 1925, Shanghai students and workers staged a protest parade. Demonstrators marched to the police station, demanding the release of sev-

---

[5] J. Stalin, "The Prospects of the Revolution in China," *International Press Correspondence*, December 23, 1926, pp. 1581–84.
[6] *Ibid.*

eral of their number who had been arrested. A British officer, losing his head in the excitement, shouted orders to fire, and twelve students fell dead.[7]

The May 30 Incident gave rise to a wave of violent antiforeign sentiment. A general strike was called in Shanghai, and there were sympathetic demonstrations in other cities. On June 23 British and French troops in the Canton concession area machine-gunned a parade of students, workers, and military cadets as they passed Shakee Road Bridge. More than fifty Chinese students and workers were killed and over a hundred wounded.

Through these acts of violence, the foreigners—representatives of Western democracies—were playing directly into the hands of Communist specialists in force, maneuver, and deceit. The May 30 and Shakee-Shameen shootings made truth out of Soviet propaganda against the "foreign imperialist," and, by inflaming latent Nationalist militancy, strengthened the Communist position within the Kuomintang. Bolshevik leaders boasted that in several labor organizations Chinese Communist agitators jumped overnight from labor union assistants to leaders. Workers who had formerly distrusted or even hated the Communists now regarded them as friends, and numbers joined the party.[8] Communists gained similar strength within organs of the Kuomintang itself.

Stalin's defeats did not result from a neglect of labor or from a bypassing of the peasant movement, which, by the early months of 1927, was militant and largely Communist-controlled. Stalin failed in this period because he misunderstood the Kuomintang.

CONFLICT WITHIN THE KUOMINTANG

Borodin's presence in Canton brought about a fundamental division in Nationalist ranks, and the First Central Executive Committee, from the days of its election in January 1925, suffered spasms of internal strife. Within six months a group of Right Wing leaders who previously had not opposed the Bolshevik alliance was issuing "A Proposal for the Impeachment of the Communist Party."[9] Com-

[7] *Report of the International Commission of Judges Appointed to Inquire into the Causes of the Disturbance at Shanghai*, May 30, 1925 (Shanghai, 1925).

[8] Translation of a document by Teng Chung-hsia, *South China Morning Post* (Hong Kong), February 6, 1928.

[9] *T'an-ho Kung-ch'an-tang liang tayao-an* (Two Proposals for the Impeachment of the Communist Party), Kuo-min-tang chung-yang chien-ch'a wei-yuan-hui (The Central Control Committee of the Kuomintang) (Nanking, September 1927), as cited in Schwartz, *Chinese Communism and the Rise of Mao*, p. 51. Cf. p. 76, note 38. These documents are the same work, available at the Hoover Institution, but given two slightly different translations.

munists were not acting as "individuals" within the Kuomintang, the Right Wingers charged, but were taking orders from the Central Committee of the Chinese Communist party. In supporting this contention, they offered a Communist document, "Resolutions of the Socialist Youth Corps," dated August 1923, which stated: "When our party members enter the Kuomintang, they must adhere to the orders of the executive committee of this corps . . . We must support all demands made by members of the Chinese Communist Party and be united with them in word and deed."[10] The Communists, in short, were acting as a party within a party.

In notations made on the margins of these documents, Sun Yat-sen declared that the "experienced leaders of the Soviet Union are interested in working with *our* party and not with the inexperienced students of the Communist Party," a statement scarcely calculated to reassure those who distrusted the Bolsheviks. What Sun probably did not fully realize was that the Comintern and the Chinese Communist party were bound together by tight organizational and disciplinary ties, as well as by a common ideology. Communist members did not and could not join the Kuomintang as individuals, but only as members of a highly disciplined fraction.

Sun Yat-sen died March 12, 1925, a little less than fourteen months after Lenin's passing. Richard Sorich has shown that—whether or not Sun was ever momentarily a Marxist—Soviet theoreticians never recognized him as such. What Bolshevik writers through the years have done is to discount the Nationalist leader's theoretical pronouncements and give weight to his relatively leftist political practices.[11] According to Liao Ch'eng-chih, a leading Communist and son of Liao Chung-k'ai (see p. 71), "Sun Yat-sen never reached the point where he wanted to follow in Lenin's footsteps."[12] Hence, Russian and Chinese Communists—including Mao Tse-tung in his *New Democracy*—rank Sun's three policies (alliance with the Soviet Union, with the Communists, and for the interest of the workers and peasants) as equal to, if not above, the Three People's Principles (Nationalism, Democracy, and the People's Livelihood).

In short, the Kuomintang-Communist entente had much less influence upon Sun Yat-sen's political philosophy than upon his revolutionary tactics.[13]

[10] *Ibid.*

[11] Richard Sorich, "Sun Yat-sen in Soviet Eyes," an unpublished paper in the Hoover Institute and Library, Stanford University, 1952.

[12] *Red Dust: Autobiographies of Chinese Communists*, as told to Nym Wales (Stanford, Calif., 1952), p. 30, cited hereinafter as *Red Dust*.

[13] This conclusion is supported by Shu-chin Tsui, "The Influence of the Canton-Moscow Entente," *The Chinese Social and Political Science Review*, quarterly publi-

Many of Sun's writings suggest that during his last days he was growing increasingly critical of Communist ideology, but there is slight evidence that he advocated major readjustments in Soviet-Chinese relations. Within forty-eight hours of his death, the Soviet government released the following message ascribed to Sun:

DEAR COMRADES:

Here on my death bed my thoughts turn to you, as well as to the future destiny of my Party and of my country.

You are at the head of the Union of Free Republics, that heritage which the immortal Lenin has left to all suppressed peoples of the world. By means of this heritage the victims of imperialism will inevitably win their emancipation from that social order which has always been based on slavery, war and injustice.

I leave behind me a party which, as I always hoped, will be allied with you in its historical task of liberating China and other suppressed peoples from the yoke of imperialism.

My charge to the Kuomintang party before all is that it shall continue to promote the cause of the national revolutionary movement for the emancipation of China, which has been degraded by imperialism into a semi-colonial country. I therefore charge my party to maintain permanent contact with you.

I cherish the firm belief that your support of my country will remain unaltered.

In taking my last leave of you, dear comrades, I express the hope that the day is approaching when the Soviet Union will greet in a free and strong China its friend and ally, and that the two states will proceed hand in hand as allies in the great fight for the emancipation of the oppressed of the whole world.

With brotherly greetings,
SUN YAT-SEN[14]

In the meantime, a civil struggle had broken out in Canton between Hu Han-min, who had been a follower of Sun Yat-sen since the turn of the century, and T'ang Chi-yao, a Yunnan militarist who had used his troops in support of Sun's Kwangtung regime. In June

cation of the Chinese Social and Political Science Association (Peiping), XVIII (1934), 96.

[14] *International Press Correspondence*, March 19, 1925, p. 286. After Sun's death the Central Committee of the Russian Communist party, through Stalin, tendered sympathy to the Central Executive Committee of the Kuomintang, which replied in part: "We are convinced that you, as true disciples of Lenin, will fight along with us, the heirs of Sun Yat-sen." In the name of the Comintern, Grigorii Zinoviev dispatched to the Kuomintang a wire which included the following: THE EXECUTIVE COMMITTEE OF THE COMMUNIST INTERNATIONAL IS CONVINCED THAT ALL ITS SECTIONS WILL RENDER SUPPORT TO THE KUOMINTANG PARTY, WHICH WILL LEAD THE CAUSE OF SUN YAT-SEN TO A VICTORIOUS END, AND DOES NOT DOUBT THAT THE COMMUNIST PARTY OF CHINA, WHICH IS COOPERATING WITH THE KUOMINTANG PARTY, WILL ALSO PROVE EQUAL TO THE GREAT HISTORICAL TASKS CONFRONTING IT.

1924 Hu, with support of the Kuomintang Central Executive Committee, to which he belonged, used Kuomintang troops against T'ang and won a victory. Strengthened by military success, the Central Executive Committee used the conflict to justify expelling from the party all Kuomintang members associated with the Right Wing group known later as the Western Hills faction.[15] In Canton the power now seemed to lie in the hands of Wang Ching-wei, Liao Chung-k'ai, Hu Han-min, and the late Generalissimo's son, Sun Fo, with Borodin in the near background, as always.

But the new balance had scarcely been established when Liao Chung-k'ai was suddenly and mysteriously assassinated on August 20, 1924.[16] The full story has never come to light, but Borodin suspected Hu Han-min of complicity, and straightway "banished" the veteran Kuomintang leader to Moscow. In the Russian capital, bewilderingly enough, the exiled leader was invited the following February to attend the Sixth Plenum of the ECCI, where, using the honorary title of "Generalissimo," inherited from Sun Yat-sen, he greeted Comintern leaders. "I feel I am one of the fighters of the world revolution," said this man who tended to align himself over the years with the Kuomintang Right Wing, "and I greet the session of the Communist International. Long live the solidarity of the proletariat of the world! Long live the victory of the world revolution! Long live the Third International! Long live the Communist Parties of the world! Long live the comrades here!"[17] In Canton, meanwhile, the Left Wingers and Communists in the Kuomintang were stronger than ever.

Striking out against this consolidation of Left Wing power, rightist members of the Kuomintang, meeting as the Chungkuo Kuomintang Tungchih Club, resolved that all acts of the Kuomintang should be considered null and void so long as the party remained under Communist influence, and plans were made for registration, under Club supervision, of all followers of Sun Yat-sen who had not allied themselves with the Bolsheviks. And later, during the autumn of 1925, a group of Right Wingers met at Sun's grave in the Western Hills, near Peking, to reiterate their opposition to Communist penetration of the Kuomintang.

THE RISE OF CHIANG KAI-SHEK

This Right-Left split became an important factor in shaping the nature of the Second National Congress of the Kuomintang and in

[15] *The China Year Book, 1928*, p. 1324.

[16] A personal, though not necessarily accurate, account is that presented by his son, Liao Ch'eng-chih, now a Communist, in *Red Dust*, p. 29.

[17] *International Press Correspondence*, March 4, 1926, p. 256.

bringing about a sharp upheaval in Central Executive Committee membership. Elections for the Second CEC, in January 1926, brought defeat for those who had identified themselves with the Western Hills viewpoint and victory for those favoring continued co-operation with the Soviet Union and the Chinese Communist party. Yet in the long run it was neither the extreme Right Wing nor the pro-Communist Left Wing that was to win final control of the Kuomintang, but the young commandant of Whampoa, Chiang Kai-shek. Until a few months prior to the Second Kuomintang Congress, the future Generalissimo had been relatively unknown, but immediately following Liao Chung-k'ai's assassination, Borodin maneuvered the appointment in Canton of a dictatorial triumvirate composed of Wang Ching-wei, Chiang, and Chiang's military superior, the commander in chief of Kuomintang forces, Hsü Chung-chih. But the Russians, who did not trust Hsü, planned a coup whereby Chiang, with the aid of his Whampoa cadets and an estimated ten thousand strike pickets from Hong Kong, seized military power. With the close of the Second Congress in late January, there remained in Canton a delicate balance wherein Borodin, Chiang Kai-shek, and Wang Ching-wei were believed to share power, with a preponderance in the hands of the Russians. There was talk of a northern expedition against Peking, with Chiang in favor and Borodin—at this particular juncture—opposed.

During February 1926 Borodin left Canton to negotiate with Feng Yü-hsiang. While the Bolshevik was gone, Chiang struck out. Claiming to have discovered a conspiracy directed against him by officers of a warship which had anchored off Whampoa during the night, Chiang detained the vessel, declared martial law, surrounded the houses of his Russian advisers with troops, closed trade unions, disarmed the Canton Headquarters of the Canton–Hong Kong Strike Committee, and arrested all Communist political workers attached to units under his command. By morning, the Kuomintang was in confusion, and Chiang enjoyed control of Canton.[18]

The Central Executive Committee of the Kuomintang immediately passed two resolutions—one laying down general principles governing the Kuomintang-Communist relationship and the other limiting the status of Communists within the Kuomintang. In effect, Communist membership in higher executive committees of the Kuomintang was limited to one-third; Communist party organs were for-

[18] Compare Isaacs, op. cit., pp. 93–94, with Tang Leang-li, The Inner History of the Chinese Revolution (London, 1930), pp. 242–48; MacNair, op. cit., p. 105; George Sokolsky, Tinder Box of Asia (New York, 1933), p. 336; The China Year Book, 1928, p. 1326.

bidden to instruct individual Communists within the Kuomintang until such instructions had been cleared by a joint-party committee; and Communist members of the Kuomintang were denied eligibility as heads of departments within the Kuomintang central organization.[19]

Borodin, on his return from the Northwest, accepted these restrictions, and his relations with Chiang became, to all appearances, more cordial than ever.[20] Moscow, in complementary fashion, simply denied that anything unusual had taken place. Less than three weeks after the March 20 coup, an official organ of the Comintern stated:

. . . Reuter's Telegraph Agency . . . recently issued the statement that in Canton Chiang Kai-shek, the supreme commander of the revolutionary troops (whom Reuter had hitherto described as Red) had carried out a coup d'etat. But this lying report had soon to be denied by the London *Times*. . . . The Kuomintang Party is not a tiny group with a few members, but is a mass party in the true sense of the word, and the revolutionary Canton troops and the revolutionary Canton government are founded on this basis. It is of course impossible to carry out a coup overnight . . . The perspectives for the people's government in Canton were never so favorable as they now are . . . The province of Kwangsi will shortly form a Soviet government which will be subordinate to the Canton Kuomin government . . . *The power of the generals as a result of the pressure of the national revolutionary movement is beginning to disappear.* The Kuomin government is now proceeding to organize all district and town administrations within the province of Kwangtung according to the Soviet system.[21]

G. N. Voitinsky, who had helped to organize the Chinese Communist movement, dismissed reports of Chiang's coup as imperialist propaganda,[22] but Soviet representatives on the scene in China tried to analyze what had happened. The development of Soviet activities in the army, according to one Kissanka, who was head of the Canton Military Group under Borodin, had caused friction within the Kuomintang by making Chiang's soldiers radical too soon,[23] i.e., before the Communist apparatus had grown strong enough to stand on its own. This criticism was supported by Stepanov, another Russian agent, in a report written immediately after the coup. Communist

---

[19] The texts of these resolutions are available in Woo, *op. cit.*, pp. 175, 176–77.

[20] Tang, *op. cit.*, p. 247.

[21] Tang Shin She, "The Canton Government and the Revolutionary Movement in China," *International Press Correspondence*, April 8, 1926, p. 415. The italics are in the original.

[22] G. Voitinsky, "The Situation in China and the Plans of the Imperialists," *International Press Correspondence*, May 6, 1926, pp. 600–601.

[23] Mitarevsky, *op. cit.*, pp. 36, 122.

centralization of control over the army was too hasty, he declared, with a tendency toward surrounding generals of the National army with commissars and advisers who "rather often wanted to play a leading part and in some places even took command of the troops." In this fashion first the latent and later the open opposition of Kuomintang generals and higher officers was provoked.[24] Moreover, the Chinese Communists, according to Stepanov, tried to spread Bolshevik ideas too fast, rooting out the Kuomintang "always and everywhere" and thus creating antagonisms which strengthened Chiang and the Right Wing of the Kuomintang.

Kremlin leaders no doubt thought that by catering to Chiang Kai-shek temporarily, they could buy time until the Chinese Communists were strong enough and sufficiently well placed to take over. Certainly Stalin, during succeeding months, made his own tactics clear enough: the Chinese Communists must intensify political work among Kuomintang troops and make the army "a real and model support" of the (Communist-inspired) ideas of the Chinese revolution; the revolutinary army, as the first force penetrating new provinces, would give rise to a pattern similar to that of the Canton government; to maintain power, this new apparatus *must* enjoy support of the Chinese peasantry; the special task of the Communists, therefore, must be to penetrate into the apparatus of this new power and put into effect the necessary policies—even including finally the nationalization of land—in order to win over the peasants. Thus Stalin intended using Kuomintang armies to gain control over the peasant countryside and later the cities. "The revolutionary armies in China," he said, "are the most important factor in the fight of the Chinese workers and peasants for their liberation."[25] Years later, Mao Tse-tung was to follow a different plan with much greater success: he organized peasants into his own revolutionary army.

Stalin, sitting in Moscow, and Borodin, on the spot in Canton, both seem to have assumed that they could use Chiang—even after he had bested them—and cast him aside at the appropriate moment. Louis Fischer explained Communist behavior this way:

They [the Communists] had wide mass sympathy but in Canton they wielded insufficient forces to overcome Chiang and the bourgeoisie which supported him . . . Both sides knew that the struggle between them was inevitable. But rather than engage now in blood letting from which only the Cantonese militarists could gain, they tacitly agreed to postpone the issue until they reached the Yangtze. The resolution to commence the

[24] *Ibid.*, p. 37.
[25] J. Stalin, "Prospects of the Revolution in China," *International Press Correspondence*, December 23, 1926, pp. 1582–84.

Northern Expedition was adopted by the Kuomintang Central Committee on May 15. At that meeting the expressed sentiments of each faction amounted to this: "Gentlemen, we know we must fight one another. But we need a wider area. Let us delay the day of reckoning and meanwhile go forward to a common goal."[26]

An American consular officer who was staunchly anti-Communist, but who respected Borodin as an individual, maintained that the Comintern representative himself knew precisely what he was doing. "Borodin had dreamed of five years in which he hoped to have the laborers and peasants of Kwangtung organized into a revolutionary force that would sweep over China," wrote Jay Calvin Huston. "But the impetuosity of Communist leaders in the Kuomintang and their Russian confreres upset his plans and made it necessary to compromise with a leader who had a growing ambition to dominate the Chinese situation in a military way."[27] These "impetuous" Communist leaders, according to Huston, were convinced that the time had come for seizing Canton as one objective in an imminent world-wide revolution, whereas Borodin "actually understood the realities of the situation" and was content, therefore, to create a strong revolutionary base under Kuomintang rule. The fact remains, however, that Borodin—and Stalin—were not only unprepared for Chiang's coup of March 20, 1926; they were equally unprepared for his second and decisive coup a year later.

THE NORTHERN EXPEDITION

On July 9, 1926, the Northern Expedition was launched. At a formal ceremony Chiang received the Kuomintang banner with a white sun and the red, white, and blue flag of the Canton government. To the crowd Chiang explained that the purpose of the expedition was to defeat Wu P'ei-fu, Chang Tso-lin, and other militarists, to unify the Chinese nation, and to secure for the country a position of equality among the other states of the world.[28]

Following in the wake of an advance army of Communist-trained propagandists and political agitators, Chiang's forces began their long campaign. The way had been carefully prepared, for as the troops moved northward, Nationalist soldiers discovered that Bolshevik agents had organized strikes and peasant revolts behind enemy lines. Even the northern armies themselves had been infiltrated, and as

---

[26] Louis Fischer, *The Soviets in World Affairs*, II (London, 1930), 651–53.

[27] Jay Calvin Huston, "Sun Yat-sen, the Kuomintang and the Chinese-Russian Political Economic Alliance," an unpublished manuscript on file at the Hoover Institute and Library, Stanford University.

[28] Huston, *op. cit.*, p. 134.

Chiang's troops pushed forward, their ranks were swelled by deserting soldiers[29]—just as, two decades later, deserting Nationalist soldiers were to join a Communist sweep.

Unlike Mao Tse-tung and his party in the 'forties, however, Stalin and his supporters failed to harness or exploit the peasant discontent they had stirred up. The countryside was on the edge of revolt, but the Stalinists—at what was perhaps the crucial moment—held them back. In October the Kremlin dispatched a telegram ordering the Chinese Communists to restrain the peasant movement in order not to antagonize Kuomintang generals in command of the Northern Expedition.[30] Later, under attack from Trotsky, Stalin was to admit that the telegram had been a "mistake."[31]

Trotsky did his best to make capital out of his opponent's errors, but it was Stalin who held effective power. Whether—if the positions of the two leaders had been reversed—Trotsky would have been more successful is problematical. Stalin's methods were undoubtedly cruder, but it should not be forgotten that Trotsky, too, was totalitarian and ruthless.

Early in November, while Chiang Kai-shek was still sweeping northward, A. S. Bubnov, F. F. Raskolnikov (Il'in), and G. N. Voitinsky were charged with the task of writing preliminary theses on the Chinese question.[32] After a short visit to China, Bubnov returned to Moscow with recommendations that were purely military: support the Northern Expedition in order to capture power across the face of China, using the Kuomintang army with its landowning officers. This meant avoiding agrarian revolution at all costs. According to Roy,

the preliminary theses prepared by Bubnov, Raskolnikov and Voitinsky were all but useless. So Stalin asked Bubnov, Bukharin and me to draw up another set of theses. These were divergent. On November 26, speaking of the theses that were presented, Stalin stated, "Roy has written these theses."[33] The emphasis was on the necessity for agrarian revolution. Stalin was convinced of this necessity at the time. In those days Stalin listened carefully when someone dealt with a subject about which he knew

[29] *Ibid.*

[30] Leon Trotsky, *The Stalin School of Falsification* (New York, 1937), pp. 165, 173.

[31] J. Stalin, *Marxism and the National and Colonial Question* (New York, n.d.), p. 237. The orders had been "cancelled," he insisted, only a few weeks after the wire's dispatch. This "cancellation" was the line laid down by the Seventh Plenum of the ECCI in November 1926.

[32] Roy interview.

[33] Compare with Isaacs, *op. cit.*, p. 117, who states that these theses were drafted by Stalin and Bukharin.

nothing, and when he had heard a fair presentation, he accepted it quickly and without equivocation.[34]

On the evening of November 22, 1926, Bukharin opened the first session of the Comintern's Seventh Plenum. Delegates and guests, long before the appointed hour, had filled Andreev Hall in the Kremlin to overflowing, and Bukharin's entrance was met by stormy applause. "We address ourselves to the great Chinese people," he declared after his opening words of greeting, "which stands in a gigantic revolutionary liberation struggle. We promise in the name of the entire Communist International, in the name of the whole working class of the world, that we will support this world historical struggle with all means, with all forces, at any price."[35]

Among the speakers was T'an P'ing-shan, a Communist who had been shipped off to Moscow because, in opposition to Borodin, he had advocated using the Northern Expedition for the sole purpose of spreading agrarian revolution across the face of China. "But most of the big guns in Moscow supported Borodin," according to Roy, "and during T'an's stay there he was more or less won over. Hence, after the Fifth Congress in May 1927, he was to join Ch'en Tu-hsiu in upholding the Kuomintang alliance. Later, of course, he was made a complete scapegoat and condemned for his 'Kuomintang illusions.' But that sort of thing was usual."[36]

T'an P'ing-shan, in offering the Plenum an analysis of the Kuomintang, divided the party's membership into five social groups: (1) the extreme Right, representing the interests of compradors and big landowners, which, he said, had been the real initiator of the March coup and the May 15 attempt to expel the Communists; (2) a Right Wing composed of big bourgeoisie, wealthy emigrated merchants, and well-to-do peasants—all oppressed by foreign imperialism and therefore "revolutionary-minded"; (3) a Middle Wing, represented by Tai Chi-t'ao, the ideologist, and Chiang Kai-shek, the military man, which represented "the industrial-bourgeoisie-in-the-making who aim at independence from imperialism"; (4) the Left Wing of middle and petty bourgeoisie who wanted a constituent assembly, the cancellation of unequal treaties, and co-operation with the Communists; and (5) the Communist wing, including all Communists working within the Kuomintang, all urban proletarians and landless peasants. "Since the establishment in July of last year of the nationalist government in

[34] Roy interview.

[35] *International Press Correspondence*, December 1, 1926, p. 1429. Among Asian peoples, Bukharin also singled out "the proletarians and peasants of Indonesia" for a special pledge of Comintern support.

[36] Roy interview.

Canton, which is nominally a government of the left wing," T'an told the Plenum, "the power has actually been in the hands of the right wing."[37] But the *real* power of the Kuomintang, he said in contradictory fashion, lay in the Left Wing groups which controlled "nine tenths" of the Kuomintang organs. The Communist task was to strengthen the Left Wing, combat the Right Wing, and isolate the Middle (Chiang Kai-shek) Wing and push it toward the Left.

In typically Stalinist fashion the Seventh Plenum adopted a dual tactic which emphasized peasant revolt but provided at the same time for support of the Kuomintang, among whose members were many influential landholders. "If the proletariat does not put forward a radical agrarian program," the theses of the Plenum declared, "it will fail to attract the peasantry into the revolutionary struggle and will lose hegemony in the national revolutionary movement."[38] Yet all this must be accomplished within the Kuomintang, many of whose bourgeois members "would continue to march with the revolution for a certain time."

The Kuomintang government, the Communists reasoned, would provide effective channels for reaching the peasantry. Later, while supporting the Left Wing against the Right, Communist members of the government could develop the Kuomintang "into a real people's party—a solid revolutionary bloc of the proletariat, peasantry, the urban petty bourgeoisie, and other oppressed and exploited strata."[39]

To ensure the carrying out of these directives, Stalin dispatched M. N. Roy to China.

CHIANG'S COUP AND THE COMMUNIST DEBACLE

The Nationalist troops, meanwhile, had moved northward with considerable *élan* and in early October had captured Hankow and Wuchang. Then Borodin, aware that the industrial populations of these two cities offered an exceptionally fertile field for Communist organization and agitation, took advantage of Chiang's absence in the field and persuaded Kuomintang leaders to move their government to the Wuhan cities (Wuchang, Hanyang, Hankow). The transfer, accomplished almost contemporaneously with the Seventh Plenum

---

[37] *International Press Correspondence*, December 1, 1926, p. 1430. Other speakers before the Plenum included "the representative of the Kuomintang Party, Shao Li-tse," and the Indonesian, Semaoen. In Indonesia at this time a Communist-led revolt was developing, but the Dutch authorities managed to quell it within the space of a few weeks.

[38] *Kommunisticheskii Internatsional v Dokumentakh, 1919–1932*, pp. 668–80. A translation of the theses of the Seventh Plenum by Xenia Eudin is on file at the Hoover Institution.   [39] *Ibid.*

in Moscow, brought Borodin in touch with Wuhan labor. Thereafter his influence grew to the point where he was once more in control of the state apparatus.

Chiang Kai-shek, headquartering in Nanchang, the capital of
Kiangsi province, tried to counter with a convention of the Kuomintang Central Committee in that city, but the Wuhan leftists and
Communists not only refused the invitation, but convened their own
meeting in Hankow and removed Chiang (on paper) from both his
party and army positions. Kuomintang leadership was then reserved
for Wang Ching-wei, who was expected momentarily from Paris.

When the Third Plenary Session of the Central Executive Committee opened in March 1927, Chiang stayed away, whereupon the
leftists and Communists abolished the chairmanships of all government councils and instituted presidiums which assured them a maximum of control. According to Wuhan leaders, "The military organs
are willingly and gladly turning over all political functions to the
party . . ." They dismissed rumors of a split as "pure fabrication."[40]

But Chiang Kai-shek had other thoughts in mind.

On March 24 Nationalist troops occupied Nanking. There was
looting, and several missionaries and consular officials were killed;
whereupon United States and British gunboats opened fire from the
river, killing a number of Chinese. In port cities the Western-lan-
guage press assumed that these "Nanking outrages" were part of a
Communist Left Wing plot to embroil Chiang with the foreigners, but
in retrospect these charges appear to be without foundation. ". . . the
Communists and Kuomintang liberals at Wuhan," writes Harold
Isaacs, "were far more concerned with propitiating Chiang than em-
barrassing him."[41] There were also rumors that Chiang himself had
organized the incident in order to provoke the Communists, but this
theory appears exceedingly improbable. According to an American
who investigated the scene a few days after the incident, retreating
northern soldiers were actually responsible.[42]

In Shanghai Communist-led labor forces, anticipating the Nationalist advance, had staged a February strike and insurrection. Ex-
pecting Kuomintang relief at any moment, these labor forces were
effectively silenced by the northern garrison commander, Li Pao-
chang, who was said to have made a special agreement with Chiang.
Apparently, this rumor was not without foundation, for within a few
weeks Li accepted command of the Eighth Nationalist Army.[43]

[40] *People's Tribune*, March 16, 1927.
[41] Isaacs, *op. cit.*, p. 144.
[42] G. A. Kennedy in the *People's Tribune*, April 5 and 16, 1927.
[43] *North China Herald*, April 16, 1927.

Meanwhile, execution squads armed with broadswords patrolled the streets, decapitating as many revolutionists as they could find.[44]

At his own measured pace, Chiang now approached Shanghai. Contrary to widespread expectations, there were, in the words of the foreign press, no "unpleasant incidents" involving Westerners, but Nationalist agents were said to be infiltrating the city, and it was widely rumored that the "red" general, Chiang Kai-shek, would attack at any moment.

But Nationalist forces were scarcely needed—not against the local war lord, Sun Ch'uan-fang, whose troops were demoralized and deserting rapidly. Chang Tso-lin was reported moving southward, however, and many observers predicted a pitched battle between him and Chiang. Others insisted that the two had made a deal, that Chiang had turned against the leftists. Meanwhile, northern troops under Chang Tsung-ch'ang moved into the Shanghai region.

Still Chiang did not attack the city. As Communist-dominated labor unions pulled themselves together and began planning for a second strike, the Nationalist general made a speech suggesting what was to come. "I have never taken the view," he declared on March 17, "that I cannot cooperate with the Communists. As a matter of fact, I may rightly claim the credit for bringing the Communists into the fold of the Kuomintang. But I have also made it clear that while I was opposed to the oppression of the Communists, I would check their influence as soon as they grew too powerful."[45]

What were the Communists saying meanwhile? On March 16 a leading article in *Pravda* complained that the "imperialist press" was exaggerating the significance of the Kuomintang. "They do not grasp the fact," *Pravda* charged, "that the leading role of the proletariat in the Chinese revolution is impossible without the Kuomintang and the Communist Party." The imperialist plan to separate the military leaders from the Kuomintang and make them independent was coming to nought. "The revolutionary pressure from below is so strong that Chiang Kai-shek is compelled, as can be seen from his declarations, to maneuver, to swear allegiance to the principles of revolutionary loyalty and to submit himself to the leadership of the mass party of the Kuomintang . . . The Chinese revolution will continue to advance and scatter all hindrances, crushing those who wish to crush it."[46]

In Shanghai the labor tide was rising again. "Many Chinese left Shanghai for their native villages, which they regarded as safer," wrote George Sokolsky. "The foreigners were nervous, tense, irri-

---

[44] *New York Herald Tribune*, February 21, 1927.
[45] *New York Times*, April 3, 1927.
[46] *Pravda*, March 16, 1927.

table. A fear psychology possessed us. We were all to be murdered by our own servants. And the truth was that the first real warnings came from boys and coolies and amahs who kept repeating, 'Plenty trouble—more better go Japan side.' The Communist Party of China was planning to make a shambles of Shanghai on a Sunday, to prevent Chiang Kai-shek from taking refuge there after he realized that Nanking was impossible for him."[47]

Yet when Chiang Kai-shek appeared, the Communists were not prepared. On the contrary, by order of the Comintern, the bulk of their weapons lay carefully buried. On March 26 Chiang arrived aboard a gunboat unannounced and walked ashore without opposition from anyone. "It was not at all improbable," Sokolsky wrote, "that he would not be able to stem the tide of Communist activity . . . Chiang had only 3,000 troops in Shanghai. He could not cooperate with the foreign forces, first because of Kuomintang principles and secondly, because the foreigners would have nothing to do with him: they hoped that he would fail, so that Sun Ch'uan-fang or Chang Tsung-ch'ang, the representatives of Tuchunism, might return to Shanghai."[48]

Nearly everyone was underestimating Chiang.

The rumors of a Communist-Kuomintang rift continued, meanwhile—and so did the denials. "A split in the Kuomintang and hostile sentiment between the working class in Shanghai and the revolutionary soldiers are absolutely out of the question at the present moment," wrote Tang Shin She in *International Press Correspondence*, March 31. ". . . A Revolutionary like Chiang Kai-shek will not act in cooperation with the counter-revolutionary Chang Tso-lin . . . The only danger for the working class in Shanghai consists in the provocation by the imperialists . . ."[49]

In Shanghai Wang Ching-wei, who had just returned from France, and Ch'en Tu-hsiu issued a joint statement:

An alliance between the Kuomintang and the Communist Party is necessary . . . At the present time China needs a democratic dictatorship of all oppressed classes to suppress the counter-revolution . . . The national revolution has reached the last base of imperialism in China—Shanghai. The counter-revolutionaries both inside and outside China are spreading false reports in order to bring our two parties in opposition to each other. Some say that the Communist Party is preparing to form a workers' government, to overthrow the Kuomintang and to recover the concessions by force of arms. Others say that the leaders of the Kuomintang intend to make war on the Communist Party, to suppress the labor unions and to

---

[47] George E. Sokolsky, "The Kuomintang," *The China Year Book, 1928*, p. 1360.
[48] *Ibid.*, p. 1361. *Tu-chün* was the title assumed by most warlords at this time.
[49] *International Press Correspondence*, March 31, 1927, p. 446.

dissolve the workers' defense organizations . . . *there is no basis whatever for these malicious rumors.*[50]

And in Moscow "3,000 active officials of the Moscow organization of the Communist Party of the USSR, after hearing Stalin and his supporters denounce Trotskyist views on China, declared their complete agreement with official policies." Stalin's speech, for obvious reasons, was never published officially. In it he declared:

Radek appears here with very revolutionary slogans: Break with the Right Kuo Min Tang, drive away the Right—a few more such r-r-revolutionary [*sic*!] slogans and the Chinese revolution is lost . . . Why drive away the Right, when we have the majority and when the Right listens to us?

The peasant needs an old worn out jade as long as she is necessary. He does not drive her away. So it is with us. When the Right is of no more use to us, we will drive it away. At present, we need the Right. It has capable people, who still direct the army and lead it against the imperialists. Chiang Kai-shek has perhaps no sympathy for the revolution, but he is leading the army and cannot do otherwise than lead it against the imperialists.

Besides this, the people of the Right have relations with the Generals of Tchang Tso-lin and understand very well how to demoralize them and to induce them to pass over to the side of the revolution, bag and baggage, without striking a blow. Also, they have connections with the rich merchants and can raise money from them. So they have to be utilized to the end, squeezed out like a lemon and then thrown away.[51]

As Trotsky subsequently pointed out, the "squeezed-out lemon," within a very few days, "seized power and the army."[52] But the Stalinist obsession was to avoid an open breach at any cost. "On March 31," according to one of the Comintern representatives in Shanghai, "when the preparations of the bourgeoisie for the overthrow became apparent, the ECCI gave the following directive: Arouse the masses against this overturn now being prepared and conduct a campaign against the Right. Open struggle is not to be launched at this time (in view of the very unfavorable change in the relationship of forces). Arms must not be given up, but in any extremity they must be hidden."[53] In a subsequent statement, Ch'en Tu-hsiu declared, "The International telegraphed us to hide or bury all

[50] *International Press Correspondence*, April 14, 1927, p. 493.

[51] Stalin, as reported in a speech of Vuyo Vuyovitch before the Eighth Plenum of the ECCI. Leon Trotsky, *Problems of the Chinese Revolution* (New York: Pioneer Publishers, 1932), pp. 389–90.

[52] Trotsky's "First Speech on the Chinese Question" before the Eighth Plenum of the ECCI, *ibid.*, p. 91.

[53] T. Mandalyan, as quoted in Isaacs, *op. cit.*, p. 163.

weapons of the workers in order to avoid military conflict between the workers and Chiang Kai-shek."[54]

In Shanghai Chiang found his support growing. "Bankers and merchants flocked to his standard," according to Sokolsky. "The Shanghai Chinese Bankers' Association, the representatives of the Chinese modern banks, arranged for an immediate three million dollar loan . . . The intellectuals supported his efforts. The students in a mass meeting declared themselves anti-Communist."[55] Nanking, on the other hand, was still occupied by Ch'eng Ch'ien's pro-Communist army. Chiang therefore dispatched all available troops to that city, while in Shanghai the situation was handled differently. "Arrangements," Sokolsky says, "were made with the Green and Red Societies . . . ," secret organizations with which Chiang was rumored to have long-standing connections.[56]

On April 12, under cover of early morning darkness, squads of armed men (variously described as Kuomintang workers, merchant volunteers, Nationalist troops, and Red and Green Society men[57] posing as "white" laborers) organized themselves into secret patrols ready for action. Then, just before dawn, an order was passed, and they quit their hiding places and went to work, systematically rounding up Communist-organized labor pickets, seizing what few weapons they still had, and executing on the spot all those who resisted. Within a matter of days the Shanghai Communists and their labor supporters were all but annihilated.

It was impossible even for Stalin to deny this coup. "In China the imperialists have not merely blockaded the whole land," declared the Comintern in its Appeal to the Proletarians of the Whole World and to All Suppressed Peoples, "they have succeeded in disrupting the unity of the Kuomintang and hiring Chiang Kai-shek."[58] But at the same time "the treachery of Chiang Kai-shek does not come unexpected," admitted Liao Han-sin in an article for *International Press Correspondence*. "This danger has already existed a year."[59] And Bukharin, defending Stalinist policies, wondered "if it were not better to hide the arms, not to accept battle, and thus not to permit oneself to be disarmed."[60]

Stalin's carefully laid plans and deceits had precipitated nothing but near-disaster for the Chinese Communists.

[54] Ch'en Tuhsiu, *Kao ch'üan-tang tung-chih shu* (Letter to the Comrades), dated December 10, 1929 (Shanghai, 1929).

[55] Sokolsky, *loc. cit.*, p. 1361.

[56] *Ibid.*, p. 1362.

[57] *Ibid.*

[58] *International Press Correspondence*, April 21, 1927, p. 525.

[59] *Ibid.*, p. 527.

[60] N. Boukharine, *Les Problèmes de la Révolution Chinoise* (Paris, n.d.), p. 56.

CHAPTER VII

STALIN AND THE KUOMINTANG LEFT

A DEFEAT BECOMES A "VICTORY"

The spring and early summer of 1927 saw Soviet-Chinese relationships develop into another series of tragicomic farces. In China—especially in Hunan and Kiangsi—the peasants were rising in revolt, while in Moscow it was the same old story: Stalin vacillated between support for agrarian revolt and the preserving of his alliance with the Wuhan Nationalists, now faced by Chiang Kai-shek's rival Kuomintang government in Nanking. When this seesawing policy failed—at the cost of Chinese Communist lives—it was not Stalin but Chinese Communist leaders who were held responsible.

After the Shanghai coup Stalin presented the debacle as a Communist victory and as one more evidence of his own correct policies. "The attempt made by Chiang Kai-shek in March, 1926 to drive the Communists out of the Kuomintang was the first serious attempt of the national bourgeoisie," he said, "to bridle the revolution."[1] But the Moscow leadership had been wary. "As is known, the Central Committee of the CPSU was already at that time of the opinion that the policy of keeping the Communist Party within the Kuomintang must be maintained, that the 'withdrawal or the expulsion of the Rights from the Kuomintang must be propagated' . . . The events which followed have fully and entirely proved the correctness of this line."[2] Echoing Stalin, the ECCI declared that recent events had "entirely confirmed the point of view of the Communist International concerning the Chinese Revolution . . ."[3]

The upheaval in China had now entered a new stage, Stalin declared, as Chinese Communist survivors of Chiang Kai-shek's purges took refuge in Wuhan. ". . . there has commenced a turn from the revolution of the entire united front to the revolution of the masses of farmers and peasants numbering many millions, to the agrarian revolution which will increase and strengthen the fight against imperialism, against the gentry and the feudal landowners, against the militarists, and against the counter-revolutionary group of Chiang

---

[1] "Theses of Comrade Stalin for Propagandists, Approved by the CC of the CPSU," *International Press Correspondence*, April 28, 1927, p. 543.

[2] *Ibid.*, p. 544.

[3] "Resolution of the Chinese Question," *International Press Correspondence*, June 16, 1927, p. 737.

Kai-shek.''[4] And yet, when the time came, when in late May the peasants rose in revolt, Stalin was to waver over using them.

Attacking the Stalinist record, the Trotsky opposition demanded immediate Communist withdrawal from the Kuomintang Left and the formation of soviets. Stalin, working for the elimination of his opponents, pressed his own devious reasoning—and took measures to deprive Trotsky of a platform. He demanded:

What does the withdrawal of the Communist Party from the Kuomintang [Left] mean at the *present moment* . . . ? It means to abandon the battlefield and to leave in the lurch its allies in the Kuomintang, to the joy of the enemies of the revolution. This means to weaken the Communist Party, to undermine the revolutionary [Left Wing] Kuomintang . . . and to deliver the flag of the Kuomintang, the most popular flag in China, into the hands of the Right Wing members of the Kuomintang. This is precisely what the imperialists, the militarists and the Right Wing members of the Kuomintang are demanding at the present moment. It follows, therefore, that the Opposition . . . is playing into the hands of the enemies . . .[5]

In Stalin's view, the formation of soviets would be premature. Rather, the "revolutionary" Kuomintang in Wuhan must be converted into an organ of "the revolutionary-democratic dictatorship of the proletariat and the peasantry" with the whole power of the country concentrated in its hands.[6]

Thus, under Stalin's domination the Communist International insisted on continued support for the Kuomintang Left. "The ECCI regards as incorrect the view which underestimates the Hankow [Wuhan] government and which in fact denies its great revolutionary role . . . ," Comintern leaders declared; ". . . the Hankow government, being the government of the Left Wing Kuomintang, is not yet the dictatorship of the proletariat and the peasantry, but is on the road to it and will inevitably in the course of the victorious class struggle of the proletariat and in the discarding of its radical bourgeois camp followers [!] develop in the direction of such dictatorship."[7]

Stalin's plan was brutally clear: to use the Wuhan government for building Communist strength and then to take it away from those to whom it belonged. But as events turned out, it was not the "radical bourgeoisie" who were eliminated, but the Communists themselves.

---

[4] *Ibid.*
[5] *Ibid.*
[6] *Ibid.*
[7] *International Press Correspondence*, June 16, 1927, p. 740.

STALIN "RESTRAINS" THE PEASANTS

Previous plenums of the ECCI had been held in Andreev Hall, the former throne room of the tsars situated in the Kremlin. But the current session—the Eighth Plenum—was held in a small room normally used for meetings of the presidium. According to the official explanation of the Stalinist bureaucracy, there was no other space available. But a French delegate and member of the Chinese Commission thought otherwise. "In reality," wrote Albert Treint, who soon was expelled from the Comintern, but who did not consider himself a member of the Trotsky opposition, "it was a question of preventing the Russian comrades, usually invited to our international sittings, from attending the discussions, where they could have learned some of the things hidden from them. Political documents bearing no secret character whatever were delivered to the delegates only on the eve of the opening session."[8]

What Treint and other Comintern officials witnessed was Stalin's personal power machine choking off the protests of its opposition. Delegates, according to Treint, were forbidden to take copies of the stenograms of their own speeches or to communicate them to anyone.

As soon as the plenum ended, all documents had to be returned immediately, on pain of not receiving permits to leave. They tried to forbid members of the Executive from making declarations when voting, but in the end, following several protests, this decision was applied only to members of the Opposition. For the first time in the history of the International, no record of the discussions was published either in the press of the USSR or in the international Communist press. Only the resolutions adopted and a few statements made during the discussion were published, but these lost their real meaning when detached in this way from the discussion from which they emerged.[9]

Conditioned by this atmosphere, the Eighth Plenum condemned the opposition, which was urging Communist withdrawal from the Kuomintang Left and the immediate establishment of soviets, and endorsed Stalin's program for China: support for the Kuomintang Left; military operations against the northern war lords; the development of the agrarian revolution throughout the territory of the Wuhan government; and the conduct of an intensive campaign of agitation and disruption within the army of Chiang Kai-shek.

In China Roy, Borodin, Chinese Communist leaders, and members of the Kuomintang Left were already in disagreement. The

---

[8] Albert Treint, *Documents de l'Opposition et la Réponse du Parti*, p. 65, as quoted in Isaacs, *op. cit.*, p. 240.

[9] *Ibid.*

Wuhan Nationalists wanted to use what forces remained under their command for pushing northward against Nanking (Chiang Kai-shek) and eventually Peking. The social problems of the revolution could not be achieved, they declared, until a military victory had been won and major political problems solved. It was argued, moreover, that Wuhan, being surrounded by hostile forces, was no longer safe and that new territories must be acquired in the Northwest and fresh military forces won over as primary steps in the projected attack on Peking.[10]

Roy took a different view, insisting that the furtherance of the revolution depended less on geographical expansion than on the consolidation of its social base, that is, upon the development of the peasant revolution. Toward this end, he said, the Communist Left Wing alliance must begin by recovering territories in the south, where the revolutionary mass movement was more advanced, but where Right Wing forces were now in control.[11] With mastery of Kiangsi and the Kuomintang-Communist base in Kwangtung, Roy believed, the Bolshevik Left Wing alliance could encircle Shanghai from inland and defeat the "combined forces of Chiang Kai-shek and International Imperialism."[12]

Borodin took the view of the Kuomintang Left: Wuhan Nationalist forces should be supported in their drive against Nanking and Peking.[13]

According to Roy:

The Communist leaders would not accept my alternative plan of action. They argued that a refusal to support the Second Northern Expedition would amount to a break with the Left Kuomintang. Borodin propounded a defeatist theory. He argued that Wuhan could not be held because the revolutionary forces were very weak. Therefore, he advocated that the remains of the ruins must be safely withdrawn to a new base in the northwest. That was a fantastic proposition which revealed a remarkable lack of faith in the masses, tragically shared by the whole leadership of the Communist Party. His other astounding proposition was to set a conglomeration of military forces into motion with the hope that something positive might come out of the chaos.[14]

---

[10] M. N. Roy, *Revolution and Counter-Revolution in China* (Calcutta, 1946), p. 462; hereinafter cited as *Revolution and Counter-Revolution*. Compare Fischer, *op. cit.*, II, 674.

[11] *Ibid.*, p. 463.

[12] Jay Calvin Huston, "Sun Yat-sen, the Kuomintang, and the Chinese-Russian Political Economic Alliance," p. 165.

[13] Louis Fischer, *The Soviets in World Affairs*, II, 67.

[14] *Revolution and Counter-Revolution*, pp. 548–49 n. Borodin's reasoning is available in Fischer, *op cit.*, II, 673–77.

This controversy — over whether Wuhan Nationalists should press a military campaign (the Northern Expedition) against Nanking and Peking, or should first deepen the revolution in their own area, then encircle Chiang Kai-shek, and subsequently move against the northern militarists—threw the whole Chinese Communist program into confusion. "I referred the disputed question to Moscow," Roy wrote subsequently. "The answer was ambiguous. It was in favor of doing both things simultaneously: to carry on the military plan and to develop the revolution in the territories of the Wuhan government. That was an impossibility. It proved to be so before long."[15]

The Comintern continued to advise bold measures—especially for agrarian revolution, but insisted at the same time that the co-operation of Kuomintang leftists was essential for victory. The crucial fact was that leaders of the Wuhan government and the military men upon whom their power depended were largely landowners or the sons of landowners. Under these circumstances it became vital for the Fifth Congress of the Chinese Communist party to develop an agrarian program which the Kuomintang Left leadership could accept. Hence, the Communists decided upon a policy of land confiscation without compensation (but only for the larger estates) and stipulated further that property belonging to officers of the Kuomintang army was not subject to seizure.[16] Adopted by the Wuhan government (and soon re-emphasized by Stalin himself), this program was activated by the Communist T'an P'ing-shan, who had recently been appointed Minister of Agriculture, and was accepted by chiefs of the Communist-dominated All-China Peasant Union.[17] In central China, meanwhile, and especially in Hunan and Hupeh, the peasants—partly by impulse, partly as a result of Communist agitation—were rising in revolt.

In retaliation, local militarists and landowners began taking action. In Changsha, capital of Hunan, General Hsü K'o-hsiang, commander of the local garrison, ordered his troops to march into the headquar-

---

[15] *Ibid.*, p. 549 n. Isaacs, p. 220, states that Roy, like the "whole staff of 'Bolshevik' advisers hanging onto the end of wires from the Kremlin," helped chart and endorsed the path that was followed. The chief point is, of course, that Roy—and all the others—were charged with carrying out impossibly confused and impractical directives. See Robert C. North, "M. N. Roy and the Fifth Congress of the Chinese Communist Party," *The China Quarterly*, No. 8, October–December, 1961, pp. 184–95.

[16] "Resolution on the Agrarian Question," in P. Mif, *Kitaiskaia Kommunisticheskaia Partiia v kriticheskie dni* (Moscow, 1928), p. 157. For other documents of the Fifth Congress see Robert C. North and Xenia J. Eudin, *M. N. Roy's Mission to China: The Kuomintang-Communist Split of 1927* (Berkeley: University of California Press, 1962).

[17] *The People's Tribune* (Hankow), June 11, 1927.

ters of the Hunan Provincial General Labor Union, to round up labor and peasant leaders, and to "reorganize" both the provincial Kuomintang and governmental hierarchies.[18] Similar episodes took place elsewhere, including Hupeh, where large numbers of peasants were killed.

The issue had been reduced to its essentials: would the Communists support the workers and peasants they had been so busily organizing and indoctrinating against the landowners, or would they support the landowners whose influence and armed forces they considered indispensable? The answer came as news of the countryside killings reach Wuhan: Communists joined Kuomintang officials in complaining that the peasant unions were not observing "discipline." According to T'an P'ing-shan, Communist Minister of Agriculture in Wuhan, the peasants had been making excessive demands, and while these demands were a logical result of the long suppression of the peasantry, "it remains a matter of necessity," he declared, "that they be controlled and checked." It became Wuhan—and Communist— policy, therefore, to "nip in the bud" all irresponsible acts and illegal deeds of the peasants "in the interests of the majority of the peasants and the larger phase of the peasants' movement."[19]

The hierarchy did not protest. "Almost all the Communist leaders," Roy wrote several years later, "believed the stories about the 'excesses' of the peasants and declared that the most effective method of combatting the counter-revolution would be to check them."[20] Peasant attacks on local landlords were denounced by the Central Committee as "infantile acts."[21]

Meanwhile, in Hunan, peasant forces mobilized by Communist agitators were converging on Changsha in order to attack the counterrevolutionary troops and landlord militia. At this critical moment, according to Communist records, the leader of the party organization in Hunan canceled the order of attack on the ground that military action against Changsha would cause national political repercussions and that instructions from the Central Committee should be awaited. On the second day a letter from the Central Committee ordered the attack postponed and the peasant forces held up "pending solution of the incident" by the Nationalist government.[22] "More than twenty thousand peasants marched upon Changsha from all sides," Roy later wrote. "Nearly at the gates they were ordered to go back and dissolve their military formations. The instruction came from the Com-

[18] *Ibid.*, June 4, 1927.
[19] *Ibid.*, May 29, 1927.
[20] *Revolution and Counter-Revolution*, p. 551.
[21] As reported in the "Circular Letter of the CC [CCP] to All Party Members (August 7, 1927) [extract]," *A Documentary History*, p. 112.
[22] *Ibid.*, p. 113.

munist headquarters at Wuhan."[23] Counterrevolutionary forces then attacked the retreating peasants and killed large numbers.

SUPPORT FOR THE KUOMINTANG LEFT

In Moscow Stalin himself now weighed the balance—and decided upon what he seems to have considered a coldly realistic policy. At a meeting of the Chinese Subcommittee of the ECCI, Bukharin informed his two colleagues, Ercoli (Togliatti) of Italy and Treint of France, that the peasants of China were forcibly seizing the land. "This frightens the Wuhan government," he said, as quoted several years later by Treint.[24] "If we do not curb the agrarian movement, we will lose our left allies and it will become impossible to win a majority in the Kuomintang. On the other hand, by curbing it, we will enlarge our influence in it, and when we will have become more powerful, we will go beyond our present allies . . ."

Treint demurred. "The problem," he said, "is not whether to sacrifice all the allies of the proletariat, but knowing which ones to sacrifice: the insurgent peasants or the national bourgeoisie. We will no more be able tomorrow than today to make the revolution in China by means of the constitutional decisions of the Kuomintang."

As the discussion progressed, Bukharin insisted that the Subcommittee ought to hear Stalin's opinion. While Bukharin was out telephoning, Ercoli and Treint continued the discussion.

Later Stalin joined them and supported the arguments put forward by Bukharin. "To fail to take a position against the peasant revolts," he said, "would be to set the left bourgeois against us. That would mean civil war. The armed Chinese are largely mercenaries, and we do not dispose of big enough financial resources to have them on our side."

[23] *Revolution and Counter-Revolution*, p. 551. Roy's part in these developments has been a subject of controversy. "I vigorously objected to the Communists undertaking the task of checking the revolutionary action of the peasants in order to placate the reactionary army officers," he declared in a footnote, p. 551. ". . . I suggested that T'an P'ing-shan might go with the instructions that, when on the spot, his mission should not be to check the 'excesses' of the peasant movements, but to set up village self-government, investing the peasants' unions with the necessary political power. That would be setting up Soviets in fact, if not in name." Isaacs, p. 218, states, on the other hand, that while "Roy later claimed that he had fought hard to get the Chinese Communist Party to pursue a bolder revolutionary course even if it meant a break with the Kuomintang," his own reports published at the time fail to back him up on this claim. The essential fact was, of course, that Roy had been charged by Stalin with carrying out an utterly inconsistent policy. See North and Eudin, *M. N. Roy's Mission to China*.

[24] This conversation is drawn, with deletions, but not alterations, from "Minutes of the Chinese Subcommittee of the ECCI," in *New Militant* (New York), February 8, 1936. According to Isaacs, *op. cit.*, p. 244 n., this is an English reprint of "Compte Rendu Analytique de la Petite Commission Chinoise, Mai, 1927," which Treint, at Isaacs' urging, had developed from notes taken in 1927.

"But the mercenaries," Treint pointed out, "are largely ruined peasants who will desert [to the Communists] if the agrarian program is put forth."

Stalin argued that the Left bourgeoisie were still too powerful: "Its armies will not disband in the twinkle of an eye, and we will then be defeated in a civil war before the insurgent agrarians are able to connect with the proletarian insurrection." The question, according to Stalin, was whether to fight or to maneuver.

"We must fight," Treint declared.

"To fight means certain defeat," Stalin said. On the other hand, the Communists could maneuver, he thought, without compromising anything. "The agrarian revolution frightens the Kuomintang only in the degree that it directly injures its members as well as the officers of the army. I propose to send instructions to Borodin to oppose the confiscation and division of land belonging to members of the Kuomintang or the officers of the Nationalist Army . . . We possess sufficient authority over the Chinese masses to make them accept our decision."

Ercoli supported Stalin.

"You are the majority," conceded Treint. "You can decide what you like . . ."

"The minority," Bukharin proposed, "must be disciplined."

Angered, Treint said, "So serious a question is involved here that no force on earth will prevent me from formulating my reservations in such a manner that they will be heard. Or are you going to employ physical violence against me?"

"Don't get dramatic," Stalin shot back.

In a telegram which reached Hankow June 1 Stalin delineated the course he had in mind. As quoted in his own book, *Marxism and the National and Colonial Question*, the directive reads as follows:

Without an agrarian revolution victory is impossible. Without it the Central Committee of the Kuomintang will be converted into a wretched plaything by unreliable generals. Excesses must be combatted, not, however, with the help of troops, but through the Peasant Unions. We are decidedly in favor of the land actually being seized by the masses from below. The fears regarding T'an P'ing-shan's visit are not devoid of foundation. You must not sever yourselves from the worker and peasant movement, but must assist it in every possible way. Otherwise you will ruin the cause.

Certain of the old leaders of the Central Committee of the Kuomintang are afraid of what is taking place. They are vacillating and compromising. A large number of new peasant and working class leaders from the ranks must be drawn into the Central Committee of the Kuomintang.

Their bold voice will stiffen the backs of the old leaders or throw them into the discard. The present structure of the Kuomintang must be changed. The leadership of the Kuomintang must be freshened and reinforced by new leaders who have come to the fore in the agrarian revolution, while local organizations must be enlarged by bringing into them the millions belonging to the working class and the peasant unions. Otherwise, the Kuomintang runs the risk of becoming divorced from realities and losing every atom of authority.

[It is necessary to liquidate the unreliable generals immediately.][25] This dependence upon unreliable generals must be put an end to. Mobilize about 20,000 Communists and about 50,000 revolutionary workers and peasants from Hunan and Hupeh, form several new army corps, utilize the students of the school for commanders, and organize your own reliable army before it is too late. Otherwise, there can be no guarantee against failures. It is a difficult matter, but there is no other course.

Organize a revolutionary tribunal headed by prominent non-Communist Kuomintangists. Punish officers who maintain contact with Chiang Kaishek or who set soldiers on the people, the workers and peasants. Persuasion is not enough. It is time to act. The scoundrels must be punished. If the Kuomintangists do not learn to be revolutionary Jacobins, they will be lost both to the people and to the revolution.[26]

According to sources in China, Stalin also directed in this telegram that possessions of Kuomintang officers and men should not be disturbed.[27]

On receipt of the telegram Roy made what usually has been interpreted as an incredible blunder : he showed it to Wang Ching-wei. According to a Kuomintang Left account, Wang went to Roy's flat, where the Indian told him, "There is a telegram from Stalin addressed to Borodin and me. Has Borodin shown it to you?"

Wang's reply was "No."

"Borodin does not like to show you this telegram, which is a secret resolution by the Moscow Bureau," Roy declared. "I, on the other hand, think that it is most advisable that you should know what it is about, as I am quite sure you would approve of it. Here it is, and have a look at it."[28] He handed Wang the original Russian text and its Chinese translation.

On reading the message, Wang Ching-wei's conclusion was that the Communists now regarded the Sun-Joffe agreements (see page 71) as obsolete and were preparing to "lead the National Revolution

---

[25] This point appears in a version of the telegram recorded by Ch'en Tu-hsiu in *Letter to the Comrades*, but not in Stalin's text.

[26] J. Stalin, *Marxism and the National and Colonial Question*, p. 249.

[27] Tang Leang-Li, *op. cit.*, p. 280.

[28] *Ibid.*, pp. 280–81.

to the goal of Communism"[29]—an objective which we now know they had never lost sight of.

The Kuomintang Left account continues:

Wang was, of course, very astonished on learning Stalin's new attitude towards the Kuo-Min Tang . . . Wang at once told Roy that on no account could the Kuo-Min Tang accept the conditions contained in the resolution. They argued about it for some time, of course, without any result. About to leave, Wang asked Roy whether he would let him have a copy of the translation. Roy hesitated a moment and then said, "Yes, I will send you a copy of it tomorrow . . ." Wang received the promised copy next day, and at once showed it to Madame Sun and Eugen Ch'en. Eugen Ch'en's face became pale on learning its contents. "That means war between the Kuo-Min Tang and the Communist Party."[30]

Roy's explanation makes his action more understandable:

On his way back to China he [Wang Ching-wei] had passed through Moscow. There he was promised full support of the Soviet Government as well as of the Communist International . . . I managed to send a radio message to Moscow demanding the reassurance. On the other hand, to him I proposed a concrete plan of action which should be undertaken to reestablish his effective leadership of the Wuhan government. He agreed with the plan [which included confiscation of land above a fixed minimum, arming of the peasants, disarming of the landlord militias, and so forth], provided that the necessary help would be forthcoming . . . It was almost too late when the urgently needed reassurance came. Meanwhile, believing that the Communists had betrayed him, Wang Ching-wei had entered into negotiations with the right wing which was clamoring for the blood of the Communists to propitiate Chiang Kai-shek . . . I thought at that juncture a final effort must be made to regain the confidence of Wang Ching-wei. I communicated to him the message from Moscow . . . It was a repetition of the promise made personally to him in Moscow . . .[31]

A Kuomintang Left source gives a different view:

Roy's idea was that the Left Kuo-Min Tang could only survive when in alliance with the Communists, as otherwise they would be crushed by the Rightists. They should, therefore, be informed of Stalin's cable. Borodin, however, realized that the Left Kuo-Min Tang was much stronger than Roy thought it was and knew that if they saw the resolution, they would at once sever their relations with the Communists . . . A majority of the Chinese Communists sided with Borodin, being also of the opinion that the time for overt action had not yet come . . .[32]

---

[29] *Ibid.*, p. 279.
[30] *Ibid.*, pp. 280–81.
[31] *Revolution and Counter-Revolution*, p. 520 n.
[32] Tang, *op. cit.*, p. 282.

Wang Ching-wei and his closest supporters began immediate preparations for the expulsion of Communists from the Kuomintang. Madame Sun Yat-sen and Eugen Ch'en, on the other hand, urged caution on the basis that Wuhan was still vulnerable to attack from Chiang Kai-shek and needed Bolshevik support.[33]

Communist leaders were on the verge of panic. In an eleven-point statement the Chinese leadership recognized the Kuomintang as occupying "the leading position" in the national revolution; emphasized that Communists in the Wuhan government were participating as members of the Kuomintang, and not as Bolsheviks; agreed that the workers' and peasants' mass organizations should accept Kuomintang leadership and control; ordered armed labor pickets and other worker and peasant forces to submit to Wuhan regulation and training; warned labor unions and workers' pickets not to assume judicial or administrative functions, arrest people, or patrol the streets without permission from the Kuomintang; and forbade the labor unions to insult employers, to make excessive demands, or to question the right of employers to hire and fire.[34]

On July 3, according to Roy, an emergency meeting of the Central Committee approved a further "policy of defeat" proposed by Borodin and Ch'en Tu-hsiu. Under this program, all Communist agrarian activities were to cease. Party members were to concentrate their activities in the treaty ports, forcing the "imperialists" to intervene so that the united front would be forcibly re-established.[35]

Roy refused to support this program. "I saw that, in the face of the opposition of the leaders of the Communist Party backed by Borodin, who controlled the funds and the mediums of communication to Moscow, I could do nothing in China. Galen also advised me to leave the country before it was too late."[36]

Roy left Hankow forthwith and set off overland for Moscow. By the end of July Madame Sun Yat-sen and Eugen Ch'en had gone into exile, the Kuomintang Left had turned against the Bolsheviks, Borodin had left for Russia, and the Chinese Communists were hiding out wherever they could escape detection.

Stalin, ruthlessly ignoring his own fundamental complicity, now placed full responsibility for the Wuhan failures on Chinese shoulders. Communist leaders in China, according to the ECCI, should have developed and led the agrarian revolution; should have openly criticized and exposed the half-hearted and cowardly attitude of the

---

[33] *Ibid.,* p. 283.
[34] Ch'en Tu-hsiu, *Letter to the Comrades.*   [35] Roy interview.
[36] Roy interview. For a detailed discussion of Roy's role in the events of 1927 see North and Eudin, *M. N. Roy's Mission to China.*

so-called radical leaders of the Wuhan government; should have warned the masses of the possible betrayal of the generals; should have armed ever greater numbers of workers and pushed the Kuomintang and the Wuhan government onto a really revolutionary path. "The Comintern considers it necessary," the ECCI declared, "that these errors committed by the Communist Party of China should be made good at once . . ."[37]

The ECCI directed the Chinese Communists to resign demonstratively from the Wuhan government, *but to remain within the Kuomintang,* establishing closer contact with the rank and file and inducing them to protest the actions of their own party leadership. The Chinese Communists were ordered to intensify their work among workers and peasants and to organize a competent and aggressive illegal party apparatus. Finally, the Comintern warned the Chinese Communists to make good the mistakes of their leadership, to close ranks on the basis of Communist International decisions, and to raise from its own ranks a new leadership capable of directing the revolution.[38]

The whole Kuomintang Left line, according to Roy, was only one more twisted offshoot of the Stalin-Trotsky feud. "If Trotsky said this, Stalin said that." And so, if the opposition called for severing the Kuomintang alliance, Stalin must find a rationalization, however devious, for preserving it.[39]

The Chinese Central Committee soon raised its dutiful echo: "The Communist Party will fight this struggle [against imperialists, militarists, and feudalists] with the really revolutionary members of the Kuomintang and with the masses of the Kuomintang. The Communists have therefore no reason to leave the Kuomintang or to refuse to cooperate with it . . ."[40]

Stalin described the new central task, e.g., to replace the reactionary Hankow hierarchy with a new, more revolutionary leadership. At the same time, however, the Chinese Communists were to "popularize" the soviets—those very organisms for which Trotsky had been pressing throughout recent months—"without rushing ahead of events and without attempting to organize soviets now, by keeping in mind that soviets can be formed only in the situation of a powerful advance . . ."[41]

Stalin considered that the immediate organization of soviets

<hr>

[37] "Resolution of the ECCI on the Present Situation of the Chinese Revolution," *International Press Correspondence,* July 28, 1927, p. 984.

[38] *Ibid.*

[39] Roy interview.

[40] *International Press Correspondence,* August 4, 1927, p. 1006.

[41] *Pravda,* July 28, 1927.

would be "premature," but he advised that the time had come to make propaganda preparations for their emergence. With the Trotsky opposition all but silenced, the Georgian could now advocate a policy which, up to that moment, he had condemned as political heresy.

The Russian Central Committee reasoned thus: "Should the efforts of the Communist Party for the revolutionizing of the Kuomintang not meet with success . . . and should, on the other hand, the revolution make a fresh advance, then it will be necessary to change the propagandistic slogan of soviets into a slogan of immediate fight and to proceed at once to the organization of workers', peasants' and artisans' soviets."[42]

Stalin now sent two new agents to China: Besso Lominadze, who carried instructions for an uprising soon to take place at Nanchang;[43] and Heinz Neumann, who called a special meeting of Chinese Communist leaders (the August 7 Conference)[44] and later the Canton insurrection of the following December. Lominadze, a young Georgian who had won favor from his powerful compatriot Stalin, was twenty-nine years old. Neumann, a native of Berlin, was three years his junior.

The August 7 Conference, according to a bitterly critical account, was called in great haste by Ch'ü Ch'iu-pai and attended by thirteen party members, of whom only three belonged to the Central Committee. "Just like me," wrote a disillusioned Communist who called himself Li Ang, "they went to the meeting after they received a notice from the Politburo, without knowing anything beforehand. They never dreamed that this conference was called in the name of the Politburo by Ch'ü Ch'iu-pai personally, and also they never dreamed of the comedy of overthrowing Ch'en Tu-hsiu during the conference."[45]

The meeting was held in a second-floor room in the Japanese concession of Hankow. On the one hand, according to Li Ang, the Communists feared arrest by Japanese police; on the other, they were afraid of being apprehended by Ch'en Tu-hsiu. "Two square tables were put together . . . The chairman was Ch'ü Ch'iu-pai, who was nervous . . . He wore an open flannel shirt of very loud color which was completely out of harmony with his appearance and age . . . he actually suffered tuberculosis . . . we could see the swollen

[42] "Resolution on the International Situation," Joint Plenum of the Central Committee and the Central Control Commission, *International Press Correspondence*, August 18, 1927, p. 1074.

[43] Roy interview.

[44] Roy interview.

[45] Li Ang, *Hung-se wu-t'ai* (The Red Stage) (Chungking, 1942), hereinafter cited as *Red Stage*.

veins in his face . . . After announcing the opening of the meeting, he abused the central organization . . ."

The conference endorsed a manifesto which censured the Central Committee for carrying out "an opportunistic policy of betrayal"; which held Ch'en Tu-hsiu and T'an P'ing-shan personally responsible for restraining the peasantry and "retreating temporarily in order to retain the alliance with the Kuomintang"; and which insisted that the Communists must continue their co-operation with the Kuomintang Left. In bewildering contradiction, the manifesto "resolutely" opposed asking Communist party members to withdraw from the Kuomintang.[46]

While endorsing a "Kuomintang Left" policy, the August 7 Conference denounced Communist party leadership for submitting to the policies of Ch'en Tu-hsiu and T'an P'ing-shan and for restraining the peasant uprising at Changsha. "The CI has severely criticized the opportunist line of the CC, which has in reality betrayed the Chinese revolution," declared a circular letter of the August 7 Conference. "We agree that this criticism is entirely just and that the policy of the Communist International regarding the Chinese problem is entirely correct. We welcome recent instructions of the Communist International which have made possible the unmasking of the past mistakes of the [Party] leadership and have saved our party [from destruction]. We positively agree that in the past the leadership of the CC carried out an opportunist, unrevolutionary policy and that it is necessary to carry out a thorough revision of our policy on the basis of lessons of the past."[47]

An important reason for past mistakes, the conference decided, was that leadership had been generally in the hands of the intelligentsia and bourgeoisie. Only upon the insistence of the Comintern had a few workers been admitted to the central hierarchy, whereas the Central Committee had often discriminated against workers on the grounds that their cultural standards were too low. Ch'en Tu-hsiu was deposed from leadership, the office of general secretary was abolished, and a new committee system was set up. Dropped from positions of leadership were Chang Kuo-t'ao, T'an P'ing-shan, Mao Tse-tung, and many others.[48] The new "ruling clique," scarcely more

---

[46] "Circular Letter of the CC [CCP] to All Party Members," *A Documentary History*, pp. 102–18.

[47] *Ibid.*, p. 117.

[48] Chang Kuo-t'ao, in an interview with the author, Hong Kong, November 3, 1950. According to Chang, these men were all penalized by the August 7 Conference. Li Ang, on the other hand, claims that Ch'ü Ch'iu-pai demoted them separately, aligning himself first with Li Li-san, Chang Kuo-t'ao, and Chou En-lai to expel T'an P'ing-shan, and attacking the others later. It is probable that the power shift

proletarian than its predecessors, included Ch'ü Ch'iu-pai, Hsiang
Chung-fa, Li Li-san, Chou En-lai, Li Wei-han, and Liu Shao-ch'i.
According to one source, Chou En-lai "almost got expelled."[49]
Throughout Chinese Communist history we shall see how in one
intraparty struggle after another this man managed to hop from the
losing to the winning side.

The new Central Committee set itself up in the French concession of Hankow, while Ch'ü Ch'iu-pai and other individual leaders
lived in the Japanese concession. "The Japanese imperialists," according to Li Ang, "were not only polite to the Communists, but
virtually protected them." Under the influence of Lominadze and
Heinz Neumann, the leadership began developing a policy of armed
insurrection.

The first uprising under this policy had already taken place at
Nanchang under the direction of Lominadze. During the remaining
months of 1927 the Communists were to stage two more major—and
largely unsuccessful—insurrections: the Autumn Crop Uprising
under Mao Tse-tung, and the Canton Commune, which Heinz Neumann directed.

---

took place about the time of the conference, but that formal action came at various
times later.
[49] Chang interview.

CHAPTER VIII

THE COMMUNISTS "PLAY" AT INSURRECTION

The Nanchang, Autumn Crop, and Canton insurrections of late 1927 failed miserably, and by the end of the year Soviet Russian influence in China was all but annihilated. Stalin and his associates began developing new plans which were passed on to Chinese Communist leaders to execute. Yet it was not Stalin, but a relatively obscure peasant graduate of Hunan Normal School who brought victory to the Chinese Communist movement.

On a diplomatic level Stalin had been no more successful than on the subversive. After the signing of the Sino-Soviet Agreement of 1924, the USSR had maintained relations with the Peking government. But in April 1927 Chinese police and soldiery, armed with a warrant countersigned by the dean of the diplomatic corps in Peking, raided both the Chinese Eastern Railway and the Dalbank buildings in the Soviet Embassy compound and seized large numbers of documents which revealed how the Comintern had been availing itself of Soviet government resources and extraterritorial immunities for subversive purposes. Li Ta-chao and nineteen other Communists arrested in the raid were tried by a summary court and executed. In protest, the USSR recalled its chargé d'affaires, leaving in the Embassy only such persons as were considered necessary for the performance of consular functions. The Peking government terminated official relations.

After these various defeats, Stalin and his colleagues shifted to a policy of armed insurrection.

The Nanchang Uprising, directed by Stalin's protégé Besso Lominadze, was carried out by two Kuomintang officers—Ho Lung and Yeh T'ing—who were actually Communists. Ho Lung, who had kept his Communist affiliation a secret, was commander in chief of the 20th Kuomintang Army. Yeh T'ing was a divisional general in the 11th Army which, along with the 4th Army, comprised the famous Second Army Group, or "Ironsides," the finest troops under the Kuomintang.

On the night of August 1, 1927, these two men, supported by Chu Teh, Lin Piao, and other officers and men who were later to become prominent in the Communist movement, staged a mutiny "under the banner of the Kuomintang Left." More than 20,000 troops rose up,. disarmed opposing forces, captured Nanchang, seized the property of banks, and extracted tribute from local businessmen. "I led my company during the Nanchang Uprising," Hsiao K'o was to boast a decade later when he had become a Communist general; "The soldiers of Yeh T'ing's division joined the uprising to a man because the Communist organization ran from the top to the bottom."[1] Supporting the insurrection were numbers of miners from near-by Hanyehping; more than two decades later Chinese Communist theoreticians would trace the careers of these men as evidence that the Chinese Communist movement had emerged under proletarian inspiration.

The mutineers proclaimed a Revolutionary Committee, including Madame Sun Yat-sen and Eugen Ch'en, who were already on their way to European exile, and Generals Chang Fa-k'uei and Huang Ch'i-hsiang of the Ironsides, who were later to put down the Canton insurrection. According to the Comintern press, "a new revolutionary center had been formed,"[2] but if there was any center at all, its days were numbered. Chang Fa-k'uei (of the Revolutionary Committee!) closed in for an attack, and the mutinous troops were forced to flee. Setting off southward, they made plans for capturing the province of Kwangtung. From Communist headquarters in Shanghai Ch'ü Ch'iu-pai wired Chang T'ai-lei, a fellow Communist in Canton, that the Southern Expedition had approached Swatow, that the enemy was ready to retreat, and that an insurrection should be staged in Canton to coincide with the approach of the revolutionary forces. But Chang T'ai-lei was doubtful. "The objective situation in Canton is not really favorable to insurrection," he telegraphed back. ". . . it is really not a good time to start an insurrection."[3]

On September 24, 1927, Yeh T'ing's troops occupied Swatow, an event which *International Press Correspondence* reported with jubilance:

The important harbor town of Swatow and the extremely rich and strategically very important district of the eastern river of the province of Kwangtung are in the hands of the revolutionary troops, who are cooperating with the workers and peasants. This favorable circumstance renders possible the direct advance on the capital town of Canton . . .[4]

What European readers did not yet know was that the Communist army, because of "the superiority of reactionary militarists and its

---

[1] *Red Dust*, p. 133.
[2] *International Press Correspondence*, August 18, 1927, p. 1069.
[3] *Red Stage*, Chap. IV.
[4] *International Press Correspondence*, October 6, 1927, p. 1236.

own wrong tactics,"[5] had already been compelled to retreat from Swatow, seeking safety where they could find it.

With news of the defeat, Chang T'ai-lei reported that an insurrection in Canton was out of the question, but Ch'ü Ch'iu-pai was insistent. Canton must start an insurrection no matter how difficult the circumstances, he informed Chang T'ai-lei, because that was the order from the Comintern.[6]

Pravda, which had been hailing temporary successes before Swatow as "a new revolutionary upsurge," argued now that the Kuomintang Left had been "successfully exploited" and that, as the revolution spread to industrial centers, it would be possible to create soviets of workers', soldiers', and artisans' deputies. The time had come for the soviet slogan to "develop from a propaganda slogan into an action slogan."[7]

But when it became clear that the revolution had failed, responsibility was pinned not on Stalin or his agents or Ch'ü Ch'iu-pai, but on T'an P'ing-shan, who was denounced and expelled for his "Kuomintang Left" illusions.[8] Later, needing more scapegoats, the Comintern (without criticizing Stalin, its own Executive Committee, or the Russian Communist party) would expose a serious error of the August 7 Conference: *it had raised false hopes for the emergence of a Left revolutionary Kuomintang and had called for action under that banner!*[9]

After the Swatow defeat, retreating Communist troops took refuge in the Hailufeng district of Kwangtung, where they helped establish a soviet, and in other rural areas.

The Autumn Crop Uprising also failed. Accounts of this rural insurrection differ. A decade after the occurrence Mao Tse-tung told Edgar Snow: "I was sent to Changsha to organize the movement which later became known as the Autumn Crop Uprising,"[10] an undertaking which, he insisted, had not been sanctioned by the Central Committee. Li Ang maintains, on the other hand, that Ch'ü Ch'iu-pai ordered the insurrection and a number of others in the name of the Central Committee:

I am sorry to report that he [Ch'ü Ch'iu-pai] was cheated by Mao Tse-tung, who promised him to mobilize 100,000 armed peasants and to seize

[5] P. Mif, *Heroic China* (New York, 1937), p. 54.

[6] *Red Stage*, Chap. IV.

[7] *Pravda*, September 30, 1927.

[8] Mif, *Heroic China*, p. 55.

[9] *The Communist International: Between the Fifth and the Sixth World Congresses*, p. 451.

[10] *The Autobiography of Mao Tse-tung* (as told to Edgar Snow) (Hong Kong, 1949), p. 35.

political power. The innocent revolutionist sent an even more exaggerated cable to Moscow saying that Hunan could mobilize a million armed peasants. This cable was dispatched by me. As a matter of fact, the peasant troops of Mao Tse-tung numbered no more than 5,000 persons.[11]

The purpose of the insurrections, according to Mao, was to achieve a final severing of the Communist-Kuomintang alliance on local levels; to organize a peasant-worker army; to confiscate the property of small, middle, and large landlords; to set up Communist power in Hunan independent of the Kuomintang; and to organize soviets. The last proposal, according to Mao, was opposed by the Comintern at that time (presumably August) and was not advanced as a slogan until later.[12]

With the collapse of the uprising, Mao was disciplined:

Because the program of the Autumn Crop Uprising had not been sanctioned by the Central Committee [he told Edgar Snow], because the First Army had suffered some severe losses and from the angle of the cities the movement appeared doomed to failure, the Central Committee now definitely repudiated me. I was dismissed from the Politburo and also from the Party Front Committee.[13]

Li Ang maintains that Ch'ü Ch'iu-pai was fundamentally responsible for the failure but "cleverly and at the same time clumsily" held Mao accountable.[14] The only reason Mao was not expelled from the party altogether, according to Li Ang, was that although he had less prestige than T'an P'ing-shan, he did control "a thousand-odd remnants" of a peasant army.

Gathering his troops, Mao withdrew to an old bandit stronghold at Chingkanshan in Kiangsi feeling, he said, "that we were following the correct line, and subsequent events were to vindicate us fully." During succeeding months Mao set about building his peasant army.[15]

With a note of triumph the November 1927 Plenum of the Chinese Central Committee declared that the "enormous experience" of the past three months had proved party tactics, on the whole, to have been correct. Hailing the foresight of the August 7 Conference—"it will be impossible to transform the Kuomintang into the ruling party of the bourgeois fraction"—the Plenum repeated a September echo of the Moscow line which rejected "revival" of the Kuomintang and put

[11] *Red Stage*, Chap. II.
[12] *The Autobiography of Mao Tse-tung* (as told to Snow), p. 35.
[13] *Ibid.*, p. 37.
[14] *Red Stage*, Chap. III.
[15] *Autobiography of Mao Tse-tung* (as told to Snow), p. 37.

forward the slogan of soviets. The Plenum declared unequivocally that a "decidedly revolutionary situation" now existed in China. This did not necessarily mean a complete victory in the near future was inevitable, the Plenum hedged, for the revolutionary situation would be measured, not by weeks and months, but by years. "It is in character what Marx called a 'permanent revolution,'" the Plenum decided.[16]

THE CANTON COMMUNE

Ever since the advance on Swatow, Comintern leaders had been pressing the Chinese Central Committee to stage urban uprisings. According to Li Ang:

Nearly every day the Comintern sent one or two cables urging Canton and other cities to initiate insurrections . . . Finally the Comintern stated that it was necessary for strategic reasons to start an insurrection even if it were certain to fail.[17]

Stalin and his supporters, who intended using the Fifteenth Congress of the Russian Communist party to force a purge of Trotsky oppositionists from their ranks, were casting about for tangible proof of their own orthodoxy. "They badly needed insurrections and a Soviet government." declared Li Ang, "even if it lasted three minutes . . ."[18] Or, in the words of Trotsky's subsequent charges, they wanted a victory to cover up "the physical extermination of the Russian opposition."[19] And the Chinese leadership needed an uprising, too, for further failures or even mere inaction on the part of the Central Committee of the CCP would lead almost certainly to Comintern intervention at the expense of men like Ch'ü Ch'iu-pai, Hsiang Chung-fa, Li Li-san, and Chou En-lai.[20]

An important speaker before the Fifteenth Congress in Moscow was Besso Lominadze, who described three defeats suffered by the Chinese revolution during the course of recent months: the first in Shanghai, the second in Wuhan, and the third at Swatow. The fundamental "objective" reason for these defeats, he said, lay in the fact that the rise of labor and of peasant movements had not coincided. "The revolution in Shanghai and Wuhan took place when the peasant movement had not assumed that profound revolutionary character

---

[16] "Resolution of the November Plenum," in P. Mif, *Kitaiskaia Kommunisticheskaia Partiia v kriticheskie dni,* pp. 239–71.
[17] *Red Stage,* Chap. IV.
[18] *Red Stage,* Chap. IV.
[19] *Problems of the Chinese Revolution,* pp. 291–92.
[20] *Red Stage,* Chap. IV.

which it now has," he told the Congress.[21] Moreover, the September and October wave of peasant uprisings had begun after the labor movement had already been crushed. It was in the merging of these two streams—the peasant revolts and a rising labor movement—that Communist leadership must find the key to new upheavals. "The question now confronting the party in Kwangtung and several other provinces," he declared as Chinese Communists were rising to seize Canton, "is that of taking up a struggle for power and the organization of armed insurrection."[22]

By November 1927, power in Canton was being shared by two rival generals—Li Chi-shen (Kuomintang Right in 1927, but elected in 1949 one of six vice-chairmen of the Communist-dominated Central People's Government), and Chang Fa-k'uei (Kuomintang Left in 1927, and today a staunch Nationalist), whom the Communists in late summer had listed on their Revolutionary Committee.

With Wang Ching-wei's support, Chang Fa-k'uei was now planning a coup for complete control of the city, and it was this situation which the Comintern, through Heinz Neumann, hoped to exploit. On November 17 Chang Fa-k'uei and Wang Ching-wei effected their coup, and nine days later the Kwangtung Central Committee of the Chinese Communist party laid plans for immediate insurrection. The Committee, according to Neumann, was "profoundly convinced that all conditions for victory were joined and that with good technical and political technique victory was assured."[23]

From Shanghai the Central Committee of the Chinese Communist party instructed the Kwangtung provincial organization of the party to make preparations:

The worker-peasant masses of Kwangtung have only one way out . . . that is, to utilize the opportunity of civil war resulting from the coup d'état in order resolutely to expand the uprisings in the cities and villages, and in the time of war to link such uprisings into a general uprising for the establishment of the Workers', Peasants', and Soldiers' Delegates' Councils (Soviets).[24]

The Kwangtung Central Committee launched slogans for the impending insurrection: Bread for the workers! Land for the peasants!

[21] *Report of the Fifteenth Congress of the Communist Party of the Soviet Union,* (London, 1928), pp. 291–95.

[22] *Ibid.*

[23] A. Neuberg [Heinz Neumann], *L'Insurrection Armée* (Paris, 1931), p. 110.

[24] Teng Chen-hsia, "The Canton Commune and the Tactics of the Communist Party," an undated manuscript in the Jay Calvin Huston Collection at the Hoover Institute and Library, Stanford, California. See also Hua P'ing, "The Canton Commune and Its Preparation," *Räte China, Dokumente der Chinesischen Revolution* (Moscow-Leningrad, 1934), pp. 139–65, cited hereinafter as *Räte China.*

Down with the power of the Kuomintang! Down with Chang Fa-k'uei and Wang Ching-wei! Full democratic freedoms of press, speech, assembly, organization, and strike! Immediate liberation of all political prisoners! All power to the workers, peasants, and soldiers! All power to the soviets![25]

The date originally set for the Canton uprising was December 16, but during the night of December 7 Communist leaders learned that Chang Fa-k'uei, on instructions from Wang Ching-wei, was preparing to disarm the training regiment. Plans were hastily revised and the insurrection set for 3:30 A.M. December 11.[26] But the Canton Police Department had ordered the arrest, meanwhile, of all labor union members, and within forty-eight hours more than 2,000 laborers had been rounded up and jailed.

Despite these setbacks, the Communists began their attack on schedule. Under cover of darkness transport workers put trucks at the disposal of the rebels, and soon assault squads were swinging into action. Within a few hours Red Guard units and rebellious cadets had captured police headquarters, barracks, and post and telegraph offices, and by noon the city had fallen to the Communists. Authority was vested in a Soviet of Workers', Soldiers', and Peasants' Deputies composed of representatives chosen rather than elected—ten from labor groups and three from each of the other two categories.[27]

During these operations Soviet consular officials assumed active leadership and used the consulate as an insurrectionary headquarters.

Communist forces held the city for two days. But word had been dispatched to Chang Fa-k'uei, and early on the thirteenth his Ironsides units opened an attack. Reported Huston:

The so-called White soldiers entered the city so quickly that the Russian Vice Consul and an assistant were caught in front of the Communist headquarters with a red flag on the consulate car. The inmates of the consulate were immediately arrested, and five members, two of whom were peasant organizers of the consulate staff, were shot.[28]

Insurrectionist defenses collapsed under the first attack, and by evening Chang Fa-k'uei was in command of the city. Members of

[25] Neuberg, L'Insurrection Armée, p. 110.

[26] Ibid., p. 114. In "Sun Yat-sen, the Kuomintang and the Chinese-Russian Political Economic Alliance," Jay Calvin Huston, who was an eyewitness to many phases of the uprising, provides an account of what he saw and what he pieced together from materials seized from the Soviet consulate in Canton.

[27] International Press Correspondence, July 5, 1928, pp. 1696–97.

[28] Huston, op. cit., p. 210. Personal papers from the pockets of Soviet Vice-Consul Abram Isaakovich Hassis were secured by Huston and are now on file at the Hoover Institute and Library.

the anti-Communist Machinist Union now helped the soldiers in mopping up the city. According to Huston:

Many private scores were paid off. Two lots of 500 and 1,000 men each were taken out and machine gunned. Realizing that this was a waste of ammunition, the soldiers loaded the victims on boats, took them down the river below the city, and pushed them overboard in lots of ten or twelve men tied together. The slaughter continued for four or five days during which some six thousand people, allegedly Communists, lost their lives in the city of Canton.[29]

The Fifteenth Congress of the Russian Communist party was still in session when news of the Canton defeat reached Moscow. In a final resolution the Stalinist majority, victorious over its party opposition, passed an optimistic resolution: despite the crushing of the Canton soviet, the Chinese revolution was still alive and gathering its forces for a new beginning and a broader offensive along all fronts.[30]

In February the Canton defeat was subjected to a more critical analysis. Before the Ninth Plenum of the ECCI, Stalin, in co-operation with Bukharin and two Chinese delegates, presented a resolution, adopted unanimously, which listed a whole series of blunders: there had been insufficient preliminary work among workers and peasants, and insufficient subversion of enemy forces; there had been a faulty appraisal of the loyalties of workers belonging to non-Communist unions; the party and Young Communist League had not organized properly; there had been insufficient organization of strikes; the soviet in Canton had been chosen, not elected. The Resolution held partially accountable "the direct leaders who are politically responsible to the Communist International (Comrade N.[31] and others)" and at the same time instructed the Chinese Communist party to strengthen "its cadres, its periphery and its center." There had been enough of unorganized action. "To *play* with insurrections instead of organizing a mass uprising of the workers and peasants," the Resolution declared, "is a sure way of losing the revolution."[32]

Stalin and his Russian and Chinese colleagues maintained that although the first revolutionary wave was over, worker and peasant movements of China were moving toward another "mighty upsurge."[33] Essentially the revolution lay in a trough between two waves. Under these circumstances, the greatest danger lay in the possibility

---

[29] *Ibid.*

[30] Paraphrased from the *Report of the Fifteenth Congress*, p. 337.

[31] Heinz Neumann.

[32] "Resolution on the Chinese Question," *International Press Correspondence,* March 15, 1927, pp. 321–22.

[33] *Ibid.*

that the "vanguard" of the labor and peasant movements might "run too far ahead" of the masses, split up its forces, and thus allow itself to be smashed into separate detachments. It was absolutely essential for the Chinese Communists to win over the masses and to link each separate guerrilla action "with the new upsurge of the revolutionary wave" in centers of the urban proletariat.[34] The main task of the Chinese Communist party was to carry out the agrarian revolution and organize Chinese Red Army detachments toward this end, having always in view that the many small guerrilla units would gradually unite into one common national Red Army.[35]

[34] *Ibid.*, p. 321.
[35] *Ibid.*, p. 322.

CHAPTER IX

LI LI-SAN: VICTIM OF THE MOSCOW LINE

From early 1928 until the fall of Li Li-san in late 1930 the attempt to link peasant uprisings with urban insurrection underlay Comintern policies toward China. This intricate program, sketched during the Sixth World Congress of the Communist International in July 1928, was developed over the next two years by Kremlin planners and communicated to Chinese leaders in a series of resolutions and directive letters. During the summer of 1930 it was activated—not without blunders on the part of local leaders—by Li Li-san and his Chinese colleagues. But when the program failed, as was probably inevitable under the circumstances, it was not Stalin or his advisers who were held responsible, but Li Li-san. Where the fundamental errors lay can best be judged by the 1928–31 Communist record.

On a diplomatic level Soviet representatives were scarcely more effective than Li Li-san and Comintern agents were to be. After the Peking raids on Soviet Embassy buildings, the USSR had maintained consular—though not full diplomatic—relations with the Peking government, which now consisted largely of Chang Tso-lin. But there was constant friction, much of it resulting from difficulties over the Chinese Eastern Railway.

The Sino-Soviet Agreement of 1924 and the parallel understanding reached between Soviet Russia and Chang Tso-lin's Manchurian regime had recognized Chinese administrative authority over the line and had also maintained, on a provisional basis, the joint managerial system provided for in the 1896 treaty. But over the years Chang Tso-lin had sought gradually to increase Chinese participation in railway administration. In 1926 Chang, retaliating against the Soviets for refusing to transport Chinese railway guards free of charge, had arrested the Russian manager;[1] eight months later he had seized a fleet of Chinese Eastern Railway vessels on the Sungari River.[2]

The Soviet Union had not taken drastic action in either case, but with the Kuomintang capture of Peking during June 1928 and the death of Chang Tso-lin shortly thereafter, the Russian position in the Chinese Eastern Railway zone became exceedingly precarious. In

[1] *North China Herald*, January 30, February 6, and February 13, 1926.
[2] *Ibid.*, September 11 and September 18, 1926.

October 1928 a new constitution of the Kuomintang government was proclaimed at Nanking, Chang Hsüeh-liang, son of Chang Tso-lin, was appointed to a state position, with his authority in Manchuria and Jehol recognized, and the decision was made to extend Chinese control over the railway.[3]

In April 1929 Chinese police raided and closed Soviet consulates in northern Manchuria, capturing large quantities of subversive documents. This action was followed in July by the arrest of Soviet consular officers, the deportation of the Russian general manager of the Chinese Eastern Railway, together with his subordinates, and the seizure of telephone and telegraph facilities pertaining to the line.[4] The Soviet government held that these raids were a violation of international law and that the incriminating documents were forgeries;[5] the Nanking government, using the captured materials as evidence, justified its action on the basis that the Soviet Union had been using its consulates, together with railway facilities, for purposes of subversion and espionage.

The Chinese case depended upon the authenticity of the documents which, taken at face value, clearly established ties between the Third International and both consular and railway authorities; indicated the existence of a widespread Communist organizational network throughout central China; gave evidence that the USSR was moving arms and explosives into the country for terroristic purposes; and showed Bolshevik agents seeking to turn the so-called Christian General Feng Yü-hsiang against the Nanking government.[6]

For many years it was widely assumed that these documents were actually forged. To contrive this vast quantity of doctrinaire and highly specialized material would have constituted a project of considerable intricacy and magnitude, however, and it is doubtful whether staffs capable of such an undertaking were available in China at this time. It is conceivable, of course, that individual documents might have been altered here and there to make the Communist position look worse than it actually was, but the vast bulk of material seems to bear the imprint of Communist authenticity. In any case, the USSR broke off remaining consular relations with China, and on July 20, 1929, the Nanking government retaliated in kind.

In its propaganda, Moscow presented these developments as evidence that war against the Soviet Union was imminent, and conse-

[3] *Survey of International Affairs, 1928* (London), p. 382.
[4] *Survey of International Affairs, 1929* (London), p. 345.
[5] *International Press Correspondence*, June 14, 1929, pp. 608–9.
[6] "International Relations Committee," *The Sino Russian Crisis* (Nanking, 1929), pp. 1, 2, 31, 33.

quently the various Communist parties were expected to rally to the support of the Bolshevik motherland. In this strictly Russo-Chinese controversy the Chinese Communist party under Li Li-san did not hesitate to raise the slogan "Protect the Soviet Union"[7] — a move which made it possible for the Kuomintang to point out how Red Chinese were supporting the old-style imperialist privileges of a foreign power.

On July 28 the deposed Communist leader, Ch'en Tu-hsiu, directed a letter to the Central Committee criticizing the slogan and urging a propaganda line which would reveal Kuomintang weaknesses without placing the Communists in a position which made them appear anti-Chinese.[8] But the Li Li-san hierarchy simply seized upon Ch'en Tu-hsiu's action and the resultant controversy as an excuse for expelling the former leader from the party.

Meanwhile, a series of border incidents took place between Soviet and Chinese forces, and on November 16, 1929, Soviet military units crossed the Manchurian frontier, and Chinese strength collapsed. The dispute had aroused international apprehension by this time, and the British, French, and United States governments sent notes to both China and the USSR. In the Soviet reply, Maksim Litvinov informed the Powers that since direct negotiations were in progress between the USSR and China, the intervention had been ill-advised.[9]

Somewhat later in the Siberian city of Khabarovsk the People's Commissariat of Foreign Affairs announced its desire for a peaceful regulation of the conflict,[10] and subsequent negotiations culminated in the Khabarovsk Protocol, signed December 22, 1929, which restored the *status quo ante* as far as the Chinese Eastern Railway was concerned; provided that each state should release such of the other's nationals as had been arrested since May 1929; called for the resumption of commerce across the frontier; and made arrangements for the re-establishment of consular—but not full diplomatic—relations.[11]

On May 9, 1930, a Chinese delegation arrived in Moscow to participate in a Soviet-Chinese conference which had been called to bring about a final settlement of the Chinese Eastern Railway problem. After a series of delays, the first sitting opened in October with negotiations based on the Khabarovsk Protocol. This meeting was fol-

---

[7] "The First Letter of Ch'en Tu-hsiu Concerning the Problem of the Chinese Eastern Railway," *China's Revolution and Opportunism* (Chung-kuo ko-ming yü chi-hui chu-i) (Min-chih Book Store, 1929).

[8] *Ibid.*

[9] Royal Institute of International Affairs, *Documents on International Affairs* (London, 1930), p. 275.

[10] *Soviet Union Review*, VIII (1930), 2.

[11] *The China Year Book, 1931*, p. 497.

lowed in December by a second session which established three commissions to investigate questions relating to trade, railway problems, and a possible resumption of full diplomatic relations between the USSR and Nationalist China.[12]

Since his 1927 coup against the Communists, Chiang Kai-shek had consolidated a measure of power not only by force of arms against the Peking government, but more especially through constantly shifting alliances with various individual officers, political and army cliques, and independent or semi-independent war lords. At the time of the Third National Congress of the Kuomintang in March 1929, Chiang had become by far the most powerful military and political leader in China. But during the next few years he found himself faced with intraparty intrigues, rebellions (such as those of Feng Yü-hsiang, Yen Hsi-shan, the Wang Ching-wei clique, and the Kwangsi militarists), and numerous Communist uprisings. As a result, the Nanking government was able to maintain direct control only over those provinces near the mouth of the Yangtze River. In other areas, Chiang's authority depended upon whatever alliances he could patch up with the very militarists who were constantly revolting against him.

CHINESE RED ARMY AND PEASANT SOVIETS

During this same period much of the Chinese countryside was in ferment. After the abortive Autumn Crop Uprising Mao Tse-tung withdrew his First Division of the First Workers' and Peasants' Army to Chingkanshan in South Kiangsi, where he held out in an old bandit stronghold on the mountainside. Other Communist-led troops took refuge in the region, including those led by Chu Teh, and by April 1928 more than 10,000 men were available for organization into the Fourth Corps. Chu Teh was named commander in chief, and Mao Tse-tung the party commissar. Communist sources estimate that no more than 2,000 of these troops were effectively armed.

Intensive training was carried out during the spring and early summer, but food supplies ran short, and it was therefore decided to disperse the troops over a number of counties. According to a subsequent account by Mao Tse-tung, both political and military authorities in the region pressed a moderate policy which "earned Chingkanshan the recriminations of putschists in the Party, who were demanding a terrorist policy of raiding and burning and killing landlords in order to destroy their morale. The First Army Front Committee refused to adopt such tactics and were therefore branded by the hotheads as 'reformists.' I was bitterly attacked by them for not carrying out a more

[12] *Soviet Union Review*, IV (1931), 16.

radical policy."[13] Subsequently Mao and his associates proved themselves perfectly capable of sacrificing landlord lives—but only when a
tactical advantage warranted. Mao was not softhearted; he simply
knew how to exploit a potential opponent before casting him aside.

Gradually Mao, Chu Teh, and other local leaders drew their various guerrilla contingents together into a Chinese Communist Red
Army which ranged over rural areas of Hunan and Kiangsi. And
wherever these troops went, according to Li Ang, a soviet appeared.
Many were short-lived. Others were suppressed by local authorities,
only to reappear within months or even a few weeks. The tendency
was persistent, but did not fully articulate with plans which the Communist hierarchy was then developing.

Illustrative of these rural organisms was the hsien (county) of
Wan-nan, Kiangsi, which established a soviet claiming jurisdiction
over 100,000 peasants organized into six district leagues and more
than 300 village leagues. Organization and discipline, according to a
contemporary Communist account, were very strict. A political program developed on the basis of five "demands": the further seizure
of power on a county seat level; the distribution of landlord acreage
among the peasantry; abolition of all levies and the nullification of
promissory notes; equipment with new weapons; and the confiscation
of stores, small factories, and industrial plants.[14]

Mao and Chu Teh now planned a six-hsien soviet area for consolidating Communist power in the Hunan-Kiangsi-Kwangtung border region and for establishing a base for expansion over larger areas.
According to Mao:

This strategy was in opposition to recommendations of the Party, which
had grandiose ideas of rapid expansion. In the army itself Chu Teh and
I had to fight against two tendencies: first, a desire to advance on Changsha [the capital of Hunan] at once, which we considered adventurism;
secondly, a desire to withdraw to the south of the Kwangtung border [sic],
which we regarded as "retreatism." Our main tasks, as we saw them, then,
were two: to divide the land and to establish soviets.[15]

In the autumn of 1928 a meeting of party representatives was called
at Chingkanshan and was attended by delegates from neighboring soviets. Later Mao declared:

Some division of opinion still existed among Party men in the Soviet
districts concerning the points mentioned above, and at this meeting our

13 *The Autobiography of Mao Tse-tung* (as told to Snow), p. 37.
14 "The Workers and Peasants Revolution in Kiangsi" (a letter from Kiangsi),
appearing originally in the underground periodical, *Pu-erh-sai-wei-k'o* (Shanghai?),
November 1928; translated into German and reprinted in *Räte China*, pp. 244–52.
15 *Autobiography of Mao Tse-tung* (as told to Snow), p. 37.

differences were thoroughly aired . . . the majority had faith in the policy. The Party Central Committee, however, had not yet given the movement its sanction. This was not received until the winter of 1928, when the report of proceedings of the Sixth Congress of the Chinese Communist Party held in Moscow, reached Chingkanshan.

Mao (together with Chu Teh) found himself in agreement with decisions of the Sixth Congress. "From that time on," he wrote later, "the differences between the leaders of the Party and the leaders of the Soviet movement in the agrarian districts disappeared. Party harmony was reestablished."[16]

The decisions of the Sixth Congress of the Communist International, and more especially the Resolution on the Land Problem and the Resolution on the Peasant Problem passed by the Sixth Congress of the Chinese Communist party, are often cited as proof that the subsequent development of Maoism was actually planned in advance by Moscow. Subsequently, we shall find Stalin and his supporters claiming as much, and even Chinese Communist theoreticians have tailored history in this direction, for by 1950 the Maoists had their own reasons for attesting to Stalin's omniscience. But what we can discern from the record looks much more complex—and far less flattering to Stalin.

THE COMINTERN PLANS FOR URBAN INSURRECTION

Stalinist leaders at the Comintern Sixth Congress saw the Chinese revolution developing against a background of general world unrest. From this point forward—and especially after the American stock market crash of 1929—Kremlin strategists discerned a revolutionary upsurge which they described as uneven but world-wide. Within the Soviet Union there was a parallel leftward shift: Stalin pushed for collectivization of agriculture and, having already disposed of Trotsky on the Left, began attacking his Right flank as symbolized by Bukharin.

The Chinese Communist party, following the subsequently notorious "Li Li-san Route," was also veering left. The record shows—contrary to a widely held assumption—that essentials of the Li Li-san policy were shaped in Moscow, but that Comintern directives for implementing them were enigmatic and even contradictory. These documents were so vaguely worded, in fact, that it was easy, when the whole policy failed, for the Kremlin to disclaim all responsibility for error. If the Li Li-san route had succeeded, it would have been equally possible for Stalin to assume full credit.

16 *Ibid.*

Under Comintern supervision the Sixth Congress of the Chinese Communist party placed responsibility for errors connected with the Nanchang Uprising, the August 7 Conference, the Autumn Crop Uprising, and the Canton Commune (described as a "rearguard fight") upon the Chinese Communist leadership,[17] and Bukharin—so soon to fall from grace—chided Ch'ü Ch'iu-pai, Chou En-lai, Chang Kuo-t'ao, Li Li-san, and Hsiang Chung-fa. "You are supposed to be a Bolshevik leader," he told Ch'ü, "not a playwright. You have led the Chinese revolution as though you were acting in a play." To Chou En-lai, he said: "You are in charge of military affairs. You should have estimated your own strength. You are the one most responsible for blind actionism." Chou En-lai blushed without a word, but Ch'ü, who had a "thicker face," just smiled.[18]

Two of the Chinese leaders were ordered to remain in Moscow—Ch'ü, because he was regarded as a "terrorist," and Chang Kuo-t'ao, who was labeled an "opportunist."[19] Nominally, Ch'ü served as the Chinese Communist delegate, but practically, according to Li Ang, he was an exile. Hsiang Chung-fa was made the new general secretary, but, according to Li Ang, it was Li Li-san and Chou En-lai who had real power.[20]

While criticizing the Chinese Communists for "blind actionism," the Comintern insisted that a new upsurge was imminent. The "Theses" declared:

In China the future growth of the revolution will place before the Party as an immediate practical task the preparation for and the carrying through of armed insurrection as the sole path to the completion of the bourgeois-democratic revolution and to the overthrow of the power of the imperialists, landlords, and national bourgeoisie—the Kuomintang.[21]

The Chinese Communist party was told to "struggle for the masses" through strikes, peasant activities, careful organization, and preparation for the establishment of soviets.[22] The task of winning over the masses, the Chinese Communist party echoed, was synonymous with preparing for armed insurrection.[23]

[17] "Political Resolution [of the Sixth National Congress of the CCP] (September 1928)," translated from the Chinese in *A Documentary History*, pp. 127–65.

[18] *Red Stage*, Chap. VI.

[19] Chang interview.

[20] *Red Stage*, Chap. VI. The new Central Committee, according to Li, included Hsiang, Chou En-lai, Li Li-san, Lo Ch'i-yuan, Mao Tse-tung, and Liu Shao-ch'i. Chang Kuo-t'ao lists the Politburo as Ch'ü, Li Li-san, Chou En-lai, Tsao Ho-sheng, and Sheng Yin.

[21] "Theses and Resolutions of the VI World Congress . . . ," *International Press Correspondence*, December 12, 1928, p. 1672.   [22] *Ibid.*

[23] "Political Resolution [of the Sixth National Congress of the CCP], *A Documentary History*, p. 144.

A primary tactic in this preparation was for the Communists to gain leadership over the peasantry, to guide them in the establishment of soviets, and to co-ordinate this rural movement with the struggle of the working class in various Chinese cities. To develop, with maximum effort, a regular revolutionary army of workers and peasants, a Red Army—this was put forward as a foremost Chinese Communist task.[24]

Over the next two years Comintern leaders addressed to the Central Committee of the Chinese Communist party a series of directive letters preparatory to insurrection: the upsurge was imminent, but not yet in sight; the Communists must take the lead, but not rush ahead; the peasants were important, but not a central force. Reading these contradictory analyses, prognostications, and programs for action, one does not wonder that Li Li-san's leadership was confused.

Sitting far away in Moscow, Stalin and his associates relied heavily on three developments: a series of rebellions (led by Feng Yü-hsiang, Yen Hsi-shan, the Wang Ching-wei clique, and the Kwangsi militarists) against Chiang Kai-shek; a further acceleration of peasant guerrilla warfare in widespread rural areas of China; and an allegedly imminent and violent upsurge among the masses. But the record reveals fundamental misinterpretations of all three phenomena.

Kremlin leaders persistently overestimated the "small wars," which they perceived as Chinese manifestations of world-wide Anglo-American antagonisms. In thoroughly characteristic fashion, they diagnosed these primarily factional rebellions as preliminaries "to the great war for world leadership between Great Britain and the United States."[25] The agrarian uprisings, in contrast, were real enough, but Communist strategists saw peasant forces remaining subordinate to urban proletarian leadership. As for the expected upsurge among city masses— this phenomenon simply did not materialize.

Early in 1929 the ECCI issued to the Chinese Communists an enigmatic warning against overanxious anticipation of a "new revolutionary high tide"—and against failing to keep abreast of its upsurge.[26] By June Moscow had perceived "many premises" for revolution, but was still cautioning that the high tide had not yet arrived. This directive, in contrast to its February predecessor, devoted considerable space to the peasant problem. There had been uprisings in

[24] *Ibid.*, p. 151.

[25] *Protokoll, 10 Plenum des Exekutivkomitees der Kommunistischen Internationale, 3 Juli 1929 bis 19 Juli 1929* (Berlin, n.d.), p. 888.

[26] "A Letter to the Chinese Communist Party from the Executive Committee of the Comintern, February 8, 1929," *Erh chung-ch'uan hui chüeh-i an* (Resolutions of the Second Central Congress of the Chinese Communist Party), June 1929. The original document was in Russian.

many different localities, the ECCI acknowledged, but many of them had been led by non-Communists—in fact, by "reactionaries." The time had not yet come for an appeal to land revolution.

On the contrary, the objective environment in China requires the Party to emphasize the leading of small partial struggles of the peasant masses . . . to fight for improved working conditions among the hired peasants . . . to struggle against the civil wars of new war lords . . . to struggle against usury capital . . .[27]

Early in July the Second Plenum of the Chinese CP Central Committee informed all party headquarters that the surge of the revolutionary tide was neither "very remote" nor "imminent," but decidedly on the upswing.

At present, the workers' struggle is beginning to revive, the agrarian revolution is developing, certain Soviet areas as well as the Red Army under the command of Chu [Teh] and Mao [Tse-tung] are still in existence, revolts of [non-Communist] troops still occur frequently, and these troops then join the agrarian uprisings.[28]

Taken together, then, current political conditions lent urgency, the Plenum thought, to the party's "general mission" of winning over the masses and preparing for armed insurrections. This meant leading guerrilla movements, expanding the soviet areas, organizing the Red Army, tightening party organization and discipline, developing the labor movement in major industries, and providing the workers with military organization and training. It was still assumed that a firm core of urban workers remained an absolute prerequisite to victory.

In general the Plenum confirmed the leadership of Li Li-san and recognized a near-identity between his policies and those laid down by the Communist International. But Moscow was not quite satisfied, for in late summer the ECCI drew to the "serious attention" of the Chinese Communist party the necessity of effecting as soon as possible a change in the work of the Communists in mass organizations of workers. "The Communist Party of China must take all measures possible to revive the Red unions and to turn them into real mass organizations," the ECCI declared. "This is particularly important in the present upturn of the struggle . . ."[29]

[27] "A Letter to the Chinese Communist Party from the Executive Committee of the Comintern, June 7, 1929," loc. cit.
[28] "Resolutions and Spirit of the Second Plenum of the CC (Circular No. 40 of the CC) (July 9, 1929)," A Documentary History, p. 170.
[29] Kommunisticheskii Internatsional, September 27, 1929, pp. 56–58. An English translation appears in International Press Correspondence, September 20, 1929, pp. 1126–27.

The ECCI also directed the Chinese Communists to infiltrate whatever yellow (non-Communist) unions enjoyed mass membership.

We join these trade unions only because and insofar as they have large memberships of workers in their ranks, and only for the purpose of capturing those masses . . . When it captures a strong position in them . . . [the Communist Party] must at a suitable moment take up the question of ousting the yellow and Kuomintang leadership . . .

Finally, the Chinese Communist party was directed to work toward legalizing Red trade unions—"even if under another name." But whatever the circumstances, the actual leadership of these Communist-controlled organizations must remain "conspiratorial."

In October the ECCI suddenly revised its estimates. "Dear Comrades!" wrote the Political Secretariat to the Chinese Central Committee: "Recent events in China prompt us to express our estimation of the present situation in China and to give some preliminary instructions concerning the major tasks of the Communist Party without waiting for information from you . . ."[30] There had been a new outburst of "fratricidal war" among the rebellious "imperialist-backed" factions; Wang Ching-wei and his supporters had formed a party for the reorganization of the Kuomintang with military support from Chang Fa-k'uei; the Kuomintang domestic policy was "failing"; Chang Hsüeh-liang, son of Chang Tso-lin, had seized the Chinese Eastern Railway in a move the Soviet Union considered antagonistic; and, finally, the tide of the labor union movement was rising—the start of a new revolutionary upsurge!

The ECCI declined to predict the speed of transformation "from a national crisis to a direct revolutionary situation," but the current task was clear: the Communists must undertake mass revolutionary preparations for the overthrow of the Nanking government and for the establishment of a "Soviet proletarian-peasant" dictatorship.

How accurate was this new estimate?

The truth was that Communist leaders—Russian and Chinese— had remained blind, for the most part, to an acute transformation in the Chinese Communist mass movement from primarily proletarian to primarily peasant composition. Near the end of 1926, according to Communist figures, at least 66 percent of Chinese Communist party membership could be classed as proletarian. Another 22 percent were considered to be intellectuals.[31] Only 5 percent were peasants, and 2

---

[30] *Kommunisticheskii Internatsional,* December 23, 1929, pp. 43–47, and *Hung Ch'i* (Red Flag), February 15, 1930. An English version is available in *International Press Correspondence,* January 9, 1930, pp. 29–31.

[31] *Report on the Activity of the Communist International,* March–November, 1926, p. 118.

percent were soldiers. But by the early months of 1930, elements which could possibly be labeled working class totaled only 8 percent of Chinese Communist party membership, while the number of industrial workers was "still smaller, accounting for only 2%" of party membership.[32] The Chinese Red Army, which, more than any other Red organ, had been responsible for Chinese Communist victories and the establishment of soviets, was overwhelmingly peasant.

Despite these developments, the Chinese Communist party continued its preparations for a "revolutionary upsurge" emerging from urban discontent. Early in January 1930 the Chinese Politburo voted formal acceptance of the Comintern's October 26 directive and declared that a new revolutionary wave was definitely on its way. Conditions among the peasants and workers, according to the Politburo argument, were growing worse: peasant bankruptcy, unemployment in the cities, prohibitive prices, lower wages, increased working hours, heavier work, and large numbers of refugees without a living—these were all important elements in the forthcoming upsurge. "We must follow the directive of the Comintern," the Politburo declared, ". . . preparing the masses to fulfill their tasks and aggressively initiating and enlarging the revolutionary methods of class struggle."[33] Communist party members were told to equip the workers and peasants to the maximum limit, disarm the troops of the war lords, and seize the means of communication. At the same time, the party must increase its international responsibility. The workers and peasants must be taught to understand their proper relationships with other oppressed peoples such as the Indians, Koreans, and Malayans. The party must strengthen its relations with the Japanese and especially with the Russian masses. Above all, the Chinese Communists must live up to their responsibility "for the armed protection of the Soviet Union," a task the more heavily imposed upon them, apparently, by the Manchurian railways incident of the time.

By March the Chinese Communist central organization was informing rank and file members that the "national revolutionary high tide" was about to confront them. "The objective conditions of the revolutionary upsurge are undoubtedly growing riper and riper," the Central Committee declared, "but the subjective power of the Party, on the contrary, reveals great weakness in that it cannot catch up with the development of the revolution, but tends to become the tail of the

[32] "Letter from the Central Committee of the Chinese Communist Party to All Party Members," *Hung Ch'i*, March 26, 1930.

[33] "Resolutions for Acceptance of the Directive Letter of the Comintern Dated October 26 [1929] Concerning the Nationalist Reorganizationalists and the Task of the Chinese Communist Party, Passed by the Central Politburo on January 11, 1930," *Hung Ch'i*, February 1930.

masses."[34] Frankly and soberly the Central Committee indicated the gravely small number of urban workers enjoying party membership and offered the following reasons for this weakness:

First, timidity. Members are afraid to become known as Communists and dare not promulgate Communism among the masses. Even though the masses cried out "We support the Communists," we still dared not induce anyone to join the Party . . . Second, contempt for the masses. Members think that the masses do not know anything, and are not qualified to be Party members. Actually, they are competent enough to lead the whole labor branch. This is a narrow sectarian idea. Thirdly, negligence concerning the importance of organization. In ordinary times, they neglected the development of the Party; in times of struggle, they are again busy with leadership and forget about the development of Party organization . . . these are very serious and dangerous rightist concepts.[35]

Party leaders felt that there was no time to lose. "The class struggle is increasingly acute," the Central Committee declared; "the revolutionary situation is developing increasingly, and the great historical mission—the seizure of national political power—is about to confront us!"[36]

Acting under these various directives, Li Li-san planned his tactics. The Sixth Congress of the CCP had declared: "The degree of consolidation of the reactionary regime in different regions is uneven; therefore the revolution, in a general new rising tide, may succeed first in one or more provinces."[37] In late March Li Li-san, citing this principle, urged the setting up of a revolutionary regime in one or more provinces first—rather than making an attempt to control the whole country. A Berlin insurrection, he maintained, would cause the whole of Germany to support it, and a victory in Paris would be a victory of the whole of France, but in China there was no such single city. Shanghai, being an industrial center, might affect the whole country, even the whole world, in case of a successful insurrection, but even then the reactionary forces could simply withdraw to another part of China and continue their fighting. The Chinese Communist task was to fight for political power in one or a few provinces and then to establish a revolutionary regime to complete a "national revolutionary" victory.[38]

Li Li-san refused to believe, at this time, that the Chinese Red

[34] "A Letter to All Party Members Concerning the Development of Party Organization," *Hung Ch'i,* March 26, 1930.

[35] *Ibid.*

[36] *Ibid.*

[37] *A Documentary History,* p. 143.

[38] Li Li-san, "Ready to Establish the Revolutionary Regime," *Hung Ch'i,* March 26, 1930.

Army could be relied upon for the capture of urban bases. "All talk of 'encircling the city with the country' or of relying on the Red Army to take the cities is sheer nonsense,"[39] he declared "[and] so much hollow bluff." It was the strength of the urban proletariat which Li Li-san—at this time—considered decisive.

> . . . the leading role of the proletariat . . . is, in fact, the only guarantee of the success of the revolution. The proletariat is the leader of the revolution—the peasantry is its ally. No strategic line can ever depart from this principle.[40]

In order to achieve a closer co-ordination between activities in the cities and activities in the rural areas, the Chinese Communists were planning a Conference of Delegates from the Soviet Areas, a gathering called jointly by the Central Committee and the All-China Federation of Labor. In 1928 the Sixth Congress had emphasized a need for establishing a closer relationship between peasant and worker under the hegemony of the proletarian movement. At the Tenth Plenum of the ECCI, July 3–19, 1929, a Chinese delegate had criticized a dangerous lack of connection between peasant and worker activities and declared that labor could not be victorious unless supported by a mighty peasant movement. It was the task of the Chinese Communist party to organize the agricultural laborers and, through them, to link up the worker and peasant movements.[41] On February 25, 1930, the call for a Conference of Delegates from the Soviet Areas was issued, and some weeks later official organs of the Communist International carried a three-part program for consideration by the conference: a general program for soviet governments, labor laws, and agrarian laws.[42]

The chief purpose of the conference, according to one advance notice, was "to secure the leading role of the proletariat" in the Chinese revolution.[43] Another preliminary announcement (published subsequent to the conference) emphasized that the Chinese Communist party, aware of the fact that only the proletariat in alliance with the masses of the peasantry could decide the fate of the revolution, was now "taking over leadership of the peasant insurrections" in order to

---

[39] "Conditions for Preparing the Victory of a Regime in One or Several Provinces," *Hung Ch'i*, April 5, 1930.

[40] "The Problem of the Proletarian Hegemony," *Hung Ch'i*, May 24, 1930.

[41] *Protokoll, 10 Plenum des Exekutivkomitees der Kommunistischen Internationale, 3 Juli 1929 bis 19 Juli 1929*, p. 844.

[42] Li, "Der 1 Kongress der Vertreter der Sowjetgebiete Chinas," *Die Kommunistische Internationale*, 9 April, 1930, pp. 712–20.

[43] Chen Kwang, "The Forthcoming First Chinese Soviet Congress," *International Press Correspondence*, April 30, 1930, p. 386.

connect the struggle of the urban proletariat with the guerrilla wars.[44] A Russian observer put it this way:

Powerful as the partisan movement already is at present, the counter-revolution which stands under the protection of the imperialists in the industrial and trading centers cannot finally be crushed with partisan forces of the Chinese village and the small districts alone. Without being burst from within, without the revolt of the industrial proletariat which must have the hegemony of the revolutionary movement not only in the town but also in the village, the main stronghold of the counter-revolution cannot be captured.[45]

The conference, he said, must establish the closest fighting connection between partisan actions, guerrilla warfare, and the undertakings of the industrial proletariat.

When it finally took place, the conference—following the program which had been laid out for it—enacted labor statutes and a series of land laws that were especially radical and which foresaw the establishment of collective farms within the Soviet areas. Later we shall see how the Communist International, which prior to the conference had published substantially the same program in its own official journal, was to hold Li Li-san personally responsible for the collective farm concept. Meanwhile, the conference repudiated the "incorrect line of neglecting the leadership of the city and concentrating exclusively on the 'encirclement of the city by the country' through attacks on the cities by Red Army forces."[46] Before many weeks were spent, Li Li-san—not without tacit Russian support—would employ precisely the tactics he was now arguing against.

Most fundamental of all, perhaps, the conference proceeded on the assumption that a revolutionary situation already existed. For the time being, there was to be no criticism of this premise from Moscow; in fact quite the contrary occurred. But after Li Li-san had failed, Stalinist writers were careful to point up the mistakes of the Chinese leadership. "The resolution of the Conference on the political situation in China contains a mistaken statement that there already existed a revolutionary situation in China," wrote G. B. Ehrenburg some three years later. ". . . Hence followed the incorrect political slogans of the Conference, namely the call to immediate armed uprising . . ."[47]

[44] Kuo, "On the First Congress of the Chinese Soviets," *International Press Correspondence*, July 12, 1930, p. 509.

[45] A. Ivin, "The Partisan Movement in China," *International Press Correspondence*, May 22, 1930, pp. 431–32.

[46] "A Summary of the Declaration of the All-China Conference of Delegates from the Soviet Areas," *Hung Ch'i*, June 21, 1930.

[47] G. B. Ehrenburg, *Sovetskii Kitai* (Moscow, 1933), pp. 25–26.

LI LI-SAN OPENS THE ATTACK—AND FAILS

On June 11 the Chinese Politburo adopted a resolution, "The New Revolutionary Rising Tide and Preliminary Successes in One or More Provinces,"[48] which brought the Communists a long step closer to overt action. Still denying that cities could be enveloped from the country or "simply captured by the Red Army," this document reiterated that armed uprisings among the urban proletariat must be accorded priority. Nevertheless:

In view of the present objective economic and political conditions of China, a rising tide of proletarian struggles unaccompanied by peasant uprisings, soldiers' mutinies, powerful assaults by the Red Army, and a [whole] combination of various revolutionary forces, also will not lead to victory.

Once the revolutionary upsurge began—whether in this province or that—it could not develop alone, but must be co-ordinated with other movements on a nation-wide basis. Moreover, since China was the "weakest link in the ruling chain of world imperialism," the Politburo reasoned that success there might well touch off revolution on a world-wide scale.

Comintern and Soviet Russian leaders—quite in contrast to their subsequent charges against Li Li-san—seemed to encourage the Chinese Politburo's reasoning and to bestow their blessing. Addressing the Sixteenth Congress of the CPSU on June 27, 1930, Stalin placed great emphasis upon a chain of economic crises developing throughout the capitalist world. Antagonisms were deepening among the various capitalist powers, and it was evident that the economic disturbances would soon be transformed into political crises. This meant that the upsurge of the revolutionary mass movement would "rush forward" with new emphasis; it meant also that the working class of the world, struggling against capitalist exploitation and war danger, would "seek the remedy" in revolution.[49] On a domestic Russian level, Stalin pressed for liquidation of the kulaks, the enforced collectivization of agriculture, and the surrender of Bukharin and other "right opportunists" who wanted to proceed less ruthlessly.[50]

Before this same gathering, Molotov hailed the new revolutionary upsurge in China. "Drawing support from the best provided regions in which the Red Army is active," he declared, "the Soviets in China are able to make contact with large industrial centers and form a Soviet workers' and peasants' government under the leadership of the Com-

---

[48] *A Documentary History*, pp. 184–200.

[49] J. Stalin, "The Political Report of the Central Committee of the XVI Party Congress of the CPSU, June 27, 1930," *International Press Correspondence*, pp. 550, 552–53.

[50] *Ibid.*, pp. 578–79, 616–17.

munist Party."[51] There was no word of warning here, no indication that Kremlin leaders saw anything wrong with what Li Li-san was doing.

On July 23, moreover, the ECCI dispatched a directive to the Chinese Politburo: "The new upsurge in the Chinese revolutionary movement has become an indisputable fact."[52] But unfortunately the struggling masses had not yet been able to occupy industrial centers. The ECCI directed, therefore, that every effort should be bent toward strengthening the Red Army for seizure of several political or industrial centers as circumstances might dictate. "In analyzing the present-stage struggle," the letter declared, "we have to keep in mind that we do not have an all-China objective revolutionary situation. The waves of the labor and peasant movements have not yet been combined." The total force was, therefore, not sufficient for attacking Kuomintang and imperialist control. "But if we are to judge from the tendency of recent events," the letter stated, "the revolution should cover a few important provinces, if not the whole country." Whether or not the Communist party succeeded must depend upon its ability to lead and develop the soviet movement.

There is a clear warning here—one of the better loopholes through which Comintern leaders could later squeeze themselves—but it concerns timing and not the fundamental strategy for which Li Li-san was so soon to be held responsible.

The Chinese Red Army now issued a communiqué, signed by Mao Tse-tung and other members of the Revolutionary Military Committee, which described the high tide as "already surging upon us" and the Kuomintang as bordering on a state of collapse.

In accordance with decisions of the First All-China Congress of Representatives from the Soviet Areas, and in order to fulfill its revolutionary tasks, this committee has sent the First Red Army marching against Nanchang and the Second and Third Red Armies against Wuhan and seeks to win victory first in Hunan, Hupei and Kiangsi. In this way the committee will hasten the upsurge of the revolutionary high tide throughout the nation . . .[53]

[51] "Report to the XVI Party Congress, July 5, 1930," *International Press Correspondence*, July 17, 1930, pp. 589–95. A Russian version is available in *XVI S'ezd Vsesoiuznoi Kommunisticheskoi Partii (b); Stenograficheskii Otchet* (Moscow, 1931), pp. 415–16.

[52] *Shih-hua* (Truth), October 30, 1930. This is an official CCP organ probably published in the Kiangsi Soviet. Cf. Tso-liang Hsiao, *Power Relations within the Chinese Communist Movement, 1930–1934* (Seattle: University of Washington Press, 1961), pp. 28–31, 60–61, 63–68. Throughout his excellent analysis Dr. Hsiao overlooks one important point: the tendency on the part of leaders in Moscow to write such ambiguities into their directives that the Kremlin could equally take credit for successes and disclaim responsibility for failures.

[53] Japan, Ministry of Foreign Affairs, Intelligence Division (Jôhô-bu), *Shina*

At this time Chiang Kai-shek was at war with Feng Yü-hsiang and Yen Hsi-shan, who had formed a coalition, and Communist leaders considered the situation favorable. Several years later Lo Ping-hui, a Communist general, described how, setting out against Nanchang, he and his forces took a so-called Li Li-san oath.

In order to cooperate with the Communist revolution all over China, we must struggle to win the support of the masses in Hunan and to capture Changsha and Nanchang and then Hankow and Wuchang, and finally carry on down the Yangtze River to Shanghai![54]

In the fighting at Nanchang Lo Ping-hui was made commander of the Twelfth Red Army. But the attack was not successful, and so Communist forces set out for Changsha. Lo Ping-hui recalled later:

We wanted to capture Changsha on August 1 to commemorate the Nanchang Uprising [1927]. I was with P'eng Te-huai, Chu Teh, and Mao Tse-tung (who was political commissar). In the attack on Changsha we experienced our first airplane bombing. A squadron of six airplanes came. At first the Red soldiers didn't know what the planes were and looked up with much interest when they saw something being dropped into the air.[55]

The Comintern organ *International Press Correspondence* carried on August 7 an ecstatic description of a new Chinese Communist victory.

Changsha, the capital of the province of Hunan, one of the most important provinces in the heart of China, was captured on the 28th of July by the victoriously advanced Fifth Red Army of the Chinese Soviet territories. Supported by the insurgent workers and peasants in town and country and by the mutiny of some of the government soldiers, who turned their rifles against their own commanders, the red workers' and peasants' army was able, after heroic fighting, to achieve a tremendous victory . . . The rich, the foreign capitalists, and the missionaries fled in greatest panic. Reactionary elements who organized counter-actions were shot . . . In a surprisingly short time the whole of Changsha was covered with a sea of red flags . . . Leaflets were distributed and placards pasted on the fronts of houses. The Soviet Power, the power of the workers, peasants and soldiers was proclaimed . . .[56]

Communist determination to seize Hankow, Wuchang, and Hanyang was restated:

Kyôsantô Shi (A History of the Chinese Communist Party), Ken'ichi Hatano, editor, (Tokyo? 1932). No date for the communique is included, but the two other documents bracketed in the book with it bear July 1930 dates.

[54] Lo Ping-hui to Nym Wales, *Red Dust*, p. 123.   [55] *Ibid.*, p. 124.

[56] Chieh Hua, "The Occupation of Changsha by the Chinese Red Army," *International Press Correspondence*, August 7, 1930, p. 697. Cf. Hsiao, *Power Relations*, pp. 32–33.

The capture of these three sister towns, the largest industrial towns of Central China, is the aim of the Red Army . . . All around Wuhan there already exist Soviet districts. The Red Army is endeavoring, with the aid of the insurgent peasants, to extend its field of operations more and more to the center and to encircle Wuhan.[57]

And a Chinese representative told the Sixteenth Party Congress of the CPSU:

The military operations must be developed in the direction of the most important transport routes with a view to winning the industrial and administrative centers . . . After the occupation of the industrial centers the Soviet government will be sufficiently consolidated to challenge the reactionary Kuomintang.[58]

But victory could be achieved only through the combined action of workers, peasants, and soldiers. "The bearer of the revolutionary advance there [in China] is the working class," Pavel Mif, a Russian specialist on China, told the CPSU.[59] For continued success, the Chinese Communists must make certain that their leading cadres were filled with workers, rather than peasant or other elements.[60]

Communist leaders in Russia and China were ebullient over the success in Changsha, but by the time readers in other countries were learning about it through official publications, the city had already slipped from Red Army hands. Some years later General Wang Cheng offered a cryptic account of what happened:

In August news came of P'eng's successful capture of Changsha on July 27. In great excitement we made a quick march [from Taowushan] to Changsha, only two days away, and entered the city while P'eng was still there. The CP ordered all peasants and workers to go to Changsha to help the Red Army. Over ten thousand arrived.[61]

The Communist troops, according to Western observers, were poorly armed, but well disciplined and intelligently led,[62] and poverty-stricken farmers were joining by the thousands.[63] The Changsha proletariat, on the other hand, was not nearly the powerful force that Communist leaders had imagined. It was easier, the Red Army discovered, to take Changsha than to hold it. Foreign gunboats appeared on the river,

[57] *Ibid.*, p. 698.

[58] "Comrade Siu to the XVI Party Congress, CPSU," *International Press Correspondence*, August 7, 1930, p. 735.

[59] *International Press Correspondence*, August 28, 1930, p. 847. Pavel Mif discussing the Molotov Report.

[60] Comrade Siu to the XVI Party Congress, *International Press Correspondence*, August 7, 1930, p. 735.

[61] Wang Cheng to Nym Wales, *Red Dust*, pp. 97–98.

[62] *New York Times*, August 3, 1930.

[63] *Ibid.*, August 4, 1930.

and Nationalist troops were reported on the way. By August 3 P'eng's forces were withdrawing from the city, leaving it asmolder and stained with the blood of an estimated 2,000 victims.[64]

According to Wang Cheng:

Under the Li Li-san line, P'eng was ordered to attack Changsha again. Our men were still carrying on partisan attacks near the city, of course. Chu Teh, Mao Tse-tung, and Huang Kung-lüeh arrived in Hunan, but P'eng was unable to reoccupy Changsha.[65]

Attempts to move on Hankow and other cities also failed.

Neither Moscow nor the Chinese hierarchy gave any indication as yet that the defeat at Changsha was the colossal blunder that it was later made out to be. Chieh Hua, writing for *International Press Correspondence,* described the operation as a "great step forward in the Soviet movement"[66] and *Kommunisticheskii Internatsional* restated the absolute necessity of a seizure of urban industrial centers.[67] Yet it was clear enough that the Chinese Communists were running into difficulties.

Earlier in the year Moscow had appointed Pavel Mif, director of the Sun Yat-sen University in Moscow and a Stalinist "expert" on China, as Comintern representative to the Communist movement in that country. With him traveled a group of young men who had been studying at the university and who were known later as the "Returned Student Clique." Centering around Wang Ming (Ch'en Shao-yü), the group included Ch'in Pang-hsien (Po Ku), Shen Tse-min, Wang Chia-hsiang, Chang Wen-t'ien (Lo Fu), and Ho Tse-shu. According to Li Ang:

These fellows were just a group of young students who, needless to say, had done nothing for the Chinese revolution. While we were carrying out the revolution, they were taking milk at their mothers' breasts. So they did not have any practical experience . . . But these men, who were still infants in terms of revolutionary background, were now sent back to be leaders of the Chinese revolution and the Chinese Communist Party . . .[68]

Actually, several months were to pass before Mif could dislodge Li Li-san and place his Returned Students in leadership.

In China Li Li-san was already under attack by Ch'en Tu-hsiu—

[64] *Ibid.,* August 6, 1930.
[65] Wang Cheng to Nym Wales, *Red Dust,* p. 98.
[66] *International Press Correspondence,* August 21, 1930, p. 777.
[67] "On the Eve of a New Revolution in China," *Kommunisticheskii Internatsional,* August 10, 1930.
[68] *Red Stage,* Chap. XII.

sniping from outside the party—by a labor-oriented group under Ho Meng-hsiung,[69] and of course by the Returned Student group, who had not yet received sufficient official sanction to make themselves effective. After the Changsha defeat officials in Moscow dispatched Ch'ü Ch'iu-pai, who was still the Chinese party representative there, and Chou En-lai, who happened to be in Soviet Russia on a party mission, back to China for the Third Plenum, which had been called for late September in Lushan, Kiangsi. According to subsequent Comintern charges, Ch'ü Ch'iu-pai announced, before leaving Moscow, his opposition to the "Li Li-san line" and his complete agreement with the Comintern. In its "Report on the Third Plenum of the Party and the Errors of Comrade Li-san," the Far Eastern Commission of the Comintern declared:

> But when comrade Ch'iu-pai arrived in China, he who was practically the leader of the Third Plenum not only did not carry out the directives of the Comintern, but on the contrary took a compromising attitude toward the Li-san Trotskyite blind actionist line.

Chou En-lai, nimble-footed as ever, also "compromised"—up to the last possible moment for making a successful switch.[70]

The Third Plenum found only minor errors in the policies of Li Li-san. In his "Report on the Third Plenum," Chou En-lai asked: "Do the errors of the CC lie in a difference in line from the CP?" His answer to the question was "absolutely not. There is no difference in line."[71] Only because of an overestimation regarding the degree and speed of the current revolutionary development had the Chinese Central Committee made mistakes, and these had not been deep-seated, but sporadic and tactical. The Third Plenum could scarcely decide otherwise, for the Comintern had not yet changed its own policy. Li Li-san might have made local miscalculations, but the over-all policy was Moscow-made, and Manuilsky could boast—as late as November 7—about the correctness of the prognosis of the CPSU and the Comintern regarding the "inevitability of the extension and strengthening" of the revolutionary upsurge.

> The Communist Party [of China] is furnishing a living example of the revolutionary-democratic dictatorship in the Soviet districts, and is now rousing millions of Chinese workers and peasants to the struggle for the social and national liberation of China. It is endeavoring to link up the

[69] For an analysis of these opposition factions, see Schwartz, *op. cit.*, pp. 145–51.

[70] "The Report of the Far Eastern Commission of the Comintern in Regard to the Third Plenum of the Chinese Party and the Errors of Comrade Li Li-san," *Pu-erh-sai-wei-k'o*, May 10, 1931. Cf. Hsiao, *Power Relations*, pp. 77–79.

[71] Chou En-lai, "Report on the Third Plenum (September 24, 1930)," (Extract), *A Documentary History*, pp. 200–208.

military struggle with the workers' movement in the industrial centers of China.[72]

Why had the "victorious advance" of the Chinese Red Army against the industrial cities been held up near Changsha? Manuilsky—at this date—had a sympathetic rationalization: the development of the Chinese revolution was in direct collision with the *whole system* of world imperialism, which knew that a Communist victory on the Chinese countryside would shake international capitalism. Imperialism—its back against a Chinese wall—was fighting for its life.

With such unqualified reassurances, Li Li-san must have felt stunned by the next change in the Comintern line, which reached China just nine days later. To the Chinese Central Committee the ECCI wrote:

During an historic moment like this, there arises a grave difference between the Executive Committee of the Comintern and a few comrades of the Chinese Politburo on one side, and Comrade Li-san and a few other comrades of the Politburo on the other side . . . The problem is not one of disagreement or of a relatively unimportant difference of opinion concerning an estimate or timing or an understanding of tactics and tasks. It is perfectly clear that we have two political lines of differing principle opposing each other during the most critical moment of the Chinese revolution. These two lines are mutually antagonistic and cannot be coexistent.[73]

This one letter was more than sufficient to topple Li Li-san.

The ECCI took sharp note of a "dangerous spirit" in Li Li-san's attitudes, quoting him as complaining that the Comintern did not understand the local situation, that China was really an exceptional case, and that Moscow leaders did not comprehend the tendencies of the Chinese revolution.

He dared to contrast loyalty to the Comintern with loyalty to the Chinese revolution. He said before the Conference of the Politburo on August 3 that to be loyal to the Comintern and to observe the discipline of the Comintern is one thing, and to be loyal to the Chinese revolution is another thing, that talking to the Comintern would be different after Wuhan had been taken.[74]

But the ECCI reserved its heaviest blows for an attack on Li Li-san's over-all plan which, through the months and even years of its growth, had been so largely shaped by Comintern directives. Li Li-san

[72] Dmitrii Manuilsky in *Pravda*, November 7, 1930. An English translation appears in *International Press Correspondence*, November 20, 1930, p. 1065.
[73] "A Letter to the Central Committee of the Chinese Communist Party by the ECCI, Received November 16, 1930," *Shih-hua*, December 14, 1930.
[74] *Ibid.*

had ignored the uneven development of both the Chinese and world revolutionary movements. Thus, he had denied the possibility of a Chinese victory apart from the victory of a world-wide revolution, and he had pushed the notion that a victory in one province was tantamount to a nation-wide sweep. He had failed to perceive how the labor movement lagged behind the peasant movement: "When Comrade Li-san proposed to start an insurrection in Wuhan, there were only two hundred Communists there; one hundred fifty persons were in the red unions, and the organization of the proletariat was weak and without preparation . . . ." Even the Soviet areas had not been properly organized, the ECCI declared, while the Red Army, for all its positive features, had not really accomplished much. Equipment had been poor, ammunition scarce, cannons lacking. Above all, "The leadership cadres should be workers," the ECCI wrote. "The main officers should be the best Communist Party members."

Supported by this letter from the ECCI, the Returned Students, under Pavel Mif's supervision, lost no time in unseating Li Li-san, changing policy, and setting themselves up in leadership. At Comintern request the new Politburo sent Li Li-san off to Moscow where, under grilling by the Far Eastern Commission, he made an abject confession: he had not understood the uneven development of the Chinese revolution; he had failed to establish a revolutionary base; he had pressed for collective farms; he had thought that a revolutionary government could not be set up until large industrial cities had been occupied; he had expected the international revolutionary movement to surge quickly with the Chinese revolution as its motive power. These and other mistakes he now recognized as clearly "Trotskyist."[75]

Li Li-san now admitted that Ch'en Shao-yü, Ch'in Pang-hsien, and other Returned Students had tried to put him on the right road, criticizing his June 11 letter, but he had refused to listen. One difficulty, he said, was that the Chinese Communist party had been riddled by personal cliques.

Undoubtedly I was under Ch'iu-pai's influence, but also I should say that organizationally I had no relations with Ch'iu-pai's clique . . . I repeatedly objected to the cliques . . . I objected to the attempts on the part of [Chang] Kuo-t'ao, Ho [Meng-] hsiung and Ch'iu-pai and so forth to form cliques.[76]

There had also been hard feelings between Russian and Chinese Communists: ". . . the comrades in China maintain a prejudice

---

[75] "The Discussion of the Li-san Line by the Praesidium of the ECCI," *Pu-erh-sai-wei-k'o*, May 10, 1931.
[76] *Ibid.*

toward the comrades in Moscow and do not trust them," Li Li-san admitted. "The comrades in Moscow do not trust the comrades doing practical work in China, either."[77] He told how the Russian Communists took care of "their own racial interests" to the neglect of the Chinese situation, which they did not understand.[78]

The chairman of the examining board, the same Manuilsky, found many aspects of this confession disturbing. Clearly, Li Li-san had found the Moscow atmosphere shocking, for after a few meetings of the Far Eastern Commission he had confessed his errors. This seemed good, but actually there were dangerous aspects to so easy a capitulation. Had all these dangerous notions been uprooted, not only by Li Li-san, but by his comrades in China? Manuilsky considered the relationship between the Russians and the Chinese Communist party particularly objectionable.

For instance, some of the Chinese comrades assumed that the Comintern would have talked to them differently if they had taken Changsha and other large cities. This is not the language of Communists, but of the League of Nations. Comrade Li-san, you assume that your case will be unquestioned if you hold your fist clenched, but you should know that this kind of language is to be used in the League of Nations where everything depends on power.

The relations between the Comintern and various countries, Manuilsky solemnly maintained, did not depend on power. "This is the point you must comprehend. This shows that you are a good revolutionist, but not a Communist!"[79]

Manuilsky went on to charge that Li Li-san, together with Ch'ü Ch'iu-pai, had destroyed the prestige of the Comintern. But if Li Li-san, in accordance with promises he had made under questioning, would go to the Comintern and make a detailed report concerning the cliques in the Chinese Communist party, then he would be helping the Comintern to lance a boil which badly needed cutting. "We want Li-san to be a true Bolshevik and hand in all material and information to the Comintern—openly and honestly!"

Li Li-san agreed, and made further confessions and recantations. It was absolutely not true that the Comintern did not understand the practical situation in China.

In the beginning I knew my line was absolutely different from that of the Comintern, but I considered mine to be more correct . . . Then En-lai and Ch'iu-pai returned and told me that it was a mistake in as much as I

    [77] Ibid.
    [78] Ibid. Li's statement as reported by D. Manuilsky. Cf. Hsiao, *Power Relations*, pp. 79–80, 85–86, 90.
    [79] Ibid.

stood face to face with the line of the Comintern and that, if I insisted that I had a special line, it meant that I did not understand the line of the Comintern. Since they had just come back from Moscow and must know more about the line than I did, I therefore agreed with them.

At this point a Chinese member of the examining commission, identified as Comrade Pi, broke into the confession. "Was Ch'iu-pai the only one who said so?"

Li Li-san replied:

No, En-lai also said so. They both said the same thing. They said I was not to contrast my line with that of the Comintern and that I was not to confess my own errors and was not to weaken the prestige of the leading organ . . . During the time of the Third Plenum I already realized that there was another line. Whenever I talked, I combined my own strategical mistakes with political errors, but I did not say there were two lines for fear of hampering the prestige of the leading organ. After I arrived in Moscow and read the letters of the Comintern to the Politburo, which criticized my errors for being against the Comintern and semi-Trotskyite and for having a special strategic and also a special political line, I recognized them [the criticisms] as perfectly correct. But I never thought in the fashion the Third Plenum did.[80]

Li Li-san further maintained that in making his initial report before the Far Eastern Commission he had been afraid to criticize the Third Plenum. Now he realized how wrong he had been and how the Comintern line was the only line that could lead the Chinese revolution to victory.

Maintaining that confession, criticism, and analysis in Moscow were not enough, Manuilsky called for a Fourth Plenum of the Chinese Central Committee "to raise all these questions and to practice severe self-criticism." As for Li Li-san, the Russian said:

. . . we want him to attend the Bolshevik school here. We want him to understand the substance of his mistakes. This is not a thing to be completed quickly by doing it in a half-hearted way, but must be learned through daily work. Although the Politburo sent him here only to make a report, I think he should not go back to China now. Comrade Li-san should stay here to study for a few months and to work with the Comintern in order to correct his mistakes.[81]

Fifteen years were to pass before Li Li-san returned to China.

Instigated by Manuilsky and the Far Eastern Commission, the Chinese Fourth Plenum echoed Comintern charges and stated specifically that Chinese Communist leadership had "adopted an inexcusably

---

[80] "Li Li-san's Conclusions," *Pu-erh-sai-wei-k'o*, May 10, 1931. Cf. Hsiao, *Power Relations*, pp. 90–92.

[81] *Ibid.*

disrespectful attitude towards the CI representative," an attitude that had been reflected in the following circumstances:

A few comrades of the [CCP] Politburo and the CI representative previously agreed on a revision and rewording of the political resolutions of the Third Plenum . . . Although this had been agreed upon, nothing was included in the political resolution. In addition, the CI representative was not informed beforehand . . . the compromising viewpoint of the Third Plenum made it possible to recognize the CI line only in words, and to display disrespect towards the CI representative—the major responsibility in this respect should be assumed by Comrade [Ch'ü] Ch'iu-pai.[82]

The Fourth Plenum traced the historical roots of the erroneous line to "opportunism and putschism" dating back before the Sixth Congress.

Comrade Li-san, basing himself upon this absolutely incorrect line, carried out a struggle against the CI line, disobeyed CI discipline, and adopted the arguments used by the leftist and rightist rebels against the CI by saying that the CI did not understand the Chinese situation and could not lead the Chinese revolution.[83]

Before the Plenum closed, the new Returned Student leadership, with the backing of Mif and the Comintern, obtained groveling confessions of error from Ch'ü Ch'iu-pai, Chou En-lai, and others who, in one way or another, had been caught during the policy switch. Ch'ü was banished to the Soviet areas, but Chou En-lai, after confessing his "cowardly rotten opportunism," obtained a respectable post on the new Central Committee.[84]

Credit for correcting the "erroneous line and mistakes" of the Li Li-san leadership, according to the Fourth Plenum, belonged entirely to the Communist International.

Communist documentation reveals, then, that Kremlin leadership played an important role in shaping Li Li-san's abortive policy; that decision makers in Moscow contrived directives which could be interpreted to their advantage no matter what course events might take; that Stalin and his supporters, when the policy failed, did not hesitate to use Li Li-san as a scapegoat; and that the Returned Student leadership came to power as creatures of the Russians.

[82] "Resolution of the Enlarged Fourth Plenum of the CC, CCP (January, 1931)," *A Documentary History*, pp. 209–16.
[83] *Ibid.*
[84] Harold Isaacs, *The Tragedy of the Chinese Revolution* (London, 1938), p. 407. This edition contains material on the early 1930 phases of the Chinese Communist movement which does not appear in the American edition (Stanford, Calif., 1951).

CHAPTER X

MOSCOW AND THE KIANGSI SOVIET

The fall of Li Li-san and the rise of Returned Student leadership opened a critical transition period in the development of the Chinese Communist party. During the four or five years immediately ensuing, the peasant composition of the Communist movement in China achieved recognition, rural soviets were drawn together under a central government, and Mao Tse-tung, supported by the Red Army, gradually increased his personal influence. Throughout this period there are regrettable gaps in the Chinese Communist record, but even more distressing is the meagerness of evidence revealing precise relationships between Moscow and Mao Tse-tung's rise to power. Soviet negotiations with the Nationalists are easier to determine.

Diplomatically, the USSR was finding its highly irregular relations with the Nationalist government further complicated by Japanese expansion in Manchuria. Charging that Chinese troops had committed sabotage against the Japanese-controlled South Manchurian Railway, Japanese forces on the night of September 18–19, 1931, began military operations.[1] During the following month Japan's ambassador in Moscow charged that China and the USSR were in active collaboration and that Soviet troops were being concentrated in the Far East.[2] In reply, Moscow described Soviet policy as one of strict noninterference, charged the Japanese with seeking to transform all of China and particularly Manchuria into an imperialist base for the exploitation of raw materials and the creation of markets,[3] and put in a jab at Chiang Kai-shek by claiming that the Kuomintang was ready to sell "the whole of China to the imperialists" in order to protect itself against the Chinese soviets.[4]

But Moscow was not slow to perceive that this new Japanese expansionism made closer relations between the USSR and Nationalist China nearly mandatory. For Chiang Kai-shek, if he turned his forces against the Japanese in Manchuria, not only would protect China against an aggressor, but at the same time would relieve the Chinese Communists of Kuomintang attack and—even more vital—would weaken the threat of Japanese aggression against the Soviet Union.

[1] *The China Year Book, 1931*, p. 497.
[2] *Soviet Union Review*, IX (1931), 231.
[3] L. Magyar, "Japanese Imperialism in Manchuria," *International Press Correspondence*, October 1, 1931, p. 923.
[4] *Pravda*, October 3, 1931.

In December 1932 normal relations were re-established between China and the USSR.

Meanwhile, Moscow impressed upon Tokyo a Russian desire for peaceful relations, and it was toward this end that in March 1935 the USSR—in a conciliatory gesture and without regard to Nanking's protests—sold the Chinese Eastern Railway to Japan, which badly needed the line in the furtherance of its anti-Chinese expansionism.[5]

What was happening concurrently in the Chinese Communist camp is not so simple to trace. During their Long March (1934–35) Mao Tse-tung and his colleagues lost the greater part of their official files, and possibilities for non-Communist acquisition of confidential party materials diminished after the settlement in Yenan. At the same time, Communist leaders in Russia and other countries of the world were changing their techniques of party communication, observing far greater secrecy in the transmission of letters and directives. Moreover, as Stalin tightened his personal dictatorship, both party and Comintern congresses and plenums became less important as policy-making bodies, with the result that the significance of their resolutions rapidly diminished.

ESTABLISHMENT OF THE CENTRAL SOVIET

Benjamin Schwartz places the "complete victory" of the Mao-Chu leadership during the 1932–33 period.[6] And certainly there had been a rapid rise in Mao's importance just prior to that time. To begin with, the Chinese Communists had depended upon his troops for turning back a series of Nationalist attacks; and concurrently, the Comintern itself began placing more emphasis upon Red Army consolidation and upon use of rural bases—a policy which inevitably brought the peasant leader into greater prominence. But precisely at what point Mao achieved effective power is not yet clear. Certainly all observers will agree that the Returned Students maintained control for a time and that Moscow continued its relatively close supervision for a few years, at least. Actually the two processes—the rise of Mao Tse-tung to power and the Chinese Communist achievement, relative to Moscow, of wider areas of discretion—in all probability moved by degrees, so that the disputing of dates is somewhat academic anyway.

One of the chief problems confronting Russian Communist leaders in regard to China was how the various soviet districts should be drawn together into a central government. In May 1930 the Presidium of the Conference of Delegates from Soviet Areas had decided upon November 7 for the calling of a National Congress of Soviets. A

[5] *Survey of International Affairs, 1934*, p. 673.
[6] Benjamin Schwartz, *Chinese Communism and the Rise of Mao*, p. 185.

meeting on July 23 organized a preliminary Standing Committee for the Central Preparatory Committee of the Congress, and on September 12 the latter body convened in Shanghai with seventy-five delegates present. This gathering called on the broad masses of the Chinese people—from the factories, villages, barracks, and streets—to prepare for the National Soviet Congress, which was to be postponed until December 11, anniversary of the Canton Uprising, and to fight for the establishment of a central soviet government. The seat of the Preparatory Committee was shifted from Shanghai to "the central part of the Soviet districts."

In printing a report of the September 12 meeting, *International Press Correspondence* carried the usual rationale—so soon to become heresy—to the effect that the accomplishment of the Chinese revolution would provoke the world revolution, that the beginning of the success of the Chinese revolution represented, in fact, the death of world imperialism. "All proletarians of the world must immediately render aid to the Chinese revolution," the report declared, "and increase their fight for the overthrow of international imperialism."[7]

The ECCI letter of November 16 legitimatized and—under the circumstance of Communist defeat in the cities—made mandatory the establishment of a Soviet government quite apart from an urban proletarian base. For the cities Moscow ordered what was essentially a return to Li Li-san's policy prior to the Politburo letter of June 11: the urban movement must be built up and brought abreast of the agrarian revolution. On the countryside, Chinese Communists were directed to organize and train a consolidated Red Army of workers and peasants. In what might be interpreted as a criticism of Mao and Chu Teh the ECCI declared:

The main directing cadres should be workers. It should be under the leadership of a strong Communist cadre and should have the best and most reliable directors and also an iron discipline. This Red Army should remain completely in the hands of the Communists and should have a strong physical basis in one or a few Soviet areas, which are supposed to be revolutionary bases. The realization of this task cannot be delayed even one second. The choicest sections of the Party should be centralized to solve this task immediately.[8]

The National Congress of Soviets did not materialize on December 11, or for many months thereafter. Undoubtedly there were various reasons for delay. Certainly, the leadership of the Chinese

---

[7] *International Press Correspondence,* October 23, 1930, p. 998. Cf. Hsaio, *Power Relations,* pp. 42–43.

[8] "Letter to the Central Committee of the Chinese Communist Party by the ECCI, Received November 16, 1930," *loc. cit.*

Communist party was in flux at that time, and it is also probably significant that several soviet areas were under attack from Kuomintang forces.

Even during the Fourth Plenum, Wang Ming (Ch'en Shao-yü) and his Returned Students were plagued by party factionalism. Rank and file followers of Li Li-san were still intensely loyal to their deposed leader; Ch'ü Ch'iu-pai was struggling to regain his lost influence; and the labor-oriented Ho Meng-hsiung group had been insisting—contrary to the new line—that the first objective must be to win back a proletarian base. With Comintern authority, Mif was able to establish the new hierarchy, and the greater part of Communist leadership accepted discipline.[9] But Ho Meng-hsiung and some of his supporters broke away. On January 17 this faction's newly constituted Central Committee was apprehended in session by the British police in Shanghai and placed under arrest. Three weeks later Ho Meng-hsiung and twenty-four others were executed by the Kuomintang. According to Li Ang and other sources, the British police had been informed by Wang Ming.[10] In any case, the Returned Students had fewer opponents to worry about.

In April 1931 Manuilsky told the Eleventh Plenum of the ECCI that a world-wide crisis had arisen over the past year and, in spite of its uneven development, had affected all capitalist countries regardless of whether their economies had been on the upgrade—as in the United States, France, Sweden, and so forth—or in prolonged depression—as in England, Germany, and Poland.[11] Characteristic of this crisis, and resulting from it, was an unevenly developing revolutionary upsurge which showed some countries getting ahead and then falling behind, "allowing those who were behind yesterday to get ahead today." Unfortunately, he declared, there was no fully developed revolutionary crisis in any country. "We are moving toward it primarily in China, where we can already speak of a revolutionary crisis, but which crisis has not yet spread throughout the whole country."[12] Events were moving similarly, but with less impetus, he thought, in India and Poland, but whether crises would really materialize depended upon a weakening of the economies of leading capitalist states and upon a sharpening and deepening of the world crisis.

In China, Manuilsky pursued, the deepening of the political crisis

---

[9] For a discussion of these factional struggles, see Schwartz, *op. cit.*, pp. 164–67.

[10] *Red Stage*, Chap. XII; Isaacs, *Tragedy of the Chinese Revolution* (1938 edition), p. 407.

[11] Manuilsky's "Report to the XI Plenum of the ECCI," *International Press Correspondence*, June 10, 1931, p. 544.

[12] *Ibid.*, p. 551.

had found expression in the organization, on territory with a population numbering tens of millions, of soviets and of a Red Army. This is at present the most important fact of the revolutionary upsurge in China, giving it first place in the national revolutionary movements of the colonial world. This is the highest form of the revolutionary upsurge; it is the victory of the armed mass uprising merging into civil war over a considerable part of the territory of China.[13]

He assigned full credit for both soviets and Red Army—not to Mao Tse-tung, or even to the Chinese Communists, but to the Third International.[14]

In China by this time Chiang Kai-shek had embarked on what became a series of "extermination campaigns" against the Communists. The first of these campaigns, begun in November 1930, had already been turned back by the Communists. Explained Mao Tse-tung later:

Following out the tactics of swift concentration and swift dispersal, we attacked each unit separately, using our main forces. Admitting the enemy troops deeply into Soviet territory, we staged sudden concentrated attacks, in superior numbers, on isolated units of the Kuomintang troops, achieving positions of maneuver in which, momentarily, we could encircle them, thus reversing the general strategic advantage enjoyed by a numerically greatly superior enemy.[15]

Chiang Kai-shek began his second offensive in April 1931, and again the Communists drove him back. "The situation of the Red Army was then thought to be very critical," Mao later admitted. "The area of Soviet power was very small, resources were limited, equipment scanty, and enemy material strength vastly exceeded that of the Red Army in every respect." But again the Communists admitted Nationalist troops deep into Soviet territory and attacked units separately.[16] According to Chu Teh, the Red Army captured 30,000 rifles and thus greatly boosted their own morale.

The third Nationalist campaign began in July 1931, and this time, as Chu Teh later told Edgar Snow, Communist leaders miscalculated, being unaware that Chiang was preparing to strike so soon. Nationalist troops moved forward in four parallel lines, concentrating their attack upon soviets in the province of Kiangsi. According to Mao:

Chiang hoped to take the Red areas by storm—a rapid "wiping-up" of the "Red-bandits." He began by moving his armies 80 li a day into the heart of Soviet territory. This supplied the very conditions under which

---

[13] *Ibid.*, p. 552. Manuilsky also put forward a program for India.
[14] *Ibid.*, p. 555.
[15] *Autobiography of Mao Tse-tung* (as told to Snow), p. 47.
[16] *Ibid.*, pp. 47–48.

the Red Army fights best, and it soon proved the serious mistake of Chiang's tactics.

The Communists captured more ammunition, guns, and equipment, and by October Chiang was withdrawing his troops.[17]

There followed what Mao Tse-tung has called a period of "comparative peace and growth."[18]

The First All-China Soviet Congress (not to be confused with the Conference of Delegates from Soviet Areas of May 1930) finally opened in Juichin, Kiangsi, on November 7, 1931, the anniversary of the Bolshevik Revolution in Russia. In spite of many difficulties, stated an official account, the majority of delegates arrived on time.

The solemn opening of the congress was greeted by the working people's resounding jubilation. There was a parade of the Red Army in the morning of the first day . . . ; in the evening a torchlight procession was arranged in which a crowd of ten thousand people participated.[19]

The Congress produced a Draft Constitution and established a Central Soviet government—the general prototype of more fully developed Chinese Communist regimes of later years. The governmental form was declared to be a transitional "democratic dictatorship of the proletariat and the peasantry" (a concept that was subsequently broadened classwise) which aimed at

the destruction of all relics of feudalism, the destruction of the imperialists' power in China, the unification of the whole country, the accomplishment of economic construction, the development of the class consciousness of the proletariat and of its organization, the function of the broad masses of the poor peasantry and of the proletariat for the transition to the dictatorship of the proletariat.[20]

Like the present Chinese Communist regime, the Juichin Central Soviet government drew a sharp line between what it called "the people" and those it scorned as enemies of the people.

It [Soviet power] is against the democracy of the bourgeoisie, but in favor of the democracy of the workers and peasants. It will destroy the economic and political power of the bourgeoisie and of the landowners in order to free the workers and peasants . . .[21]

Like various constitutions of the USSR, the Chinese Communist document guaranteed—on paper—the right of national minorities in China to "separate and form independent states."

[17] *Ibid.*, p. 48.   [18] *Ibid.*
[19] *Räte China*, p. 611. Cf. Hsiao, *Power Relations*, p. 172.
[20] "Draft of a Constitution of the Chinese Republic," *Räte China*, pp. 614–18.
[21] *Ibid.*

The Congress prepared detailed drafts of labor and peasant laws, statutes on economic policy, and theses on the further building of soviets. Every effort was made to broaden the "proletarian base" of the new government. To this end it was decided that membership in the Soviet Congress should be determined by formula: one representative for every twenty-five workers; one representative for every fifty Red Army men; and one representative for every one hundred peasants, artisans, and small traders enjoying the right to vote.

At the same time, the Congress made every effort to encourage the Red Army and inspire its growth. Officially it was described as a political class army, the most important asset of the soviet movement, which was being trained to act in accordance with the international tasks of the laboring masses. "In the interests of the revolution," declared a Draft Resolution on the Red Army, "a class-conscious revolutionary discipline must prevail in the Red Army. The activities of all commanders, leaders, and supply organs must be strictly centralized." It was further stipulated that "proletarian control" in the Red Army must be strengthened, and the Congress specifically called upon labor organizations to recruit revolutionary workers and farm laborers (the poorest, most nearly proletarian peasants) in a steady stream. Provisions were also made for the organization of new regiments, divisions, and corps and the establishment of military schools for instruction in the "modern art of war."[22]

The question arises, to what degree was the Congress of Soviets inspired and shaped by Moscow, and to what extent was it a homegrown phenomenon? One inevitably speculates, too, on the power relationships within the Chinese Communist movement at this time. How strong were the Returned Students, and how strong was Mao Tse-tung? Who controlled the party hierarchy and who controlled the new Central Soviet? Unfortunately we have no certain answers.

We have seen how Moscow, speaking through Manuilsky, had repeatedly called for an integration of Red Army elements, the formation of a central soviet government and—after the failure of Li Li-san's policy of urban insurrection—the establishment of a rural territorial base. Unquestionably the general form and content of the constitution and resolutions produced by the First Congress of Soviets drew heavily upon Soviet Russian documents of a similar nature, with minor modifications to fit circumstances peculiar to China and its relatively retarded economy. The agrarian program of the Juichin Republic is sharply illustrative.

Between 1931 and 1934 the new Chinese Soviet government pro-

---

[22] "Draft of a Resolution on the Question of the Red Army," *ibid.*, pp. 639–44. A Chinese text is now available in the Chen Cheng Collection at the Hoover Institution.

mulgated four documents—"The Land Law of the Soviet Republic (November, 1931),"[23] Mao Tse-tung's "Report to the Second All-China Soviet Congress (January 22, 1934)," "How to Analyze Class Status in the Countryside (1933)," and "Decisions Concerning Some Problems Arising from Agrarian Reform (1933)"—from which the Communists developed their peasant policy. To a large degree the various Chinese Communist agrarian programs of later years were also derived from these documents, and in 1950 the latter two were adopted with only a few alterations and additions by the Chinese People's Republic for current land reform.[24]

Above all else, these four documents reveal Communist agrarian reform not primarily as an instrument for relieving the broad peasantry of economic distress, but rather as a tactical weapon for the waging of class warfare against the landlord and—under proper circumstances—against upper strata of the peasantry itself.

In later years the Chinese Communists severely criticized certain aspects of the 1931–34 agrarian policies. For example, the land of the rich peasant (as well as that of the landlord) was subject to confiscation under the law of November 1931—a provision which was subsequently condemned as premature and ultraleftist. But these criticisms appear relatively inconsequential. The important aspects are the concepts of the peasantry, fundamental to these documents, which Lenin and Stalin developed in Russia and which were then transposed by the Chinese Communists for service in China.

On January 22, 1934, Mao Tse-tung, addressing the Second All-China Soviet Congress, emphasized the importance of class struggle on the countryside. "Our class line in the agrarian revolution," he said, "is to depend upon the hired farm hands and poor peasants, to ally with the middle peasants, to check the rich peasants, and to annihilate the landlords. The correct practice of this line is the key to the success of the agrarian revolution and the foundation for all other policies of the Soviet government in the villages."

Let us now see where these words came from. As early as 1905 Lenin had written:

We support the peasant movement in so far as it is revolutionary and democratic. We are making ready (making ready at once, immediately) to fight it in so far as it becomes reactionary and anti-proletarian. The whole essence of Marxism lies in this double task . . . At first we support to the end by all means, including confiscation, the peasantry generally against the landlords and then (or rather, not "then," but at the

[23] An English translation is available in *A Documentary History*, pp. 224–26.
[24] Translations of these documents in the 1950 versions are available in *People's China*, Supplement to Vol. II, No. 8 (October 16, 1950).

same time) we support the proletarian movement against the peasantry in general . . . we shall with all our might help the whole of the peasantry to make the democratic revolution *in order that* it may be *easier* for us, the party of the proletariat, to pass on as quickly as possible, to the new and higher task—the socialist revolution.[25]

In later years Lenin clarified what he meant by the "revolutionary" and the "reactionary" aspects of the peasantry. In 1919 he wrote:

The peasant as a toiler gravitates toward Socialism, prefers the dictator-ship of the workers to the dictatorship of the bourgeoisie. The peasant as a seller of grain gravitates towards the bourgeoisie, to free trade, i.e., back to the "habitual," old "primordial" capitalism.[26]

Lenin described two primary phases of Communist relationship with the peasantry. First, the urban working class and its Bolshevik lead-ers had marched "with the 'whole' of the peasantry against the mon-archy, against the landlords, against the medieval regime . . . ,"[27] and to that extent the revolution, including some capitalist (rich peas-ant) elements, had remained bourgeois-democratic in nature. In the second stage, the urban working class and its Bolshevik leaders had marched only "with the poorest peasants, with the semi-proletarians, with all the exploited, against capitalism, including the rural rich, the kulaks, the profiteers,"[28] and to that extent the revolution had been Bolshevik-socialist in nature.

In the second stage the urban workers and their Bolshevik leaders had set their task as the destruction of the landlord and the smashing of rich peasant, or kulak, resistance. "For this purpose," Lenin wrote in 1918, "we can rely firmly only on the semi-proletarians, the 'poor peasants.' But the middle peasant is not our enemy. He vacillated, is vacillating, and will continue to vacillate."[29] Why? Because, as pointed out by the Eighth Congress of the Russian Communist party in 1919:

The middle peasant is partly a property owner, partly a toiler. He does not exploit other representatives of the toilers. For decades he had to defend his position under the greatest difficulties; he suffered the exploi-tation of the landlords and the capitalists; he has borne everything; yet at the same time he is a property owner.[30]

---

[25] V. I. Lenin, *Selected Works*, III, 145–46. The italics are Lenin's.

[26] V. I. Lenin, *Sochinenia*, XXIV, 314.

[27] *Ibid.*, VII, 190–91.

[28] *Ibid.*

[29] *Ibid.*, VIII, 150.

[30] *VIII S'ezd, Rossiiskoi Kommunisticheskoi Partii (Bolshevikov)* (Moscow, 1919), p. 300.

Because of these capitalist tendencies, the Russian Communists had not found it easy to collaborate with the middle peasant. ". . . the blows which were intended for the kulaks very frequently fell on the middle peasantry," Lenin declared. "Here we have sinned exceedingly . . . The line of our Party, which has not done enough toward arriving at a bloc, an alliance, an agreement with the middle peasantry, can and must be straightened out and corrected."[31]

In 1929 Stalin used this analysis of the peasantry to show that Bukharin and other members of the Russian "right deviation," by predicting a "growing into socialism" on the part of the rich peasants, were revealing their own blindness. It was ridiculous that kulaks should ever "grow into socialism"; eventually they must be rooted out of the system! "The poor peasant is the *support* of the working class," Stalin clarified, "the middle peasant is the *ally*, the kulak is the *class enemy* . . . All this is obvious and generally understood. Bukharin, however, regards the matter somewhat differently . . . According to him the kulak is not a kulak . . ."[32]

The Communists must make an alliance with the peasantry, Stalin reiterated, but not just *any kind* of alliance. The Communist alliance must be planned to further class warfare, to press to a victory the stubborn struggle against capitalist elements on the countryside.

In terms of economic determinism, the Communist China of 1934 was less comparable to early Soviet Russia than to the Russia Lenin had known in 1905. Yet even in 1918–19 Lenin had described the Bolshevik task in words that did not differ greatly from those of Mao before the Second All-China Congress.

Our task in the rural districts is to destroy the landlord [Mao said "annihilate"] and smash the resistance of the exploiter and the kulak profiteer ["check the rich peasants," Mao said]. For this purpose we can rely firmly *only* on the semi-proletarians, the "poor peasants" [Mao said "depend upon the hired farm hands and poor peasants"] . . . the period of collaboration with the middle peasant will be a long one ["ally with the middle peasants," Mao said, while Stalin's words were: "the middle peasant is the ally"].

The difference in emphasis between Mao's "checking" of the rich peasants and Lenin's "smashing of kulak resistance" is easily rationalized by the different revolutionary stages in which the Russia of 1918 and the China of 1934 were theoretically located. Through subsequent years the Chinese Communist attitude toward the rich peasant should serve as a criterion of revolutionary development.

---

[31] *Sochinenia*, VII, 40.
[32] J. Stalin, *Problems of Leninism* (Moscow, 1940), p. 261.

THE EXERCISE OF POWER IN THE CHINESE SOVIET

Who exercised power within the Chinese Communist movement during the Juichin period is not yet certain. Official party organs such as the Politburo, Central Committee, and Secretariat remained for the time being in Shanghai, but transferred to mountain areas in 1932.[33] Wang Ming served as Secretary General until the time of the transfer, or thereabouts, and was then shipped off to Moscow. Precisely how Mao Tse-tung fitted into the picture is still open to speculation.

Schwartz concludes that the First All-China Soviet Congress of November 7, 1931, casts a "glaring light on the abyss which lay between the actual power of the government leaders in Juichin and the titular power of the Central Committee leaders"[34] who still maintained their headquarters underground in Shanghai. "Real power," he declares, "remained concentrated in the hands of the Soviet area leaders."[35] Much depends, no doubt, upon what "real power" means.

It is true, of course, that the First Congress of Soviets elected Mao Tse-tung chairman of the Chinese Soviet Republic's sixty-one-man CEC, but whether he actually made party or even military policy is not so certain. Chang Kuo-t'ao, who had returned from Moscow in April 1931 and who was now designated vice-chairman under Mao, states that "the real power was in the hands of Po Ku (Ch'in Pang-hsien), who handled party affairs, and Chou En-lai, who supervised the military."[36]

Li Ang, who is vague about dates[37] and sequences, appears to confuse many aspects of the First All-China Soviet Congress (November 1931) with the Second All-China Soviet Congress, held in January 1934 concurrently with the Fifth Plenum, and so it is difficult to follow his version of what happened. Untangled, his account describes Mao's gradual but bloodletting ascendancy over rivals on the countryside, followed by his final capture of the party apparatus at the Fifth Plenum in January 1934.[38]

It was Mao, according to Li Ang, who enticed the party hierarchy

---

[33] *Red Stage*, Chap. XIV, fixes the transfer as occurring somewhat prior to the Fifth Plenum of January 1934. On the other hand, from an examination of Soviet and Chinese documents, Charles McLane, in a letter to the author June 2, 1953, offers the tentative hypothesis that the move may have occurred in August or September 1931, when Kuomintang pressure had reached a climax and when the First All-China Soviet Congress was being planned. Schwartz, *op. cit.*, p. 208, and *A Documentary History*, p. 37, agree on the autumn of 1932.

[34] Schwartz, *op. cit.*, p. 185.

[35] *Ibid.*

[36] Chang interview.

[37] It should be noted also that Chang Kuo-t'ao has disclaimed any certainty of precise dates.

[38] *Red Stage*, Chap. XIV.

into the mountains where he could trap them. First he sent a series of telegrams to the Central Committee urging its transfer to Juichin because of Shanghai's "white terror," because of the need for calling the Fifth Plenum in a locality where his personal supporters might participate, and because the Soviet government suffered from a shortage of capable leading cadres. When these dispatches failed to achieve the desired result, Mao then wired an implication that because of communication difficulties it might not be possible, henceforth, for the soviet areas to supply the party hierarchy with funds.[39]

The Shanghai group had been depending on the Comintern to back them up, Li Ang states, but Moscow was not inclined, at this point, to offend Mao, and there were a number of the Returned Students who rather took to the notion of moving, anyway. Once the transfer had taken place, Mao sprung his trap: The Fifth Plenum, under Maoist control, abolished the position of Secretary General and completely reorganized the hierarchy.[40]

Chang Kuo-t'ao's story differs considerably. After the fall of Li Li-san, according to this version, there were still so many Chinese Communists supporting the now-repudiated policies that in March 1931 Moscow sent Chang Kuo-t'ao back (he had been in the Soviet Union since 1928) in order to straighten out the trouble. "If it were not for this circumstance," he now states, "I could not have come back." Under his supervision a new standing committee of the Politburo was appointed.[41]

According to Chang Kuo-t'ao, it was Chou En-lai who called the First All-China Congress of Soviets in November 1931, which elected Mao Tse-tung chairman and Chang himself as vice-chairman. But almost simultaneously, Chou En-lai "squeezed Mao out" and saw to it that the peasant leader, because of his "peasant psychology," was not elected to the party Central Committee.

The Secretariat moved from the Shanghai underground to Juichin in August or September 1932, Chang Kuo-t'ao records, not primarily because of intraparty struggle, of which there was much, but from Kuomintang pressure. Still under criticism for his "countryside" interpretations of communism, Mao continued out of official favor. Power was now in the hands of Po Ku, with Chou En-lai in charge of military affairs. Chu Teh was considered only a field commander. Contacts with Moscow were now somewhat irregular, but what di-

---

[39] *Ibid.*, and Schwartz, *op. cit.*, pp. 185–86.

[40] *Red Stage*, Chap. XIV.

[41] Chang lists the spring 1931 Politburo as: Hsiang Chung-fa, Wang Ming, Chou En-lai, Po Ku, and Chang Wen-t'ien. On the new standing committee he lists himself, Hsiang Chung-fa, and Chou En-lai.

rectives came through were received by Po Ku. Chang Kuo-t'ao does not believe that Wang Ming was sent off to Moscow as a political exile at this time. Rather, the Chinese Communist party was having trouble with its underground apparatus, someone had to go to Moscow, and Wang Ming seemed the logical choice.

With the Central Committee's transfer into the mountains, individual members were distributed among the various soviet areas.[42] Some left Shanghai a little earlier, some a little later, and it is possible that a "staying-behind group" was organized. "But Kuomintang suppression was tight," Chang declares. "We couldn't operate in Shanghai. That was the main reason for the move." As for the Fifth Plenum, Chang Kuo-t'ao maintains that Po Ku not only used the meeting for an attack on Mao, but succeeded in making him the Minister of Education in the Central Soviet—a position that was supposed to be analogous to a back shelf. It was only after the beginning of the Long March, Chang insists, that Mao achieved effective party leadership.[43]

Available Soviet Russian materials offer little evidence to clarify what was going on beneath the surface of Comintern relations with China. We do know, however, that Bolshevik leaders in Moscow were developing two primary concerns: The Soviet Union badly needed a span of peace in order to complete its program of rural collectivization as envisaged in the first Five-Year Plan; and yet, at this precise juncture the Japanese, through their expansion in Manchuria, were presenting what looked like a threat to Soviet Russian security.

Speaking before the Central Executive Committee of the Soviet Union toward the end of 1931, V. M. Molotov gave promise of completing the first Five-Year Plan in four years. In harmony with this objective, Moscow was doing everything possible, he said, to ensure "general peace," but Japanese pressure in Manchuria was presenting a critical problem.

It is known that the League of Nations attempted to intervene in the military activities taking place in Manchuria. However, this in no degree affected the present occupation of Manchuria, nor did it bring about a cessation of military activities there.[44]

[42] The official location of the Central Committee remained in Juichin, according to Chang, and Chou En-lai, Po Ku, Chang Wen-t'ien, Ch'ü Ch'iu-pai, and Teng Fa maintained themselves there, or at least in the Kiangsi soviet area. Jen Pi-shih, Hsia Hsi, and Kuan Hsiang-yun went to Ho Lung's area on the Hunan-Hupeh-Szechuan-Kweichow border. Ch'en Chang-hao and Shen Tse-min went to the Oyuwan Soviet, where Chang Kuo-t'ao was in charge.

[43] Chang interview.

[44] V. M. Molotov, "The Carrying Out of the Five Year Plan," Report Delivered at the II Session of the Central Executive Committee of the Soviet Union, *International Press Correspondence*, January 7, 1932, pp. 10–11.

With the passage of time, this Soviet Russian apprehension regarding Japan came more and more to shape Bolshevik policy in the Far East.

The Chinese Soviet Republic had lost no time, after the Mukden Incident of September 18, 1931, in denouncing what it called the "robber campaign of Japanese imperialism." "The intentions of the Japanese imperialists are perfectly obvious," declared the Central Workers' and Peasants' Revolutionary Committee on September 20.

With the occupation of Manchuria they aim at consolidating their rule in Manchuria and Mongolia, bringing the Chinese people still more under the yoke of their exploitation and oppression, in order to increase their own profits and thereby overcome the economic crisis in their own country and beyond this to prepare the imperialist war for hegemony in the Far East and the war against the Soviet Union. The present events are a warning signal for the world proletariat; they are the harbingers of a second world war, of a war against the Soviet Union.[45]

The Japanese could never have succeeded in this overt aggression, the Communists declared, if Chiang Kai-shek had not "grovelled in the most shameful manner" before "world imperialism." Only the Chinese Communist movement—mobilized against the Kuomintang and the imperialists alike—could render effective action.

But the truth of the matter was that in less than four years the Chinese Communists would be raising Chiang Kai-shek as a symbol of Chinese unity against Japan. The gradual move in this direction began with what was called "the united front from below"—a program of close Communist collaboration with various non-Communist mass movements with limited interests in common.

THE LONG MARCH

It was a Japanese Communist, Okano, who presented the definitive Far Eastern report to the Twelfth Plenum of the ECCI held in Moscow during September 1932. On the basis of this document the Plenum decided that

The CP of China must continue to exert every effort to guarantee the hegemony of the proletariat in the mass anti-imperialist movement in Kuomintang China. For this purpose the CP of China must set itself the task of further developing and deepening the Soviet movement, strengthening the Red Army of the Chinese Soviets, linking up the Soviet government with the mass anti-imperialist struggle in Kuomintang China, widely and consistently *using the tactic of the united front from below* [alliance with non-Communist mass movements] in the anti-imperialist

---

[45] *International Press Correspondence*, October 29, 1931, p. 991.

struggle of the masses under the slogan of a revolutionary national liberation war for the independence, unity and territorial integrity of China,
against all imperialists, for the overthrow of the agent of imperialism—
the Kuomintang.[46]

Steps were soon taken to implement this policy. Appealing to the
"Chinese people," the Provisional Soviet government and the Revolutionary War Council condemned what it called "the palpable fraud
of the Kuomintang" and offered to co-operate with any military force
willing to fight against the Japanese. "Already in April 1932 we called
upon the mass of the Chinese people to join us in the fight against
Japanese imperialism," the appeal stated. "In reply, Chiang Kai-shek
mobilized an army against the workers and peasants of China—not,
however, against Japanese imperialism." The Communists now declared:

The Red Army is prepared to enter into a fighting alliance with any army
or any body of troops against the Japanese invasion. Our conditions for
such an alliance are: (1) Immediate cessation of the offensive against
the Soviet districts; (2) immediate granting of democratic popular rights,
right of combination, freedom of speech and of the press, the right to hold
meetings, etc.; (3) immediate arming of the people and formation of
armed volunteer troops for the fight for the defence of the independence
and unity of China.

The appeal was directed specifically to "the soldiers and the masses of
the people" on the basis of a national revolutionary struggle against
the Japanese and the "treachery and sabotage of the Kuomintang
agents."[47] The document was signed by Mao Tse-tung, Chang Kuo-
t'ao, Chu Teh, and others.

Actually, there were sharp disagreements within the Kuomintang
over the Nationalist government's Japanese policy. Winning control
of the Nationalist administration for a brief time, Eugen Ch'en had
tried to initiate a program of vigorous opposition to Japanese aggression, but both Chiang Kai-shek and Wang Ching-wei had been blocking these efforts, and since Chiang's appointee as Minister of War,
Ho Ying-ch'in, controlled most of Nanking's military forces, Ch'en's
new administration, already short of funds, was unable to act and
soon lost power. It was a clear case of domestic rivalries blocking the
development of a badly needed foreign policy.

[46] "The War in the Far East and the Tasks of the Communists in the Struggle
against the Imperialist War and the Military Intervention against the USSR,"
International Press Correspondence, October 20, 1932, p. 1005. The italics are mine.

[47] "Appeal of the Provisional Soviet Government of China and the Revolutionary
War Council of the Chinese Red Workers' and Peasants' Army to the Chinese
People," *International Press Correspondence*, January 26, 1933, pp. 91–92. Cf. Hsiao,
Power Relations, pp. 224–25.

During the spring of 1932 a more complicated disagreement developed between Wang Ching-wei and Chang Hsüeh-liang, the young "Marshal of Manchuria," over the latter's conduct of operations against the Japanese. Wang, who later defected to the Japanese, maintained this time that his opponent ought either to put up stubborn resistance against the invader or to resign in favor of a more able commander. Chang Hsüeh-liang, on the other hand, argued that his troops were not sufficiently paid, and that if the Nanking government wanted more fighting, it should be willing to underwrite a campaign with arms and money. In the midst of this debate both men resigned their Nanking posts, and Wang set off for another of his health trips to Europe. For the next three years the various factions in the Kuomintang were in continual conflict—often debates, sometimes abortive rebellions.

Among the armed struggles was the Fukien revolt, which developed into an issue among the Communists, as well as among Nationalists. Three military leaders organized a People's Government with a program for tariff autonomy, abolition of unequal treaties, freedom to strike, religious liberty, state ownership of lands, forests, and mines, and militant resistance against the Japanese. Fukien leaders hoped for support from Kwangtung and Kwangsi militarists, but this aid was not forthcoming, and after a brief engagement with Nationalist forces, the rebellion died. In harmony with the new Communist policy of a "united front from below," it would have been logical for the Chinese Communists to negotiate toward an alliance, but this was not done. In the meantime, Japanese troops captured Shankaikwan and, in February 1933, opened an attack on Jehol.

The argument used by the Chinese Communist Central Committee against support for the Fukien revolt was that only two roads existed, that there was no middle way.[48] For several months Returned Student leaders had been emphasizing a need to "bolshevize" the Chinese Communist movement. The revolutionary crisis was "ripening," Po Ku told graduates of the Chinese Workers' and Peasants' Red Army Academy in February 1933, and the whole international situation had reached an intermediate stage between new uprisings and outright war. This meant that Communists in various countries—in line with decisions of the Twelfth Plenum of the Comintern—must open positive offensives in order to open a "bolshevik invasion" along every battle line.[49]

Teng Ying-ch'ao (Madame Chou En-lai), employing unusually

----

[48] "The CC of the CP of China on the Coup de Main in Fukien," *International Press Correspondence*, February 23, 1934, pp. 300–301.

[49] "For the Bolshevik Offensive Line of the Party," *Tou-cheng* (Struggle), February 23, 1933. This is a Chinese Communist underground publication.

forthright and incisive language, pressed for the strengthening of "proletarian" leadership. Party leaders in soviet areas, she charged, were "still displaying negligence" in regard to the leadership of the proletariat, and it was therefore small wonder that the work of the party lagged. There was too much nonsense about how the feeling of struggle among the workers was inferior to that of the peasants. Only leadership by the proletariat, Madame Chou En-lai declared, could guarantee the fundamental victory of the soviet revolution and the liberation of the peasants.[50]

This "bolshevizing" of the Chinese Communist party was further emphasized by Wang Ming when he addressed the Thirteenth Plenum of the ECCI in Moscow a few months later. "The Communist Party . . . leads a sharp struggle," he declared, "against the right deviation as the principal danger in the present period."[51]

In view of this aggressive "left" line, it was almost inevitable that the Chinese Communist leadership should scorn the non-Communist Fukien rebels as part of "a fresh swindle from the counter-revolutionary camp."[52]

Meanwhile, Chiang Kai-shek, on the premise that he could not effectively oppose a foreign enemy until he had achieved unity at home, was preparing his forces—not against the Japanese—but for another series of "annihilation campaigns" against the Communists. During the summer and autumn of 1933 Nationalist offensives had ended inconclusively, whereupon Chiang, with the technical assistance of foreign advisers, such as the German General von Seeckt, began encircling soviet areas with a network of blockhouses and field fortifications. When these preparations had been completed, he co-ordinated his further military operations with a tight economic blockade.

This combined military and economic attack was so effective that by the convocation of the Second Congress of Soviets in January 1934 the capital city of Juichin was seriously endangered. Mao Tse-tung, who appears to have dominated the gathering, readily admitted the serious effects of Chiang Kai-shek's blockade and called for an aggressive program (which had been put forward by the Chinese Politburo nearly twelve months previously) not only for saving the Soviet Republic,[53] but also for enlarging it in the face of the Nationalist offensive. The plan called for building Red Army strength to a million men, increasing the size of reserve units such as the Red Guards and the

[50] "An Examination of the Practical Struggle for the Consolidation and Strengthening of Proletarian Leadership," *Tou-cheng*, February 4, 1933.

[51] *International Press Correspondence*, February 5, 1934, pp. 197, 199.

[52] "The CC of the CP of China on the Coup de Main in Fukien," *loc. cit.*, p. 301.

[53] See Po Ku, "For the Bolshevik Offensive Line of the Party," *loc. cit.*

Communist Youth Guards, and boosting both agricultural and industrial production.[54]

The Fifth Plenum of the Chinese Communist party Central Committee, held concurrently with the Congress, chose—not Mao—but another Returned Student, Chang Wen-t'ien, to replace Po Ku as Secretary General. Moreover, the Plenum, according to Chang Kuo-t'ao, attacked Mao for the very "countryside policy" and "banditry doctrine" that were so soon to give him leadership.[55]

Even during the Plenum and Congress, Nationalist forces were tightening their encirclement of soviet areas. There was hard fighting throughout the spring and summer of 1934, and casualties mounted on both sides. Then the Nationalists maneuvered Red forces into abandoning their guerrilla tactics for positional warfare and thus gained a further advantage. Before many months Mao would be holding the Returned Students responsible for this shift in policy.

By early autumn 1934, Nationalist forces were exerting such pressure that Chinese Communist leaders began talking about evacuation. The possibility was referred to Moscow, and Chinese officials waited for an answer. Chang Kuo-t'ao told the author:

Moscow's telegrams at that time were routed through Sinkiang or Outer Mongolia, and were relayed by wireless to Juichin, where the Communists had a radio station. It was rare at this time for personnel to pass from Russia to Juichin, although during a part of the period 1931–1934 a German Comintern agent, Albert, was in the Chinese Soviet capital. With the beginning of the Long March all contact with Moscow was lost for several months.[56]

The next to the last radiogram received in Juichin from Moscow in the autumn of 1934 advised the Chinese Communists to pull out and seek safety somewhere—as far away as Outer Mongolia, if necessary. Po Ku and Chou En-lai made the local decision to evacuate, according to Chang Kuo-t'ao.

Preparations for the Long March were kept secret, according to Hsü Meng-ch'iu, the one-time official historian of the soviet districts, except from the highest authorities. "The first public indication of the idea was in an article by Lo Fu [Chang Wen-t'ien] in the newspaper Red China on October 1, telling of the emergency," he recalled some years later.

Only one week was given for mobilizing to leave, though from one hundred twenty to one hundred thirty thousand personnel started on the

[54] "Report of Mao Tse-tung to the Second Congress of Chinese Soviets," International Press Correspondence, June 29, 1934, p. 957; July 6, 1934, p. 977.

[55] Chang interview.

[56] Chang interview. Cf. Hsiao, Power Relations, pp. 293–95.

Long March. Personnel were withdrawn from the front and gathered in the rear, and all were given guns. Meetings were held and food supplies organized.[57]

Everyone in Juichin knew that the Red Army was mobilizing for a move, but the destination remained unknown to all but a few of the top leaders. Because of the Nationalist encirclement, there were only limited supplies available.

Many Kiangsi soldiers took money from their families to buy salt and tobacco and other things from districts outside the blockade. During the mobilization week the spirit was good, not passive, and nobody deserted secretly. The original plan was to break through the blockade by surprise . . . We left Juichin, Kiangsi, on October 15, 1934, nearly the whole Red Army moving out of Kiangsi.[58]

Ch'ü Ch'iu-pai, plagued by tuberculosis, was left behind when the march began—by Mao's personal order, Li Ang records. Captured forthwith by Nationalist troops, Ch'ü remained in prison until his execution on January 18, 1935. On that day, according to a story then current, he was brought from prison to the place of execution on a stretcher. There he drained a glass of whisky, asked for brush and paper, and wrote down this poem:

The colorful splurge of the setting sun etches the mountains of Fukien.
The rustle of the falling leaves and the sound of the running stream show
    that winter is near.
These are eternal.
Ten years I have passed in worldly undertakings, and now I am prepared
    to join heaven,
But I leave with desires unfilled.

Then, according to the story, he met his death singing the "Internationale" in Russian, a cigarette drooping languidly from his fingers.

By this time the evacuating columns were well on their way.

First came a week-long "Night March," when the Communists moved secretly to avoid Chiang's bombers and reconnaissance. Then Red troops began breaking through the Nationalist lines. "We now marched four hours and rested four hours, alternately, both day and night. The 'Fast March' lasted three days, and we did ten li [approximately 3⅓ miles] an hour, resting only for meals. This left the enemy behind."[59]

In Tsun-yi, Kweichow, the main column of the Long March halted for a few days of consultation and rest, and it was at this point, when

---

[57] Hsü Meng-ch'iu to Nym Wales, *Red Dust*, pp. 64-65.
[58] *Ibid.*, p. 65.
[59] *Ibid.*

the Communists were out of touch with Moscow, that Mao Tse-tung pressed charges against the Returned Student leadership. Chang Kuo-t'ao, who commanded another column of the march, was not present at the conference, but kept in touch by telegraph. In leveling his attack, Mao maintained that Po Ku and his group, in planning military campaigns, had failed to use proper guerrilla tactics and had refused to co-operate with the Fukien revolt. By telegraph, Chang Kuo-t'ao presented a third charge which Mao refused to support: the soviets were not effective political instruments for Communist purposes in China.[60]

This, at least, is Chang Kuo-t'ao's account of what happened. Other sources, limited as they are, tend to support the general outlines of this version. In 1938 Edgar Snow quoted Mao to the effect that the Chinese Communists had made two critical errors during the 1931–34 period: they had failed to ally themselves with the Fukien revolutionists; and they had used improper military tactics. A decade later Anna Louise Strong, in another report sympathetic to Mao, pictured the peasant leader condemning "dogmatists" of the Returned Student period for their "pure proletarian line" and, again, for failing to unite with the Fukien rebels against Chiang Kai-shek.[61]

A Communist historian, Hu Chiao-mu, in his officially approved "Thirty Years of the Communist Party of China,"[62] states that in January 1931 "a new left faction" headed by Wang Ming and Po Ku and characterized by its doctrinarism, had analyzed Li Li-san's errors as Right deviations instead of Left deviations. (Hu does not point out that the Returned Students were only following Moscow!) Securing the leading positions in the party, this new faction denied the important changes which Japan's invasion of Manchuria had brought about in China's domestic situation. Furthermore, they made the mistake of regarding the various cliques and middle groups in the Kuomintang as equally counterrevolutionary, and therefore they demanded that the Communists should wage a life-and-death struggle against all of them without distinction.

As to the question of Red Army tactics, this Left group, according to Hu, opposed Mao's ideas of guerrilla warfare and mobile warfare and persisted in demanding that the Red Army seize all the key cities. On the question of party work in the cities of Kuomintang-controlled areas, Hu continues, they opposed the use of legal forms and the accumulation of revolutionary strength, as urged by Mao and his advisers,

---

[60] Chang interview.
[61] "The Thought of Mao Tse-tung," *Amerasia* (New York), June 1947, p. 166.
[62] *New China News Agency*, supplementary issue, July 23, 1951, p. 14. Cf. Hsiao, *Power Relations*, pp. 159–63.

especially Liu Shao-ch'i, and continued to carry out "adventurist" policies which isolated them from the majority of the masses. Under this erroneous leadership, Hu charges, almost all party organizations in the Kuomintang-controlled areas were destroyed.

The provisional central leading organs formed by the "left" elements were moved to the Central Red Army bases in 1933. The provisional central leading organs, following their arrival in the Red Army bases, joined up with the Central Committee members such as Mao Tse-tung and others who had been working in the Red Army and the revolutionary bases and formally established control over leading organs. But Comrade Mao Tse-tung's leadership, especially his leadership of the Red Army, was thrust aside.

Hu, like Chang Kuo-t'ao, dates Mao's control of the party from the Tsun-yi Conference of January 1935. It is true that Chang himself was to challenge the new leadership on at least two occasions, but Mao was able to retain considerable control and, in 1938, to secure Chang's expulsion from the party.

Neither Hu's party-line account nor the testimony secured from Mao by Edgar Snow and Anna Louise Strong can be accepted at face value. It is entirely possible that Mao, well within the Stalinist tradition, is falsifying history and holding others responsible for policies of his own that happened to go sour. But one cannot fail to note how this evidence harmonizes with the story told by Chang Kuo-t'ao, who not only holds no love for Mao, but became his bitterest antagonist. Beyond this, there is Mao's life history, which causes one to doubt that the peasant leader would err in the direction of a "pure proletarian line" or the doctrinaire application of Russian principles.

Whatever the details of these various struggles for power, the Westerner cannot refrain from noting how Mao Tse-tung appears to have risen in spite of—rather than because of—Joseph Stalin and other Communist leaders in Moscow. Once the Chinese leader had achieved control, however, the same Communist hierarchy which formerly had subjected him to discipline lost no time in bestowing its approval.

CHAPTER XI

MAO ACHIEVES POWER

Mao Tse-tung is fundamentally a peasant leader, but he is also from boyhood a rebel and a canny dialectician. He was born in Shao Shan village on the Hunan countryside, where his father kept a small farm. As a young peasant lad the elder Mao had been forced to join the army because of debts, but later, by saving his money, he was able to repurchase his land. Dealing in rice on the side, his father continued to save and gradually to increase his holdings to approximately three and one-half acres, a total which made him a "rich" peasant in Hunan terms.

As with many another Communist in China and elsewhere, Mao recalls his father with resentment, but describes his mother as a kind, generous, and sympathetic woman. Old Mao Jen-sheng, according to his son, was a domestic tyrant who gave his children no money and barely sufficient food. Mao Tse-tung told Edgar Snow: "The dialectical struggle in our family was constantly developing,"[1] and made the observation that in these conflicts the autocratic parent showed more respect for a rebellious offspring than for a submissive one.

At thirteen Mao was forced to leave school temporarily, but he continued a voracious reading of everything available. In Shao Shan he was influenced by a radical teacher who opposed Buddhism and also by various small rebellions on the countryside. ". . . I began to have a certain amount of political consciousness," he told Edgar Snow many years later, "especially after I read a pamphlet telling of the dismemberment of China . . . of Japan's occupation of Korea and Formosa, of the loss of suzerainty in Indo-China, Burma and elsewhere."[2]

At sixteen Mao returned to school, this time in a neighboring town. There many of the richer students scorned him because of his ragged clothes. Very few peasants, he recalled later, could afford to send their children to such a school. He sensed the hostility of the other students against him, but he did well in his studies, and the teachers appeared to like him. He learned to write essays in the Chinese classical manner and read about Napoleon, Catherine of Russia, Peter the Great, Glad-

[1] *The Autobiography of Mao Tse-tung* (as told to Snow), pp. 4–5.
[2] *Ibid.*, p. 7.

stone, Rousseau, Montesquieu, and Lincoln. "I first heard of America," he stated later, "in an article that told of the American revolution and contained a sentence like this: 'After eight years of difficult war, Washington won victory and built up his nation.' "[3]

Restless for higher schooling, Mao set off on foot for Changsha, the capital of Hunan, which impressed him as a most magnificent place. As a student there he watched the revolution of 1911–12, and subsequently he joined the insurrectionary army, in which he served for about six months. When it looked as though the revolution was over, he returned to civilian life and began looking around for a place to continue his studies. After a series of misadventures in fly-by-night institutions advertised in newspapers, he studied first in a middle school, then independently in the Hunan Provincial Library, and then, for five years, in the Hunan Normal School. At the close of his first year in the normal school, he set off with a fellow student on a walking trip across the Hunan countryside, where he was much impressed by the hospitality and kindness of the peasantry.

Upon his graduation from Hunan Normal School, Mao set out for Peking, where he secured a job from Li Ta-chao, the university librarian who was so soon to join his colleague, Ch'en Tu-hsiu, in founding the Chinese Communist party. Mao has described his job as so insignificant that people ignored him, but, in fact, he was not altogether isolated. In time he met fellow students with whom he was later to become closely associated—men like T'an P'ing-shan and Chang Kuo-t'ao. Even more important, he met Ch'en Tu-hsiu, whose influence, Mao states, was more irresistible than that of anyone else.

After a journey to Shanghai, Mao went back to Changsha, where he helped lead a strike against a local war lord, and then returned to Peking. In the winter of 1920, while organizing workers, he began to be guided, for the first time, by what he read of Marxist theory and of the recently effected Russian Revolution.

These books were *The Communist Manifesto,* translated by Chen Wang-tao, the first Marxist book ever published in Chinese; *Class Struggle,* by Kautsky, and a *History of Socialism,* by Kirkupp [sic]. By the summer of 1920 I had become, in theory and to some extent in action, a Marxist, and from this time on I considered myself a Marxist.[4]

Li Ta-chao and, more especially, Ch'en Tu-hsiu continued to be instrumental in shaping his interests, and he has since cited the two of them as among the most brilliant intellectual leaders in China at the time.

[3] *Ibid.,* pp. 11–12.
[4] *Ibid.,* p. 28.

In May 1921 Mao went to Shanghai for the founding First Congress of the Chinese Communist party. Thereafter he returned to Hunan where, as secretary of the provincial party, he helped organize various unions and took part in the planning of strikes. "The work of the Communist Party was then concentrated mainly on students and workers," he records, "and very little was done among the peasants."[5]

MAO, THE PARTY HIERARCHY, AND THE PEASANTRY

With the achievement of a Communist-Kuomintang alliance in late 1923, Mao worked simultaneously in the executive bureaus of both parties, and it was in this dual capacity that he seems first to have clashed with the discipline of his own party hierarchy. Mao's personal account states that during the winter of 1924–25 he "fell ill" and withdrew to Hunan for a rest. But Chang Kuo-t'ao maintains that the Communist party considered Mao too friendly with his Kuomintang associates, especially with certain of the older Nationalist leaders. As a consequence, he failed re-election to the Central Committee and was shipped off to Hunan.[6]

In his native province Mao set to work organizing the nucleus of a peasant movement. He recalled to Edgar Snow:

Formerly I had not fully realized the degree of class struggle among the peasantry, but after the May 30th Incident [1925] and during the great wave of political activity which followed it, the Hunanese peasantry became very militant. I left my home where I had been resting and began a rural organization campaign. In a few months we had formed more than twenty peasant unions and had aroused the wrath of the landlords, who demanded my arrest.[7]

Mao fled to Canton, where he became editor of *Political Weekly,* a publication of the political department of the Kuomintang, chief of the Agitprop department of the Kuomintang, and candidate for the Kuomintang Central Committee. "I was also put in charge of training organizers for the peasant movement, and established a course for this purpose which was attended by representatives from twenty-one different provinces, and included students from Inner Mongolia."[8]

Mao served for a time as director of the peasant department of the Communist party, maintaining his headquarters in Shanghai, and then, early in 1927, he was sent to the Hunan countryside on an inspection tour. In Moscow the Seventh Plenum of the ECCI had just

---

[5] *Ibid.,* p. 30.
[6] Chang interview.
[7] *The Autobiography of Mao Tse-tung* (as told to Snow), p. 31.
[8] *Ibid.,* p. 31.

declared the urban proletariat to be the only class in a position to carry on the radical agrarian policy prerequisite for further development of the Chinese revolution.[9] And Stalin, pressing a similar argument before the same Plenum, had insisted that revolutionary peasant committees were insufficient to "permeate this ocean of peasantry." The Communists, therefore, could influence the peasants only through the "national revolutionary power," i.e., the Kuomintang government in Wuhan, and through the revolutionary (Nationalist) army. The part of initiator and guide of the Chinese revolution, he concluded, must inevitably fall into the hands of the Chinese proletariat.[10]

In his "Report on an Investigation of the Peasant Movement in Hunan,"[11] Mao Tse-tung ignored the proletariat. "To give credits where they are due," he wrote, "if we allot ten points to the accomplishments of the democratic revolution, then the achievements of the urban dwellers and the military units rate only three points, while the remaining seven points should go to the peasants in their rural revolution." In terms of recent Chinese Communist attempts at tailoring their ideology more nearly in conformity with that of the Soviet Union, it is significant that the 1951 Chinese version of Mao Tse-tung's *Collected Works* has omitted this statement. Whether or not it is ever allowed to reappear in official Communist doctrine, this concept remains fundamental to Mao's political strategy and tactics between 1927 and 1950. According to Mao in 1927 the millions of poor peasants had nothing to lose by revolt and everything to gain. "Sun Yat-sen devoted forty years to the national revolution," Mao stated in his report. "What he wanted but failed to achieve has been accomplished by the peasants in a few months."

Within a short time, hundreds of millions of peasants, Mao predicted, would rise throughout China with the fury of a hurricane, and no power, however strong, could restrain them. Revolution, he warned, was "not a dinner party, nor literary composition, nor painting, nor embroidering." He improvised on the *Analects* of Confucius: "It cannot be done so delicately, so gentlemanly, and so 'gently, kindly, politely, plainly and modestly.' " Revolution amounted to insurrection, the violent action of one class overthrowing the power of another. "If the peasants do not apply great force, the power of the landlords, consolidated over thousands of years, can never be uprooted. There must be a tidal wave over the countryside . . ."

In the spring of 1927 Mao submitted his report first to an inter-

[9] *Kommunisticheskii Internatsional v Dokumentakh, 1919–1932*, pp. 668–80.

[10] J. Stalin, "Prospects of the Revolution in China," *International Press Correspondence*, December 23, 1926, p. 1583.

[11] An English translation of this document is available in *A Documentary History*, pp. 80–89.

provincial meeting of peasants in Wuhan. This meeting passed a resolution in support, but the Central Committee overruled it. At the Fifth
Congress in May the conflict deepened. Mao, Ch'ü Ch'iu-pai, and
others maintained that a government based on the Soviet system must
be established by organizing a peasant army and that revolutionary
land reform must be enforced by the confiscation and redistribution
of land. But Ch'en Tu-hsiu, T'an P'ing-shan, and other party leaders,
in line with official policy, insisted that a split must be avoided by con-
fining the confiscation to the larger holdings. "Even for the confiscation of the large and middle landed estates," Ch'en Tu-hsiu declared,
"it is necessary to await the further development of the military actions. The only correct solution of the present movement is to deepen
the revolution after it has first been spread."[12]

A decade later Mao told Edgar Snow that he had been much dissatisfied with party policy at the time of the Fifth Congress.

My opinions, which called for a rapid intensification of the agrarian program, were not even discussed, for the Central Committee, also dominated
by Ch'en Tu-hsiu, refused to bring them up for consideration. The Conference dismissed the land problem by defining a landlord as "a peasant
who owned over 500 mou [almost 76 acres] of land"—a wholly inadequate
and impractical basis upon which to develop the class struggle, and quite
without consideration of the special character of land economy in China.
Following the Conference, however, an All-China Peasants' Union was
organized, and I became first president of it.[13]

Ch'en Tu-hsiu withdrew Mao from Hunan, holding him responsible for "certain happenings there"—probably the peasant uprisings
of late spring which had led to the May 21 killings at Changsha (see
page 103). But after participating in the August 7 Conference, which
deposed Ch'en Tu-hsiu, Mao was sent once more to Hunan, where he
began organizing the Autumn Crop Uprising. We have already seen
how, when this undertaking failed and he was once more being disciplined by the party, Mao retreated with his troops to Chingkanshan.
From this point forward he devoted himself to the development of
his peasant army and the establishment of soviets. It was during these
years that he and Chu Teh worked out the military tactics that were
to make them both feared and famous:

When the enemy advances, we retreat!
When the enemy halts and encamps, we trouble them!
When the enemy seeks to avoid battle, we attack!
When the enemy retreats, we pursue![14]

[12] Ch'en Tu-hsiu, "Political and Organizational Report of the CC," *International
Press Correspondence,* June 9, 1927, pp. 716–17.
[13] *Autobiography of Mao Tse-tung* (as told to Snow), p. 33.   [14] *Ibid.,* p. 43.

It is difficult to fix Mao Tse-tung's precise relationships with the Li Li-san and Returned Student leaderships. Li Ang maintains with his usual, undisguised bitterness that Mao obeyed Li Li-san's Central Committee nominally, but regularly disobeyed in practice. Personnel appointed to the soviet areas by Li Li-san were hidden in unimportant positions, or they "disappeared" in the mountains, or they "died in battle" at convenient moments when the Nationalists were attacking.[15] So, too, the leader of the first Returned Student cadre sent into the mountains, Shen Yen-ping, came down with "jaundice," Li Ang declares, and died soon after his arrival.

MAO'S RISE TO POWER

Li Ang records that during the 1930–31 period Mao and his personal faction eliminated large numbers of military commanders and other opponents who blocked his rise to power: "People who were killed in the Red Army and the Soviet area by Mao and his disciples amounted to tens of thousands . . . Even a slight personal quarrel caused Mao to kill them."[16] In actual fact, Mao probably did not eliminate "tens of thousands," but after making all possible allowance for bias, one is still forced to the conclusion that Mao did not spare even party comrades when they presented a serious challenge to his personal progress.

During the sanguine Fut'ien Incident of December 1930, Mao struck out against a party faction which had been formed in opposition to his growing power over the countryside. According to Chang Kuo-t'ao, ". . . Mao arrested and executed hundreds of anti-Mao Communists who were dubbed members of the A-B (Anti-Bolshevik) Corps."[17]

Li Ang records that during this period Mao began angling to draw the Central Committee and other party organs from Shanghai into the mountains. We must keep in mind, of course, that, according to Chang Kuo-t'ao's story, Communist party organs had moved only as a result of Kuomintang pressure, but this does not deny the possibility that circumstances may simply have facilitated Mao's personal scheming.

Li Ang and Chang Kuo-t'ao disagree also over the beginnings of

[15] *Red Stage,* Chap. XIV.
[16] *Ibid.*
[17] Chang Kuo-t'ao, "Mao—A New Portrait by an Old Colleague," *New York Times Magazine,* August 2, 1953, p. 46. *Soviety v Kitae* (Soviets in China), translated from German (Moscow, 1934), p. 246, an official Communist publication, holds the Anti-Bolshevik Corps responsible. It seems likely, however, that this term was used as a label to cover anti-Mao personnel whether or not they actually belonged to such an organization.

the Long March. Li maintains that Mao was the first to propose this evacuation before the Politburo—and for personal reasons: the Central Soviet, from which his power derived, was threatened by Nationalist troops, and Chang Kuo-t'ao was growing too strong in the Oyuwan Soviet.

Chang himself minimizes these charges and attributes formal initiative for the Long March to Po Ku and the Returned Students. The former Oyuwan leader admits to a long-standing disagreement with Mao: as early as 1932 Chang sent a wire (there was telegraphic communication between Oyuwan and Kiangsi, according to Chang, but no close liaison) suggesting that the soviets ought to be replaced by some organism more suited to the Chinese scene. But it was not until the Long March had begun that this disagreement broke into rivalry and conflict.[18]

Setting forth on the Long March from Oyuwan, the troops of Chang Kuo-t'ao and Hsü Hsiang-ch'ien proceeded separately from the Kiangsi columns under Mao, P'eng Te-huai, and Lin Piao. In telegraphing his charges against the Returned Student leadership to the Tsun-yi Conference of January 1935 (see page 165), Chang once more condemned the soviet concept, but he was attacking Po Ku, rather than Mao. The conflict between the two rivals was not to be joined until the convergence of their troops in western Szechuan the following summer.

The Kiangsi columns of the Long March looped through western Kweichow, bisected a corner of Yunnan, crossed the Yangtze and Tatu rivers, and moved northward through eastern Sikang. "We always had radio connections with all units," Hsü Meng-ch'iu recalled later, "and also telephones. Each division had a radio and used telephones the whole time."[19] In late June the Kiangsi columns merged at Mao-erh-kai, western Szechuan, with the troops of Chang Kuo-t'ao and Hsü Hsiang-ch'ien, and both forces halted to rest and confer on policy.

As the Tsun-yi decisions came up for ratification, Mao, supported by the ever adaptable Chou En-lai, maintained that the Returned Students had been more in error militarily than politically. Chang Kuo-t'ao, on the other hand, pressed his argument that the whole soviet principle was inapplicable to China.[20]

There was also a further disagreement in that Mao and Chou proposed that the Long March should proceed toward Shensi, which would be close to Kao Kang's soviet and accessible to Inner Mongolia.

[18] Chang interview.
[19] Hsü Meng-ch'iu to Nym Wales, Red Dust, p. 72.
[20] Chang interview.

Chang, for his part, saw advantage in settling as close as possible to Sinkiang.

From Mao-erh-kai the Communists re-established contact with Moscow and referred the controversy to Soviet leaders there. In response, the Russians sent Lin Piao's uncle, Lin Yu-yin, to settle the dispute, but this move only caused further difficulties. The Communists then set out across a swampy and next to impassable region known as the Grasslands. Chang maintains that Moscow approved the journey to Sinkiang and that the two groups, having separated, made another juncture and began a crossing of the Yellow River. Kuomintang forces interposed, however, and nearly destroyed two Communist armies. A conflicting source states that, after the second juncture of the two forces, the old conflict broke out again, whereupon Chang and Hsü returned to Mao-erh-kai, whence they struck westward into Sikang, while Mao proceeded to Shensi.[21] The precise story may never be established for the reason that few party records survive. "We lost nearly all of our official documents in the Grasslands and in crossing rivers," Hsü Meng-ch'iu told Nym Wales subsequently. "Many carriers were drowned, being hampered by the dispatch cases. We also burned many documents that could not be conveniently carried. Now we have scarcely any historical records."[22] Historians do know that both groups settled in Shensi eventually and that it was there in the Northwest that the final Mao-Chang clash took place.

The Chinese Communists selected Paoan as their first capital, remaining there until December 1936, when, after their seizure of Yenan, they transferred their headquarters to that city. In the meantime, Chinese Communist leaders were faced with the problem of translating a new Comintern policy into Chinese terms, and it was on this issue that Mao Tse-tung and Chang Kuo-t'ao finally broke.

It will be recalled that both Russian and Chinese Communists had expressed deep concern over the Mukden Incident of September 1931 (see pages 147, 160). Committed to completion of the first Five-Year Plan in four years, the Moscow leadership could ill afford a diversion of strength to counter Japanese moves in Asia and had reason, therefore, to suffer genuine apprehension. For the Chinese Communists, however, the Japanese threat to China offered possibilities which were not long overlooked: if Chiang Kai-shek could be induced to mount a full-scale countermove against Japanese aggressions in Manchuria, the Nationalist pressures on soviet areas would be relieved at the same time that the Japanese threat to Soviet Russian frontiers was diverted.

[21] O. Briére, "Twenty-five Years of the Chinese Communist Party, 1921–1946," Aurora University *Bulletin*, Vol. VII, No. 3 (1946).

[22] Hsü Meng-ch'iu to Nym Wales, *Red Dust*, p. 76.

Proposals for a more comprehensive united front were put forward separately—though probably not independently—by the Chinese Communists and by the Russians. On August 1, 1935—in the middle of the Long March—the Mao-erh-kai Conference in northwestern Szechuan decided on an anti-Japanese People's United Front and issued a proclamation urging all classes to fight against Japan. The convention called on "all fellow countrymen, in spite of differences of political opinions, strivings, and interests" to "unite as one man" and made also a special appeal to Chiang Kai-shek—that mortal enemy whom, up to this moment, they had been vigorously denouncing—promising to co-operate with the Kuomintang if only the Nationalist leader would halt the fight "against his own people." The proclamation called also for the "formation of a United All-Chinese People's Government of National Defence jointly with the Soviet Government and the Anti-Japanese local authorities in Manchuria" and for the "organization of a United All-China Anti-Japanese Army jointly with the Red Army and the Anti-Japanese partisan units in Manchuria."[23]

On the following day, August 2, Georgi Dimitrov, advocating a world-wide united front policy to the Seventh Congress of the Communist International in Moscow, said:

. . . We therefore approve the initiative taken by our courageous brother Party of China in the creation of a most extensive anti-imperialist united front against Japanese imperialism and its Chinese agents, jointly with all those organized forces existing on the territory of China who are ready to wage a real struggle for the salvation of their country and their people.[24]

Five days later Wang Ming told the same Congress:

In my opinion and in the opinion of the entire Central Committee of the Communist Party of China, the latter, together with the Soviet government of China, should issue a joint appeal to the whole nation, to all parties, groups, troops, mass organizations and all prominent political and social persons, to organize together with us an all-China united people's government of national defense.[25]

Chang Kuo-t'ao states that to his knowledge the Chinese Communists, prior to the Seventh Congress, had carried on no communi-

---

[23] Shigeo Watanabe, *Sho Kaiseki to Mo Shitaku* (Chiang Kai-shek and Mao Tsetung) (Tokyo, 1941), Harvard Yenching Library. Cited by Chao Kuo-chun, "Thirty Years of the Communist Movement in China" (unpublished manuscript in the Russian Research Center, Harvard University, 1950); also *International Press Correspondence*, December 21, 1935, p. 1728; and *Wei k'ang-Jih chiu-kuo kao ch'üan-t'i t'ung-p'ao shu* (Letter to All Chinese on Resisting Japan and Saving the Nation) in *Chung-kung chung-yang k'ang-chan hsüan-yen chi* (Collection of Proclamations on the War of Resistance issued by the CC of the CCP), n.p., Su-nan hsin-hua shu-tien, 1949, pp. 1–6.

[24] *International Press Correspondence*, December 2, 1935, pp. 971–72.

[25] *Ibid.*, November 9, 1935, p. 1489.

cations with Moscow in regard to a broad united front policy as opposed to the old "united front from below."[26] It is also worth noting that at the Congress Chinese delegates other than Wang Ming (who had been in Moscow since the autumn of 1932) were continuing to call for an anti-imperialist and *anti-Kuomintang* united front as late as August 11, nine days after Dimitrov's speech.[27] This circumstance suggests that the new policy may well have been made behind closed doors, rather than through close Russian-Chinese discussion, and that Wang Ming may have been chosen consciously as a suitable mouthpiece. One should not overlook the possibility, however, that Chinese inclinations may have had a bearing on Russian decisions. According to Chang Kuo-t'ao, both Chinese and Russian leaders had been considering the problem of opposing Japanese expansion more effectively and, independently, had reached several of the same conclusions concerning a broad united front. He believes there was no co-ordination, however, until Lin Yu-yin returned to China with a copy of the Seventh Congress Resolution dealing with the new united front policy.[28]

This resolution, passed August 20, demanded a broad front in colonial and semicolonial countries, including China, "under the slogan of a national-revolutionary struggle of the armed people against the imperialist enslavers, in the first place against Japanese imperialism and its Chinese servitors."[29] In China the soviets were to be the rallying center of this movement, but by implication the path was left clear for the Kuomintang if Chiang Kai-shek were to call off his anti-Communist campaigns and join in the fight against Japan.

Chiang showed no inclination to heed Communist proposals until his kidnaping in December 1936. Subsequent to the Japanese occupation of Mukden, he had been reluctant to take action against the aggressors for the reason that Communist uprisings and war lord rebellions would have endangered his columns from the rear. This hesitant policy had evoked loud criticisms from many veteran Kuomintang leaders, but Chiang had remained adamant. Toward the end of 1936, however, Chang Hsüeh-liang (son of Chang Tso-lin), whose forces had been driven out of Manchuria into Shensi, and Yang Hu-ch'eng, the pacification commissioner of Shensi, captured Chiang Kai-shek and pressed upon him the view that the main war was against the Japanese rather than the Communists. While soldiers at the front were enduring "death and bloodshed," they declared in a "Telegram to the Nation," the "diplomatic authorities" were still seeking compromises with the Japanese aggressor. In the negotiations that led to

---

[26] Chang interview.
[27] *International Press Correspondence,* December 2, 1935, p. 1666.
[28] Chang interview.
[29] *International Press Correspondence,* September 19, 1935, p. 1181.

Chiang's release,[30] Chinese Communist leaders—notably Chou En-lai—acted as mediators, a service which paved the way for effecting a Communist-Kuomintang truce.

MAO AND THE UNITED FRONT

In March 1937 the Kuomintang, while announcing that it would continue to "uproot the Communists," set down formal terms for accepting Red submission: abolition of the Red Army and its integration under Nationalist command, dissolution of the Soviet Republic, cessation of all Communist propaganda, suspension of the class struggle.[31] The Chinese Communists accepted these proposals, and in Moscow Wang Ming, then a member of the ECCI, published an article answering Nationalist demands. The article expressed a willingness to see the Red Army transformed into a National Revolutionary Army, with officers and political workers retained, and incorporated into a Chinese United National Revolutionary Army under a single command. There would be no objection to turning the Soviet power into a "general democratic power acting in concert with a United All-China Central Government." Moscow would agree to the "cessation of Red propaganda" provided the term were interpreted to mean "propaganda," and not the propagation of broad progressive ideas. As for suspension of class struggle, Wang Ming declared that this phenomenon was a cause of the Chinese Communist movement, rather than the other way around, and that in any case the Communists were doing nothing to disrupt Chinese society "at the present time."[32]

No precise arrangements for integration were yet begun, but the two parties scheduled a National Salvation Conference for autumn. Then, on July 7, 1937, Japanese forces launched an attack near Peking and thus opened the long-drawn-out hostilities that eventually merged into World War II. With these stepped-up developments the Communists made a series of new moves. On August 15 they put forward "The Ten Great Policies for Anti-Japanese Resistance and National Salvation," which demanded total mobilization of the country, the convening of a National Assembly "truly representative of the

[30] "Manifesto on the Seizure of Chiang Kai-shek (1936)," in Lawrence K. Rosinger, *China's Wartime Politics, 1937–1944* (Princeton, 1944), Appendix, pp. 94–95. Also James Burnham, *First Act in China* (New York, 1938), pp. 126–27.

[31] "The Chinese Communist Movement" (Washington, D.C.: Military Intelligence Division, War Department, 1945) as reproduced in the United States Senate, Committee on the Judiciary, *Institute of Pacific Relations, Hearings Before the Subcommittee to Investigate the Administration of the Internal Security Act and Other Security Laws*, Part 7A, Appendix II (Washington, 1952), p. 2331. Cited hereinafter as *The Chinese Communist Movement* (McCarran Hearings, 7A).

[32] Ch'en Shao-yü (Wang Ming), "The Only Road for the Salvation of the Chinese People," *Bolshevik*, April 15, 1937, pp. 69–81.

people," the extirpation of traitors, improvements in the welfare of the people, and the conclusion of mutual assistance pacts with all countries opposed to Japanese aggression.[33]

A few weeks later, on September 22, the Communists published a further statement on interparty co-operation. "In order to deprive the enemy of all pretexts for conspiracy," the Communists declared, "and to dispel misunderstandings on the part of [our] friends who have doubts, it is necessary for the CC of the CCP to declare frankly its sincerity in regard to the cause of national emancipation."[34] Hailing the Three People's Principles of Sun Yat-sen as the "paramount need of China" at that time, the Communists offered to abandon their policy of overthrowing the Kuomintang, to abolish the Soviet government in favor of "democracy based on the people's rights," and, doing away with the Red Army designation, to reorganize their troops into the National Revolutionary Army under the Nationalist government.

On the tail of these announcements, however, Mao made it clear—as he had made it clear before—that he and his followers were not forsaking their program altogether. "Communism is to be implemented in a future stage of revolutionary development," he explained. "Communists do not wishfully envisage the realization of Communism at present, but are striving for the realization of the historically determined principles of national revolution and democratic revolution."[35]

Chiang Kai-shek hailed the September 22 statement of the Communists as "an outstanding instance of the triumph of national sentiment over every other consideration" and expressed the hope that all members of the Communist party would "faithfully and unitedly" put into practice the various decisions reached, fighting "shoulder to shoulder with the rest of the nation for the successful completion of the Nationalist Revolution."[36]

The new and sharp turn in Communist tactics brought about drastic readjustments in the soviet areas. After completion of the Long March the new Communist-controlled border regions of Shensi, Kansu, and Ningsia had been confiscating landlord holdings and redistributing them to the peasants. But now, under an anti-Japanese united front, the requirements had changed, and the Communists

---

[33] *A Documentary History,* pp. 242–45.

[34] "The CCP's Public Statement on KMT-CCP Cooperation (September 22, 1937)," in *A Documentary History,* pp. 245–47.

[35] Mao Tse-tung, "Urgent Tasks of the Chinese Revolution Since the Formation of the KMT-CCP United Front (September 29, 1937)," in *A Documentary History,* pp. 247–57.

[36] "Chiang Kai-shek on Kuomintang-Communist Unity (1937)," Rosinger, *op. cit.,* Appendix, pp. 98–99. The document appears also in Chiang Kai-shek, *Resistance and Reconstruction* (New York, 1942), pp. 20–21.

looked with favor on the well-to-do peasants.[37] Parallel alterations were made in both the structure and the functioning of the Chinese Communist government.

To what degree were the Communists acting in good faith? A large part of the answer emerges from final stages of the struggle between Mao Tse-tung and Chang Kuo-t'ao. In translating Dimitrov's united front in Chinese terms, Mao pressed what Chang called a "Defeat for All!" policy, meaning defeat for the Japanese and eventual defeat for non-Communist groups in the alliance, especially the Kuomintang. Mao believed that Communist troops should remain autonomous throughout the war, engaging in campaigns that would advance the Communist position—and in no others. The chief Communist objective, Mao believed, was to achieve power—regardless of the fate of the Nationalists.[38]

Chang Kuo-t'ao advocated sincere co-operation with the Kuomintang in accordance with the Communist Manifesto of September 22, 1937.[39] Attacking Mao's proposal, he advocated a "Victory for All!" policy with the hope that, through a sincere alliance, the Communists might lead the Kuomintang and other non-Communist groups along a more progressive path than they had followed in the past. What Chang Kuo-t'ao proposed, according to Li Ang, was simply that the party should honor its own proposals to the Kuomintang on a genuine, rather than a deceptive, basis. The two policies were debated at a conference in Lochuan during October 1937, but when it became clear (according to Chang) that a majority of those present—including Chou En-lai—favored a "Victory for All!" policy, Mao cut off further discussion and closed the meeting.[40] Chang lost all freedom, according to Li Ang, except that he could walk in his own house and "breathe air." Mao Tse-tung then obtained a Chinese Communist resolution charging that his rival had "betrayed" communism and the "cause of the anti-Japanese front" by being too friendly to the Kuomintang, and in Moscow the Comintern gave its unqualified endorsement.[41] Chang managed to escape, but large numbers of his followers, according to Li Ang, were captured and executed.[42] Once more Chou En-lai ended up on the winning side of the controversy, and Mao, from this point forward, enjoyed undisputed leadership of the Chinese Communist movement.

[37] Francis Ross Carpenter, "The Peasant Policy of the Chinese Communists with Special Reference to the Post–World War II Era" (Master's thesis, Stanford University, 1950), p. 49.

[38] Chang interview.

[39] *Red Stage,* Chap. XV.   [40] Chang interview.

[41] *Communist International,* July 1938, pp. 688–89.

[42] *Red Stage,* Chap. XV.

CHAPTER XII

THE WARTIME ALLIANCE

Mao Tse-tung and his colleagues treated the Japanese conflict as a national crisis which could be turned to Communist advantage. While co-operating nominally with Chiang Kai-shek and his government, the Chinese Communists expanded, trained, and battle-tested their armed forces; developed border region governments as proving grounds for administrative techniques and structures; proclaimed the so-called New Democracy as a theoretical framework; and carried out the Cheng Feng, or "ideological remolding movement," which enabled them to adapt Russian theory to Chinese practice and at the same time to tighten the ideological discipline of the whole Communist movement in China.

The Communist-Kuomintang alliance, uneasy though it was, did allow Chiang Kai-shek respite in which to unify both party and government and on the surface, at least, to strengthen his power in China. True, a group of Kuomintang leaders, notably Wang Ching-wei and Chou Fo-hai, defected to the Japanese and took part in the organization of a puppet government which, as the narrative will show, was later to play a considerable role in the Communist-Kuomintang contest for power. But generally speaking, Chiang Kai-shek, on grounds of national interest, was able to tighten Kuomintang discipline and increase his own governmental authority. Unfortunately, this organizational tuning up was not matched by efforts toward functional efficiency or training in democratic practice. By the end of the war, Chiang, seemingly at a peak of power and prestige, found China disrupted by hostilities and inner conflicts and his government unable to cope effectively with the problems thrust upon it.

Relations between Nanking and Moscow had been formalized in December 1932, but both Soviet Russians and Nationalist Chinese had continued to regard each other with dark suspicion. Soviet newspapers regularly charged that Nanking had sold out to the Japanese, while to Chiang Kai-shek and his colleagues the ties between Russian and Chinese Communists were painfully obvious. These circumstances were not improved when the USSR—intent upon avoiding unnecessary trouble on its eastern borders—proposed the sale of the Chinese Eastern Railway to Japan.[1] In reply to Chinese Nationalist pro-

---

[1] Ai-ch'en Wu, *China and the Soviet Union* (New York, 1950), p. 238.

tests over this violation of their interests and legal rights, the Russians merely pointed out that Nanking was not in a position to carry out its railway obligations.[2] Further difficulties arose when on March 12, 1936, the Soviet Union published a new protocol which amounted to a defense alliance between Moscow and Outer Mongolia—all despite the fact that the 1924 Sino-Soviet Agreement had specifically recognized Chinese sovereignty over the Mongolian area.[3] In Nanking it was known, too, that Soviet Russia was pushing its influence deep into Sinkiang, a region which the Moscow government officially recognized as an integral part of China.

Despite these hostile circumstances, Nanking and Moscow were pushed into ever closer relationships by the Japanese threat. Aggressor troops pushed deeper and deeper into Chinese territory and at the same time exerted intermittent pressures on regions along the Soviet border to the point where, during the summer of 1939, an undeclared Russo-Japanese war was fought.[4]

In March 1937 the United States Ambassador to Moscow, Mr. Joseph E. Davies, after talking to the Chinese Ambassador to the USSR, noted that relations between the two governments had improved "immeasurably" within a few days. It was his impression that a definite understanding had been arrived at, that the USSR had agreed to refrain from "communistic activity in China that was antagonistic" to the Central Government, and that the Russians would lend no more support to independent (i.e., Communist) political and military forces.[5] On August 21, 1937, a treaty of nonaggression along these lines was actually signed.

By this document the two nations condemned recourse to war as a solution for international controversies and renounced it as an instrument of national policy in their relations with one another. They agreed to refrain from aggression against each other individually or jointly with one or more powers. Should either nation be subjected to aggression by one or more third parties, the other nation was under obligation to refrain from extending direct or indirect aid to the aggressor and to refuse entrance into any agreement which might be used by the aggressor to the disadvantage of the nation under attack.[6]

[2] *Ibid.* The sale was finally consummated in March 1935 after long negotiations (*Pravda*, March 24, 1935).

[3] *Pravda*, April 8, 1936.

[4] Moscow *News*, July 19, August 2, August 17, 1939; *North China Herald* (Shanghai), July 19, August 2, August 16, 1939; September 6 and September 20, 1939.

[5] Joseph E. Davies, *Mission to Moscow* (New York, 1941), p. 134.

[6] *China Handbook, 1937–1943*, pp. 169–70.

How the Soviet Union regarded this treaty in practice will become evident as subsequent relations unfold.

In China this document was described as "a beginning of collective security for Pacific countries through mutual assurances of non-aggression,"[7] while *Izvestia* noted that the treaty was "in complete accord with the character of Soviet-Chinese relations and with the role of the USSR, the indefatigable and consistent fighter for peace in all sectors of international relations."[8] With the treaty concluded, Soviet Russia proceeded to build Chinese Nationalist strength as a counter against Japan.

In November 1937 Mr. Davies was told by "a well-informed colleague" that in August the USSR had agreed to extend a credit of 100 million Chinese dollars for the purchase of military supplies and that deliveries from the Soviet Union had already exceeded that amount. Specifically, Mr. Davies mentioned 400 Soviet bombing and pursuit planes, together with 40 Soviet instructors and an unstated number of light aircraft. Over 200 trucks were said to be in operation in caravan transport between the USSR and China. It was also reported that the Soviet Ambassador to China had been in Moscow on October 7 to work out a better supply route and to urge more direct support for the Nationalist government through direct military participation on the part of the USSR. The informant added that he considered the possibility of Soviet military participation quite unlikely inasmuch as the USSR was anxious to avoid an open rupture with Japan.[9]

The total of Soviet Russian aid to the Nationalists, according to the *China Handbook, 1937–1945*, was $250,000,000 (U.S.), spread over three loans granted during 1938 and 1939. These funds fell far short of the loans which the United States granted Chiang's government subsequently, but as late as December 2, 1940, the Generalissimo was able to state: "With Soviet Russia there has been no change in her consistent policy of support for Chinese resistance."[10]

While extending material aid to the Nanking government, the USSR was also able to pose as a champion of the Chinese cause within the League of Nations. Ever since the Rome-Berlin Axis had first appeared as a menace, the Soviet Union had been expressing itself in support of collective action, and when, at the opening of the British Empire Conference in 1937, the Australian Prime Minister had pro-

---

[7] *Chinese Year Book (1938–1939)*, p. 262.

[8] *Izvestia*, August 3, 1937.

[9] Davies, *op. cit.*, p. 241.

[10] Chinese Ministry of Information, *Collected Wartime Messages of Generalissimo Chiang Kai-shek, 1937–1945* (New York, 1946), II, 525.

posed a Pacific regional pact, *Izvestia* had been quick to voice approval. Soon the more cautious attitudes of Western Powers were playing directly into Soviet hands.

Maksim Litvinov, supporting Chinese Nationalist pleas for foreign aid, reminded the League Assembly that Japan had attacked China without a declaration of war (a charge which has since been leveled quite properly against certain Communist powers) or excuse of any sort, had invaded the country with a hundred thousand troops, had blockaded Chinese coasts, and had paralyzed Chinese trade. Yet none of these events, he said, had been mentioned in Secretariat reports to the current session.

Emphasizing the homogeneity of aggressive forces throughout the world, Litvinov stated that the League's relative inactivity during the Manchurian crisis had encouraged a later violation of Manchuria; that insufficient support for Abyssinia had facilitated the revolt in Spain; and that the League's passivity in regard to Spain had helped to bring about this new attack on China. The League, he declared, was capable of meeting Nationalist China's requests for aid, and such support would lessen possibilities for new international complications.[11]

League action appeared dilatory. After condemning Japanese action in China the Advisory Committee referred the question to a subcommittee which recommended that the Assembly invite into consultation the various League members which had been parties to the Nine Power Treaty of the Washington Conference[12] (pledging respect for the sovereignty, independence, and territorial and administrative integrity of China). This move resulted in the Brussels Conference, which recommended consultation among the various powers in preference to direct negotiation between parties to the conference.

Litvinov's contrasting attitude appeared at the time to justify the growing impression of Soviet Russia as a "peace-loving" nation.

By the spring of 1939 the Soviet Union, while still pressing for collective action, began preparing for what later appeared to be an overnight reversal. On March 10 in a speech before the Eighteenth Congress of the Russian Communist party, Stalin suggested that a shift had begun. Reviewing the progress of Japanese aggressions in China, he pointed out that attempts had been made to justify the successive advances as part of a crusade against communism. And while Japanese troops were taking over Peking, Tientsin, and Shanghai,

---

[11] Records of the 18th Ordinary Session of the Assembly," *League of Nations Official Journal*, Special Supplement No. 169 (Geneva, 1937), p. 79.

[12] "Sino-Japanese Conflict," *League of Nations Official Journal*, Special Supplement No. 177 (Geneva, 1937), p. 43.

bourgeois leaders appeared afraid to move—apprehensive, perhaps, that action on their part might lead to war and war to revolution.

The Western Powers, Stalin charged, had decided to allow each nation to defend itself as it liked and as best it could, thus placing each in a position to trade with aggressors and victims alike. But that, Stalin stated with indignation, was conniving at aggression. Indeed, a policy of nonintervention actually revealed an eagerness *not* to hinder the aggressors, in his opinion.

It was in consideration of all these circumstances, Stalin implied, that the USSR felt compelled to depend henceforth upon its own might and (he might have added but did not) upon whatever combinations and alliances and other maneuvers Soviet diplomats could put over. The Soviets would strive, he said, for peace and diplomatic relations with all countries, for close and friendly intercourse with neighboring states, for aid to victims of aggression, and for an exchange of blow for blow against violators of its borders. In order to maintain this policy, the USSR would rely upon its own economic, political, and cultural might, upon the "moral and political unity" of Soviet society, and upon the Red Army and Navy.[13]

Five months later Moscow concluded a pact with Nazi Berlin, and so once more Russian Communist leaders allied themselves with a bitterly despised enemy. In the course of less than thirty months (March 1939–July 1941) Stalin and his colleagues negotiated with the Western Allies and with Hitler; signed the Soviet-German alliance and sent the Red Army into Finland; saw their own country invaded; and lined up with the United Nations against the European axis. In all these developments the distinctions between pressure of circumstance, tactic, and pure accident is extremely diffcult to delineate.

Contrary to a widespread notion, the Communist line in the United States and elsewhere did not normally abuse Chiang Kai-shek and the Nationalists during the Nazi-Soviet Pact period. On the surface, at least, the Soviet and World Communist position remained unchanged: support for Chiang Kai-shek as the leader of a united China. The propaganda line with its obtuse inflections is perhaps best suggested by a *New Masses* article of February 6, 1940. Admitting serious frictions between Communist and Nationalist forces, the author notes that the old order dies hard—"much harder than we sometimes think." He continues:

Chiang Kai-shek, never a radical, fought the Communists for ten years. He has certainly not joined the left. Rather, he seems to base his own future upon holding both right and left in check and making himself the

[13] "VKP(b), 18th Congress, Moscow, 1939," *Land of Socialism Today and Tomorrow; Reports and Speeches* . . . (Moscow, 1939), p. 12, *et. seq.*

indispensable intermediary. As far as one can tell, he has not since the beginning of the war wavered in his determination to resist Japan; he appears in fact to have committed himself to a fight to victory.[14]

As for the Communists, the author predicts: "They will not use the war situation against the Kuomintang; as far as they are concerned, China will not see civil war again."

An analysis of New York *Daily Worker* treatment of China and the Sino-Japanese war is illustrative of how Communist propaganda writers walked the tightrope during the Nazi-Soviet Pact period: Chiang Kai-shek is featured by article and photo as the leader of a united China with criticism, if included at all, varying from subtle to mild; Wang Ching-wei's Japanese puppet regime is regularly and vigorously condemned; defeat and internal disorder are predicted for Japan; Chinese troops (Nationalist, Communist, and guerrilla or "partisan") are hailed for their victories; articles about the Chinese Communists, the border regions, and the Red Army are published right along with Nationalist material; Roosevelt and Wall Street are attacked for spreading war hysteria in Europe, for "refusing to end" if not actually encouraging the Japanese invasion, and for betraying China.[15]

On a completely different communications level Soviet writers used for the Sino-Japanese war and the internal affairs of China a treatment which carried implications somewhat more critical of Chiang Kai-shek and the Nationalists. The broad premise was similar: sympathy for Chiang as the leader of united China in its struggle against the Japanese aggressor. But beneath the surface of this attitude lay an inclination to press for domestic reforms which would strengthen the Chinese Communist position in China—the establishment of an all-China democratic government on the basis of the revised Three Principles,[16] for example—and to suggest that the Kuomintang was not doing all it might toward the eradication of traitorous elements and the effective prosecution of the anti-Japanese war.[17] Three years later Soviet observers would be leveling more outspoken charges.

On the scene in China Mao Tse-tung and his comrades were proclaiming similar arguments. Interviewed on September 1, Mao had

[14] John Sterne, "Not So Quiet on the Far Eastern Front," *New Masses* (New York), February 6, 1940, p. 8.

[15] For this analysis the author is indebted to notes compiled by Elliot Lewis as background for a paper entitled "The Attitude of the New York *Daily Worker* Toward Russo-Chinese Relations, 1939–1945," Stanford University, 1949.

[16] "The Three Principles of Sun Yat-sen," *Bolshevik*, No. 10, 1940, p. 85.

[17] V. Rogov, "On the Eve of the Third Anniversary of the War in China," *Mirovoe Khoziaistvo i Mirovaia Politika* (Moscow), No. 4/5, 1940, p. 85.

hailed the Nazi-Soviet Pact as evidence of Soviet Russia's growing power as a champion of peace.

The Pact is of tremendous political importance. It frustrates the plans of Chamberlain, Daladier and others, who carry out the business of the international reactionary bourgeoisie and who wanted to provoke war between the USSR and Germany. The Pact helped China to strengthen the positions of the supporters of the war of emancipation and to deal a blow against the Chinese capitulators. All this strengthens the confidence of the whole of humanity in the possibility of winning freedom.[18]

The great current danger, according to Mao, was the possibility of an Anglo-Japanese agreement.

The Japanese will feverishly continue military operations in the districts occupied by them in order, by British mediation and pressure, to compel China to capitulate. At the appropriate moment Japan will attempt to put through an Eastern Munich by agreeing to more or less concessions in order to "catch" China and compel it to conclude a shameful peace.[19]

Luckily, according to Mao, the Nazi-Soviet Pact had given the USSR greater possibilities for supporting the peace movement, for helping China in her struggle, and for promoting the emancipation movements in all parts of the world.

In the realm of China's domestic affairs, Mao followed the same general pattern. "The Communist Party is not an enemy of the Kuomintang," he declared in an interview September 11, 1939. "The Kuomintang is not an enemy of the Communist Party. Therefore they must not combat each other, nor must they engage in mutual struggle . . . we must support Chiang Kai-shek."[20] He proceeded then to urge the formation of a nation-wide democratic regime in which both parties would participate. And Chou En-lai made another parallel delineation: China, resisting Japanese aggression, must pursue her own independent policy in the war; ". . . she must not join the imperialist countries who are waging predatory war, and she must never renounce the principles of national independence and freedom."[21] But he hastened to add that a policy of this sort did not preclude China's acceptance of foreign aid!

CHINESE COMMUNIST RELATIONS WITH THE KUOMINTANG

It was on such deviously structured premises as these that the Western World was condemned by Soviet sources for supporting

[18] "The International Situation and China's War of Liberation," *World News and Views*, October 14, 1939, p. 1029.

[19] *Ibid.*, p. 1029.

[20] *World News and Views*, March 2, 1940, pp. 138–40.

[21] Chou En-lai, "The Position of China," *World News and Views*, June 7, 1941, p. 364.

Finland, on the one hand, and sending insufficient aid to Nationalist China, on the other. So, too, Communists throughout the world were arguing that it was Western—and not Soviet—attitudes that were changing. The USSR still recognized Japan as a major threat against which any sort of combination or alliance was justifiable, and so, according to the argument, the Communists remained prepared to accept—and even champion—Chiang Kai-shek as the most effective symbol of Chinese unity and resistance.

But the united front in China was not harmonious; in the battlefield, in fact, there were open clashes.

In the Soviet-Japanese Declaration of April 3, 1941, the USSR, in establishing closer relations with the Asian pole of Hitler's Axis, recorded its respect for "the territorial integrity and inviolability" of Manchukuo—in return for a Japanese recognition of the inviolability of the People's Republic of Mongolia.[22] In one stroke then—all rationalizations to the contrary notwithstanding—the Kremlin, eager to protect its eastern as well as its western flank, not only strengthened ties with China's number one enemy, but also, by recognizing Mongolian independence, violated the Chinese integrity which the Soviet Russians had guaranteed by previous treaty (see page 51).

To many Chinese it must have looked as though Japan and Soviet Russia were combining to parcel out and divide the territory of China. But to apologists—another victory for Soviet diplomacy and its policy of world peace and freedom and independence for China! "From the Soviet point of view," wrote Asiaticus (Hans Mueller), "friendship with China and aid to China's struggle for independence and freedom do not preclude relations of peace and friendship with the Japanese nation."[23] The agreement represented a serious defeat for the equivocal Anglo-American policy of nonintervention in the Sino-Japanese war, Asiaticus maintained, and proof that such a policy could bring results quite different from those presumably expected!

The German attack on Soviet Russia in June 1941 did much to shift Kremlin attention from the Far East. In October the Soviet embassy in Chungking announced that because of requirements on the Western front the USSR was forced to discontinue the shipment of military supplies to China. It was still vital for the Soviet Union to keep its Asian flank neutralized to the greatest possible extent, but Japan itself performed that function ably by attacking Pearl Harbor on December 7. Until the end of the war in 1945 there was no need, in terms of Soviet security, for the USSR to exert itself in Asia, and

[22] *China Handbook, 1937–1943*, p. 170.
[23] Asiaticus (Hans Mueller), "Soviet Relations with Japan," *Pacific Affairs*, September 1941, pp. 284–85.

it is probable—though not yet proven—that Soviet Russian leaders tended to neglect the Chinese Communist movement during this period.

The record of Chinese Communist clashes with Nationalist troops emerges from the history of Red Army development during early years of the Japanese war.

In September 1937, after months of Communist-Kuomintang negotiations, the Nationalist government designated as the Soviet base a garrison area known as the Shensi-Kansu-Ningsia (Shen-Kan-Ning) Border Region, and the Red Army was reorganized as the Eighth Route Army with Chu Teh and P'eng Te-huai as commander and vice-commander and Lin Piao, Ho Lung, and Liu Po-ch'eng as division commanders. In turn, Chu Teh was appointed deputy commander of the second war zone under the Nationalist general, Wei Li-huang. Somewhat later the Communists, having expanded their area of control through guerrilla warfare, established the Shansi-Chahar-Hopeh (Chin-Ch'a-Chi) Border Region under Nationalist sanction—the only border region *government* to receive official recognition.

For the next three years the Nationalist government paid the Eighth Route Army a regular subsidy on the basis of a 45,000-man strength (the actual strength seems to have been closer to 100,000), together with a small ammunition allotment.[24] Meanwhile, the course of events served to strengthen the Communist position vis-à-vis the Nationalists. After the occupation of Peking on July 28, 1937, the advance of Japanese armies across north China was rapid, and by the year's end nearly all the chief cities and their connecting communication systems were in Japanese hands. A measure of order was achieved by the Japanese when they established a puppet government over the region, but rural districts remained for some time a no man's land of Japanese soldiers confiscating grain and mopping up, and wandering units of Chinese soldiers and peasants who had turned bandit.

It was into this area that the Eighth Route Army now directed its operations, fighting sometimes in co-operation with General Yen Hsi-shan and other non-Communist forces, but more often on its own. There were Central Government and provincial troops operating in the region, too, but these units almost invariably preferred to attack the Japanese from fixed positions—a tendency which cost them dearly. Lacking air support and even sufficient artillery and other ground fire, these troops met one defeat after another and suffered crippling casu-

---

[24] *The Chinese Communist Movement* (McCarran Hearings, 7A), p. 2332. See also *United States Relations with China (White Paper)*, Department of State Publication 3573, Far Eastern Series 30 (released August 1949), pp. 51–52.

alties, while the Communists, relying on guerrilla warfare, were more successful.

In September 1937 the Eighth Route Army defeated two Japanese divisions in the battle of P'ing-hsing Kuan (Pass) in eastern Shansi— a victory described by German military journals as a classic in mobile warfare[25]—and, while delaying the enemy advance, thus gained for themselves considerable quantities of much-needed equipment. But according to American intelligence reports, it was not so much these victories which enabled the Communists to equip themselves, but rather the defeats of Central Government and provincial forces.

Tens of thousands of rifles were left by fallen and fleeing Chinese soldiers on the battlefields in Shansi, Hopeh, Chahar and Suiyuan. The Chinese Communists collected vast quantities of these abandoned arms and munitions and used them to replenish their own supplies and to arm guerrilla units and local self-defense corps which they organized among the peasants.[26]

By the close of 1937 Communist forces had infiltrated extensive areas of northern and eastern Shansi, southern Suiyuan and Chahar, and central and southern Hopeh, restoring a measure of order, and during the ensuing spring, columns of the Eighth Route Army entered Shantung east of the Tientsin-Pukow Railway—a region outside the limits assigned them by the Nationalist government. Simultaneously, groups of Communist organizers were operating in the Kiangsu-Chekiang-Anhwei area adjacent to Japanese-occupied zones,[27] and Red agents were sent to establish contact with non-Communist patriotic units which had been formed underground in Japanese-controlled cities.

During January 1939 some 148 delegates from 39 hsien gathered in the Fu-p'ing Conference to organize guerrilla warfare and plan united front co-operation for the establishment of a "free, independent, and democratic China." Out of 28 organizations represented, the Communists enjoyed predominance in 19; in other terms, about 90 of the 148 delegates represented Communist-sponsored organizations. Included in the total group were delegates from Governor Yen Hsishan of Shansi and a few unofficial Kuomintang representatives.

The Fu-p'ing Conference passed resolutions for setting up a border region government and for the organization of a united "people's self-defense army." On January 30 this new Shansi-Chahar-Hopeh Border Government (Chin-Ch'a-Chi Pien Ch'ü) received a telegram

---

[25] *The Chinese Communist Movement* (McCarran Hearings, 7A), p. 2333.
[26] *Ibid.*, p. 2333.
[27] *Ibid.*, p. 2333.

of approval from Chiang Kai-shek and on February 1 a Central Government confirmation signed by H. H. Kung. The first of several Communist-sponsored border governments to be established in north China, this one, despite its nonpartisan front, was believed by United States Military Intelligence to have emerged under the actual control of the Communist General Nieh Jung-chen.[28] The techniques through which the Communists maintained this control will be discussed later.

Dissension between Communist and Nationalist forces in the field was not uncommon even in 1938, but it was not until the following year that large-scale fighting broke out between the two. Both sides pleaded self-defense, and the record indicates that neither was altogether blameless. The Communists, with their skill at guerrilla warfare, were more successful than Chiang's troops and acquired large areas at the expense of the Nationalists.[29]

Controversy over the demarcation of Nationalist and Communist zones of action reached a crisis in the New Fourth Army Incident of January 1941, an armed clash which marked the beginning of long years of struggle. The Nationalists maintained that the conflict had occurred because Communist troops, ordered to engage Japanese forces north of the Yangtze, ignored directives through a desire to expand their own holdings in the south. The Communists, on the other hand, accused their allies of seeking to restrict Communist areas and to render the military position of the New Fourth Army ineffective. The battle raged for eight days and resulted in the killing of 2,000 New Fourth Army men and the wounding of another 3,000 or 4,000. Government forces were said to have suffered a total of nearly 20,000 casualties.[30]

From this time forward the "united front" in China was an armed truce at best; in the long run it proved to be a series of positional maneuvers prior to a postwar struggle for power.

THE COMMUNISTS FORM BORDER REGION GOVERNMENTS

Wherever Communist forces won control, they set up border region governments belonging to one or another administrative level. These differed in particulars from region to region, but the general structure tended to be uniform throughout, and comparison shows that the present-day Chinese People's Republic, with only minor changes, is derived directly from them. At first glance these organisms offer a deceptive appearance of broad democratic function, and it was in this guise that Communist writings often presented them

[28] *Ibid.*, p. 2334.
[29] *Ibid.*, pp. 2347–48.
[30] *Ibid.*, p. 2351.

during the united front period. A closer examination reveals them as mere modifications of the Soviet system—with allowances for peculiarities of Chinese political, economic, and social development.

As set forth in the *Laws and Regulations of the Shensi-Kansu-Ninghsia Border Region,* the government consisted of a pyramidal framework of variously graded people's councils elected by direct universal and secret suffrage and held together by democratic centralism. Starting from the bottom, each government organ was required to obey the next higher echelon, from the hsiang (town) level through hsien (county) and on up.[31]

The border region suffrage principles were concessions to the united front and the result of a Communist need for the greatest possible non-Communist support at that particular time. The present-day People's Republic is considerably stricter in its franchise limitations. A parallel feature of the border region governments was use of the "three-thirds" system through which the Communist membership of any given administrative organ was limited to one-third of the total. The announced purpose of this device was to "enable all parties and groups and non-partisan people to participate in the activities of the people's representative organs and in the direction of the Border region administrative affairs."[32] It was stipulated that in case of a Communist being elected as head of a certain administrative institution, he must guarantee that two-thirds of his staff would be non-Communist. Border region law specifically directed that Communists in such positions of authority must co-operate "in a democratic manner" with non-Communists under them and "refrain from disregarding their opinion, domineering them and monopolizing everything."[33] The system was highly touted as an example of Communist self-restraint and respect for true democratic processes.

But the Chinese Communist party, in instructions to its own members, made clear how the "fraction" technique must be used to ensure control over these same bodies! According to a Central Committee Resolution on the Unification of Leadership in the Anti-Japanese War Bases:

Party committees and Party organs have no right to give direct orders to representative assemblies and government organs . . . they cannot force the obedience of men outside the Party; for the practical realization of the leadership of the Party in the "three-thirds" system, the Party relies on the unanimity of speech and activity of Party members and Party

---

[31] *Laws and Regulations of the Shensi-Kansu-Ninghsia Border Region* (n.p., n.d.), p. 17.
[32] *Ibid.,* p. 7.
[33] *Ibid.*

cadres in the political system and their absolute obedience to Party resolutions; strict Party discipline among Party members and Party cadres
in the political system is of grave significance.[34]

MAO ADAPTS RUSSIAN THEORY TO CHINESE CIRCUMSTANCES

While the Chinese Red Army was expanding Communist control
over areas of northern China and incubating border region governments, Mao Tse-tung was adapting Russian Communist political
theory to meet peculiar Chinese requirements and the convenience of
his own climb to power. In 1937 Mao had written *Concerning Practice*, an essay which emphasized the inseparability—in Bolshevik doctrine—of knowledge and practice, and at the same time struck out at
past Chinese Communist leadership.[35]

Using Communist terminology, Mao lashed out at two groups
whom he labeled "dogmatists" (who relied on theory, rather than
action, and "scared people with isolated words and phrases torn out
of the text of Marxist books"),[36] and "empiricists" (who, working
zealously but blindly, "clung to their own limited experience" and refused to understand the importance of theory).[37] The first label clearly
refers to Wang Ming and other members of the Returned Student
group, while Ho Meng-hsiung and Lo Chang-lung were presumably
representative of the "empiricists."

In a work entitled *On Contradiction,* which appeared in August
1937, Mao leveled another broadside against these groups. Still basing
himself on Communist doctrine, Mao insisted that conflict is inherent
to the whole universe, including human relations, and must therefore
govern politics on international and domestic levels—and even within
the Communist party itself. "The time when a bomb has not yet ex-
ploded," he declared, "is the time when contradictory things, because
of certain conditions, coexist in an entity. It is not until a new condition (ignition) is present that the explosion takes place."[38]

On an international scale inherent contradictions would bring
about a defeat for imperialism, according to Mao's view, and on a local
level the eradication of "feudalism." In terms of the Communist
hierarchy, inner party contradictions would produce a triumph of
"correct" ideology (Lenin–Stalin–Mao) over erroneous ideologies

---

[34] "Central Committee Resolution on the Unification of Leadership in the Anti-
Japanese War Bases," passed by the Political Bureau of the Central Committee,
September 1, 1942, as translated by Boyd Compton, *Mao's China: Party Reform
Documents, 1942–44* (Seattle, 1952), pp. 168–70.

[35] Mao Tse-tung, *Concerning Practice* (Bombay, 1951).

[36] *Ibid.,* editor's note.

[37] *Ibid.*

[38] *Ibid.,* p. 66.

(Trotsky–Bukharin–Ch'en Tu-hsiu–Wang Ming, and others). "The task of the Communists," he said, "is precisely to . . . propagate the dialectic inherent in things, and to hasten the transformation of things, to attain the aim of revolution."[39] It was clear, then, that intraparty struggle and official purges belonged to the normal order of Communist revolutionary practice.

The political and economic vehicle for Mao's concepts—the present-day People's Republic—was blueprinted toward the end of 1940 in *China's New Democracy*.[40] In this essay Mao defined his approach in terms set forth by the earlier writings. What was the future of Chinese culture to be? There is only one truthful answer to any question, he said, and the truth can be found only through practice. "It is the revolutionary practice of thousands of people that is the measure of truth." So the Chinese Communists, by participating in the transformation of China, would—we infer—become an integral part of the truth-seeking process. The aim was to create a new culture, but what kind should it be? "Any variety of culture, as it appears in its thought form," Mao declared, paraphrasing Marx, Engels, and Lenin, "is the reflection of the political organization and economy of a specific type of society, the politics of which in its turn is the concentrated expression of economic relations prevalent in the same. Conversely, the culture of a certain society exerts no small influence over the corresponding political and economic relations." Thus the old politics and old economy of China were necessarily the basis of the old culture, while a new politics and a new economy must be the basis for the new culture of a new Chinese nation.

Mao described the nature of Chinese society then current as "semi-colonial and semi-feudal." The revolutionary transition, he maintained, would take place in two stages—the democratic and the (Bolshevik) socialist. ". . . but the democracy must be of a new and specific kind born of China's own history—i.e., the new democracy."

This was his reasoning: Prior to World War I the Chinese bourgeois-democratic revolution had moved within the stream of "the world bourgeois-democratic revolution" as typified by developments in the capitalist democracies of the West. But the victory of Bolshevism in Russia had transformed these circumstances.

When the world capitalist front was smashed on the sector of one-sixth of the globe, and when it has already shown itself to be shaking in other

---

[39] *Ibid.*, p. 59.

[40] Mao Tse-tung, *China's New Democracy*, Sharaf Athar Ali translation as reproduced in U.S. Congress, House Committee on Foreign Affairs, *The Strategy and Tactics of World Communism*, Supplement III, "Communism in China" (Washington, 1949), pp. 67–91.

parts, when the remaining capitalist part cannot survive except by holding onto the colonies and semi-colonies, when a [Bolshevik] Socialist state has come into being and has declared its willingness to help the movement of national liberation of all the colonies and semi-colonies, when the working class of the capitalist countries is becoming more and more free from the yoke of the influence of the social democratic parties and is supporting the national liberation movements of colonies and semi-colonies, when therefore during such a time there has grown in any colony or semi-colony an anti-imperialist movement—such a revolutionary movement can no more be within the orbit of the old world bourgeois-democratic revolution but within the new. It forms a part no longer of the old bourgeois and capitalist world revolution, but of the proletarian, Socialist world revolution.

There was nothing essentially new in this concept: Marx had differentiated between the two movements, the two opposing camps, and at the Second Congress of the Comintern in 1920 Lenin had described how revolutionary masses in economically retarded areas—with proletarian leadership from more advanced countries — could move toward communism without passing through all the various stages of capitalist development:

It is impossible to indicate beforehand the means to be used for this purpose; practical experience will show the way, but it is firmly established that all working masses, including those of the remotest nationalities, are susceptible to the soviet idea, and that these soviet organizations must be adapted to pre-capitalist relationships . . .

This is precisely what Mao—drawing from Soviet Russian experience and from Chinese experience in the Kiangsi Soviet and in the border regions—was trying to do. For the first stage in China, the transitional stage, he proposed "a united dictatorship of all revolutionary classes" serving as a bypass to channel Chinese society around the "bourgeois dictatorship" and more directly into a "republic of the proletarian dictatorship" like that in the Soviet Union. Pyramidal in form and tied together by democratic centralism, this republic of the "new democracy" would derive power through suffrage that was "real, popular and equal"—but strictly denied to the "chosen few" (in practice, those who openly opposed it).

Under democracies of the "old" sort, Mao charged, the dictating bourgeoisie had deceived the masses by employing the word "citizen" to hide actual domination of the many by the few. This kind of discrimination would be justifiable, according to Mao, if it were used against "anti-revolutionary individuals and traitors" rather than in the interests of a bourgeois minority. "In a real democratic system, the very spirit of 'denial to the chosen few' must be the core of the

method of the formation of the government and the armed forces."
What this meant in practice we shall discover when a decade later the
"new democracy" emerged as the People's Republic of a Communist-
dominated China.

In economic terms, Mao conceived of the new democracy as a
special "new" economy. Three types of enterprise—private, co-opera-
tive, and state—would exist side by side, with the first strictly controlled and the third dominant.

All big banks, big industries, and big commercial establishments must be
state-owned. In order to ensure the freedom of the people's livelihood
from the influences of private profit, all native-owned or foreign-owned
enterprises, either monopolist or of a dimension too large for private
efforts—for instance, banks, railroads, airways, and so forth—will be
managed and controlled by the state alone . . . However, in the meantime, the state will not confiscate other forms of private property and will
not forbid the development of capitalist production so long as it is taken
for granted that it "does not affect the people's livelihood." The reason
for this procedure is that the Chinese economy is still in a very backward
state.

Mao, in short, like Lenin during the New Economic Policy of early
Soviet Russian days, did not hesitate to use capitalist techniques
toward the strengthening of Bolshevism and the eventual destruction
of capitalism itself.

In developing these political and economic doctrines, Mao was
careful to relate them to the Three Principles of Sun Yat-sen, but
contrary to a once widely held notion, he did not take over Sun Yat-
senism or develop any of his fundamental theories from the Kuomintang leader's theories. Like Stalin and other Russian theoreticians
before him, Mao emphasized Sun's three political practices—alliance
with the USSR, co-operation with the Chinese Communist party, and
alliance with the workers and peasants—over his Three People's Principles of nationalism, democracy, and the people's livelihood.[41]

THE CHENG FENG MOVEMENT

Mao Tse-tung and his colleagues went one step further in the
consolidation of their leadership: Observing Mao's own precepts
about the wedding of theory and practice, they initiated the Cheng
Feng,[42] or "ideological remolding movement," in order to indoctrinate
and train Chinese Communist party membership down to the lowest
cadres. Once the movement was well launched and once the guiding
documents had been published, it was painfully evident that the move-

---

[41] See "Sun Yat-sen in Soviet Eyes," by Richard Sorich, *loc. cit.*
[42] A contraction of *cheng tun* (to correct) and *tso feng* (style of work, spirit).

ment was intended to cut much deeper than the political level of human thought and behavior. The design of the Cheng Feng movement was to probe the very depths of the human psyche, to remold the individual party member, and to destroy traditional morality in order to set up a new order of ethics and behavior.

On February 1, 1942, more than a thousand Chinese Communist party members crowded into a lecture hall in Yenan in order to hear Mao Tse-tung inaugurate Cheng Feng. He began by rationalizing the Bolshevik movement:

Why must there be a revolutionary party? There must be a revolutionary party because our enemies still exist, and furthermore there must be not only an ordinary revolutionary party but a Communist revolutionary party, for if there were no Communist revolutionary party, the complete overthrow of the enemy would be impossible. For the complete overthrow of the enemy, our ranks must be in order, we must all march in step, our troops must be seasoned, and our weapons fit. Unless these conditions are fulfilled, the enemy will not be overthrown.[43]

In a series of exaggerated Socratic questionings—an expository technique much favored by Stalin—the Chinese leader struck out at errors in the party's style of work and thought. The general line was correct, but were there not shortcomings also? Yes, there were short-comings. What were these shortcomings? They were unorthodox tendencies—especially in thought, in the party's internal and external relations, and in the field of literature.

We shall call the incorrect spirit in learning subjectivism, the incorrect spirit in the Party sectarianism, and the incorrect spirit in literature Party formalism . . . These views are not held by the entire Party; however, they still constantly vex and harass us. It is therefore necessary to analyze and clarify them, and it is necessary to study them. These then are our duties: antisubjectivism to reform the spirit in learning, antisectarianism to reform the Party spirit, and anti-Party formalism to reform the spirit in literature.

What resulted was a highly organized campaign of party thought control which provided a foundation for even larger mass indoctrination once the Communists were in control of mainland China. In the twelve months immediately following Mao's opening address, the Cheng Feng movement trained more than 30,000 Chinese leaders and at the same time dislodged from high party position those like Wang Ming whom Mao and his supporters condemned as unorthodox.

---

[43] Mao Tse-tung, "Reform in Learning, the Party and Literature," a lecture delivered at the opening day ceremonies of the Party School, February 1, 1942, translated by Compton, *op. cit.*, pp. 9–32.

The details of Cheng Feng history are still to be uncovered. Writes Boyd Compton:

There is too little information on what actually transpired during the Cheng Feng period. The picture can only be pieced together from scraps of available fact. Reform was evidently carried out through small study groups which worked their way through the maze of standards set in *Reform Documents*; criticism and self-criticism then followed on the basis of these often contradictory standards. Self-criticism meant complete confession and symbolized allegiance to Mao's standards, whatever they might be. The psychological effect of public confession as an organizational device in Communist Parties is difficult to understand in the West, but it should not be underestimated. It was a major tool of the Cheng Feng reform.[44]

Twenty-two key documents were designated for study. Eighteen were those upon which the various cadre trainees were required to stand examination, and four—Stalin's "Leadership and Inspection," Lenin and Stalin on "Party Discipline and Party Democracy," Stalin's "Equalitarianism," and Dimitrov's "Cadre Policy and Cadre Educational Policy"—were included for purposes of discussion. The trainees were examined on two Russian items—"Conclusion" from *The History of the Communist Party of the Soviet Union* and Stalin's "The Bolshevization of the Party" in twelve sections. The remaining sixteen documents included seven pieces by Mao Tse-tung, a series of party reports and resolutions, Ch'en Yün's "How to Be a Communist Party Member," and *The Training of the Communist Party Member,* by Liu Shao-ch'i.[45]

Mao struck new blows at the "dogmatists" and the "empiricists" who apparently had not yet succeeded in combining theory with practice. "If a man read ten thousand volumes by Marx, Engels, Lenin and Stalin, and read each volume a thousand times so he could recite every sentence from memory," Mao declared, "he could still not be considered a theoretician."[46] A theoretician, to deserve the designation, must first succeed in applying the concepts and methods of Marxism-Leninism to China's actual problems in order to discover the laws peculiar to Chinese historical development. And on the other hand, comrades engaged in practical work run grave risks if they rely solely upon their experience. "They should realize that the greater part of their knowledge is gained from immediate perception and is therefore limited . . ."[47]

[44] *Ibid.*, p. xxxv.
[45] "Report of the Propaganda Bureau of the Central Committee on the Cheng Feng Reform Movement," *ibid.*, pp. 1–8.
[46] "Reform in Learning, the Party and Literature," *loc. cit.*, p. 13.
[47] *Ibid.*, p. 18.

Mao considered sectarianism especially dangerous. Men like Chang Kuo-t'ao and Li Li-san had placed the individual first and the party second, Mao charged. In communism there was no place for those who demanded this kind of independence. "We must see that the marching order of the entire Party is regular and uniform," Mao declared, "and that it struggles toward a common objective."[48] Rooting out sectarianism meant not merely the subordination of individual interests to those of the party, but harmony among various groups and regions—as between provincial cadres, for example, and those brought to the province from outside.

At first glance the Chinese Communist code appears to be strictly utilitarian and materialistic. But on closer examination we perceive that Communist "materialists" can exhort their followers in a most "subjective" fashion. In this respect Liu Shao-ch'i's *The Training of the Communist Party Member* is illustrative of a common trend:

The interests of the Party above all—this is the highest principle . . . The Party member should see that he has only the Party and Party interests in mind and no individual purpose. He should see that his own individual interests are identical with Party interests to the extent that they are fused. When contradictions arise beween the interests of the Party and the individual we can, without the slightest hesitation or feeling of compulsion, submit to Party interests and sacrifice the individual.[49]

So far, so good. But we read on.

To sacrifice the individual for the sake of the Party, for the sake of class, for national liberation, or the liberation of mankind [a touch of idealism here?], even to sacrifice one's own life, without the slightest hesitation, with a feeling of happiness—this is the highest expression of Communist morality, the highest expression of principle by the Party member, a pure and honest expression of the Party member's proletarian consciousness.

Where is Marx's materialist determination now?

But this is only the beginning. We learn from Liu Shao-ch'i, who quotes freely from the Chinese classics, that the individual member, if he submerges himself in the party and supports it "unselfishly," can obtain the best Communist "moral virtues":

He can express loyal, sincere affection for all comrades, revolutionaries and laborers, can give them unconditional assistance, meet them on a basis of equality, and be unwilling to harm anyone for the sake of his own interests. He can treat them with "loyalty and reciprocity," establish "heart to heart" relationships, imagine himself in another's place, show consideration for others, and "not do to others what he would not have

[48] *Ibid.*, p. 24.
[49] *Ibid.*, pp. 109–10.

others do" . . . He bears the sorrows of the world now for the sake of later happiness . . . he toils now for the sake of later satisfaction. He doesn't wrangle with others whose lot is better . . . In times of adversity he can straighten up and carry on . . . he has the greatest determination and a stature which "riches cannot corrupt, poverty cannot change, and terror cannot surmount."[50]

The party member, according to Liu, has integrity and fortitude:

. . . he can show the world his mistakes and shortcomings openly and correct them with daring. They are "as public as an eclipse." "Being right, he is strong." He never fears the truth, but daringly upholds the truth, speaks the truth to others, and fights for the truth. Even if such a stand is temporarily disadvantageous, even if to uphold the truth he is attacked from all sides, encounters majority opposition, is blamed and forced into isolation (a splendid isolation!), and even faced with the necessity of sacrificing his life—he still swims against the current to uphold the truth and refuses to follow along with the crowd . . . He can also be sincere, straightforward, and happy . . . he can be broadminded, patient and give his full effort under difficult circumstances . . . enduring insults and ill treatment patiently and without "feelings of resentment and hatred" . . . he does not accept flattery. In personal questions he does not ask for help, nor does he crawl to others for assistance . . . [He] can . . . endure insult, carry a heavy burden . . .[51]

Thus the party member becomes a modern Knight of the Round Table, a champion of party honor and a defender of Bolshevik faith, a man who, being able "to love men or hate them," has dedicated himself to upholding party good and destroying nonparty evil—"treating humanity's parasites," as Liu puts it, "with the greatest determination."

If we place these developments of the war years into relationship with each other—the Communist initiative in forming a united front and offering aid to Nanking, the Communist willingness to use the anti-Japanese conflict for their own party advancement, the elaboration of Chinese Communist ideology, the tightening of discipline through Cheng Feng, and the glorification of a "higher" Communist duty—we begin to perceive how Machiavellian and at the same time all-encompassing the Bolshevik creed is intended to be.

[50] *Ibid.*, p. 111.
[51] *Ibid.*, pp. 112–13.

CHAPTER XIII

THE USSR, THE UNITED STATES, AND MAO'S VICTORY

The summer of 1943 saw a sharp turning point in both Russian and Chinese Communist policies and the speeding up of a dual program which—in all its essentials—lasted six years and culminated with the establishment in 1949 of the Chinese People's Republic. During this period the Soviet Union maintained and even elaborated upon its official policy of diplomatic support for Chiang Kai-shek, but the Chinese Communists, never for long out of touch with Moscow, pressed terms which they may not have wanted the Nationalists to accept.

As the new period opened there were surface maneuvers—such as the dissolution of the Communist International and Chinese Communist persistence in demanding a "truly democratic" all-China government—which camouflaged fundamental Bolshevik policies and persuaded many observers to believe that Mao and his comrades had broken with Moscow, were not really Communists, and offered the only hope for a strong and emancipated China. Somewhat later—as Kuomintang weaknesses became increasingly evident and as the Chinese Communists, through repeated demands for a coalition government, appeared to be championing a democratic cause—this unrealistic appraisal began figuring as an element in world politics and a factor in American attitudes toward Asia.

But parallel to these developments were others which told a truer story of what was happening. These included continued, though carefully camouflaged and probably somewhat loosened, ties between Russian and Chinese Communists; a systematic Communist campaign for expansion at Kuomintang expense; Nationalist retaliation and the emergence of a "war within a war"; the rapid growth of Communist military and political power, and Mao's foreshadowing, through his statements on "coalition government," of what co-operation with Communist forces really meant. From these and other circumstances a few observers foresaw that the historical power structure in Asia was about to be overturned, that the USSR would soon emerge as the greatest single Asian land power, and that the United States was now an increasingly important factor in Soviet relations with China—entirely apart from whether or not it so chose. What responsibilities the American people were prepared to assume and what the United States government should do—and could do—policy-wise was another, more complex matter.

Even in retrospect it is difficult to formulate an American course which, if followed, would necessarily have stopped or even seriously frustrated the Communists. In facing up to a few of the more obvious Asian realities the United States was beginning late, and by 1943 a number of elements—including some important ones—lay partially or wholly outside American control. But the record shows nevertheless where various Western observers and decision makers erred in their appraisals of Communist intent—and thus raises warnings for the future.

THE ROGOV ARTICLES: A TURNING POINT

In August 1943 Vladimir Rogov, a *Tass* correspondent with many years' experience in China, leveled an attack against "appeasers, defeatists and capitulators" within Chinese Nationalist ranks who had evolved theories for an honorable peace with Japan and were resisting Chiang Kai-shek's program for the reorganization of the armed forces. These destructive elements were working to deepen and sharpen China's internal conflicts, to weaken China's power for resistance, to undermine Communist-Kuomintang collaboration, and to incite persecution of the Eighth Route Army. If these "anti-democratic and anti-popular forces" were to gain the upper hand in Chungking, Rogov declared, a fratricidal war might then develop and lead to fatal consequences for the Chinese war of liberation. "Discontent with the Kuomintang's policies," he said, "is widespread throughout China." Rogov's criticisms were taken up by other Soviet authors and by Communist spokesmen elsewhere,[1] and were cited favorably by various Americans who, being genuinely disturbed by developments in China, were disposed, perhaps, toward accepting the argument without questioning its source.[2] In time the attack was broadened to include Chiang Kai-shek.

Unfortunately—all aside from Rogov's doctrinaire charges—the integrity and efficiency of Chiang Kai-shek's government were open to a measure of legitimate criticism. In facing the Japanese invasion, Kuomintang leaders had resorted to a series of special measures—

---

[1] See I. Aleksandrov, "On the Situation in China," *Voina i Rabochii Klass*, No. 14, 1944, p. 9; B. Grigoriev, "China in Its Eighth Year of the War," *Bolshevik*, No. 17–18 (1944), p. 55; V. Avarin, "China at the Present Stage of the War," *Voina i Rabochii Klass*, No. 23 (1944), p. 9; I. Aleksandrov, "On the Situation in China," *Trud*, April 5, 1945.

[2] See, for example, "An Appraisal of Conditions in China by Raymond Gram Swing," a portion of a broadcast on August 11, 1943, as reproduced in *Amerasia*, VII, No. 9 (1943), 281–84.

the expansion of the New Life movement devoted to a regeneration of Confucian teachings, the formation of the rigidly disciplined San Min Chu I Youth Corps, the granting of extraordinary powers to Chiang, the arbitrary designation (rather than election) of a portion of National Congress membership, the reintroduction of party cells (Hsiao-tsu), and the further development of party purging facilities through the party supervisor's net (Tang-jen Chien-ch'a Wang)[3]— all of them features which impressed many Westerners as essentially nondemocratic and potentially authoritarian in spirit. Beyond this, Chiang Kai-shek's new book, *China's Destiny,* disturbed many Westerners with its tendency to raise paternalistic concepts of the past as approaches to problems of the present. Finally, there was the growing realization that war-induced inflation remained unchecked and that whole sectors of the Chinese population—particularly the intellectual and salaried classes—were being drained financially and neutralized politically.

According to an analysis which has since been severely criticized there were two Chinas emerging, one (Nationalist) being "feudal" in nature and the other (Communist) being essentially "democratic."[4] This was an extreme point of view, but many Americans—largely ignorant of what went on among the Chinese Communists—were doubtful whether the Nationalist need for increased efficiency and effectiveness in the war effort justified the undemocratic measures which Kuomintang leaders were taking.

What happened in China during the war years and immediately after has become highly controversial. Observers have differed in their viewpoints—from those who saw Chiang Kai-shek assuming the burden of the anti-Japanese war effort while Communist forces struggled only for the expansion of their own territory, to those on the other extreme who have presented the Communists as fervent and hard-hitting patriots and the Kuomintang as semifascist traitors. It may be many years before the truth is ascertained, but in the meantime there is one report that deserves more attention than it has so far received.

THE WAR WITHIN A WAR

Toward the end of 1944 the United States Military Intelligence Service initiated "a major project under which the most competent analysts—both civilian and military—were assigned to the examination of *all* material available, and to the compilation of a report on

[3] Paul M. A. Linebarger, *The China of Chiang Kai-shek* (Boston, 1941), p. 141.
[4] T. A. Bisson, "China's Part in the Coalition War," *Far Eastern Survey* (New York), July 14, 1943, XVI, 135–41.

the Chinese Communist movement."[5] The pages of this document reveal that after the New Fourth Army Incident of January 1941 and more particularly after the United States had entered the war both Communists and Nationalists devoted more attention to fighting each other than to resisting the Japanese. In the words of this report: "The history of this inter-party struggle, against the background of the war against Japan, presents both the Kuomintang and the Chinese Communists in a most unfavorable light."[6]

According to this analysis, the Chungking government effected a virtual truce with Japanese-Chinese puppet troops, whereupon the greater part of Nationalist forces were withdrawn well within the frontiers of free China. "As a result, practically all the coastal provinces of North China came under either Communist or Japanese control."[7] The blockading of Communist areas and the building of Nationalist strength in west China now became the chief Central Government objective:

After the United States entered the war and American military aid was extended to China, Chungking's unwillingness to commit its best armies to fight the Japanese became even more apparent. American observers came to believe that many leading Chinese Government officials felt that China had done her part in fighting Japan and that it was henceforth up to the United States and Britain to defeat Japan. American officials in China repeatedly complained in their reports about the Chinese Government's lack of interest in supporting the American war effort in China, and emphasized that Chinese troops "that could be used for the protection of our air bases are stationed elsewhere to blockade Chinese Communist areas."[8]

American officers even reported instances where Chinese troops refused to fire on Japanese raiding planes lest the pilots, "getting angry," might come back and drop bombs![9]

The *National Herald*, an English-language newspaper in Chungking, reputedly sponsored by the Chinese Ministry of Foreign Affairs, argued this way in August 1944:

As we have had occasion to point out in these columns before, the Japanese militarists will in all probability give up the struggle when Japan proper has been invaded and they have been crushingly defeated by the Allies in their homeland. However, if the Japanese should keep on fighting on the Asiatic mainland even after their homeland has been occupied, the Allies of

---

[5] *The Chinese Communist Movement* (McCarran Hearings, 7A), p. 2305. Italics in the original.
[6] *Ibid.*, p. 2355.
[7] *Ibid.*, p. 2354.
[8] *Ibid.*, p. 2355.
[9] *Ibid.*, p. 2355.

course must carry out a land campaign in China . . . Some Americans are right in saying that "most infantry work can be done by the Chinese . . ." Nevertheless, the fact remains that the use of the newest weapons of war cannot be learned in a few days or weeks. By the time when it is possible to bring these weapons to China in large quantities it will be too slow a process to teach the millions of Chinese troops how to use them . . . The best way, we believe, is for the United States to send a large expeditionary force—say 1,000,000 men—to China as soon as landings in this country can be effected and immediately start to drive the Japanese into the sea.

On a political level also the Nationalist government was carrying out policies that many Americans found difficult to justify. Extreme conservative elements—particularly the so-called CC clique led by Ch'en Li-fu and Ch'en Kuo-fu—were gaining strength within party and government, and official attitudes toward minority groups (entirely apart from the Communists) were growing increasingly stringent. According to Military Intelligence:

The result was that it [the Central government] lost most of the popular support it had enjoyed at the beginning of the war. Its intolerance has driven several of the minority groups in Chungking-controlled China to consider the formation of a political coalition against Chungking. They seek American support for this coalition not so much as a means of overthrowing the Chungking Government as of forcing the Government to abandon its system of one-party dictatorship. Some of the minority groups within the coalition now contemplate forming a new united front with the Communists against both Chungking and Japan.[10]

Kuomintang inefficiency and what Marshal Li Chi-shen of the Kwangsi Military Group called the "drift toward dictatorship and departure from democratic principles" induced a negative reaction from the Chinese populace. United States Military Intelligence stated in 1945:

All observers agree that the greatest cause of the poor showing made by the Chungking forces last year during their defense against the Japanese was the hostility of the people toward their own army, and the hopeless disunity between the regular Kuomintang or Central Army and the Provincial armies.[11]

Meanwhile, Mao and his colleagues, equally unwilling to fight the Japanese at this stage, competed with the Nationalist government in winning favor from puppet forces and continued, at the same time, to expand their areas of control—more at the expense of Chiang Kai-

[10] *Ibid.,* p. 2354.
[11] *Ibid.,* p. 2396.

shek than of the Japanese. "From control of about 35,000 square miles with a population of about 1,500,000 people at the beginning of 1937," Military Intelligence declared in 1945, "the Communists have expanded their control to about 225,000 square miles with a population of some 85,000,000 people."[12]

Both Communists and Nationalists were jockeying and otherwise preparing for the same contingency: if, under Allied pressure, the Japanese were to withdraw from mainland China, the force gaining control of the port cities, the cities of the Yangtze, the railroads, mines, and agricultural plains of northern and central China would win a powerful position in relation to its domestic opponent. It was further assumed that Chinese puppet forces would remain where they were— with the possibility, therefore, of transferring their loyalty and the territory they occupied to either the Communists or the Nationalists.

There is no indication that either Nationalist or Communist head-quarters ever considered capitulation to the Japanese, but numbers of qualified observers reported the extension of "feelers" in the direction of puppet personages by both camps. Against this background, a Tokyo radio announcement of March 1944 may take on some significance:

The Sino-Reds recently adopted a "10-20-70" forward policy under which they use 10 percent of their power to deal with Japan, 20 percent for the protection of their bases, and the remaining 70 percent for the extension of their influence. In order to counter . . . the new strategy mapped out by the Chinese Reds, the Chungking regime is putting into practice the dual policy of political and military pressure, carrying on political negotiations with the Communists, and simultaneously carrying out an encirclement offensive.[13]

In January 1945 Congressman Mansfield, on his return from a mission to China, evaluated the situation as follows:

On the basis of information which I have been able to gather, it appears to me that both the Communists and the Kuomintang are more interested in preserving their respective parties at the present time, and have been for the last two years, than they are in carrying out the war against Japan. Each party is more interested in its own status because both feel that America will guarantee victory.[14]

CHINA PRESENTS NEW FACTORS IN UNITED STATES POLICIES

Just as the United States—particularly after Pearl Harbor—was beginning to loom as a critical factor in Far Eastern developments,

---

[12] *Ibid.,* p. 2354.
[13] *Ibid.,* p. 2361.
[14] *United States Relations with China,* p. 61.

so, conversely, Chinese domestic affairs suddenly emerged as signally important to American welfare. During the early phases of its war participation, the United States took a number of steps calculated to regularize and improve its relations in China.

American steps included the relinquishment by the United States of extraterritorial privileges in China, the granting on February 4, 1942, of a $500,000,000 loan, followed by a detailed Lend-Lease arrangement, and the visit to China in September of Wendell L. Willkie, serving as President Roosevelt's personal envoy. On December 1, 1943, President Roosevelt, Prime Minister Churchill, and Generalissimo Chiang Kai-shek, after a meeting in Cairo, Egypt, issued a declaration stating their resolve to bring unrelenting pressure "against their brutal enemies by land, sea and air" and their determination that Manchuria, Formosa, and the Pescadores should be restored to the Republic of China.[15]

With the passage of time the United States and its Western Allies began to feel it imperative that Nationalist and Communist China achieve closer unity and put up stiffer resistance against the invader. During the spring of 1944, therefore, President Roosevelt sent Vice-President Henry A. Wallace to China for the purpose of investigating possible measures toward consolidating the Chinese war effort against Japan. During Wallace's conversations with Chiang Kai-shek the question of Chinese Communist relations with the USSR arose—as it was to arise many times in the future. Chiang "deplored" propaganda then current to the effect that the Chinese Communists were only agrarian reformers and emphasized that despite the recent dissolution of the Third International the Reds remained more "internationalist" than Chinese. Wallace stressed the opinion that nothing should be permitted in China which might lead to conflict with Russia, and Chiang agreed, adding that whatever was not detrimental to Chinese sovereignty would be done to avoid such conflict.[16]

During the late spring of 1944 the Japanese launched a series of southward attacks, and there was evidence that Chinese resistance might be on the point of collapse. In the light of these circumstances, President Roosevelt proposed to Chiang Kai-shek that American General Joseph Stilwell—then in command of Chinese troops in Burma—be recalled to China and placed in command of Chinese and American troops directly under the Generalissimo. Chiang agreed to the proposal, but suggested that a high-ranking American official with political as well as military experience be sent to Chungking for consultations. In August Roosevelt complied by appointing Major

[15] *Ibid.*, Annex 33, p. 519.
[16] *Ibid.*, pp. 56–57.

General Patrick J. Hurley as personal representative to China with the particular mission of promoting harmonious relations between Stilwell, whose confidence in Chiang was limited, and the Generalissimo.

On his way to Chungking, General Hurley in company with Donald Nelson, who was then chairman of the War Production Board and a special representative of President Roosevelt, stopped over in Moscow for a discussion of the Chinese situation with Foreign Minister Molotov. Maintaining that the Soviet Union had been held unjustifiably responsible for various developments in China during immediately previous years, Molotov spoke of conditions there and insisted that many of the people calling themselves Communists were nothing of the sort, but only impoverished men and women seeking an outlet for their dissatisfaction.[17]

Seven months later, when General Hurley was passing through Moscow a second time, he took up the question again, this time with both Molotov and Stalin present, and restated what he recalled of the Foreign Minister's previous assertion. In his report of April 17, 1945, Hurley declared:

My analysis was briefly as follows: "Molotov said at the former conference that the Chinese Communists are not in fact Communists at all. Their objective is to obtain what they look upon as necessary and just reformations in China. The Soviet Union is not supporting the Chinese Communist Party. The Soviet Union does not desire internal dissension or civil war in China. The Government of the Soviet Union wants closer and more harmonious relations in China. The Soviet Union is intensely interested in what is happening in Sinkiang and other places and will insist that the Chinese Government prevent discriminations against Soviet Nationals." Molotov agreed to this analysis.[18]

Hurley proceeded a step further, informing Stalin that the United States and Great Britain considered support for the Nationalist government of China under the leadership of Chiang Kai-shek absolutely prerequisite to the establishment of a united, free, and democratic China. Stalin stated that the Soviet government would support such

[17] *Ibid.*, p. 71.

[18] *Ibid.*, pp. 94–95. The view that the Chinese Communists were "not real Communists" found rather wide acceptance at this time. In a broadcast of August 11, 1943, for example, Raymond Gram Swing is reported to have said in part: "For these are not Marxian Proletarians, these so-called Communists, they are agrarian radicals, trying to establish democratic practices . . . They should not be called Communists, whatever their origin may be. They have developed in another direction." Text in *Amerasia*, p. 282. Another writer who maintained that the Chinese Communists were not really Communists was Freda Utley. See *McCarran Hearings*, Vol. 10, pp. 3705–6.

a policy and spoke of Chiang Kai-shek as "selfless" and a "patriot" whom the USSR had in the past befriended.[19]

On April 23 the American chargé d'affaires in Moscow, George Kennan, wired Ambassador Harriman, then in Washington, to the effect that it had caused him "some concern to see this report go forward." Kennan continued:

There was, of course, nothing in Ambassador Hurley's account of what he told Stalin to which Stalin could not honestly subscribe, it being understood that to the Russians words mean different things than they do to us. Stalin is of course prepared to affirm the principle of unifying the armed forces of China. He knows that unification is feasible in a practical sense only on conditions which are acceptable to the Chinese Communist Party . . .[20]

And Ambassador Harriman, advocating similar caution, stated that in his opinion General Hurley's report, though accurate as to fact, gave a "too optimistic impression of Marshal Stalin's reactions" and predicted that the Russian dictator would not co-operate indefinitely with Chiang Kai-shek and that the Soviet Union, if and when it entered the Far Eastern war, would make full use of the Chinese Communists even to the point of setting up a puppet government in Manchuria and possibly northern China.[21]

Between his visits to Moscow, General Hurley spent long months in an effort to mediate between the Chinese Nationalist government and the Chinese Communist party. In December 1944 he reported:

At the time I came here Chiang Kai-shek believed that the Communist Party of China was an instrument of the Soviet Government in Russia. He is now convinced that the Russian Government does not recognize the Chinese Communist Party as Communist at all and that (1) Russia is not supporting the Communist Party in China, (2) Russia does not want dissensions or civil war in China, and (3) Russia desires more harmonious relations with China. . . .

These facts have gone far toward convincing Chiang Kai-shek that the Communist Party in China is not an agent of the Soviet Government. He now feels that he can reach a settlement with the Communist Party as a Chinese political party without foreign entanglements. When I first arrived, it was thought that civil war after the close of the present war or perhaps before that time was inevitable. Chiang Kai-shek is now convinced that by agreement with the Communist Party of China he can (1) unite the military forces of China against Japan, and (2) avoid civil strife in China.[22]

[19] *United States Relations with China*, p. 95.
[20] *Ibid.*, pp. 96–97.
[21] *Ibid.*, pp. 97–98.
[22] *Ibid.*, p. 73.

Under General Hurley's guidance the negotiations continued through the middle of February 1945, with proposals and counter-proposals from both sides. The Communists refused to submit their troops to Kuomintang command, but expressed willingness to yield them to the National government whenever the "one-party rule" of the Kuomintang had been abolished in favor of a coalition administration representing all parties. The Nationalists, on the other hand, insisted that the real purpose of the Chinese Communists was not simply to abolish one-party rule by the Kuomintang, but to overthrow the Chiang Kai-shek government and substitute a Communist one-party rule.

Negotiations were broken off following General Hurley's departure for Washington, but the Ambassador himself remained optimistic. He said:

I pause to observe that in this controversial chapter two facts are emerging : (1) the Communists are not in fact Communists, they are striving for democratic principles ; and (2) the one party, the one man personal Government of the Kuomintang is not in fact fascist, it is striving for democratic principles. Both the Communists and the Kuomintang have a long way to go, but if we know the way, if we are clear minded, tolerant and patient, we can be helpful. But it is most difficult to be patient at a time when the unified forces of China are so desperately needed in our war effort.[23]

The program which Chinese Communists had prepared for a "democratic" all-China government was not one which the Kuomintang or any other independent party could be expected to favor. Writing on coalition government in April 1945 Mao Tse-tung laid out a system[24] which differed in no essential respect from the Chinese People's Republic established four years later. Outlining two possible courses for China to follow, Mao declared:

Persistence in dictatorship and in preventing democratic reform; the policy of oppressing the people instead of fighting the Japanese aggressors ; the possibility of another civil war which will drag China to her former dependent, undemocratic, disunited poor self, even if the Japanese aggressors are beaten—this is one of the probabilities, one of the future courses . . . Those who hope for the materialization of this probability are the anti-people groups in the Kuomintang in China and the reactionary elements in the foreign nations who believe in imperialism.[25]

23 *Ibid.*, p. 86.

24 Mao Tse-tung, *On Coalition Government, Report to the Seventh Congress of the Chinese Communist Party* (Yenan, 1945).

25 *Ibid.*, p. 33.

The other possibility, of course, was a "new, independent, free, democratic, united and prosperous China" on the basis of Mao Tse-tung's New Democracy.

Specifying what he had in mind, Mao described the pyramidal system so peculiar to Communist-dominated governments founded on a class coalition of "democratic" parties and groups:

The formation of this New Democratic government should be based on the system of democratic centralization with various grades of people's assemblies making decisions on the administrative policy and electing the government. This system is at once democratic and centralized, that is to say, it is centralization of power based on democracy, and at the same time is democracy directed by centralized power.

He made clear that this government would not be a Bolshevik socialist or Communist regime, but a "new bourgeois democracy." At the same time, he said, "We Communist Party members never conceal or disguise our political aims. Our future, or ultimate program will advance China into the realm of [Bolshevik] socialism and Communism; this has been settled and cannot be doubted."[26] In his usual manner, Mao identified the proposed "coalition" with the "revised" Three Principles of Sun Yat-sen.

Like other observers, United States Foreign Service officers, reporting from the field, drew differing conclusions concerning Chinese developments. Ambassador Gauss, reporting to Secretary of State Hull in August 1944 had criticized the Kuomintang for not adhering to its own principles, but had been particularly vehement in scoring the Communists. "The request that China meet Communist demands," he wrote, "is equivalent to asking China's unconditional surrender to a party known to be under a foreign power's influence (the Soviet Union)."[27]

The reports of two foreign service officers—John Stewart Service and John P. Davies, Jr.—figured with particular prominence when General Hurley issued charges condemning certain career diplomats for siding "with the Communist armed camp and at times with the imperialist bloc against American policy." Precisely what General Hurley meant has never been fully clarified. Between mid-1943 and early 1945 Service stressed Kuomintang weaknesses and degeneration, the popular appeal of programs which the Communists were espousing, the modifying influence of nationalism on Communist behavior, and the advisability of an American policy that would "get tough," so to speak, with the Kuomintang and at the same time prevent

[26] *Ibid.*, p. 41.
[27] *United States Relations with China*, Annex 45, pp. 561–63.

the Chinese Communists from falling back "into the arms of the USSR."[28]

Davies noted nearly all the same trends. "The Communists are in China to stay," he declared. "And China's destiny is not Chiang's, but theirs."[29] For seven years, he reported, Chiang had been losing his cities and principal lines of communication to the Japanese and the countryside to the Communists, whose growth since 1937 had been almost "geometric in progression."[30] Davies gave clear warning that ties between Russian and Chinese Communists were, in all certainty, still strong, but suggested that a schism might develop in later years between Chinese Communists who were more Nationalist than Communist and those irrevocably dedicated to the direction of Moscow.[31]

In July 1945 the chief of Military Intelligence, Brigadier General P. E. Peabody, put forward the following analysis: the "democracy" of the Chinese Communists was Soviet democracy; the Chinese Communist movement was part of the international Communist movement, sponsored and guided by Moscow; there was good reason to believe that Soviet Russia planned to create Russian-dominated areas in Manchuria, Korea, and probably north China; a strong and stable China could not exist without the natural resources of Manchuria and north China; in order to prevent the separation of these areas from China it was essential that—if Soviet Russia participated in the war—China should not be divided, as Europe had been, into American-British and Russian zones of influence.[32]

General Peabody pointed out that the Chinese Communist movement was something more than a political party with sharply defined policies, able leadership, and high morale.

. . . it is represented by what is a state in all but name, possessing territory (the combined area of which is about the size of France, or one-fifth of China proper), a population of probably more than 70,000,000 people, armies, law and money of its own. The Chinese Communist state is economically primitive but (on a primitive level) fairly self-sufficient . . . in October 1944 the strength of the Chinese Communist regular forces was reliably reported at 475,000 men.[33]

Noting general American uncertainty concerning Soviet postwar aims in China, General Peabody put forward two major possibilities.

[28] "Memoranda by Foreign Service Officers in China, 1943–1945 [Extracts]," *ibid.*, Annex 47, pp. 564–76.
[29] *Ibid.*, p. 573.
[30] *Ibid.*, p. 567.
[31] *Ibid.*, p. 565.
[32] *The Chinese Communist Movement* (McCarran Hearings, 7A), pp. 2305–6.
[33] *Ibid.*, pp. 2306–7.

There was strong evidence that Moscow intended to establish domination across a Sinkiang–Inner Mongolia–Manchuria–Korea and possibly north China belt. Russian diplomats might seek to accomplish this either by establishing in those areas a regime wholly obedient to the USSR, or by improving their relations with the government of Chiang Kai-shek and working from within. Supporting the latter possibility, he said, was the fact that Soviet Russian experience in China had always been that co-operation or a united front relationship between the Kuomintang and the Chinese Communists tended to favor the Communists—without respect to whether the Nationalists were pursuing a "liberal" or a "reactionary" course.

Regardless of how the Russians proceeded, it was evident to General Peabody that, with the defeat of Japan, there would be a new power balance, with Soviet Russia regaining the dominance tsarist Russia had lost and emerging as the sole military land power in Asia:

Necessary as is the defeat of Japan to the re-establishment of peace in the Pacific, the fact remains that her defeat will upset the whole structure of the international balance of power in the Far East which was developed in the decades before 1931. Deprived of her empire in China, and with her cities and industries smashed to pieces, Japan will be back where she started at the dawn of her modern era, a group of relatively worthless islands, populated by fishermen, primitive farmers, and innocuous warriors. The clock will be turned back some eighty years to the time when the rivalry between Russia and the Western democracies in China began . . .[34]

The problem of postwar peace in the Far East, according to General Peabody, revolved, as far as the United States was concerned, around two major questions: How could the military-political vacuum in the Far East be filled following the defeat of Japan? And how could the United States promote internal unity in China? The answers lay to a considerable degree with the future moves of Soviet Russia. For if the USSR were to join in the war against Japan, the course of events would very largely be determined by the extent to which the Western Allies could prevent in China a division—like that which had already taken place in Europe—between an American-British sphere and a Soviet zone of operations. According to Peabody:

On the other hand, if American forces cooperate on equal terms with Soviet Russian, Chinese, and British forces in the reconquest and occupation of North China, Manchuria and Korea, a peace settlement in complete accord with the Cairo Declaration of 1 December, 1943 [guaranteeing the return of Manchuria to Nationalist China] can much more readily be achieved. For it is clear that if the war were to end with us in control of

[34] *Ibid.*, p. 2309.

Japan, and with Chungking-Chinese, American and British forces in control of Central and South China, while Soviet Russian and Chinese Communist forces held the controlling power in Manchuria and Korea, a peace settlement in regard to these areas might entail a considerable compromise of the terms of the Cairo Declaration. In that case, the plan of the Chinese Communists for a "coalition government" might well be the only feasible way of settling the situation in China; North China and probably also Manchuria and Korea would come under the control of native Communists dependent upon Soviet Russian support, and in these areas there would be established the new typical "united front" or "democratic" coalition administrations in which the Communists hold dominant power. Deprived of the vast raw material resources of North China and Manchuria the present Nationalist Government of China would find itself unable to compete with the Communists in the North and to establish a strong and stable state. For this reason it is necessary, for the maintenance of peace in the Far East and for the long range interests of the United States, that the Cairo Declaration be implemented without modification.[35]

As events turned out, the Cairo Declaration was not implemented. Precisely why it was not has not yet been resolved, and the full truth is not likely to be established for many years to come. A part of the answer undoubtedly lies in the circumstances and temper of the moment. Necessarily the United States had been assuming an ever greater responsibility for prosecuting the war against Japan, but amphibious drives across the Central and South Pacific were taking a heavy toll in American lives. By the end of 1944 both soldiers and civilians were demanding to know why the Soviet Union had not accepted a share of the war in Asia—just as a year later they would clamor for an early demobilization of American troops in the Far East. So, too, the various Allied military drives in Europe seemed to require American and British concessions to the USSR, if need be, in order to further co-operation among the powers. And finally, with Red Army troops at the Manchurian and Korean back doors, the Soviet Union enjoyed a position at the war's end which American and British diplomacy was scarcely in a position to alter. The Russians, in fact, could walk in as they chose.

THE UNITED STATES AND THE USSR CONSIDER CHINA'S FUTURE

At the Teheran Conference Stalin had declared that the USSR would enter the war against Japan once Germany was finally defeated, and during those conversations the question of making Dairen a "free port under international guaranty" and the Soviet use of Manchurian railways were also discussed informally. During conversations with

[35] *Ibid.*, p. 2310.

Vice-President Wallace in June 1944, Chiang Kai-shek stated that he had discussed the Dairen question with Roosevelt at Cairo, offering no disagreement provided the USSR co-operated with China and there were no impairment of Chinese sovereignty. He then asked Mr. Wallace to convey to the American President the following message: "If the United States could bring about better relations with the USSR and China and could bring about a meeting between Chinese and Soviet representatives, President Chiang would very much welcome such friendly assistance. Under such circumstances, moreover, the Chinese leader would go more than halfway in reaching an understanding with the Soviet Union.[36]

On February 11, 1945, Roosevelt, Churchill, and Stalin—without consulting China—signed at Yalta an agreement (which remained secret until several months after the war was over) setting forth the conditions under which the USSR would enter the war against Japan:

The leaders of the three Great Powers—the Soviet Union, the United States of America and Great Britain—have agreed that in two or three months after Germany has surrendered and the war in Europe has terminated the Soviet Union shall enter into the war against Japan on the side of the Allies on condition that:

1. The status quo in Outer Mongolia (The Mongolian People's Republic) shall be preserved;

2. The former rights of Russia violated by the treacherous attack of Japan in 1904 shall be restored, viz.:

   (a) the southern part of Sakhalin as well as all the islands adjacent to it shall be returned to the Soviet Union;

   (b) the commercial port of Dairen shall be internationalized, the preeminent interests of the Soviet Union in this port being safeguarded and the lease of Port Arthur as a naval base of the USSR restored;

   (c) the Chinese Eastern Railroad and the South Manchurian Railroad which provides an outlet to Dairen shall be jointly operated by the establishment of a joint Soviet-Chinese Company, it being understood that the preeminent interest of the Soviet Union shall be safeguarded and that China shall retain full sovereignty in Manchuria;

3. The Kurile islands shall be handed over to the Soviet Union.

It is understood that the agreement concerning Outer Mongolia and the ports and railroads referred to above will require concurrence of Generalissimo Chiang Kai-shek. The President will take measures in order to obtain this concurrence on advice from Marshal Stalin.

The Heads of the three Great Powers have agreed that these claims

---

[36] *United States Relations with China,* Annex 43, p. 558.

of the Soviet Union shall be unquestionably fulfilled after Japan has been defeated.

For its part the Soviet Union expresses its readiness to conclude with the National Government of China a pact of friendship and alliance between the USSR and China in order to render assistance to China with its armed forces for the purpose of liberating China from the Japanese yoke.

Subsequently, there arose important questions concerning the choice of words in this document. As a result of the insertion of "(The Mongolian People's Republic)" the USSR claimed that the provision signified independence, while the Chinese continued to base their position on the Sino-Soviet Treaty of 1924, which recognized the region as an integral part of China. As for the safeguarding of "preeminent interests of the Soviet Union" in Dairen and on the railways, Mr. Harriman, who participated in the discussions, later maintained that there was no reason for presuming that the words guaranteed anything more than safe passage for goods in transit. The Russians, on the other hand, were to interpret the phrases in terms of Soviet interests inherent in the line itself and in the Dairen facilities. So, too, Mr. Harriman believed that President Roosevelt had interpreted the Port Arthur lease as implying no more than the United States had regularly assumed in concluding similar arrangements with other powers. For the Soviet Union, of course, the agreement simply paved the way for Port Arthur's disappearance behind the Soviet curtain.[37]

Stalin, in rationalizing his terms to Churchill and Roosevelt, maintained that Soviet entry into the Pacific war would have to be justified to Russian "public opinion." The United States Department of State, in admitting that the Russian terms, by and large, had been conceded, offered the following explanation:

It should be remembered that at this time the atomic bomb was anything but an assured reality; the potentialities of the Japanese Kwantung Army in Manchuria seemed large; and the price in American lives in the military campaign up the island ladder to the Japanese home islands was assuming ghastly proportions. Obviously military necessity dictated that Russia enter the war against Japan prior to the mounting of Operation Olympic (the assault on Kyushu), roughly scheduled for November 1, 1945, in order to contain Japanese forces in Manchuria and prevent their transfer to the Japanese home islands.[38]

A year later, when more precise information of the Japanese

[37] *Ibid.*, pp. 113–14.
[38] *Ibid.*, p. 115.

potential had become available, the former head of the Office of Strategic Services, Major General William J. Donovan, was to charge that the "Yalta bargain" had been struck in the absence of sound intelligence and on the basis of a wholly false estimate of Japan's Kwantung army. In actual fact, he said, the Japanese forces holding Manchuria, having suffered critical depletion through troop transfers to Okinawa and the Philippines, were by early 1945 no longer a formidable opponent.[39]

Alexander H. Leighton in *Human Relations in a Changing World* (pages 58–75), draws similar conclusions. As early as January 5, 1945, the Foreign Morale Analysis Division of OWI reported that the Japanese home front was "full of tensions" and that "something was going to happen." Research leader of a team sent to Hiroshima in December 1945 by the United States Strategic Bombing Survey, Leighton presents evidence to suggest that the Japanese might have surrendered before the end of that year whether or not the atom bomb had been dropped or Soviet Russia had intervened, or an invasion of the Japanese homeland had been undertaken.

The United States has admitted that the failure to consult China, at least, was certainly unfortunate.

President Roosevelt and Marshal Stalin, however, based this reticence on the already well-known and growing danger of "leaks" to the Japanese from Chinese sources due to the debilitating and suppurative effects of the war. Here again [as in the writing of the agreement as a whole] military exigency was the governing consideration.[40]

Through the Yalta Agreement, we know in retrospect, the United States and Great Britain paid a heavy price for Russian aid in a war which—although few outside Japan realized it—was all but won. For the two Western Powers (again it must be noted: without consulting China) recognized a Soviet Russian claim to nearly all imperialist concessions on Chinese soil which Tsarist Russia had lost to Japan through the Treaty of Portsmouth in 1905. Great Britain and the United States also made it possible, without consulting China, for the USSR to establish through a technicality the "independence" of the Communist-dominated "Mongolian People's Republic."

After Roosevelt's death, Harry Hopkins, at the request of President Truman, visited Moscow in May 1945 and discussed the Far Eastern situation with Stalin, who stated that the reconstruction of China must devolve largely upon the United States; he proposed that there be "no alteration over the sovereignty of Manchuria, Sinkiang,

[39] *New York Times*, March 1, 1946.
[40] *United States Relations with China*, p. 115.

or any other part of China"; that the Soviet system did not exist in Mongolia; that Chiang Kai-shek was the only Chinese leader qualified to lead China in its unification, the Chinese Communists being less suitable for undertaking the task; and that he would welcome Chinese civilian participation in the administrative take-over of Manchuria.

In Washington on June 14 President Truman passed Stalin's comments on to T. V. Soong, the premier and foreign minister of China, who expressed gratification. He noted, however, that the USSR, while reclaiming Russian rights lost to Japan in 1905 and conceded to China in the Sino-Soviet Treaty of 1924, had nevertheless renounced at Yalta all special concessions including extraterritoriality. These points left ambiguities, he said, which would have to be clarified.[41] On the following day Ambassador Hurley communicated to Chiang Kai-shek the provisions of the Yalta Agreement, together with Stalin's assurances concerning Chinese sovereignty in Manchuria and his "oral concurrence" to the principle of the Open Door in China.

During July 1945, Stalin, Molotov, and T. V. Soong opened Sino-Soviet negotiations in Moscow. The participants were under notification from Washington that the United States, because of its role at Yalta, expected to be notified prior to the signature of a formal agreement. "The American position was that the Yalta Agreement should be complied with—no more, no less."[42]

This policy proved to be more easily enunciated than carried out. From the very beginning Soviet Russia, standing firm upon its own interpretations of the Yalta Agreement, demanded controlling interest in the Chinese Eastern and South Manchurian Railways; Dairen and Port Arthur lease boundaries identical with those of the whole Kwantung Peninsula lease which had been effected prior to the Russo-Japanese War of 1904; and recognition of the independence from China of Outer Mongolia. The United States supported the Chinese contention that the Russian interpretation exceeded the actual provisions of the Yalta Agreement and stated that concessions beyond the intention of the original document must be with the understanding that they were made by the Chinese government "because of the value it attached to obtaining Soviet support in other directions."[43]

Soviet troops were already moving into Manchuria when, on August 15, 1945, crowded beneath stories of Japanese surrender, newspapers across the face of the world carried accounts of the signing (the previous day) of the Treaty of Friendship and Alliance between

[41] *Ibid.*, pp. 115–16.
[42] *Ibid.*, p. 116.
[43] *Ibid.*, p. 117.

the Soviet Union and the Chinese Republic. The same meeting saw the conclusion of other agreements emerging from Sino-Soviet conversations and the original decisions at Yalta: a Changchun (or Manchurian) Railway agreement, an agreement on Port Arthur, an agreement on Dairen, and an Agreement on the Three Eastern Provinces (Manchuria). There was also an exchange of notes regarding Soviet aid to the Central Chinese government and the independence of Outer Mongolia.

Within the treaty the two governments agreed to wage war against Japan to the point of final victory; to refrain from concluding separate peace agreements with Japan; to undertake mutually all existing measures to make it impossible for Japan to repeat its aggressions; each to render assistance should the other become involved in military operations resulting from a breach of the peace by Japan; each to refrain from concluding any alliance or taking part in any coalition directed against the other; to work in close co-operation, to respect each other's sovereignty and territorial integrity, and each to refrain from interfering in the internal affairs of the other; and to render each other all possible economic aid with a view to speeding up national rehabilitation in both countries.

The conclusion of this treaty was greeted with enthusiasm in many quarters, few if any of which were yet aware of the Yalta clauses still held secret. A Communist newspaper in Chungking described the document as representing "dawn rising over the gloomy continent of Asia" and a realization of "an old dream of the Chinese people."[44] In London the Communist *World News and Views* called the treaty a "triumph for the policy of friendship with the Soviet Union for which Chinese Communists have striven since the foundation of the Communist Party of China in 1921."[45] And Kuomintang enthusiasm was scarcely less restrained. The treaty and its accompanying documents were hailed as "an act of statesmanship of the highest order" and as "a rational basis of peace in Asia."[46]

Through the Changchun Railway Agreement the main trunk lines of the Chinese Eastern and South Manchurian roads were joined in a single system under the joint ownership of the USSR and the Chinese Republic. The Port Arthur Agreement stipulated that both nations should make joint use of Port Arthur as a naval base; that the facilities would be at the disposal of the war and merchant ships of the two countries only; that matters pertaining to the base should be dealt with by a Chinese-Soviet military commission; that the

[44] *World News and Views*, September 8, 1945, p. 275.
[45] *Ibid.*, September 1, 1945, p. 265.
[46] *Contemporary China* (New York), September 3, 1945.

USSR should be responsible for the defense of the base, should provide the necessary equipment, and should bear the cost; that China should be responsible for the civil administration; that the USSR should choose a certain area for its military, naval, and air bases; that at the expiration of the agreement all equipment and public property provided by the USSR should be handed over to the Chinese government without compensation; and that the period of the agreement should be for thirty years. The area of the leasehold was extended beyond the limits which the United States had expected but not as far as the pre-1904 boundaries.

The agreement on Dairen proclaimed the city a free port open to the trade and shipping of all nations, with the USSR enjoying the lease of certain piers and warehouses. The chief of the port, like the manager of the Chinese Changchun Railway, was stipulated to be a Soviet citizen. In case of war with Japan, Dairen would be included in a special sphere of operations set forth in the Port Arthur Agreement.

According to the Agreement on the Three Eastern Provinces supreme authority on the entry of Russian troops into Manchuria would rest with the Soviet commander in chief. Representatives of the Chinese government would be appointed to establish and direct the administration of "cleared territory," however, and a Chinese military mission would be assigned to the headquarters of the Soviet commander in chief. It was stipulated that the Chinese Nationalists should assume full authority as soon as the area ceased to be a zone of direct hostilities. Soviet armed forces personnel were to remain under authority of the Soviet commander in chief, while all Chinese nationals were to be under Chinese jurisdiction.

In a note under the same date Molotov signified that the Soviet government was ready to render moral and material assistance—including military equipment—"to the National Government as the Central Government of China." He confirmed the territorial and administrative integrity of China over the Three Eastern Provinces and specified that the USSR had no intention of interfering in the internal affairs of the Chinese Republic. Concurrently, the Chinese minister of foreign affairs wrote Molotov that the Central Government was willing to recognize the independence of Outer Mongolia—provided the desire for such independence were expressed through a legal plebiscite.

The Soviet Union had now re-established Russian influence on the Liaotung Peninsula and in the management of the Manchurian railway system and had strengthened its position along borderlands from Korea through Mongolia to Sinkiang. The true position of

China was more difficult to assess. Secretary of State Byrnes described the treaty and its accompanying agreements as "an important step forward in the relations between China and the Soviet Union," and General Hurley was even more optimistic. "The publication of these documents," he declared, "has demonstrated conclusively that the Soviet Government supports the National Government of China and also that the two governments are in agreement regarding Manchuria."[47] Reporting to Washington, the ambassador suggested that he had succeeded in communicating this confidence to Chiang Kai-shek, who had "always doubted the Soviet's position in regard to relations with the Chinese Communists."

Chiang Kai-shek indeed sounded hopeful. On September 18, he declared, somewhat prematurely:

With the military assistance of our ally, Soviet Russia, the Cairo and the Potsdam declarations have been realized, and our Northeastern Provinces liberated, and our countrymen there brought back in the fold of the fatherland . . . With regard to Allied assistance in the reconstruction of our Northeastern Provinces, so far as economic aid and technical collaboration are concerned, we have already concluded a friendly pact with the Soviet Union for a period of thirty years. By virtue of the pact the geographical contiguity will first bring the desired benefits to them. We must honestly observe the past [sic] and wholeheartedly cooperate with our friendly neighbor for the improvement of the already amicable relations between the two great nations, thereby realizing the principle of joint struggle enunciated by the Father of the Republic [Sun Yat-sen].[48]

But the United States Embassy in Moscow was extremely skeptical about Soviet intentions. American diplomatic officials there pointed out that by the war's end Russian forces were so deployed in the Far East that the Soviet occupation of Manchuria and the Liaotung Peninsula could have proceeded with or without formal treaty arrangements. Moreover, the Russian willingness to withdraw at an early date and to admit Chinese officials to civil control did not represent in any sense a critical concession. On the contrary, the initial Russian position as occupying power, the close proximity of Manchuria to the USSR, and the greater discipline of Soviet power—all these factors together, in the Embassy's opinion, were sufficient to guarantee the effectiveness of Russian influence long after the Red Army had been withdrawn. So, too, recognition of Mongolian "independence" would do nothing toward changing the status quo—in which Soviet

---

[47] United States Relations with China, p. 120.
[48] The Collected Wartime Messages of Generalissimo Chiang Kai-shek, 1937–1945, compiled by the Chinese Ministry of Information (New York, 1946), II, 867, 871–72.

influence had long been the dominant force—unless to increase the country's usefulness as an instrument for further Russian expansion. As for Russian assurances of support for the Nationalist government and noninterference in internal Chinese affairs, the Embassy pointed out that Moscow was merely reaffirming what had existed for a considerable time. "It is probable that any Kremlin control over the Chinese Communists has been through the Party apparatus," the Embassy declared, "and not through government channels. It seems likely that this situation will obtain in the future—namely, control through the Party."[49] In point of fact, the restatement of Russian assurances, by removing any excuse for a Sino-American crusade against the Chinese Communists as a spearhead of Russian penetration, may easily have strengthened the total Communist position.

A PRELIMINARY POWER STRUGGLE IN MANCHURIA AND NORTH CHINA

There is evidence that Moscow and the Chinese Communist leaders were themselves in disagreement over the proper course to be followed in China—and that it was Mao Tse-tung, and not Stalin, who prevailed. In 1948 Stalin told Georgi Dimitrov and Edvard Kardelj:

. . . after the war we invited Chinese comrades to come to Moscow and we discussed the situation in China. We told them bluntly that we considered the development of the uprising in China had no prospect, and that the Chinese comrades should seek a *modus vivendi* with Chiang Kai-shek, that they should join the Chiang Kai-shek government and dissolve their army. The Chinese comrades agreed here with the views of the Soviet comrades, but went back to China and acted otherwise. They mustered their forces, organized their armies, and now, as we see, they are beating the Chiang Kai-shek army. Now, in the case of China, we admit we were wrong. It proved that the Chinese comrades and not the Soviet comrades were right.[50]

This statement shows Stalin—in 1945—seriously underestimating the capabilities of the Chinese Communists, assigns full responsibility for postwar Chinese Communist aggressiveness to Mao Tse-tung, and suggests that the pattern of Soviet Russian, American, and Chinese Communist attitudes toward coalition government may have been much more complicated than we have hitherto assumed.

The entry of Soviet Russian troops into Manchuria, together with the war's end, precipitated a whole series of developments—clashes between Nationalists and Communists, uncertainty over Russian

[49] *United States Relations with China*, pp. 122–23.
[50] Vladimir Dedijer, *Tito* (New York, 1953), p. 322.

troop withdrawals, the establishment of Soviet control over industries in Manchuria, and a "war booty" controversy in Manchuria—which badly confused the picture.

With the surrender of Japanese forces, Mao Tse-tung's peasant armies began racing Nationalist troops for control of areas which had been occupied by the enemy. At that time Nationalists held an estimated five-to-one advantage in troops and rifles and a virtual monopoly of heavy equipment, transport, and air strength. Mao Tse-tung's Red Army, on the other hand, enjoyed a geographic advantage—won largely through wartime guerrilla campaigns—in being closer to the Japanese areas, including Manchuria.

In an effort—widely criticized at the time—to help Nationalists reoccupy Japanese-held territory, the United States transported three Kuomintang armies by air to east and north China and over 400,000 troops by water. United States Marines, moreover, were moved into north China to hold key railroads and coal mines for the Nationalists. With this and other American assistance Chiang Kai-shek's troops were able to accept the capitulation of a great majority of the 1,200,000 Japanese troops in China proper. By the end of 1945—and in spite of armed clashes with the Communists—Chiang Kai-shek's forces had been able to clear the Lunghai Railway and obtain control of Peking, Tientsin, and the lines of communication to the Manchurian border. But major north-south communications lines—those upon which Nationalist forces entering Manchuria would depend for logistic support—were largely in Communist hands. The Nationalist government was thereby confronted by the dilemma of whether to postpone the occupation of Manchuria or, in pressing forward, to risk a serious overextension of its military lines. In the end Chiang Kai-shek determined on the latter course—a decision which cost him dearly.

Sino-Soviet friction over Russian troop withdrawal was generated almost immediately after the formal surrender of Japan on September 2, 1945. During Moscow discussions leading to the conclusion of the Treaty of Friendship and Alliance, Stalin had assured T. V. Soong that Soviet forces would begin evacuation of Manchuria within three weeks after the Japanese capitulation and that the withdrawal would be completed in not more than three months.[51] But soon after the initial three-week period had expired, Chinese Nationalist officials became perturbed by disquieting reports from north China.

Early in October Allied sources disclosed that Chinese Communist armies were penetrating Manchuria and co-operating closely

[51] Department of State *Bulletin*, February 10, 1946, p. 201.

with the Russian troops policing Mukden.[52] Two weeks later neutral observers were somewhat reassured when the Soviet Union informed Chungking that Russian troop withdrawals had already begun and would be completed by November 30.[53] But it soon became evident to Chungking officials that the Nationalist government would be unable to take over from the Russians unless some agreement were reached to facilitate the movement of Chiang Kai-shek's troops to key points in Manchuria.[54]

In late October Chinese and Soviet officials held discussions in order to arrange for the transportation of Nationalist troops by sea and air. Plans were made for moving heavy contingents on ships of the United States Seventh Fleet,[55] but fighting broke out between Chiang and the Chinese Communists while negotiations were still in progress.

According to the recently concluded agreements, Chinese Nationalist troops were to enter Manchuria through Yingkow on the Gulf of Liaotung. But although United States transports reached that port before Soviet troops were due to withdraw, it was discovered that the Russians had already pulled out, leaving Chinese Communists in control.[56] In other parts of China the Communists, refusing to obey Nationalist orders concerning the capitulation of Japanese and Chinese puppet troops, were manipulating every surrender possible according to their own designs, seizing enemy materiel, and occupying enemy territory.[57]

There were further difficulties in Chinwangtao, where United States ships landed the 52nd Chinese Nationalist Army. Fighting broke out almost immediately. Chinese Communist papers and radio reports accused the United States of intervening on the side of Nationalist forces by providing transportation and weapons, but Washington insisted that the American purpose was to secure the full surrender of Japanese forces throughout China and not to favor either the Nationalists or the Communists in their domestic struggle. Lieutenant General Albert C. Wedemeyer, commanding general, China Theater, declared that his forces had not "taken the initiative" in any clashes between Nationalist troops and "dissident elements" and promised that American troops would be withdrawn by spring.

On November 14, 1945, General Wedemeyer reported to Wash-

[52] *The Times* (London), October 3, 1945.
[53] *New York Times*, October 18, 1945.
[54] *Contemporary China* (New York), March 18, 1946.
[55] *The Times* (London), October 25, 1945.
[56] *Ibid.*, November 7, 1945.
[57] *United States Relations with China*, p. 130.

ington that in view of Communist opposition the Chiang Kai-shek government was finding itself totally unprepared for the occupation of Manchuria. Six days later he advised:

I have recommended to the Generalissimo that he should concentrate his efforts upon establishing control in north China [south of the Great Wall] . . . Logistical support for National Government forces and measures for their security in the heart of Manchuria have not been fully appreciated by the Generalissimo or his Chinese staff.[58]

The General further urged the "prompt execution" of political and administrative reforms in order to eliminate official corruption and the imposition on the Chinese people of taxes that were prohibitive. And beyond this, Wedemeyer drew the following conclusions: that Chiang Kai-shek should accept the assistance of foreign administrators and technicians in effecting political, economic, and social reforms under "honest, competent" civilian officials; that Nationalist stabilization of north China depended absolutely upon the carrying through of these reforms and upon a satisfactory settlement with the Chinese Communists; that short of reaching an agreement with the Russians and the Chinese Communists, Chiang could not occupy Manchuria for many years to come; that the possibility of such agreements remained "remote"; that the Soviet Union, in violation of the recent Sino-Russian Treaty and accompanying agreements, was already creating favorable conditions for the realization of Chinese Communist and possibly its own plans in north China and Manchuria; and that in view of these circumstances, the United States, Great Britain, and the USSR ought to establish a trusteeship over Manchuria until such time as the Nationalist government had become sufficiently strong and stabilized to assume full control of the area in question.

Conditions in north China and Manchuria continued to worsen. The Russians, by mid-November, were scheduled to withdraw from the Manchurian city of Changchun within a few days. But Nationalist officials now protested that—since Soviet officials were allowing Chinese Communist forces to enter Manchuria by land and to seize airports and seaports in advance of Nationalist arrivals—a Russian evacuation would mean a virtual presentation of the city to Mao Tsetung.[59]

As negotiations on troop withdrawal continued between Chinese and Soviet representatives, Chiang Kai-shek's troops began a drive to break through Communist forces and enter Manchuria. Tensions

[58] *Ibid.*, p. 131.
[59] *The Times* (London), November 17, 1945.

were only temporarily eased when in late November a new two-point accord was reached. Soviet officials agreed to "order" Chinese Communist forces to leave Changchun and Mukden and to hold Russian troops in control of Manchuria until Nationalist armies could be flown in to assume control, January 3, 1946, being set as an evacuation date.[60] The Russians also promised to grant Chinese Nationalist troops full protection "wherever and whenever" they might land and to ensure their smooth takeover of Manchuria. Arrangements were made, with Soviet consent, for moving Nationalist contingents in United States planes, and contingents of Chiang Kai-shek's troops were soon landing on the Changchun airfield while other units moved into Mukden on foot.[61]

The situation remained confused. In December at the Moscow Conference of Foreign Ministers, Molotov, reaffirming Soviet adherence to the policy of noninterference in Chinese internal affairs, stated that Russian troops had completed the disarming and deportation of Japanese troops in Manchuria, but that withdrawal of Red Army units had been postponed until February first "at the request of the Chinese Government."[62] From their own viewpoint, the Russians could not possibly lose: if they withdrew, a large part of Manchuria would fall into Chinese Communist hands; if they stayed where they were, they could increase their own influence over the area. Conversely, the Nationalist position amounted to a dilemma. In late January, Central Government spokesmen were quoted as urging the immediate withdrawal of Soviet troops;[63] four days later the United States Department of State reiterated that Soviet troops were remaining in Manchuria until February first at Chungking's request.[64] Later in the month the withdrawal was further postponed—with Nationalist approval. It was not until May 1946 that the Soviet evacuation was completed.

In February, meanwhile, the Soviet Union had begun pressing for important economic concessions in Manchuria, including a share of control in many industrial plants, mines, and similar enterprises.[65] It was stated that the USSR intended to rely on Manchuria for agricultural products to care for its growing population in the Soviet Far East and for that reason was desirous of obtaining conditions more favorable than an open door would provide. At this juncture, moreover, the United States published the hitherto secret clauses of the Yalta Agreement, which, without China's knowledge, had shaped the

[60] *The Christian Science Monitor*, December 1, 1945.
[61] *New York Times*, December 13, 1945.
[62] Department of State *Bulletin*, December 30, 1945, p. 1030.
[63] *New York Times*, January 18, 1946.
[64] *Ibid.*, January 22, 1946.   [65] *Ibid.*, February 14, 1946.

Treaty of Friendship and Alliance and which now revealed itself to many Chinese as the instrument primarily responsible for giving Soviet troops access to Manchuria. Chinese official spokesmen declared that China would not be bound by the Yalta Agreement,[66] and the Chinese Nationalist press condemned decisions made there as an international bargain at China's expense. Tillman Durdin, writing for the *New York Times*, declared that the Yalta "deal" was already damaging American prestige in Chinese eyes and that if anything went wrong with Sino-Soviet relations much of the opprobrium would go to the United States.

In identical notes delivered through the American embassies in Chungking and Moscow, the United States expressed "concern" over Sino-Soviet discussions about the control of industrial enterprises in Manchuria and pointed out that any agreements of this nature would be contrary to Open Door Policy.[67] But the issue had already been further complicated by Soviet removals of industrial equipment from the area. On January 21 the USSR had declared in a memorandum addressed to the Chinese government that all Japanese enterprises in Manchuria which had rendered service to the Japanese Army were regarded by Moscow as "war booty" of the Russian forces.[68] Both the Chinese Nationalist and the United States governments protested these claims as far exceeding the scope of war booty as generally recognized by international law and usage.

In late February the Red Army commander in Mukden admitted to foreign correspondents that his troops were already removing industrial equipment on the basis of an understanding reached at "Yalta or Potsdam"—he was not sure which. The United States Secretary of State James Byrnes immediately denied the "understanding," and Chiang Kai-shek stated that further Sino-Soviet negotiations would have to be based on Chinese law, the Sino-Soviet Treaty of August 1945, and other agreements not in conflict with international treaties to which China was signatory.[69]

United States concern over the "war booty" controversy led to an investigation and report by Edwin W. Pauley, personal representative of the President on reparations, which estimated that direct damage effected upon Manchuria by Soviet removals would amount to $858,000,000 and that a total including replacement costs and deterioration would reach the neighborhood of $2,000,000,000 (U.S.). By the time this report was published, civil war was raging between the Nationalist government and the Chinese Communists.

[66] *The Times* (London), February 21, 1946.
[67] Department of State *Bulletin*, March 17, 1946, p. 488.
[68] *Contemporary China* (New York), March 18, 1946.
[69] *The Times* (London), February 27, 1946.

THE UNITED STATES AND THE PROSPECT OF CIVIL WAR IN CHINA

In his April 1945 report to the Seventh Congress of the Chinese Communist Party (*On Coalition Government*), Mao Tse-tung had condemned the Kuomintang's "reactionary course of dictatorship" and had charged the Nationalists with "preparing to launch another civil war" once Allied armies had driven Japanese forces out of China.[70] But in spite of all possible Kuomintang machinations, according to Mao, the people's destiny lay in a China that was "independent, free, democratic, united and prosperous"—a series of euphemisms for Communist control. Eight months later when, in effect, the struggle between Nationalists and Communists had already been joined, President Truman charged his special representative, General George C. Marshall, with bringing United States influence to bear toward a solution of the conflict and—with a meaning quite different from Mao's—called for a "unified, democratic and peaceful" Chinese nation.[71]

In retrospect we can perceive that the premise upon which the Marshall mission proceeded—namely, that the Nationalists and Communists could reach through "tact and discretion, patience and restraint" a reasonable compromise—was probably faulty. First, if Stalin's statement to Dimitrov and Kardelj is true (page 222), then Mao Tse-tung and his comrades had decided by the autumn of 1945 *not* to co-operate with the Kuomintang at that time. Even if they had determined otherwise, a careful reading of *On Coalition Government* should have suggested to American negotiators that Mao's concept of collaboration (like his concept of the wartime united front) was strictly tactical, a carefully controlled maneuver in the class war.

Why, then, were the Marshall negotiations between Communists and Nationalists undertaken? It is unlikely, of course, that observers in Washington were aware of a Chinese Communist determination to fight the Nationalists to a decision at any cost, but intelligence materials and Mao's own writings might have indicated the inherent dangers in bringing Communists into the Nationalist government.

On the other hand, there was no reason, perhaps, why the Communists should not be bested at their own game. Is it not conceivable that the Kuomintang — entering a coalition with its eyes open — might have conducted itself in a manner to weaken the Communists and to ensure the development of a truly "united, free and democratic China"? In 1945 some Americans thought so.

Prior to the war's end General Peabody had warned that imple-

---

[70] *On Coalition Government*, pp. 31–32.
[71] *United States Relations with China*, pp. 605–9.

mentation of the Cairo Declaration, i.e., the restoring of Manchuria (as well as Formosa and the Pescadores) to the Republic of China, was an absolute prerequisite for peace and security in China. But events had moved in another direction. By mid-August the flow of Red Army troops into Manchuria and northern Korea was dividing the Far East (as Europe had already been divided) into an expanded and strategically located Soviet zone face to face with a crescent-shaped (Japan, Formosa, South Korea, China proper) American-Nationalist Chinese sphere. By late autumn there remained three major alternatives: a full-dress American occupation not only of Japan and South Korea, but also of China proper; or the "abandonment" of China to whatever fate the logic of the Far Eastern situation might dictate; or the building up of Nationalist China as a counterforce to balance the Soviet sphere.

With United States naval, military, and air power dissolving under domestic pressure from isolationists, the families of service personnel, and the "economy bloc" in Congress, the possibility of an American occupation—if it was considered—must have appeared dubious. The complete abandonment of China seems not to have been contemplated seriously. The third, and most likely alternative—the building of a counterforce—presented difficulties.

Nearly all reports, whether from the Foreign Service, Military Intelligence, or other sources, had noted a decline in Kuomintang effectiveness and prestige paralleled by a rise in Communist strength and popular support. Hence, many non-Communist observers in the United States and in China itself concluded that an end to civil strife and the institution of democratic reforms on the part of the Nationalist government were prerequisite to the achievement of an effective counter-force.

In 1952 the United States Senate Committee on the Judiciary (the McCarran Committee) charged in its *Report* that there was more than coincidence in the fact that both the Communists and certain influential Americans were calling for a "strong, united and democratic" China. Until late 1945, the *Report* stated, American policy with respect to China was one of support to the Chinese Nationalist government, but at that time United States policy changed to one of intervention in favor of the Chinese Communists. "This new policy," according to the *Report*, "continued from 1945 until 1950."[72] In the opinion of the Committee on the Judiciary, John Carter Vincent (director of the Far Eastern Office of the United States Department

[72] *Institute of Pacific Relations, Report of the Committee on the Judiciary* (McCarran Hearings), Report No. 2050 (Washington, United States Government Printing Office, 1952), p. 198. Cited hereinafter as the *McCarran Report.*

of State in 1945), under the influence of Owen Lattimore, was largely responsible for this shift.

The *McCarran Report* points out that Vincent drafted two of the three documents which constituted General Marshall's directive for his mission to China. Under date of December 9, 1945, Vincent produced a memorandum for the War Department which was signed by Secretary of State James F. Byrnes on December 10. This document stated in part:

The President and the Secretary of State are both anxious that the unification of China by peaceful, democratic methods shall be achieved as soon as possible . . . During the war the immediate goal of the United States in China was to promote a military union of the several political factions in order to bring their combined power to bear upon our common enemy, Japan. Our longer-range goal, then as now, and a goal of at least equal importance, is the development of a strong, united and democratic China.

To achieve this longer-range goal, it is essential that the Central Government of China as well as the dissident elements approach the settlement of their differences with a genuine willingness to compromise. We believe, as we have long believed and consistently demonstrated, that the government of Generalissimo Chiang Kai-shek affords the most satisfactory base for developing democracy. But we also believe that it must be broadened to include the representatives of those large and well organized groups who are now without any voice in the government of China.

This problem is not an easy one. It requires tact and discretion, patience and restraint. It will not be solved by the Chinese leaders themselves. To the extent that our influence is a factor, success will depend upon our capacity to exercise our influence in the light of shifting conditions in such a way as to encourage concessions by the Central Government, by the so-called Communists, and by other factions.[73]

"Clearly, this was calling for intervention," the *McCarran Report* states. "Clearly it was implying that the Chinese Communists were not really Communists."

True, the document did call for intervention. For months now a whole series of officials—General Peabody, General Wedemeyer, General Hurley, and many others—had been either intervening or calling for intervention. As for the term "so-called Communists"—this was a common tendency in 1945. We need consider only how General Hurley himself had tried to convince Chiang that the Communists were not really Communists.

What about the second document drafted by Vincent?

This memorandum was handed to General Marshall by Secretary

[73] *United States Relations with China*, pp. 606–7.

of State Byrnes late in November, whereupon it was reworked by the Army and War departments. Subsequently it served as the basis for President Truman's "Statement on United States Policy Toward China," dated December 15, 1945, and as a directive for General Marshall. The final text included the following statements:

It is the firm belief of this Government that a strong, united and democratic China is of utmost importance to the success of the United Nations organization and for world peace . . .

The Government of the United States believes that it is essential: (1) That a cessation of hostilities be arranged between the National Government and the Chinese Communists and other dissident Chinese armed forces for the purpose of completing the return of all China to effective Chinese control, including the immediate evacuation of the Japanese forces; (2) that a national conference of representatives of major political elements be arranged to develop an early solution to the present internal strife—a solution which will bring about the unification of China.

The United States and other United Nations have recognized the present Nationalist Government of the Republic of China as the only legal government in China. It is the proper instrument to achieve the objective of a unified China.

. . . United States support will not extend to United States military intervention to influence the course of any Chinese internal strife . . .

The United States is cognizant that the present National Government of China is a "one-party government" and believes that peace, unity and democratic reform in China will be furthered if the basis of this Government is broadened to include other political elements in the country . . .

The existence of autonomous armies such as that of the Communist army is inconsistent with, and actually makes impossible, political unity in China. With the institution of a broadly representative government, autonomous armies should be eliminated as such and all forces in China integrated effectively into the Chinese Nationalist army . . .

As China moves toward peace and unity along the lines described above, the United States would be prepared to assist the National Government in every reasonable way to rehabilitate the country, improve the agrarian and industrial economy, and establish a military organization capable of discharging China's national and international responsibilities for the maintenance of peace and order . . .[74]

The McCarran Committee charges that the demand for support of the idea of a coalition government, made in May 1945 by Mao Tse-tung, taken up by the Communist party of the United States, and "recommended to the President by Owen Lattimore," was thus adopted and sponsored by Vincent, affirmed by the Secretary of State, and used as a basis for United States policy toward China. The impli-

[74] *Ibid.*, pp. 607–8.

cations are obvious. It should be recalled, however, that in July 1945, General Peabody, chief of United States Military Intelligence, had declared that if the war ended with the USSR in control of Korea and Manchuria "the plan of the Chinese Communists for a 'coalition government' might well be the only feasible way of settling the situation in China."[75]

This is not to say that the attempt to bring Chinese Communists into the Nationalist government turned out to be sound policy. In retrospect, it is difficult to perceive how a coalition could have proved compatible with the interests of the United States or of China. In 1945, however, many persons of integrity were willing to believe that a workable compromise might be effected.

In January 1952 Vincent gave this testimony before the McCarran Committee in an effort to explain his reasoning eight years earlier:

Mr. Vincent: In my memorandum [of late November] I suggested assistance to Chiang in recovering Manchuria and steps to assist the Chinese in bringing about a military truce and a settlement of political difficulties through a general political conference.

I also stated that political peace in China was impossible as long as there existed autonomous armies such as the Communists had, and suggested that all armies be united and organized under the National Government.

Senator Ferguson: Did you recommend the taking of Communists into the Government?

Mr. Vincent: The Communists were included in my statement here, "a settlement of political difficulties through a general political conference."

.   .   .   .

Senator Ferguson: Did you not indicate that the Communists if they went in wanted such power that they would in effect take over?

Mr. Vincent: That brings up a question of tactics . . . We were, as I say, terribly concerned over the results of an outbreak of general civil war in China. I was particularly. I had been in China and had seen the effects of civil war on the country.

Senator Ferguson: But coming back, I understood you to tell me before that you knew that if you took the Communists in that they wanted a greater power than they were entitled to, indicated to you that Russia was in command?

Mr. Vincent: . . . in my conception you had a better chance of taking the Communists in in more ways than one by bringing them into a government on a minority basis, not against the wishes of Chiang Kai-shek's government, but they themselves were at that time negotiating.

[75] *The Chinese Communist Movement* (McCarran Hearings, 7A), p. 2310.

Senator Ferguson: . . . were you not also of the opinion that if you ever took the Communists in they would dominate the government?

Mr. Vincent: I would have been willing to say that the Communists would try to dominate the Government, but I still believed that you could have taken them in, not forced them on Chiang, but Chiang could have taken them in in more ways than one on a minority basis.

There were at the time Communists in the Italian and French Governments who were eliminated. But I was trying to avoid what I honestly thought was the worst possible disaster that could come to Chiang, which was the outbreak of a general civil war.

Senator Ferguson: Could that be any worse as far as America was concerned than to have the Communists take over the government and not have a civil war?

Mr. Vincent: Senator, my concept was that the Communists would come into the Government on a minority basis and that we could through support of the Chiang Kai-shek Government, and I think you will find this philosophy stated in my memorandum, that with help from us we could eventually strengthen the Chinese Government enough to eliminate the Communists.

Senator Ferguson: To kick them out?

Mr. Vincent: I think I stated that in so many words.[76]

The *McCarran Report* emphasizes the following points: Vincent's November 28 memorandum stressed that the Nationalist government was a "one-party government" (this, of course, is cold fact, since the whole state system had been premised on the concept of Kuomintang "tutelage") and that the United States would not support it in an internecine struggle; that the Vincent memorandum, in calling for a truce, had stated that the United States was prepared to ask for British and Soviet Russian support toward this end (as late as September 19, 1947, General Wedemeyer was suggesting a five-power guardianship over Manchuria to include the USSR); and that the Vincent memorandum of December 9 gave instructions to General Wedemeyer which were directly contrary to the recommendations which the General himself had submitted.[77]

This last point refers to the following circumstances: In November, General Wedemeyer had advised against the movement of Chiang Kai-shek's troops into Manchuria (page 225). On the other hand, the December 9 memorandum stipulated that General Marshall— while holding in abeyance the transportation of Nationalist troops

[76] *McCarran Hearings*, Part 6, pp. 1713–14.
[77] *McCarran Report*, pp. 201–3.

into northern China until such action could be carried out consistently with Kuomintang-Communist negotiations, or until the negotiations failed and Nationalist troop transfers were necessary to secure the long-term interests of the United States—*should assist Chiang Kai-shek in the movement of his troops to Manchurian ports.*[78]

Before the McCarran Committee in January 1953, Vincent denied any intent to "stymie"[79] General Wedemeyer through these instructions. The testimony included the following:

Mr. Sourwine: Where did that overruling of General Wedemeyer originate; do you know?

Mr. Vincent: I do not know. It was a military matter, I should think, and it was one of the Pentagon Building or General Marshall himself.

Mr. Sourwine: Couldn't it have originated with Chiang Kai-shek himself?

Mr. Vincent: It could have. Chiang Kai-shek was anxious to move troops into Manchuria.[80]

The movement of Chiang Kai-shek's troops into Manchuria, extending his lines as it did, was probably—as General Wedemeyer warned—a military mistake. On the other hand, a refusal on the part of the United States to move Chiang's forces would have amounted, in 1945, to the handing over of Manchuria to the Chinese Communists without a struggle. One cannot help wondering, therefore, what the attitude of the McCarran Committee would have been if the United States had taken this course, i.e., had refused Chiang the opportunity of pitting his forces against the Communists in Manchuria.

Russian, Chinese, and American Communists undoubtedly did their level best to influence both official and unofficial public opinion by propaganda, infiltration, and subversion. And to a considerable degree they may have succeeded. It would be difficult, for example, to estimate the large numbers of Americans who, in 1945, were to some degree confused or mistaken about the true intentions of the Chinese Communists. Bolshevik efforts—as well as the circumstances of World War II and the pattern of our Communist alliances—had affected the whole climate of American public opinion. But this does not prove that every American, layman or specialist, who hoped for the achievement of a "united, free and democratic China" was necessarily the dupe of Communist manipulation. Despite Bolshevik abuse and exploitation of the words, the objective itself (however unattain-

---

[78] *United States Relations with China*, p. 607. The italics are mine.
[79] *McCarran Hearings*, Part 6, p. 2205.
[80] *Ibid.*, pp. 2206–7.

able it may appear in retrospect to have been) was nevertheless respectable and worthy. Nor does it prove that the American official who committed what now appears to have been an error in judgment was guilty of subversion. It proves only that, like most statesmen, including many of his critics, he was not infallible.

THE COMMUNISTS SEIZE POWER

During most of 1946, Chiang Kai-shek's prospects looked relatively hopeful. At the midyear Kuomintang forces enjoyed approximately three times the estimated Communist strength,[81] and with these troops the Nationalist command was able to clear important lines of communication into Manchuria as far as Changchun, while at one point defeated Communist units were pushed into rapid retreat across the Sungari River. In this fashion the Nationalists extended their control over considerable areas of northern China.

President Truman's proposal for convoking a national conference was consonant with an agreement already reached by the Nationalist government and the Chinese Communists for the convening of a "Political Consultative Conference" as a step toward the formation of a constitutional government. In the wake of preliminary negotiations by General Marshall, Nationalist and Communist representatives worked out a cease-fire agreement, and the Political Consultative Conference convened January 10–31, 1946. The Kuomintang, the Chinese Communist party, the Democratic League, and the Youth party all had representatives present, together with nonparty delegates.

Resolutions of the conference called for the convening of a national assembly on May 5, 1946, in order to draft a constitution. Provision was also made for the Kuomintang to revise the organic law of the Nationalist government, making the State Council the supreme organ of the government. Membership in this council was to consist of forty persons chosen by Chiang Kai-shek. Half were to be Kuomintang members, and half were to consist of representatives from other parties (including the Communists) and of nonparty personnel. Nationalist and Communist negotiators agreed also to the drawing up of a military reorganization agreement, according to which Nationalist armies would gradually be reduced to ninety divisions and Chinese Communist forces to eighteen divisions.[82]

Chinese public opinion appeared to be relatively enthusiastic over

---

[81] *United States Relations with China*, p. 313. "Government armies in mid-1946 comprised approximately 3,000,000 men opposed by something over 1,000,000 Communists of whom an estimated 400,000 were not regular troops."

[82] *Ibid.*, p. 623.

both the cease-fire agreement and the resolutions adopted by the Political Consultative Conference. Certain intraparty groups within the Kuomintang were dissatisfied with the results of the conference, however, and there was a tendency on the part of many Nationalist military men to resent the proposed army reorganization program. Then, on April 15, 1946, within twenty-four hours after the evacuation of Changchun by Russian forces, Chinese Communist troops attacked the city and seized it, in direct violation of the cease-fire agreement.[83] The results of this action included bloodshed, recriminations, further negotiations, attempts at mediation on the part of General Marshall, and another truce, but no lasting agreement and no end to civil conflict.

Hostilities seesawed back and forth. The Chinese Communists now had large stocks of Japanese arms and munitions made available to them by the departing Russians, and Chiang, having seriously overextended his lines into Manchuria, provided a vulnerable target. As time progressed the Communists, using the guerrilla tactics in which they were so adept, succeeded more and more in isolating and defeating important Nationalist units.

Economic conditions worsened in Kuomintang China, with inflation doing serious damage to the population and to the prestige of the government. Politically, Nationalist leaders were wary of granting political rights to their relatively impotent middle-of-the-road critics, let alone to the Communists, and Kuomintang power tended more and more to accumulate in the hands of ultraconservative groups like the CC clique. The Communists, for their part, made use of every possible opportunity, both political and military, to further their party ends. Mediation offered by third-party groups, including the Democratic League, were as fruitless as those undertaken by General Marshall.

After nearly twelve months of negotiations, General Marshall was recalled. Analyzing in a public statement his inability to achieve Chinese unity, Marshall struck out at both "a dominant group of reactionaries" in the Kuomintang camp and "dyed-in-the-wool Communists" who did not hesitate to take the most drastic measures to gain their ends:

Between this dominant reactionary group in the Government and the irreconcilable Communists who, I must state, did not seem so last February, lies the problem of how peace and well-being are to be brought to the long-suffering and presently inarticulate mass of the people of China. The reactionaries in the Government have evidently counted on substantial American support regardless of their actions. The Communists by their unwillingness to compromise in the national interest are evidently counting on an economic collapse to bring about the fall of the Government

[83] *Ibid.*, p. 149.

accelerated by extensive guerrilla action against the long lines of rail communications—regardless of the cost in suffering to the Chinese people.[84]

In Marshall's view the only salvation of the situation lay in the assumption of leadership by "liberals in the Government and in the minority parties, a splendid group of men" who, in fact, lacked the power or political prestige to act. In retrospect, moreover, it appears doubtful whether the effecting of a "coalition government" acceptable to the Communists would have provided anything more positive than a vehicle for Communist subversion. One questions whether by this time anything short of full-scale American military intervention could have stopped the Communists—an action which the United States government had pledged itself not to take and which might have demanded of the American people an effort comparable to that expended later in Korea.

By early 1947, the Nationalists were reaching a peak of military successes and territorial expansion. The United States authorized $1,432,000,000 in aid to the Chiang Kai-shek government (more than half of it military), in addition to munitions supplied under surplus property arrangements.[85] There were delays and wastage in delivery—some resulting from American inefficiency, some from a seeming desire to "pressure" Chiang, some from Chinese persistence in bargaining for better arrangements, and some from black market and other illicit operations on the scene in China, but, compared with the Communists, Chiang Kai-shek's troops tended to be well equipped. Early in 1948 President Truman requested an additional $570,000,000 of aid to China, spread over fifteen months. What the Congress actually appropriated was somewhat less : $125,000,000 in special grants to the Chinese government plus $275,000,000 for economic aid spread over twelve months, a total of $400,000,000.[86] The sum of United States grants and credits to China between V–J Day and 1949 was $2,007,000,000.

Already the tide of fortune was turning against the Nationalists. Chinese Communist generals had begun to bring superior forces to bear precisely at the points of greatest Kuomintang extension—just as they had done during the "bandit suppression campaigns" in the

---

[84] "Personal Statement by the Special Representative of the President (Marshall), January 7, 1947," *ibid.*, pp. 686–89.

[85] *Ibid.*, pp. 381–82.

[86] *Ibid.*, pp. 388–89. General Claire Lee Chennault has charged that General Marshall, during his mission to China, applied pressure on the Nationalist government by shutting off the flow of military supplies and that the United States government "implied" during 1946 that a $500,000,000 loan could not be made available until a truce was effected. See *McCarran Hearings*, Vol. 10, p. 3709, and *United States Relations with China*, p. 691.

days of the Juichin Republic—destroying isolated bodies of troops, cutting down communications and seizing arms. Nationalist morale was reported to be low and rapidly ebbing. The United States Consul General at Mukden reported May 30, 1947:

There is good evidence that apathy, resentment, and defeatism are spreading fast in Nationalist ranks causing surrenders and desertions. Main factors contributing to this are Communists' ever mounting superiority (resulting from greater use of native recruits, aid from underground and Korean units), Nationalist soldiers' discouragement over prospects of getting reinforcements, better solidarity and fighting spirit of the Communists, losses and exhaustion of Nationalists, their growing indignation over the disparity between officers' enrichment and soldiers' low pay, life, and their lack of interest in fighting far from home among "alien" unfriendly populace . . .[87]

On July 9, 1947, President Truman instructed Lieutenant General Albert C. Wedemeyer to proceed immediately to China and Korea on a fact-finding mission, appraising the political, economic, psychological, and military situation—"current and projected."[88] In a report dated September 19, 1947, General Wedemeyer sharply criticized the Kuomintang, "whose reactionary leadership, repression and corruption" had been responsible for a "loss of popular faith in the Government" and condemned the Communists, bound ideologically to the Soviet Union, whose eventual aim was admittedly a Communist state in China. Moderate groups, he said, were finding themselves caught between "Kuomintang misrule and repression" and ruthless Communist totalitarianism. Neither moderates within the Kuomintang nor the various minority parties were able to make their influence felt because of "National Government repression."

Wedemeyer urged that every possible opportunity be used for seizing the initiative in China:

Notwithstanding all the corruption and incompetence one notes in China, it is a certainty that the bulk of the people are not disposed to a Communist political and economic structure. Some have become affiliated with Communism in an indignant protest against oppressive police measures, corrupt practices and mal-administration of National Government officials. Some have lost all hope for China under existing leadership and turn to the Communists in despair. Some accept a new leadership by mere inertia.

In urging an aid program for stabilizing China, General Wedemeyer emphasized that Chiang Kai-shek must concentrate upon political and economic reforms if communism were to be stopped:

[87] *Ibid.*, p. 316.
[88] *Ibid.*, p. 255.

Adoption by the United States of a policy motivated solely toward stopping the expansion of Communism without regard to the continued existence of an unpopular repressive government would render any aid ineffective. Further, United States prestige in the Far East would suffer heavily, and wavering elements might turn away from the existing government to Communism.[89]

As for Manchuria, General Wedemeyer suggested that the United Nations might take immediate action to bring about a cessation of hostilities there as a prelude to the establishment of a guardianship or trusteeship:

The Guardianship might consist of China, Soviet Russia, the United States, Great Britain, and France. This should be attempted promptly and could be initiated only by China. Should one of the nations refuse to participate in Manchurian Guardianship, China might then request the General Assembly of the United Nations to establish a Trusteeship, under provisions of the Charter . . . If these steps are not taken by China, Manchuria may be drawn into the Soviet orbit, despite United States aid, and lost, perhaps permanently, to China.[90]

Chiang Kai-shek hesitated to undertake the necessary reforms, and nothing was done toward establishing a trusteeship over Manchuria. By early 1948 the Communists were supplementing Russian-donated Japanese rifles with American weapons captured from American-trained and American-equipped Nationalist armies. In November 1948 the United States Embassy in China reported that in the four battles of Tsinan, Liaoning Corridor, Changchun, and Mukden, Chiang Kai-shek had lost thirty-three divisions, more than 300,000 men (including eight divisions that were 85 percent American-trained and American-equipped) and 230,000 rifles (100,000 of them American-made). A month later the United States military attaché in Nanking stated that "seventeen originally United States equipped divisions" had been totally lost. Subsequent estimates indicated a total of a million men and 400,000 rifles lost by the Nationalists during the last four months of 1948.[91]

Major General David Barr, commanding the United States Advisory Group in China, had this to say about Kuomintang defeats in Manchuria: "The Nationalist troops, in Manchuria, were the finest soldiers the Government had. The large majority of the units were United States equipped and many soldiers and junior officers still remained who had received United States training during the war with Japan. I am convinced that had these troops had proper leadership from the top the Communists would have suffered a major defeat." Criticizing the Nationalists for what he called a "wall psychology," General Barr described a Kuomintang habit of retiring into cities and fighting there to the end, hoping for relief that never came. The difficulty, he felt, lay in the faulty judgment of officers:

No man, no matter how efficient, can hope for a position of authority on account of being the man best qualified for the job. He must simply have other backing. In too many cases, this backing was the support and loyalty of the Generalissimo for his old army comrades which kept them in positions of high responsibility regardless of their qualifications. A direct result of this practice is the unsound strategy and faulty tactics so obviously displayed in the fight against the Communists.[92]

In October 1948 Nationalist defenders of Mukden defected to the Communists, taking with them both weapons and other equipment. Thereafter, Communist victories followed one upon another: Tientsin fell on January 15, 1949; Peking surrendered later that month without a fight; in April the Communists crossed the Yangtze; Shanghai fell in May, and on October 15 Canton, Nationalist capital for the previous six months, capitulated without resistance. Chiang Kaishek had already moved his headquarters to Formosa, and Mao Tsetung on October 1 had proclaimed the People's Republic of China.

In the course of a few years the Chinese Communists had been transformed from a relatively small, dissident, back-province group whom few outsiders knew much about to a subject of international controversy and finally to an important power on the world scene. Mao Tse-tung—seemingly in contradiction to Stalin's judgment—had accomplished this partly by virtue of China's wartime confusion, weakness, and disillusionment, partly through exploitation of Kuomintang inadequacies, to some degree as a result of Western (particularly American) misapprehensions and errors in judgment, and to a considerable extent through canny deployment and commitment of his ever expanding peasant army.

[92] *Ibid.*, p. 337.

CHAPTER XIV

THE EMERGENCE OF THE PEOPLE'S REPUBLIC

THE NEW DEMOCRACY—WEAPON OF CLASS WARFARE

On September 21, 1949, the Chinese People's Political Consultative Council opened in Peking to announce the establishment of the People's Republic of China and to bring into being the Central People's Government. Ten days later the streets of Peking were jammed with men, women, and children waiting to hear the new government officially proclaimed. From a reviewing stand before the gate of the former imperial palace Mao Tse-tung announced that the Central People's Political Council of the People's Republic of China had just taken office, had unanimously supported the formation of the government, and had adopted the Common Program of the Chinese People's Consultative Conference as the policy of the new regime. The New Democracy had found embodiment.

Around the world there was speculation about the government. In practice, what would the New Democracy be like? Were Mao Tse-tung and his colleagues free men establishing a sovereign state or were they mere puppets of the Russians? Would the regime be in any Western sense democratic, or would it incline toward Stalinist totalitarianism? Would it be something new and specifically Chinese? Should the United States recognize the People's Republic, and what were the prospects for peaceful cooperation between this new China and the democracies of the West?

Even parts of the Communist world were in doubt about the nature and role of the new government. Until the establishment of this new regime in Peking there had been only one source of Communist orthodoxy in the world—Moscow. Now, suddenly, there existed for the movement what might turn out to be a competing Mecca.

Initially the People's Republic of China was established under a Common Program which designated the All-China People's Congress as the supreme organ of state power.[1] Subsequently, on September 20, 1954, the First National People's Congress adopted in its first session the Constitution of the People's Republic of China. Accord-

---

[1] See *China (People's Republic of China, 1949), Laws, statutes, etc., The Important Documents of the First Plenary Session of the Chinese People's Political Consultative Conference* (Peking: Foreign Languages Press, 1949).

ing to Article II of this document, all power in the new state belonged to the people.

And who were the "people"? According to Mao in mid-1949,

At the present stage in China, they are the working class, the peasant class, the petty bourgeoisie, and national bourgeoisie. Under the leadership of the working class and the CP, these classes unite together to form their own state and elect their own government [so as to] carry out a dictatorship over the lackeys of imperialism—the landlord class, the bureaucratic capitalist class, and the KMT reactionaries and their henchmen representing these classes. . . . These two aspects, namely, democracy among the people and dictatorship over the reactionaries, combine to form the people's democratic dictatorship.[2]

The task at that time, Mao asserted, was to strengthen the apparatus of the people's state, that is, the people's army, the people's police, and the people's courts—the "tools of the classes for the oppression of classes"—in order to use them against the reactionaries. The people's state defends the people, he declared.

We decidedly do not adopt a benevolent rule towards the reactionary acts of the reactionaries and the reactionary classes. We only adopt a benevolent administration among the people and not towards the reactionary acts of the reactionaries and reactionary classes outside the people.[3]

What Mao did not say, but what was explicit in his theory and borne out by Communist practice, was this: as the revolution progressed over the years, section after section and class after class would be excluded from the "people" or, in Marxist-Leninist terminology, would "go over to the enemy"—until in the final stages of proletarian dictatorship the last vestiges of the middle class would be rooted out, even down to the peasantry.

The essence of Maoist strategy had been to distrust a tactical alliance with the bourgeoisie until "revolution from below" had gained control over the whole "four-class alliance" of national bourgeoisie, petty bourgeoisie, peasantry, and proletariat. Thus, the government of the New Democracy was designed primarily as a political instrument for imposing sovereignty—under Party hegemony—over all the classes and for guiding the revolution toward its objectives, phase by phase, through the exercise of the power inherent in the Communist movement.

---

[2] Conrad Brandt, Benjamin Schwartz, and John K. Fairbank, *A Documentary History of Chinese Communism* (Cambridge: Harvard University Press, 1952), p. 456; Mao Tse-tung, "On the People's Democratic Dictatorship," *New China News Agency,* July 9, 1949.

[3] *Ibid.*

While achieving control of the Chinese Communist movement during the mid-1930's, Mao Tse-tung had accepted Lenin's concept of class structure and primary antagonisms in China and other underdeveloped countries. As compared with Stalin, however, he had placed relatively less trust in national bourgeois leaders as potential revolutionists. Rather than rely upon national bourgeois troops and governmental structure, Mao had gone into the countryside to organize his own Red Army and governmental institutions—thus ensuring "proletarian hegemony."

The intent of the regime was to mobilize at each revolutionary stage the broadest possible coalition of classes for accomplishing the program at hand. Then, as soon as the class enemy of that particular phase had been disposed of, the regime could assume that the least "revolutionary" class of the coalition—or the most reactionary class —had deserted the "people" and "gone over" to the imperialists.

The further assumption was that as the class struggle progressed —as the strength of the counterrevolutionary forces abated and the power of the workers and peasants increased—the governmental class composition and structure would alter, reflecting the dialectical changes taking place in the society as a whole.

THE REDISTRIBUTION OF LAND

The long-range goal of the People's Republic was to transform China into a modern, industrial power as quickly as possible. In order to achieve this purpose Mao Tse-tung and his colleagues had to find ways of raising vast amounts of capital to serve as a base for building industry and achieving rapid developments in technology. A large proportion of this capital had to be squeezed out of the agricultural economy or raised at the expense of Chinese consumers— including the peasantry.

One of the early undertakings of the Peking regime was the implementation of Mao Tse-tung's agrarian program. In all its fundamentals, Chinese Communist "land reform"—like the programs of the Soviet Russians two decades earlier—was class warfare applied to the countryside, rather than an attempt at terminal "solution" of the basic imbalance between underproductivity and a rapidly increasing population.

A vice-minister of agriculture stated the regime's intentions specifically. The new development of Chinese agriculture, he said, could be divided into three stages: the initial step of agrarian reform; the organization of agricultural production through mutual-aid teams and production cooperatives; and a third stage, which lay in the future—collectivization of agriculture on a nationwide scale after the pattern of collective farming in the Soviet Union.[4]

On June 6, 1950, Mao Tse-tung told the Central Committee of the Chinese Communist party that three steps must be taken immediately in order to improve the economic situation: agrarian reform must be completed, readjustments must be made between commerce and industry, and economies must be effected in government expenditures. A certain length of time was needed, he said, to attain these three conditions. It would take about three years or a little longer.[5] He made clear that the first step, agrarian reform, represented a prerequisite to the main task of industrializing China.

Under the Juichin Republic (1931–34), it will be remembered, the Chinese Communists had attacked the rich peasants, as well as the landlords, a policy which party historians later condemned, and held the Returned Students responsible for. Therefore, the official line made numerous shifts. During the anti-Japanese united front, of course, the Communists made every effort to win over the rich peasant, a policy based not only on premises of the anti-Japanese alliance but also upon the need for maximum agrarian production.

The official attitude toward rich peasants changed again during the post-V-J Day civil war. The Red Army then needed mass peasant support, and therefore land, including the rich peasants' land, was held out to the landless masses as a special inducement. Unlike the Juichin period, however, a distinction in principle was emphasized between the "struggle against the rich peasants" and the "struggle against the landlord." Jen Pi-shih put it this way:

With regard to rich peasants, apart from land, which is equally distributed in common, only the surplus portion of the above named property [plowing animals, agricultural implements, buildings, and so forth] is requisitioned, that is, that portion of their property in excess of the middle peasants in general is requisitioned and not totally confiscated . . . we can only adopt the method of requisitioning their surplus property, and cannot confiscate all their property and buildings; still less can we use the method of "cleaning them out of house and home" in dealing with the rich peasants in general. Neither can we get at the hidden wealth of rich peasants in the same way as we do toward landlords, because the rich peasants themselves engage in labor and a portion of their accumulations is the product of their own labor.[6]

---

[4] Wu Chueh-nung, "Mutual Aid Teams in Chinese Agriculture," *People's China* (Peking), Vol. IV, No. 9 (November 1, 1951), pp. 8–10, 33.

[5] Mao Tse-tung, "Report to the Central Committee of the Communist Party of China, June 6, 1950," *Current Background*, No. 1 (June 13, 1950), p. 3.

[6] Jen Pi-shih, "Agrarian Reform in Communist China," *NCNA*, transmitted to the United States in English Morse, April 16, 1948.

Once the Communists had driven Chiang Kai-shek from the Chinese mainland, party policy toward the rich peasant was altered again. Mao Tse-tung told the Central Committee on June 6, 1950:

The war has been fundamentally ended on the mainland, and the situation is entirely different from that between 1946 and 1948, when the People's Liberation Army was locked in a life and death struggle with the Kuomintang reactionaries and the issue had not yet been decided. Now the government is able to help the poor peasants solve their difficulties by means of loans to balance up the disadvantage of having less land. Therefore, there should be a change in our policy toward the rich peasants, a change from the policy of requisitioning the surplus land and property of the rich peasants to one of preserving a rich peasant economy, in order to help the early restoration of production in rural areas. This change is also favorable for isolating the landlords and for protecting the middle peasants and small "renters-out" of land.[7]

In 1950 the Communists were able to describe the immediate objective of the newly revised Agrarian Reform Law as the setting-free of rural productive forces, the development of agricultural production, and a preparation for the industrialization of the new China. The "struggle against the landlord" now received full emphasis: his land, draft animals, farm implements, and surplus grain must be confiscated, but without infringement upon industry and commerce, both of which must be encouraged for the development of production.

Article 10 of the Agrarian Reform Law assigned confiscated or requisitioned land and other productive instruments—with the exception of those set aside for nationalization—to the *hsiang*[8] peasant associations for distribution "in a unified, equitable, and rational manner" to poor peasants with little or no land and to those lacking other means of production. It was also provided in the law that landlords should be given an equal share in order that they might make a living through their own industry, rather than through "exploitation," and thus "reform themselves through labor."

Fundamental to the redistribution process, according to Article 11, was the principle of allotting requisitioned land to the peasant who had actually been tilling it. The law stated specifically that land owned by "rich" peasants, "well-to-do" middle peasants, and middle peasants generally should be protected from infringement. Legal definitions for these and other class categories were set forth in a slightly revised version of the two documents "How to Analyze Class Status in the Countryside" and "Decisions Concerning Some Problems Aris-

---

[7] Mao Tse-tung, "Report to the Central Committee of the Communist Party of China, June 6, 1950," *Current Background,* No. 1 (June 13, 1950), p. 3.
[8] The *hsiang* is an administrative unit embracing several villages.

ing from Agrarian Reform," promulgated by the Central Government in Juichin seventeen years earlier.[9]

Later, of course, the land confiscated from the landlords and distributed to the peasants was largely "socialized" along with plots that had belonged to peasant owners in the first place.

A primary instrument for the carrying-out of Chinese Communist agrarian reform was the people's tribunal. According to Article 32,

A people's tribunal shall be set up in every *hsien* in the course of agrarian reform to ensure that it is carried out. This tribunal shall travel to different places and try and punish, according to the law, hated despotic elements who have committed heinous crimes, whom the masses of the people demand to be brought to justice, and all such persons who resist or violate the provisions of the Agrarian Reform Law and decrees.[10]

The presiding judge, deputy presiding judge, and half of the ordinary judges of the *hsien* people's tribunal were to be appointed by the appropriate *hsien* government; the remainder of the ordinary judges were to be elected by conferences of representatives of the people, or by mass organizations. The tribunals were empowered to arrest and detain and to pass sentences including confiscation of property, imprisonment and death.

EARLY ECONOMIC POLICIES

In his treatise *On the New Democracy* Mao Tse-tung had stated that all big banks, big industries, and big commercial establishments would be state-owned and all foreign enterprises confiscated, but that there would be no need, at first, for obstructing the development of capitalist production that did no damage to the people's livelihood. "The reason for this procedure," he said, "is that the Chinese economy is still in a very backward state." What Mao meant was that the new democratic state intended to use certain capitalist production techniques in order to prepare the Chinese economy for the first phases of Bolshevik socialism as practiced in the USSR. In this fashion he foresaw state-controlled private enterprises being used as an instrument for the eventual destruction of the institution of private enterprise—a program somewhat similar to the New Economic Policy used in the early 1920's in Soviet Russia.

[9] *People's China* (Peking), Vol. II, No. 8 (October 16, 1950), Supplement.

[10] "The People's Tribunals: Instruments of Agrarian Reform," and "Regulations Governing the Organization of People's Tribunals," *Current Background,* No. 151 (January 10, 1952), pp. 1, 4–6, passed by the Government Administrative Council July 14, 1950, and ratified by Mao Tse-tung as Chairman of the Central People's Government July 19, and promulgated July 20, 1950.

A few months prior to achieving power on the mainland Mao Tse-tung had commented on the "great importance" of the nationalist bourgeoisie under the New Democracy and had stated that the Communist party must "unite with the national bourgeoisie in the common struggle." He then proceeded with important qualifications. "But the national bourgeoisie cannot serve as the leader of the revolution," he warned, "and should not occupy a major position in the state administration. This is because the social and economic status of the national bourgeoisie has determined its weak character, its lack of foresight and of sufficient courage. In addition, quite a few members of this class fear the masses."[11]

With the establishment of the People's Republic of China, Mao Tse-tung again drew distinctions between limited capitalist (or new democratic) and Bolshevik socialist stages of economic development. "The idea of some people who think it possible to bring about an early elimination of capitalism and to introduce socialism," he reported to the Central Committee in mid-1950, "is wrong and unsuitable to the conditions of the country."[12] The chairman of the economic and financial committee of the State Administrative Council and Minister of Heavy Industry, Ch'en Yün, added: "In China, which is backward in industry, it will be progressive and beneficial to the country and the people for the national capitalists to develop industry and make investments in it for a long time."[13] Yet within two years the Chinese People's Republic was initiating a new and drastic policy against private entrepreneurs and enterprises.

At first the punitive power of the new regime was directed toward Kuomintang "war criminals," "feudal landlords," "bureaucratic capitalists," and "other leading incorrigible counter-revolutionary elements who collaborate with imperialism, commit treason against the fatherland, and oppose the people's democracy."[14]

In July 1950 the Government Administrative Council and the Supreme People's Court in Peking issued a joint directive which specifically provided the death sentence for the leaders of gangs "who take up arms against the people's government" and stipulated that leading counterrevolutionaries sentenced to death under this decree

[11] "On the People's Democratic Dictatorship," *loc. cit.*; see also *A Documentary History of Chinese Communism, op. cit.*, pp. 449–63.
[12] Mao Tse-tung, "Report to the Central Committee, June 6, 1950," *Current Background*, Supplement No. 1 (June 13, 1950), p. 4.
[13] Ch'en Yün, "Report to the National Committee of the People's Political Consultative Conference, June 15, 1950," *Current Background*, No. 2 (June 20, 1950), p. 5.
[14] See Chapter I, Article 7, of "The Common Program of the Chinese People's Political Consultative Conference," in *The Important Documents of the First Plenary Session of the Chinese People's Political Conference.*

were not to be permitted appeal. At about the same time provisions were made for setting up new people's tribunals, as noted above, which (unlike the people's courts with jurisdiction over the usual civil and criminal cases) were established to deal with cases emerging from the agrarian reform program.[15]

In October the Supreme People's Court and its regional branches condemned the widespread deviation of "boundless magnanimity" so far characteristic of judicial procedure; and some weeks later Chou En-lai, developing Mao's premises of July 1, 1949, reasoned that whereas in earlier periods the majority of the people suffered minority control, under the Communist regime the majority, quite rightly, must control the minority. On these terms, law was described, in now familiar fashion, as "a tool in the hands of the ruling class to control the ruled class" and "boundless magnanimity" was officially condemned as "harmful to the people."

Toward the end of the year there were editorial charges that this dangerous deviation had not yet been rectified, and finally on February 21, 1951, the "Regulations of the People's Republic of China for Punishment of Counter-Revolutionaries" were promulgated by Mao Tse-tung. Calling for "rigorous and timely" suppression of all counterrevolutionary activities, the government listed more than a score of charges of counterrevolutionary propaganda, plotting, spying, crossing the state frontier with counterrevolutionary purposes, organizing jail breaks, and many others—each one of which was punishable by imprisonment, life imprisonment, or death.[16]

With somewhat grim humor the Peking *Current Affairs Journal* (*Jen-min Shou-ts'e*) on May 20, 1951, made the following comment on execution as one of the three methods (together with control and imprisonment) of carrying out the suppression of counterrevolutionaries: "Execution means fundamental physical elimination of counter-revolutionaries and is, of course, the most thorough and severe measure of depriving counter-revolutionaries of their conditions for counter-revolutionary activities."[17]

THE "3-ANTI" AND "5-ANTI" CAMPAIGNS

After the outbreak of war in Korea, and especially during the early months of 1952, the Communist regime broadened and deep-

[15] See Articles 7 and 8 of "Regulations Governing the Organization of People's Tribunals," *Current Background*, No. 44 (December 22, 1950), p. 2.

[16] "Suppression of Counter-Revolutionaries," *Current Background*, No. 101 (July 24, 1951).

[17] *Ibid.*

ened its offensive, initiating a "3-Anti's Campaign" against "corruption, decay, and bureaucracy." The seriousness of Communist intent can be judged from remarks made by Kao Kang in a "Report at the Higher Level Cadres Meeting of the Northeast Bureau of the Central Committee of the Chinese Communist Party," January 10, 1952:

The following shall be accomplished during the present campaign . . . Purge all departments of corruption, waste and bureaucracy. The cases of corruption and waste should be given penalties ranging from dismissal, prison terms, labor reform to death sentence.[18]

The purpose of these measures appeared to be threefold: to ensure cleaner and more efficient government, to promote class struggle against groups considered inimical to Chinese Communist interests at this particular stage of the revolution, and to cleanse the party itself of undesirable personnel.

While the "3-Anti" movement was striking out against corruption, waste, and bureaucracy—primarily in the Party and in the government—the Chinese Communists launched a new "5-Anti" struggle against (1) bribery, (2) tax evasion, (3) theft of state assets, (4) cheating, and (5) theft of state economic secrets. During this campaign the argument was developed that, on moving from a rural to an urban environment, many party members had fallen victim to the "fierce attacks" and the "corrosion" of the bourgeois class, which must therefore be held fundamentally responsible for all corruption in Communist China. The Communists switched their chief target, therefore, from "corrupt officials" to "lawbreaking merchants."[19]

In its struggle against the "corrupt" bourgeoisie the Communist regime established statutes which graded cases according to seriousness and the willingness of the accused to "confess" and laid down five forms of punishment: surveillance by government organs, reform through labor service, imprisonment for a fixed period, life imprisonment, and death.

Following hard on the "5-Anti" campaign came the announcement in early 1953 of a Five-Year Plan of national construction aimed at transforming China from an agricultural to an industrial nation. Chinese Communist writers, with voluminous quotations from Lenin and Stalin, made it clear that in undertaking this task, the People's Republic "follows the path of the Soviet Union, which, guided by

[18] "Overcome the Corrosion of Bourgeois Ideology; Oppose the Rightist Trend in the Party," *Current Background,* No. 163 (March 5, 1952), p. 58.

[19] "The Communists and the Bourgeoisie," *Current Background,* No. 166 (March 14, 1952), p. 2.

Marxist-Leninist economic theory, accomplished such a transformation at a speed unprecedented in history."[20]

Like other Communist-controlled governments, the People's Republic of China developed cultural and educational activities as weapons in the all-pervading class struggle. In September 1950, Kuo Mojo—historian, dramatist, and essayist of world-wide reputation, who joined the Communist government, serving as vice-premier and chairman of the Committee of Cultural and Educational Affairs of the State Administrative Council—declared: "The concrete task of our cultural and educational work today lies chiefly in 'the eradication of feudalistic, compradore, and fascist ways of thought, and in the development of the ideology of serving the people' . . ."[21] Other closely related tasks included training industrial and agricultural cadres and strengthening educational, scientific, and public health activities.

For the carrying out of indoctrination, or "political study," the Chinese Communists established after-work schools and "winter study" movements for workers, peasants, and intellectuals. Concurrently, programs were inaugurated for opening higher educational institutions to industrial and agricultural cadres and to young men and women chosen from among worker and peasant masses. Educational reorganization and the development of techniques and procedures were based frankly upon Soviet Russian precedents. In this connection we must keep in mind that thousands of young Chinese men and women had been sent to the USSR for study over the prior thirty years.

First of all, the Chinese Communists sought to eradicate traditional habits of thought and to instill a new pattern based on Marxism-Leninism. But beyond this, and even fundamental to it, Mao and his colleagues were compelled to train as rapidly as possible personnel, both trusted and qualified, to accomplish the economic, social, and political programs of the New Democracy.

After 1950 there were numerous readjustments in the content of popular indoctrination, each determined by shifts in party policy and changing tactical requirements. The masses, in short, must be prepared for successive new developments: for agrarian reform, for the "3-Anti's" and the "5-Anti's," for participation in the Korean war.

[20] Li Chen, "How China Will Industrialize," *People's China*, No. 3 (February 1, 1953), p. 10.

[21] Kuo Mo-jo, "Cultural and Educational Work During the Past Year," *Current Background*, No. 15 (October 19, 1950), p. 1.

Newspapers, radio, schools, music, art, books, and drama are all used for indoctrination purposes. "Who is a propagandist?" Mao asked in *Opposing Party Formalism*, which appeared in February 1942. "Not only is the teacher a propagandist, the newspaper reporter a propagandist, the literary writer a propagandist, but all our cadres in all kinds of work are propagandists . . . Any person engaged in talking with another is a propagandist."[22]

The Communists established new schools on all levels, and special efforts were made to set up institutions of higher learning modeled after those in the Soviet Union and to reorganize old institutions after the same pattern. Heavy emphasis was placed upon technical schools and institutions for applied scientific research. On all levels and in all categories of practical instruction, the Communists paralleled each phase of specialized training with appropriate political indoctrination.

Of utmost importance—as point of contact between the party and the masses—was the cadre, and in all parts of China special schools were organized to train personnel for these units. In April 1950 the Communists established in Peking a Worker-Peasant Middle School with 116 students in attendance—all between the ages of sixteen and thirty and each with three to thirteen years of experience in revolutionary work. One twenty-two-year-old student had joined the Eighth Route Army at the age of ten and had worked since as a mimeograph operator for the Party. A peasant woman of twenty-three had been a party member for six years and was already a veteran at cadre work in the countryside.[23] By the end of 1950 the Communists had established twenty-four schools of this variety alone, with a total enrollment of more than 4,000 men and women who had already spent three to eight years in revolutionary work.

The core program for the political training of cadres was developed from the basic writings of Marx, Engels, Lenin, Stalin, and various other orthodox Russian Communist theoreticians and from the works of Mao and Liu Shao-ch'i. Cadremen were taught to scorn all concern for position, treatment, and compensation, and to devote themselves to "the life job that has no limit," the reforming of their own society and the world. "We as the proletarian vanguard armed with Marxism-Leninism aim at the liberation of the entire human race," boasted an editorial in *Jen-min Jih-pao,* October 10, 1950. "We are politically conscious and strictly disciplined and possess the weapons of criticism and self-criticism, which old-fashioned revolutionists

---

[22] An English translation is available in Boyd Compton, *Mao's China: Party Reform Documents, 1942–44* (Seattle, 1952), pp. 33–53.
[23] Chen Tan, "A Worker-Peasant School," *People's China,* Vol. II, No. 4 (August 16, 1950), pp. 22–24.

never have had or could have. Therefore, we will not repeat the mistakes of history."

Struggle, as Liu Shao-ch'i had emphasized as far back as 1941, continued within the Party and even into the most disciplined cadre. During 1952 a series of charges were leveled against agrarian reform cadres, especially in Kwangtung, where party workers were accused of "belittling" the landlord enemy, of self-satisfaction, of lassitude, of tiring of country life and longing for the city, and of an "ideological tendency toward haste." Struggles staged against the rural "despots" and landlords were not carried out for the overthrow of the enemy, but merely to "pass over" an assignment. In some localities conferences of the cadres had replaced meetings of the peasants themselves. A local party leader warned:

Let the cadres proceed into the midst of the masses, the poor peasants and hired hands, and in a penetrative manner look into their basic conditions, understand their situation. Let them undertake a penetrative investigation of the enemy situation, his strength and his organization.[24]

During the course of these inner "struggles" for "purification" large numbers of cadremen were warned, dismissed from their posts, or even expelled from the party.

In seeking to transform the individual, Chinese Communist thought reformers drew sharp contrasts between the corrupt and evil "old society" and the new society of "new men." Since many intellectuals had come from the old "exploiting classes" or from the contaminated, wavering petty bourgeoisie, the assumption was that they must retain "evil remnants" of their family origins and of the old regime. Each must therefore cleanse himself of such "ideological poisons," purge out the old forces, and save himself by merging utterly with the "new society."[25]

If a subject resisted, if he refused to press the inner struggle against the "evil forces" within him, he might be subjected to the ultimate humility of a mass "struggle" meeting. There, in ritualistic form, he was denounced publicly and his deficiencies laid bare before the thought reformers and also before his fellows. Under pressures of this sort the anxiety and general tension level were to reach an unbearable level where the subject sought relief through conversion without further resistance.[26]

---

[24] Ou-yang Wen, "Correction of Cadres' Mistakes in Ideology and Work Style Is Key to Success in Agrarian Reform," *Current Background*, No. 184 (June 12, 1952), p. 14.

[25] Robert J. Lifton, "Thought Reform of Chinese Intellectuals, A Psychiatric Evaluation," *Journal of Asian Studies*, Vol. XVI, No. 1 (November 1956), p. 77.

[26] *Ibid.*, p. 80.

Over the years these mass thought reform and transformation programs were carried out on a larger and larger scale—and often with a pseudo-religious intensity. For many young Chinese, and even for mature scholars and professional men, the point of final transformation was marked by a detailed and vitriolic denunciation of the father.[27]

As in the Soviet Union, the human cost of these widespread transformations—political, economic and psychological—was high. Without doubt the Chinese Communist planners were increasing national production—but not without intimidation and regimentation, the reduction of individual human consumption, which had been abysmally low to begin with, and the systematic use of forced labor. Estimates of the number of individuals sentenced to forced labor during this period vary from about 14 million upward.[28]

In applying this program in the Northwest, Kao Kang, at that time the fifth-ranking leader in the party, decreed: "Purge all departments of corruption, waste and bureaucracy. The cases of corruption and waste shall be given penalties ranging from dismissal, prison terms and labor reform to the death sentence."[29] Precisely how many Chinese were executed under these laws cannot be fixed, but even the most conservative estimates ran into several million.

Later Kao Kang himself was purged "for conspiratorial activities aimed at seizing the reins of leadership of the Party and the state."[30] The expulsion, made public in 1955 and discussed with unconcealed satisfaction before the Eighth Congress in September 1956 by Liu Shao-ch'i, appeared somewhat superfluous since Kao Kang, it was revealed, had committed suicide a year earlier.

COLLECTIVIZATION AND THE HUNDRED FLOWERS

In the countryside, too, Chinese Communist leaders began moving toward a first stage of Bolshevik socialism. The distribution of land

[27] For detailed analyses of the thought-control program and processes see Theodore H. E. Chen, *Thought Reform and the Chinese Intellectuals* (Hong Kong: Hong Kong University Press, 1960); Robert Jay Lifton, *Thought Reform and the Psychology of Totalism* (New York: W. W. Norton, 1961); Edgar H. Schein with Inge Schneier and Curtis H. Barker, *Coercive Persuasion* (New York: W. W. Norton, 1961).

[28] Yuan-li Wu, *An Economic Survey of Communist China* (New York: Bookman Associates, 1956), pp. 322–25; see also Karl A. Wittfogel, "Forced Labor in Communist China," *Problems of Communism*, No. 4 (July–August, 1956), pp. 34–42.

[29] "Overcome the Corrosion of Bourgeois Ideology; Oppose the Rightist Trend in the Party," *Current Background*, No. 163 (March 5, 1952), p. 58.

[30] "Resolution on the Kao Kang–Jao Shu-shih Anti-Party Alliance," *Current Background*, No. 324 (April 5, 1955), p. 4.

to the poor peasants had scarcely been completed before collectivization began. During 1955–56 the peasants were organized into collectives at an astonishing rate. In the summer of 1955, according to one estimate, no more than 15 percent of China's 110 million or so households had been organized into producers' cooperatives, which were not, strictly speaking, collectivized. A year later, however, more than 100 million households, or approximately 90 percent of the peasantry, had been gathered into cooperative organizations. More than 73 million of these belonged to "higher," fully socialized cooperatives similar to those in other Communist countries.[31] According to Liu Shao-ch'i, some 110 million households had been organized into one million cooperatives at the time of the Eighth Congress.[32]

Inevitably, in carrying out these offensives, the Peking leadership began to lose the support of many Chinese who had once sympathized with the regime.

Early in 1956 the Chinese Communist leadership initiated the "Hundred Flowers Movement" in an effort to regain the cooperation of intellectuals before continuing on the "forced march" toward industrialization. In the early days of the regime large numbers of intellectuals had supported the Chinese Communists as a hopeful alternative to the confusions and inadequacies of Chiang Kai-shek's Kuomintang. With the "3-Anti," "5-Anti," and other campaigns of suppression and uprooting, however, more and more of the intellectuals had become disenchanted with the new government.

The response to Peking's invitation to "Let A Hundred Flowers Bloom and A Hundred Schools of Thought Contend" could hardly have been anticipated by Mao and his colleagues. After initially cautious comments, Chinese intellectuals in early May began answering the party's invitation to "boldly criticize" its defects with a volume and intensity of criticism that momentarily stunned the leadership, and sustained efforts were required to shut the new Pandora's box once it had been opened.[33] A part of the basic issue was the degree to which the intellectual must be "Red" as well as "expert" to take part in planning and implementing the march toward industrialization.

[31] N. P. Smith, "Mao's Forced March to Collectivization," *Problems of Communism*, No. 5 (September–October, 1956), p. 23.

[32] Liu Shao-ch'i, "Political Report," *NCNA*, Peking, in English Morse to Europe, September 16, 1956; see also *Current Background*, No. 412 (September 28, 1956), p. 10.

[33] Roderick MacFarquhar, *The Hundred Flowers Campaign and the Chinese Intellectuals* (New York: Frederick A. Praeger, 1960); also Dennis Doolin, "Hundred Flowers: Mao's Miscalculation," an unpublished manuscript prepared for the Studies in International Conflict and Integration, Stanford University, March 17, 1961.

By 1961 it was evident that the regime still badly needed both the talents and the political loyalty of the intellectuals in its drive for great-power world status. With recollections of the 1957 "Hundred Flowers" still vividly in mind, however, Chinese intellectuals tended to feel "once bitten, twice shy,"[34] a consequent uneasiness about further invitations to "bloom and contend." Under these circumstances the party proceeded with more realism, being careful to present ground rules for the new campaign and providing for a strict differentiation of academic discussion from ideological contention. This time it was made clear that the discussions must unite the people, not divide them, strengthen party leadership, consolidate the People's Democratic Dictatorship, facilitate socialist transformation, and encourage socialist solidarity and the "solidarity of the peace-loving peoples of the world."[35] Within these limits the flowers were free to bloom and the various schools of thought to contend.

By conceding that the non-Communist intellectual need not be entirely "Red," the regime was hoping to draw more effectively upon his specialized knowledge and expertise.

THE FORCED MARCH TO SOCIALIZATION

The Eighth Congress of the Chinese Communist Party, convened in Peking in September 1956, was the first such gathering since 1945. Reviewing and assessing progress during this crucial eleven-year span, Mao Tse-tung in his opening address declared that in spite of certain mistakes, his cadres on the whole had performed their tasks "correctly": ". . . since the Seventh Congress we have, in this country with its vast territory, huge population and complex conditions, completed the bourgeois democratic revolution and we have also gained a decisive victory in the social revolution."[36]

When the Seventh Congress convened at Yenan (April 23–June 11, 1945) Chiang Kai-shek's government had its seat at Chungking, Japanese forces maintained control over large areas of China, and the Chinese Communists, taking what advantage they could of the wartime confusion, were consolidating their strength in the Border Region Governments of the Northwest.

By 1956, according to Mao, the immediate task facing the CCP was to complete the transformation of China from a backward agri-

---

[34] Dennis Doolin, "The Revival of the 'Hundred Flowers' Campaign: 1961," *The China Quarterly*, No. 8 (October–December, 1961), pp. 34–41.

[35] *Ibid.*, pp. 34–35.

[36] Mao Tse-tung to the CCP Congress, September 15, 1956. The text appears in the *New York Times,* September 15, 1956, and in *Current Background,* No. 412 (September 28, 1956), p. 1.

256   MOSCOW AND CHINESE COMMUNISTS

cultural society into an industrialized socialist state. The Chinese
Communist leader described this undertaking as similar to that which
the Soviet Union had faced in the early years of its history. "So we
must be good at studying," Mao declared. "We must be good at learning from our forerunners . . ."[37]

Chinese Communist leaders told the Eighth Congress that three
five-year plans would be required for the completion of industrialization in China. Heavy industry goals of the First Five-Year Plan,
according to official predictions, would be overfulfilled by its termination date the following year. The Second Five-Year Plan was being
designed to continue development of five major objectives: industrial construction with emphasis on heavy industry; ideological indoctrination, social transformations, and "remolding of individuals";
industrial, agricultural, and handicraft production, transportation, and
commerce; the wiping out of illiteracy and the training of technical
and scientific personnel; and higher levels of material and cultural life
within the Communist pattern.[38]

The Second Five-Year Plan was proclaimed at the Congress as
a program for pushing China into competition with the West—and
well along the road toward "pure" communism.[39] "Twenty years
concentrated into a day" was the Maoist slogan. The actual amount
of money spent on the Second Five-Year Plan, according to Chou
En-lai, would be twice that spent on the First Five-Year Plan. By
1962, he predicted, the value of China's industrial production would
be double that planned for 1957, and the value of agricultural production would be 35 percent higher than the 1957 goal.[40]

Attending the Eighth Congress, along with representatives from
other Communist parties of the world, was a Soviet delegation led by
A. I. Mikoyan, a member of the Presidium of the Central Committee
of the Communist Party of the Soviet Union and first Vice-Chairman
of the Council of Ministers of the USSR. Stalin, during later years
of his life, had seen to it that Soviet hegemony in the world Communist movement had remained unchallenged, and that only he among
Communist leaders received official credit as theoretician and party
ideologist. Mikoyan, by contrast, gave credit to Mao Tse-tung for

[37] *Current Background, ibid.,* p. 2.

[38] Liu Shao-ch'i, *NCNA,* Peking, in English Morse to Europe, September 16,
1956; see also Liu Shao-ch'i, "Political Report," *Current Background,* No. 412 (September 28, 1956), pp. 4–55.

[39] "Proposals on the Second Five Year Plan for the Development of the National Economy," adopted by the Eighth Party Congress, September 27, 1956, *Current Background,* No. 413 (October 5, 1956), pp. 33–48.

[40] Chou En-lai, "Report on the Second Five Year Plan," September 16, 1956,
Current Background, No. 413 (October 5, 1956), pp. 1–32.

major theoretical contributions and hailed him as a creative adapter and developer of Marxism-Leninism. In achieving—through the transitional stage of the New Democracy—the "participation" of the national bourgeoisie and in adapting various tactics in order to collectivize farmers and wipe out private enterprise, the Chinese leadership had developed "new forms and new methods of socialist construction."[41]

During the early months of 1958 Peking announced the intention of taking a "Great Leap Forward" in economic development.[42] Plans included the building of "back-yard" furnaces for the production of pig iron in rural areas and early communization of the peasants. Existing targets were scrapped in favor of higher and higher new goals: in the course of a few months more than 700,000 collective farms were transformed into a total of over 26,000 rural communes. In many of these collectives the rigorous discipline equaled and probably surpassed the regimentation achieved by Soviet planners during the most radical phases of Stalin's drive for socialization.

In the summer of 1959 it became evident, however, that immediate targets for the Great Leap Forward were far out of Chinese reach. By August 26 of that year Peking was admitting that 1958 production figures had been seriously exaggerated and drastic reductions were being made in 1959 output goals.[43]

Over ensuing years the Great Leap Forward gave more and more the appearance of a downward spiral. The Chinese mainland fell under a cycle of unfavorable weather, and flood and famine began to take a serious toll. At the same time many of the shrewdest and most competent of the Chinese peasantry—men and women whose ancestors for generations had met most effectively the challenges of soil and climate—had been displaced or even eliminated by the class struggle campaigns in the countryside. Other peasants, with no other ready means of defense against the regime, were accused of withholding their own human fertilizer from the state and using it on the small private plots which Peking planners found it increasingly advisable to assign.

Chinese Communist planners must have been mindful of the his-

[41] A. I. Mikoyan, "Address to CCP 8th Congress," transmitted by Moscow, *Tass,* in English Hellschreiber, September 17, 1956. For an English translation of the Chinese text released by *NCNA,* see *Current Background,* No. 415 (October 8, 1956), pp. 1–16.

[42] Liu Shao-ch'i, "The Present Situation, the Party's General Line for Socialist Construction and Its Future Tasks," a report of May 5, 1958, to the second session of the Eighth Party Congress, *Current Background,* No. 507 (June 2, 1958), pp. 1–25.

[43] "Mass Rallies Greet CCP Production Call" *NCNA* radioteletype in English to West and North Europe, August 27, 1959.

torical fact that it has been first of all on the basis of agricultural failure that the Chinese masses have perceived the Mandate of Heaven withdrawn.

RELATIONS WITH ASIAN STATES

There are good reasons why Communist China's relations with other Asian states are likely to appear ambivalent. Over the years both Russian and Chinese Communist leaders had ascribed to China a key position in the development of revolutionary movements in Asia. As far back as 1926, it will be remembered, Dimitrii Manuilsky had predicted the defeat of Japan, followed by a transformation of the conflict into a vast "liberation movement" of Asian countries oppressed by world imperialism. A "liberated" China, he said, would develop into a major power in the Pacific, a magnet for all the peoples of the yellow race in East Asia, a menacing threat to the capitalist world of three continents. And similarly, Nicolai Bukharin had described China as "a great center of attraction for awakening the masses of the Colonial East" and had predicted that in time the capital of a revolutionary China would become "a sort of Red Moscow" for the rising masses of Asian countries.[44] Less than twenty-five years later world Communist leaders could hail Mao's China as the model for other Bolshevik-led revolutions in Asia.[45]

It will be recalled that until the beginning of the last century China had lived in splendid sovereignty, the great and powerful Middle Kingdom surrounded by tribute-paying "barbarians" beneath the dignity of equal treatment. With the Opium War of 1839—only a little more than one hundred years ago—the gates flew open and Westerners came tramping in. Because of his technological superiority the foreigner demanded—and obtained—privilege. China became a wide-open field for exploitation, while the Chinese people were relegated to second-class citizenship within their own borders and otherwise humiliated. Once China's foreign relations had consisted largely of receiving tribute from surrounding states. Now the circumstances were reversed; China, in effect, found itself a tributary of the West.

Many sensitive Chinese looked Westward for salvation. If the West had been strong enough to humiliate China, could not the Chinese people regain status by learning and adapting from the West? Politically naïve though he undoubtedly was, Sun Yat-sen looked to Europe and the United States for help; his aim was to establish a de-

<hr>

[44] *International Press Correspondence*, December 30, 1926, pp. 1592–97.
[45] "Mighty Advance of the National Liberation Movement in the Colonial and Dependent Countries," *For a Lasting Peace, For a People's Democracy*, January 27, 1950, p. 1.

mocracy. The West, had it enjoyed sufficient insight, might have recognized this juncture as a road fork. But the world's democracies tended to distrust revolutionists, even those who were democratically inclined, and to commit themselves to the notion that the Chinese "understood" nothing but force, tradition, and a corporate society. To many Western diplomats the war lords, several of whom learned well the value of prating Confucius, looked like "realists" in reassuring contrast to Sun Yat-sen, the "idealist." In consequence, the West tried to shore up the Peking government while Sun Yat-sen went begging—to the Soviet Union.

Now, in many Chinese eyes—both Communist and non-Communist—the People's Republic, whatever else one might say about it, had achieved the power and prestige it sought. The foreigner was now restricted, his privileges extinguished. Great Britain, shadow of an empire that once expanded at Chinese expense, had proposed mutual recognition, and Mao Tse-tung, the Hunan peasant, had been secure enough to table the suggestion. Infantry and tanks of the United States had driven to the Yalu River in Korea, and the peasant Red Army of China, for all its inferior weapons, was able to throw them back. For many Chinese—even for some who despised the new ideology—these were proud and revengeful moments in Chinese history.

The significance of China's victories over white men's diplomacy and white men's armies has not been lost on the peoples of other subject and recently subject peoples from South Africa to Indochina. There were good reasons why Communist China, even more than the Soviet Union, was frequently looked upon as the most likely and effective champion of the "underdogs" from Asia and Africa to Latin America.

The record showed, on the other hand, that Mao had not forgotten the ancient relationships which bound the tributary states of Asia to the Chinese Empire. With exaggeration, but almost in the same words which both Sun Yat-sen and Chiang Kai-shek had used, he wrote:

In defeating China in war, the imperialist powers have taken away many Chinese dependent states and a part of her territories. Japan took Korea, Taiwan, and the Ryukyu Islands, the Pescadores Islands, Port Arthur; England seized Burma, Bhutan, Nepal, and Hongkong; France occupied Annam; and even an insignificant country like Portugal . . . took Macau.[46]

[46] Mao Tse-tung, "The Chinese Revolution and the Chinese Communist Party" (published in Chinese, November 15, 1939; translated into English and mimeographed March 22, 1949), p. 4. Cf. Chiang Kai-shek, *China's Destiny* (New York: Macmillan Co., 1947), p. 34. The original Chinese edition, published in Chungking in 1943, included Korea among the territories lost to China. Sun Yat-sen was even more

This was not simply a Communist speaking. Among other things, this was a bitter nationalist who had convinced himself that communism—and only communism—could win back for China what most Chinese felt their country had lost.

The advance of Chinese Communist troops into one former tributary state, Korea, could be rationalized on various grounds: the move may have been dictated by Moscow; the Chinese may have been driven to it by a fear, however unjustified, that the United States intended to invade Manchuria; the Chinese may simply have risen to the defense of Communist comrades, hard-pressed. Probably each of these factors played its role. But the fact remains that Mao still remembers Korea as a "dependent state" seized from China by Japan.[47]

In a New Year's message early in 1950 the Chinese People's Republic declared that Tibet (a country over which Chinese suzerainty —from the eighteenth century until 1912—had been loose at best, but which all nationalist leaders have made much of) was, in fact, a part of "continental China." In October Chinese Communist forces invaded the country and set up military and administrative headquarters.

A year later there were reports of Chinese Communist infiltration

---

explicit than Mao or Chiang in identifying territories which at one time or another had belonged to the Chinese Empire: "Beginning with recent history, we have lost Weihaiwei, Port Arthur, Dairen, Tsingtau, Kowloon, Kwangchow-wan. After the European War, the Powers thought to return some of the more recent cessions and gave back Tsingtau and just lately Weihaiwei. But these are only small places . . . Further back in history, our territorial losses were Korea, Taiwan (Formosa), the Pescadores, and such places, which, as a result of the Sino-Japanese War, were ceded to Japan. It was this war which started the 'slicing of China' talk among the Powers.

"Still further back in the century, we lost Burma and Annam. China did put up a slight opposition at the time to giving up Annam . . . Annam and Burma were both formerly Chinese territory; as soon as Annam was ceded to France, England occupied Burma, and China did not dare to protest. Still earlier in the history of territorial losses were the Amur and Ussuri river basins and before that the areas north of the Ili, Khokand, and Amur rivers—the territory of the recent Far Eastern Republic—all of which China gave over with folded hands to the foreigner without so much as a question. In addition there are those small countries which at one time paid tribute to China—the Loochoo Islands, Siam, Borneo, the Sulu Archipelago, Java, Ceylon, Nepal, Bhutan.

"In its age of greatest power, the territory of the Chinese Empire was very large, extending northward to the north of the Amur, southward to the south of the Himalayas, eastward to the China Sea, westward to the T'sung Lin. Nepal in the first year of the Republic was still bringing tribute into Szechwan, and then stopped because of the impassability of the roads through Tibet. When China was strongest, her political power inspired awe on all sides, and not a nation south and west of China but considered it an honor to bring her tribute." Sun Yat-sen, San Min Chu I (Chungking: Ministry of Information of the Republic of China, 1943), p. 35.

[47] For a brilliant analysis of Communist China's entry into the Korean war, see Allen S. Whiting, China Crosses the Yalu (New York: Macmillan Co., 1960).

of Nepal from Tibet,[48] of rapid growth on the part of the Nepalese Communist party, and local estimates of a Chinese Communist take-over within a matter of a few years.[49] Lending depth to these accounts, the May 30, 1951, issue of *Pravda* charged Great Britain with illegal seizure of Bhutan in 1890, while in August Robert Trumbull, quoting "unimpeachable sources" in the area, reported systematic Chinese Communist infiltration of Afghanistan, Nepal, Bhutan, and Sikkim as a forerunner to penetration of India itself.[50] Concurrently, there were persistent accounts of Chinese Communist support of Viet Minh forces in Indochina, and in the spring of 1953 there came word of an "independent" Thai People's Republic in Yunnan province near the Burma-Thailand-Indochina borders.

The only considerable respite in this persistent application of Chinese pressure against border countries to the south came in 1954 and early 1955 with the *Panch Shila* and Spirit of Bandung. In June 1953 a truce had been signed in Korea which provided a measure of stability in Northeast Asia. At about the same time Ho Chi-minh had intensified his campaign against the French in Indochina, and the Peking regime began sending him supplies. With the Geneva settlement in 1954 Vietnam was divided at the 17th parallel. Momentarily it appeared that a turning point had been reached.

On June 28, 1954, Prime Minister Jawaharlal Nehru of India and Prime Minister Chou En-lai of the People's Republic of China issued a joint communiqué identifying "Five Principles" which should guide relations between the two states: (1) mutual respect for each other's territorial integrity and sovereignty; (2) nonaggression; (3) non-interference in each other's internal affairs; (4) equality and mutual benefit; and (5) peaceful coexistence.[51] The two prime ministers also endorsed the proposition that these same principles ought to be observed by the two states in their relations with other countries in Asia and the rest of the world. Subsequently these *Panch Shila* were affirmed by Chou En-lai and U Nu as the foundation for Sino-Burmese relations.

At about the same time Peking was supporting Viet Minh forces in Indochina, however, and there were persistent rumors of Chinese Communist employment of Burmese and Thai minorities in Yunan province for extending political influence across the frontiers of Burma

[48] *New York Times,* December 13, 1951, p. 1.
[49] *Ibid.,* December 15, 1951, p. 3.
[50] *Ibid.,* August 26, 1952, p. 1.
[51] Extract from the joint statement of the Prime Ministers of India and China, June 28, 1954, as issued by the Press Information Bureau, New Delhi, and reproduced in S. L. Poplai, *Asia and Africa in the Modern World* (Bombay: Asia Publishing House, 1955), Appendix VI, p. 206.

and Thailand. An English-language newspaper in Rangoon, the *Nation,* reported that Chinese Communist forces had seized 1,000 square miles of Burmese territory, penetrating nearly sixty miles inside the country. And a spokesman for the Indian government asserted on December 31, 1954, that maps published by the Peking regime represented parts of Nepal, Burma, and India—including parts of Kashmir —as Chinese territory.[52]

Yet some months later, in an address to delegates from twenty-nine states represented at the Asian-African Conference in Bandung, Indonesia, Chou En-lai added two further points to the *Panch Shila* affirmations: recognition of equality of races and respect for the rights of the people of all nations to choose their own way of life and their own economic and political systems.[53] A final public announcement of the Bandung Conference urged that the participating nations should "practice tolerance and live together in peace with one another as good neighbors and develop friendly cooperation" on the basis of ten principles which derived from earlier statements. To these it added respect for the right of each country to defend itself singly or collectively, in conformance with the Charter of the United Nations; abstention from the use of collective defense arrangements to serve the special interests of the big powers; abstention by any country from exerting pressure on other countries; settlement of international disputes by peaceful means; and respect for justice and international obligations.[54]

Chou En-lai admitted at the conference that certain frontiers were not "satisfactorily established," but he offered reassurances that the Peking regime stood ready to negotiate and, in the meantime, "to restrain our government and people from taking even one step across our border."

The *Panch Shila* and the Spirit of Bandung were hailed and invoked in many countries as symbolic of a new era of cooperation and good will cutting across ideological, as well as national, frontiers. Further difficulties soon developed along Chinese borders, however.

The Chinese Communist leaders may not have been prepared for the bitter opposition they encountered as the Peking regime extended control over minority nationalities. In fact, however, the farther the Communists pushed from China proper into outlying regions the more

[52] Girilal Jain, *Chinese "Panchsheela" in Burma* (Bombay: Democratic Research, 1956), pp. 24–29.

[53] Chou En-lai's speech to the Political Committee of the Asian-African Conference, April 23, 1955, in George McTurnan Kahin, *The Asian-African Conference* (Ithaca: Cornell University Press, 1956), pp. 60–61.

[54] Final communiqué of the Asian-African Conference, Bandung, April 24, 1955, *ibid.,* Appendix, pp. 84–85.

overt the opposition became. By carrying Marxist-Leninist-Maoist organization into these areas, indeed, the Peking regime made it possible for hitherto disorganized peoples to protest Chinese control with some effectiveness.[55]

Even Communist leaders among the Thai and other minorities in Yunnan, Mongol groups in Inner Mongolia, and Kazakhs and Uighurs in Sinkiang were vociferous about the encroachments of Han, or Chinese, influence over local enclaves.[56] In a keynote address before a four-month conference of the Party Committee of the Sinkiang Uighur Autonomous Region—with 381 local party functionaries attending—Sinkiang Party Secretary Saifudin admitted that local nationalism was particularly strong among the intellectuals. "The growth is remarkable in some places and has become the most dangerous ideological trend of the present time." Some nationalists, he said, seemed to think that the Han people had brought disaster to Sinkiang and that "everything would be all right" if the Han people would only leave. With the influx of Chinese, "some people have even expressed the fear that the local nationalities may just 'vanish.' "[57]

At this same conference the First Secretary of the Regional Committee, Wang En-mao, complained that the local nationalities never talked of Sinkiang as an integral part of China. "In their mind's eye they see Sinkiang as antagonistic to the motherland, as an independent state, not a part of China."[58] Other minority groups had even cherished hopes of "the occurrence of a Hungarian incident in the country to enable Sinkiang to achieve 'independence.' "[59]

By 1958 similar conditions were evident in Tibet, where the Communist "correctional" method of demanding and publicizing self-criticism furnished an index of local attitudes. "In the past two years," admitted a postal employee in Lhasa, "I have learned some new knowledge and become arrogant, thereby giving rise to the growth of the ideology of local nationalism. I did not find the Han cadres any more

---

[55] Wang Feng, Vice-Chairman of the Nationalities Affairs Commission, State Council, "On the Rectification Campaign and Socialist Education Among the Minority Nationalities," at the Fifth (Enlarged) Meeting of the Nationalities Committee of the First National People's Congress, February 9, 1958, *Current Background*, No. 495 (March 5, 1958), pp. 5–6.

[56] See "The Building of Socialism Is Impossible Without Opposition to Local Nationalism," *ibid.*, No. 500 (March 31, 1958), p. 5; also K'uei Pi, "Mongol People's Prosperity Is Inseparable from Han People's Help," *ibid.*, p. 10.

[57] "Saifudin Reports on Local Nationalism at the Enlarged Meeting of the CCP Sinkiang Region Committee," *ibid.*, No. 512 (July 10, 1958), pp. 9, 16.

[58] Wang En-mao, "Struggle to Implement the Party's Marxist-Leninist Line for Solution of the Nationalities Question," *ibid.*, p. 27.

[59] *Ibid.*, p. 3.

competent than we were. Especially when the Han cadres called Tibet a backward region I got mad."[60]

Tibetan nationalism erupted March 10, 1958, in armed rebellion. According to an official communiqué issued by the *Hsinhua News Agency* on March 28,

The Central People's Government repeatedly enjoined the local government in Tibet to punish the rebels and maintain social order. But the local government of Tibet and the reactionary clique of the upper social strata took the magnanimity of the Central People's Government as a sign of weakness. They were saying: "The Han people can be frightened off . . . if we fail we can run to India. India sympathizes with us and may help us . . ."[61]

More and more the Peking regime tended thereafter to perceive India as a perpetrator of insult and obstruction—an "external enemy" with whom the Tibetan rebels were in league. The unmistakably Indian sympathy with the Tibetans was humiliating enough, but even more galling was the sanctuary which the Indian frontier offered—out of Chinese reach—for the escaping rebels and for the Dalai Lama. The precise location of the boundary—never satisfactorily determined—now became an explosive issue, just as the attitude of the Indian government became an infuriating interference in Chinese rights and ambitions.[62]

During the summer of 1959 the Peking regime increased the strength of its military concentrations along the Indian-Tibetan frontiers. Chinese Communist penetrations were reported from Sikkim and Bhutan, from the Indian states of Uttar Pradesh, Jammu and Kashmir, and the Kameng area along the northeastern Indian border. The Peking regime put forward claims to nearly 40,000 square miles of territory which the Indians considered theirs, and accused the Indian government of aggression.[63]

---

[60] "Tibetan Workers and Office Employees of Lhasa Postal and Telecommunications Bureau Determined to Remove Ideology of Local Nationalism," *Tibet jih-pao*, Lhasa, December 15, 1957, in *Current Background*, No. 505 (May 1, 1958), p. 2.

[61] *Concerning the Question of Tibet* (Peking: Foreign Languages Press, May 6, 1959), pp. 7–8.

[62] "The Revolution in Tibet and Nehru's Philosophy," *Current Background*, No. 570 (May 11, 1959), pp. 2–16 (An English translation of an editorial in *Jen-min Jih-pao*, May 6, 1959).

[63] *New York Times*, September 10, 1959, pp. 1, 4; also "Data on the Sino-Indian Boundary Question," *NCNA* in English Hellschreiber to East Asia, September 10, 1959, which carried the accusation that Indian maps were "cutting about 38,000 square kilometers deep into Chinese territory in the Ladakh region" and incorporating into India "some 90,000 square kilometers of Chinese territory, equivalent in size to China's Chekiang Province" along the Sino-Indian boundary east of Bhutan.

The Ministry of Foreign Affairs in Peking announced on October 26, 1959:

The entire area east of the customary line between China and Ladakh, including the places to the east, south, and north of the Konga Pass, has always been Chinese territory and under the respective jurisdiction of Chinese local authorities in the Sinkiang and Tibetan regions. Since the liberation of Sinkiang and Tibet, the frontier guards of the Chinese People's Liberation Army have all along been stationed in and have patrolled this entire area. The Sinkiang-Tibet highway, built by China in 1956–57, runs through this area.[64]

The whole border dispute, according to Peking, had been "provoked entirely by the Indian side, which should naturally bear all the responsibility."[65]

Ironically, it was more and more in Soviet-built aircraft that the Government of India was moving its troops against Chinese incursions of the common frontier. The position of the USSR became increasingly difficult as Chinese Communist forces undertook concerted invasions of Indian territory. The Russians could not support India without straining the Sino-Soviet alliance, nor could they support China without risking the antagonism of other nations of the neutralist world.

[64] *NCNA* in English Hellschreiber to East Asia, October 26, 1959.

[65] *NCNA*, radioteletype in English to West and North Europe, September 12, 1959.

CHAPTER XV

CONFLICT AND COHESION WITHIN THE
SINO-SOVIET BLOC

EARLY RELATIONS BETWEEN SOVIET RUSSIA AND
THE PEOPLE'S REPUBLIC OF CHINA

The Soviet Union granted recognition to the People's Republic of China on October 2, 1949, the day after the establishment of the new government, and within a week most of the satellite states had done the same. On February 14, 1950, the relationship was further formalized through the Sino-Soviet Treaty concluded in Moscow by Mao Tse-tung and Joseph Stalin and by trade pacts signed that spring.[1]

Terms of this new agreement were inevitably compared by Western observers with the treaty concluded in August 1945 between the Soviet Union and the Nationalist government, which accorded to the USSR nearly all the concessions that Tsarist Russia had lost to Japan through the Treaty of Portsmouth in 1905. The provisions of the 1945 document—the Soviet lease of Port Arthur as a naval base, the establishment of Dairen as a "free port" with pre-eminent interests of the Soviet Union safeguarded, the joint Chinese-Soviet operation of the Chinese railways, and recognition, if a plebiscite should so determine, of the independence of Outer Mongolia—had undoubtedly influenced Western expectations for the 1950 agreements. During the negotiation period many observers had predicted that Moscow would further prove its imperialistic intentions by stripping China of valuable assets and perhaps of independence. Hopes of a "Titoist" reaction in China were expressed in the American press.

The published terms of the Stalin-Mao agreements failed to confirm such speculations, for the Soviet Union promised to restore to China most of the rights previously surrendered to Russia. By providing for the return to China of "war booty" which the Russians had extracted from Manchuria after World War II, and by recognizing Chinese sovereignty in Manchuria, the agreements seemingly refuted the charge that the Soviet Union was not only stripping the northern Chinese provinces of the wealth but actually absorbing them into the Russian sphere. By guaranteeing the return of Port Arthur, Dairen, and the Chinese Changchun Railway freely into Chinese hands, either

---

[1] *The Sino-Soviet Treaty and Agreements* (Peking, 1950), pp. 6–8.

on conclusion of a peace treaty with Japan or "toward the end of 1952" at the latest, the Soviet Union apparently renounced the sphere of influence which it had established in 1945. The agreement thus appeared to disprove the accusation that the Soviets were using Communist methods to achieve Russian goals.

The treaty also forged a military alliance between two nations with a total population of some 800 million and suggested to the West that hopes for Titoism in China were premature, if not baseless. For Moscow and Peking pledged mutual assistance not only against Japanese aggression but also against "any other state" that might unite with Japan, directly or indirectly, "in any act of aggression." They thus achieved at one stroke the protection of China against a historic enemy, the strengthening of Soviet Russia's eastern flank against a bitter rival, and a favorable redressing of the power balance in a cold-war world.

In return for these benefits and for 300 million dollars in credits (a relatively small sum compared with United States transfers to Nationalist China), Mao, according to published terms of the agreement, conceded nothing but the independence from China of the Mongolian People's Republic, an area already within the Soviet orbit and inhabited largely by non-Chinese peoples who had often rebelled against Chinese rule.

The publication of these terms undoubtedly strengthened Mao's position in the world balance of power. Already his victories over the Nationalist armies had brought the earth's most populous nation under Communist control. Areas adjacent to China, moreover, were seething with discontent, and Western programs for the containment of communism in Asia had not advanced beyond the talking stage. Now, at that critical juncture, Mao had concluded arrangements which, from a Chinese viewpoint, were probably more advantageous than any treaty secured by the Nationalists from a foreign power.

If Mao's prestige was strengthened, Soviet prestige was also enhanced, for not only was the Soviet Union seemingly returning to China what the United States, in the capacity of an ally, had compelled her to surrender (Port Arthur, Dairen, and the Manchurian Railways); the agreements also presented the Russians in the role of altruistic allies, defenders of Chinese national integrity against foreign imperialism—this at a time when American officers were asking for permanent bases in Japan, and when the United States was recognizing Bao Dai, whom many Asians considered a tool of French imperialism in Indochina.

Critical observers pointed out, on the other hand, that Communist Russia and Communist China were presumably partners before the instruments were signed; that 60 million dollars' worth of goods a year (for which China must pay the Soviet Union with raw materials by 1963) was scarcely enough to put China on its feet; that for the most part the Soviet Union was merely returning to China what rightfully belonged to China; that a subsequently announced agreement allowing Russians to help exploit oil and nonferrous minerals in Sinkiang for thirty years smacked of Russian imperialism; and that even if China received full legal title to Port Arthur, Dairen, and the Changchun Railway, Soviet police and economic controls would probably continue to operate in Manchuria.

Among many Westerners there was an inclination to suspend final judgment until the moment arrived—either on conclusion of a peace treaty with Japan or toward the end of 1952, at the latest—for the actual return of Port Arthur, Dairen, and the Changchun Railway to China.

On April 20 the USSR and China signed a series of economic agreements which provided for exchange of commodities, Soviet loans to China for the purchase of machinery, and the establishment of Sino-Soviet joint corporations for various purposes, including the exploitation of mineral resources in Sinkiang for a period of thirty years. Under the Sinkiang agreement, China proposed to provide land, buildings, and supplies, while the USSR provided technical personnel and equipment. A Chinese radio broadcast declared:

We should not exploit the fruits of Soviet workers; we must give them something in return. Therefore, the agreements provide for a share of the profits from the various enterprises to go to the USSR. Our shipment of raw materials to the USSR will also be a form of assistance to them.[2]

In terms of Sino-Soviet relations, what did these various agreements portend? The entry of China into the Korean conflict in November 1950 made the answer exceedingly difficult to formulate. Communists unquestionably achieved added prestige in many Asian quarters, but the ensuing deadlock placed Mao and his armies in an equivocal position. Chinese forces not only were losing the victorious *élan* of a year earlier, but were growing increasingly dependent upon the USSR for weapons and equipment.

These factors may explain partially the inconclusive results of the Sino-Soviet conference held in Moscow from August 18 to September 23, 1952. In a joint announcement on September 16 the USSR and

---

[2] A commentary by Liao Tse-lung on "Support the Sino-Soviet Agreements on Economic Cooperation," *Peking International News Service* in Mandarin, April 24, 1950.

the Chinese People's Republic declared that the two nations were taking steps toward returning the Changchun Railway, but that the Peking government had "requested" Moscow to delay withdrawing Russian troops from Port Arthur until treaty relations were established between the two countries and Japan. No mention was made of Dairen, but presumably this city, too, would remain with the Russians.

To most Westerners this agreement looked like a defeat for Mao. The Chinese "request," if bona fide, was admission of China's inability to defend its integrity without Soviet help. If the request were a face-saving device, it did not conceal that Mao's government, in submitting to extended Russian occupation of Port Arthur, was relinquishing a 1950 gain without compensation. The outsider found himself wondering, too, whether Manchurian railways could be independent, with Russian troops occupying territory at both ends and with terminals tying the system into Russian railroads.

There were other circumstances that had to be considered. Characteristically, the Soviet Union had sought in the past to implement its foreign policy on several levels—both legal and subversive—with complicated machinery within machinery and effective techniques of penetration and indirect control. Had the Russians, by the autumn of 1952, achieved appreciable control over the Chinese Communist party and government? Certainly Soviet advisers were playing important roles: hundreds of them, by Chinese Communist admission, were holding important positions in the Chinese government,[3] and there may have been many more.

Terms of the agreement suggested that the Sino-Soviet honeymoon might be over, but it would have been dangerous to infer a breakup. Russian and Chinese Communists had often rubbed each other the wrong way, and even their common ideology was not likely to eradicate stresses historically created by their common border. But Mao had always worked within the framework of world communism, and the two governments shared a common compulsion to drive Western influence from Asia.

The 1952 agreements may well have reflected a gain in Russian influence over the Chinese Communists. When Mao reached Moscow in 1950, he held a position that no Communist then living, other than Stalin, had enjoyed. His party was powerful and second in size only to that of the USSR; his army was large, victorious, and relatively independent; his government ruled one of the largest, most populous nations on earth. By September 1952, when China's Foreign Minister

[3] Su Chung-yu, "The First Year of the Sino-Soviet Treaty," *People's China* (February 16, 1951), p. 6. Foreign observers estimated as many as 100,000 and even more.

Chou En-lai visited Moscow, the circumstances had changed considerably: Chinese armies were locked in a costly struggle in Korea and, far from being victorious or independent, were growing increasingly dependent on the USSR for support.

Yet it could be argued equally well—especially after the death of Stalin—that the Chinese Communists, developing confidence and power and relative freedom of action, might constitute a major influence in their own right. According to this reasoning, it was an error to assume that Chinese policy was necessarily Russian policy. On the contrary, when Mao Tse-tung and his colleagues took power in China, they ceased being simply a Communist party and became, for all their ideology, a Chinese government with distinctly Chinese interests—just as the Russian Bolsheviks, more than thirty years earlier, had become a Russian government with Russian interests. So in Chinese Communist foreign policy one might expect to find a powerful coincidence of Marxist-Leninist-Maoist and Chinese motivations, just as Soviet policy had represented a merging of ideological and historical interests.

The death of Stalin undoubtedly strengthened these fundamentally Chinese inclinations. Mao Tse-tung, with his powerful army and his well-knit party, had long been a formidable figure. But publicly, at least, he and his supporters had paid deference to Stalin: ". . . teacher of genius . . . great scientist of dialectical materialism . . . greatest figure in the world . . ."[4] Mao's theoreticians, perhaps with tongue in cheek, had even hailed Stalin's writings on China as completely correct and had implied a kind of master-disciple *mystique* between the two men.

It was difficult to imagine Mao Tse-tung and his colleagues paying homage to Stalin's successors. For Mao's prestige was greater than theirs. He had led the revolution. He headed a party that he himself had disciplined and shaped. He governed, seemingly without serious intra-party competition, a population of some 600 million people, who, on the whole, were far more homegeneous than those of the Soviet Union. As an Asian leader who had successfully defied the West, he enjoyed respect among uncounted numbers of non-Communist Asians. These were claims that no contemporary Russian leader could match.

The Chinese Communist view of Russian "de-Stalinization" policies was notably unenthusiastic. It was true that Stalin had made mistakes, but he had also "creatively applied and developed" Marxist-Leninist theory and practice. Stalin's works should be studied with great care, and Communists should be prepared to "accept as an his-

---

[4] Ch'en Po-ta, "Stalin and the Chinese Revolution," *NCNA* in English Morse to North America, December 19, 1949.

torical legacy all that is of value in them, especially those many works in which he defended Leninism and correctly summarized the experience of building up the Soviet Union."[5]

In the autumn of 1954 N. A. Bulganin and N. S. Khrushchev paid a visit to China. In the course of their Peking sojourn the Russians agreed to a second Soviet loan amounting to 130 million dollars and a total of 100 million dollars in supplies and equipment in addition to previous commitments.[6] It was also agreed that the Soviet Union would sell all its shares in the Sino-Soviet joint-stock companies to China and would return Port Arthur to Chinese control by the end of 1955. Plans were laid at the same time for the joint construction of a new railway linking China and the Soviet Union by way of Sinkiang.

Early in 1956, during the course of a visit to China, Mikoyan promised Soviet support for additional projects involving 625 million dollars in supplies and equipment. All together, during the First Five-Year Plan, the Soviet Union instituted 211 China aid projects.[7]

With the passage of time it became increasingly clear, however, that Moscow had no intention—beyond certain relatively narrow limits—of underwriting China's economic and technological development.[8] For the most part, Communist China must pull itself up by its own bootstraps—a task that could be accomplished, as the more radical planners saw it—only by a combination of breakneck speed and organizational "balance."[9]

Between 1951 and mid-1960, when Moscow withdrew its technicians from China, the Peking regime received valuable Soviet Russian loans, including two totaling approximately 450 million dollars,

[5] "On the Historical Experience of the Dictatorship of the Proletariat," editorial in Peking *People's Daily*, April 5, 1956, in *Current Background*, No. 403 (July 25, 1956), pp. 1–8.

[6] "Communiqué on Negotiations between China and the Soviet Union," October 12, 1954, *SCMP*, No. 906 (October 12, 1954), pp. 1–9.

[7] Sino-Soviet communiqué of April 7, 1956, *SCMP*, No. 1265 (April 11, 1956), p. 30.

[8] See A. Doak Barnett, *Communist Economic Strategy: The Rise of Mainland China* (Washington, D.C.: National Planning Association, 1959); also Li Choh-ming, *Economic Development of Communist China: An Appraisal of the First Five Years of Industrialization* (Berkeley: University of California Press, 1959); and Wu Yuan-li, *An Economic Survey of Communist China* (New York: Bookman Associates, 1956).

[9] Liu Shao-ch'i before the Second Session of the Eighth Party Congress, May 5, 1958, in *Peking Review*, No. 14, June 3, 1958, pp. 6–22; and also his statement, "The Victory of Marxism-Leninism in China," *Ten Glorious Years, 1949–1959* (Peking: Foreign Languages Press, 1960), pp. 26–27. See also Po I-po, "Working for the National Economic Plan for 1956 and Draft Economic Plan for 1957," speech to the National People's Congress in English Morse to North Africa and Southeast Europe, *NCNA*, July 1, 1957.

and long-term credit for the purchase of military supplies left over from the Korean war and for liquidation of the Sino-Soviet joint stock companies. Communist China also received, on a commercial credit basis, economic assistance in the form of complete sets of factory equipment and technical assistance. Yet all this amounted to comparatively little aid—hardly what a nation embarking on a vast modernization program might have expected from a close ally. The balance of Sino-Soviet trade tended, moreover, to tip in favor of the Russians. There were persistent rumors of increasing friction in relations between the two states.[10]

The Soviet Union, Doak Barnett wrote in 1959, "has not given Communist China a single free grant for economic development, as far as is known on the basis of the public record, and even the volume of Soviet loans and credits for economic purposes has been relatively small in relation to China's needs."[11]

On the basis of rough estimates, according to Barnett, "it now appears that during 1953–1957 Communist China's own foreign aid programs plus the servicing and repayment of Soviet loans and credits actually exceeded its receipts from all types of Soviet financial assistance during 1953–1957."[12]

Perceived from Moscow, the situation in China must frequently look discouraging—with the population exploding with each advance in technology and needs outstripping productivity almost *ad infinitum*.

THE PERIOD OF THE "BANDUNG SPIRIT"

While the Chinese Communists were attempting to "pull themselves up by their own bootstraps," with minimal but crucial Soviet economic and technical assistance, some notable differences could be observed between the foreign policy attitudes of Peking and Moscow.

In the mid-1950's, during the period of the "Bandung Spirit," Communist China gave the appearance of pursuing the more moderate and peaceful course, whereas in the Soviet Union there were disturbing assertions about the dangers of "imperialist war" and the necessity of preparing the nation for a "pre-emptive strike," if necessary, against the imperialist aggressor. We shall see how, over succeeding years, the two leaderships tended to switch roles—with the Chinese sound-

---

[10] For careful assessments of Sino-Soviet economic relations see Oleg Hoeffding, "Sino-Soviet Economic Relations in Recent Years" in Kurt London (ed.), *Unity and Contradiction* (New York: Frederick A. Praeger, 1962), pp. 295–312; and A. Doak Barnett, *Communist Economic Strategy: The Rise of Mainland China, op. cit.*, p. 228.

[11] *Ibid.*

[12] *Ibid.*, p. 230.

ing more and more militant, and the Russians becoming somewhat more cautious.

The Korean war had left Communist Chinese troops blocked at the 38th parallel—and also at Taiwan Straits, where Chiang Kai-shek had strengthened Nationalist garrisons on islands just off the China coast. The Chinese Communist launched two major attacks against these islands—in September 1954 and in the period August–October, 1958.

While proclaiming their determination to "liberate" Taiwan itself, the Chinese Communists in 1954 began their first bombardment of Quemoy. Nationalist resistance was stubborn, however, and Peking could not be certain that the United States would not intervene. The Bandung Conference with its atmosphere of good will and peaceful intent provided Peking with a plausible excuse for disentanglement : under the Bandung Spirit the Chinese Communists could retreat without loss of prestige—and even make a magnanimous gesture of it.

After Stalin's death—and especially during 1954—there took place in the Soviet Union, on the other hand, a vociferous debate on military policy. According to G. M. Malenkov, the USSR resolutely opposed the cold war as leading to "a new world holocaust" which could result only in the destruction of civilization. The Soviet Union, moreover, possessed everything necessary to preserve security without recourse to large-scale violence. N. S. Khrushchev—at that time —took a notably different view : only capitalism would collapse in the course of a third world war, not the whole of civilization.[13] Concurrently, Soviet military specialists were underscoring the importance for the Soviet Union of being able to deliver a pre-emptive attack against the United States—a view that became embodied in official policy.[14]

By mid-1955 a somewhat similar debate was developing in Communist China between professional military men and the party leadership. Members of the General Staff, in particular, were urging the regime to build and maintain well-equipped and modernized forces, including a stronger air force, and to coordinate economic and defense policies more effectively.

Under the Constitution of 1954 the People's Revolutionary Military Council of former times had been replaced by a larger National Defense Council and a Ministry of National Defense under P'eng Teh-huai. Compulsory military service was introduced, together with a new hierarchy of ranks and a functional classification of officers after

[13] H. S. Dinerstein, *War and the Soviet Union* (New York: Frederick A. Praeger, 1959), pp. 71, 99.
[14] *Ibid.*, pp. 77, 95.

the Soviet model. These alterations in the Chinese Communist armed forces were subsequently interpreted by close observers in the West as a victory for professional military elements seeking modernization on the basis of experience gained during the Korean war.[15] This victory was perceived as having been gained at the expense of those leaders—both military and political—who favored the preservation of the "liberation army" with its special form, long tradition, and emphasis on close relations with the masses as an aspect of class struggle.[16] To some degree, at least, the "modernizers" are believed to have begun as early as 1954 to appreciate the implications of emerging Soviet thought on problems of nuclear warfare.[17]

Subsequently—perhaps to some degree as an outcome of Soviet Russian capabilities—the scales of military influence tipped the other way, with party-oriented generals replacing the professionals in ascendancy.

To the Peking political leadership it was becoming increasingly clear—unmistakably after the testing of military strength against United States capabilities and intentions during the Quemoy-Matsu crisis of 1958, but to some degree even earlier—that there were basic limitations to Chinese strength and range of alternatives. First-rate military capability could not be maintained except at the expense of rapid economic and technological development. As early as 1956 the regime appears to have begun sorting out priorities: by virtue of an immediate, concerted, and highly disciplined effort China could build new economic and technological capabilities, which, in turn, would serve as the base for a subsequent development of military and external political power.

At the same time Mao Tse-tung and his colleagues seemed to be seeking a new role in affairs of the Communist bloc.

With the Polish and Hungarian crises in the autumn of 1956 Communist China offered mediation and ideological leadership. Warning against "great-nation chauvinism" on the one hand and excessive small-nation nationalism on the other, Peking urged recognition of the "supreme interests" of the bloc—but asserted also that

[15] Alice Langley Hsieh, *Communist China's Strategy in the Nuclear Era* (Englewood Cliffs, N.J.: Prentice-Hall, Inc., 1962), p. 21.

[16] Su Yü, "General Su Yü Writes on Army Day," *NCNA*, Peking, July 31, 1954, in *SCMP*, No. 860 (July 31–August 2, 1954), p. 3. See also Hsiao Hua, "The Chinese People's Liberation Army Marching Toward Mobilization," *NCNA*, Peking, July 31, 1952, in *Current Background* No. 208 (September 10, 1952), pp. 37–42; and Chu Teh, speaking at a meeting in celebration of PLA day, *NCNA*, Peking, August 1, 1953, in *SCMP*, No. 623 (August 1–4, 1953), pp. 2–3.

[17] Alice Langley Hsieh, *Communist China's Strategy in the Nuclear Era, op. cit.,* p. 23.

"the Socialist countries are independent and sovereign states, and relations between them are based upon the Leninist principle of national equality."[18] The Chinese Communists thus presented the image of a reasonable and somewhat benign influence within the bloc—together with an apparent predisposition toward a kind of inter-nation pluralism under loose Soviet pre-eminence. The Russians, by contrast, seemed to be demanding a considerably higher degree of centralism.

In playing this new role, Chou En-lai interrupted a visit to south Asia in order to visit Moscow, Warsaw, and Budapest—ostensibly as a mediator. On returning to Moscow from the troubled satellites he and the Russians issued on January 19, 1957, a joint communiqué which urged relations of equality within the bloc, with each Communist party respecting the national interests of other countries.[19]

THE CHINESE COMMUNIST PARTY PERCEIVES
A "TURNING POINT"

Against this background it is all the more remarkable that in the course of a few months—between June and December, 1957—the Soviet Union and Communist China seemed to switch roles. Thereafter, and especially with the development of the so-called Sino-Soviet controversy, the Chinese increasingly argued for greater centralization within the bloc, coupled with a more aggressive attitude toward the West, while the Russians—*relatively*—appeared to be championing pluralism, a loose confederation of fraternal soviet states, coupled with a more lenient policy toward the West.

At the same time, paradoxically enough, it seemed to be the party leaders, as opposed to the professional military men, who were having their way in Communist China.[20]

Repeatedly, over succeeding years, the Soviet Russians emphasized the following points: neither side could win in a nuclear war, and the outcome would be disaster for all mankind; a major war was not "fatalistically inevitable"; the USSR had sufficient strength to deter any aggressor; and communism had the capacity to win by other

---

[18] Chou En-lai in a joint Sino-Soviet communiqué, January 19, 1957, *New York Times*, January 19, 1957, p. 2; and "International Significance of the Soviet-Polish Talks," *NCNA*, November 21, 1956, in *SCMP*, No. 1418 (November 27, 1956); see also "More on the Historical Experience of the Dictatorship of the Proletariat," *People's Daily*, December 29, 1956, in *Current Background*, No. 433 (January 2, 1957).

[19] *New York Times, ibid.*

[20] For a detailed analysis of Sino-Soviet relations and the Sino-Soviet debate see Donald S. Zagoria, *The Sino-Soviet Conflict, 1956–1961* (Princeton: Princeton University Press, 1962).

means, including the economic, political, psychological, and technological.

The Chinese Communists took a different view: men—not weapons—were the decisive element in warfare, and nuclear devices had
been greatly overrated; Communist China had nothing to fear from
a nuclear war; indeed, the Chinese could lose half their population and
still be the largest nation in the world; imperialist war was "beyond
human will to avoid"; it was the unmistakable duty of the Chinese
people to make a "timely exposure" of all those who, in advocating
coexistence, had moved "from fear of war to fear of revolution" and
"from not wanting revolutions themselves to opposing other people's
carrying out revolutions."[21]

On the occasion of Lenin's birthday anniversary in late April 1960
leading Chinese spokesmen leveled especially bitter charges against
"revisionists," whom they saw as a menace to the international Communist movement. By implying that the imperialists had changed
their nature, these misguided comrades had betrayed the Marxist-
Leninist revolutionary spirit and emasculated its doctrine. Allied, in
effect, with the imperialists, these revisionists were driving a wedge
into the heart of the Communist bloc.[22]

At the time of Khrushchev's visit to the United States in the early
autumn of 1959—and again as the United States and the Soviet Union
were making plans for a summit meeting in mid-1960—the Chinese
Communist criticisms of "revisionism" reached crescendos. It was as
if the one eventuality Peking could least tolerate was a lessening of
tension between the Soviet Union and the United States.

Repercussions were felt throughout the Communist bloc as the
controversy developed—with the Chinese Communists attacking
"Yugoslav revisionists" when they meant the Russians, and Khrushchev using Albania as a whipping boy for the Communist Chinese.[23]

To a considerable degree the Chinese Communist and Soviet Russian conflicts emerged from differences in emphasis and in the calcu-
lation of probabilities. The Russians did not deny the *possibility* of
a nuclear war; they merely assigned the possibility a *lower probability* than the Chinese; or, in somewhat different terms, they saw
more opportunities for avoiding it. Conversely, the Chinese Communists did not deny the possibility of relatively nonviolent struggles

---

[21] Lu Ting-i, "Get United Under Lenin's Revolutionary Banner," *NCNA,* April
22, 1960. Radioteletype in English to Europe and Asia.

[22] *Ibid.*

[23] For a discussion of Albania in this context see Donald S. Zagoria, "Khrushchev's Attack on Albania and Sino-Soviet Relations," *The China Quarterly,* No. 8
(October–December, 1961), pp. 1–19.

in some places, but they estimated such probabilities much lower than the Russians did.

Nevertheless, a systematic content analysis of Soviet Russian and Chinese Communist foreign policy statements for three selected periods—January 1960, May 1960, and April 1961—has revealed some notable differences between the attitudes and states of mind of the two leaderships. Generally, on each of several measurement scales devised for the study (more or less hostility, more or less frustration, and so forth), the Chinese tended to be almost twice as negatively oriented.[24]

In the wake of the U-2 incident of May 1960, the differences between Soviet Russian and Chinese Communist attitudes were especially revealing. Moscow chided the United States for breaking international law, "defying accepted custom" and behaving like "war-mongers" and "imperialist aggressors." The Chinese took the attitude, on the other hand, that since the United States was, in fact, an imperialist and war-mongering nation, this was precisely the sort of behavior to expect. "We told you so," Peking seemed to be telling Moscow, "but you refused to pay attention to us."

How did these various differences between the Russians and the Chinese come about? Did the controversy have its roots in ideology, or in the wholly separate levels of economy and technology? To what degree were personal differences between Khrushchev and Mao responsible? Were distinct Russian and Chinese national interests at stake? Unfortunately, it is seldom easy to discover clear starting points for international conflicts, or to determine causal relationships. To some extent all of these factors played a part, but some were perhaps more influential than others.

The USSR tested its first successful ICBM in late August 1957. Some weeks later—at the conference of Communist parties and states held in Moscow in November—a new Chinese assessment of the world situation became evident.

Addressing a group of Chinese students at Moscow University, Mao Tse-tung (who, somewhat unaccountably, had canceled a scheduled trip to Poland a few months earlier) described the first Soviet sputniks, recently launched, as "a new turning point."[25] On the following day he presented to the assembled Communist leaders an

---

[24] "Report to the U.S. Navy on USSR–Chinese Relations from the Studies in International Conflict and Integration," unpublished manuscript, Stanford University, November 1961.

[25] "Chairman Mao Meets Chinese Students in Moscow," *NCNA*, in English from Moscow, November 18, 1957; translation of *Jen-min Jih-pao* account, November 20, 1957, in *SCMP*, No. 1656 (November 21, 1957).

elaboration of his argument.[26] Somewhat differing versions of his speech were subsequently released, but essentially this was his reasoning:

I consider that the present world situation has reached a new turning point. There are now two winds in the world: the east wind and the west wind. There is a saying in China: "If the east wind does not prevail over the west wind, then the west wind will prevail over the east wind." I think the characteristic of the current situation is that the east wind prevails over the west wind; that is, the strength of socialism exceeds the strength of imperialism.[27]

In fact, as became evident during subsequent debates, the Chinese Communists had convinced themselves that an important shift in world power had begun even prior to the Soviet achievement of ICBM capability. During World War II, according to Peking, the Soviet Union—rather than Great Britain and the United States—had played the major role in defeating Hitler. In the Chinese "war of liberation" the Communists—and not Chiang Kai-shek with his support from the United States—had been the winners. In Korea the Chinese and North Korean forces had thrown U.N. forces back from the Yalu. In Vietnam Ho Chi-minh had defeated United States-supported troops of France. During the Suez crisis the Soviet Union's warning, coupled with world opinion, had halted the British, French, and Israeli aggression. Western forces had withdrawn from various colonies. "It goes without saying," *Jen-min Jih-pao* asserted, "that these withdrawals resulted from the double blows to imperialism dealt by the socialist forces and the nationalist forces which oppose colonialism. The superiority of the anti-imperialist forces over the imperialist forces demonstrated by these events has expressed itself in even more concentrated form and reached unprecedented heights with the Soviet Union's launching of the artificial satellites . . ."[28]

To this basic argument—especially as an outcome of the Quemoy-Matsu crisis of August–October, 1958—was added the notion that Communist China, while despising its enemies "strategically," must "tactically" take them seriously.[29]

[26] Mao Tse-tung, *Imperialism and all Reactionaries Are Paper Tigers* (Peking: Foreign Languages Press, 1958), p. 28; see also *Peking Review*, No. 37 (November 11, 1958), pp. 6–11. For an early Communist use of the term "paper tiger" see Robert C. North and Xenia J. Eudin, *M. N. Roy's Mission to China* (Berkeley: University of California Press, 1962).

[27] Mao Tse-tung, "Imperialists and All Reactionaries Are Paper Tigers," *Current Background*, No. 534 (November 12, 1958), p. 12.

[28] "The Great Revolutionary Declaration," editorial translated from *Jen-min Jih-pao*, November 25, 1957, in *SCMP*, No. 1660 (November 27, 1957), pp. 27–28.

[29] Mao Tse-tung, "Imperialists and All Reactionaries Are Paper Tigers," *Current Background, ibid.*, p. 11.

From this point forward the Chinese Communists tended to depreciate the dangers of nuclear war and to urge upon the Russians a more militant policy against the West. At the same time Peking shifted from supporting Gomulka and other East European autonomists toward an insistence upon unqualified submission to Soviet leadership. Concurrently—however unrealistic it might seem—Peking began claiming that Mao Tse-tung had developed a special road for speeding socialist construction and achieving communism "in the not distant future."[30]

How did this new Chinese Communist demand for bloc centralism and global militancy square with the Peking decision to emphasize economic development at the acute expense of professional military élan and the early development of a modern striking force? No answer can be made with absolute confidence. It seems probable, however, that the Peking regime had reached the following assessment: Communist China could now depend upon the Soviet Union's enhanced technological and military capability as a protective shield and thus free badly needed manpower and resources for the regime's unprecedented program for industrial development. In accepting this assumption, however, the People's Republic of China made itself uneasily dependent upon Russian military strength—a dependence which professional Chinese military men were resisting vigorously, but without much success.

Once the fateful decision had been made to rely increasingly on Soviet Russian "protection," and once more and more potential military manpower had been diverted into economic and technical development, the Peking leadership may have found itself constantly in need of reassurance from Moscow that the USSR intended to press a vigorous "anti-imperialist" policy consonant with the Chinese Communist view of the world struggle. Behavior that could be interpreted as a "softening" of Soviet Russian attitudes toward the United States and its allies made the Peking regime feel dangerously exposed and possibly even betrayed.

No matter what the Russians agreed to do in Asia, from the viewpoint of Peking it was probably never sufficient. Perceived from Moscow, on the other hand, now that the Russians enjoyed the confidence of ICBM capability, the potential costs of nuclear warfare may have come to look increasingly awesome.

Meanwhile, having weighted priorities in favor of economic and technological development at the expense of an early modernizing of its own military establishment, the Peking regime tended increasingly

[30] Chen Po-ta, "Under the Banner of Comrade Mao Tse-tung," *Hung Ch'i* [Red Flag], No. 4, July 16, 1958, *Extracts from China Mainland Magazines,* No. 138 (August 11, 1958), p. 14.

to favor military leaders who could be relied upon to support party policies.

During the months that followed, the Chinese Communists placed more and more emphasis upon the study of Mao Tse-tung's writings on military affairs and upon increasing the political consciousness of military personnel.[31] Professional military men were criticized for "one-sidedly stressing the suddenness and complexity of modern warfare"[32] and "one-sidedly" stressing also "the part of atomic weapons and modern military techniques" to the neglect of the role of the people.[33]

Undoubtedly the Chinese Communist leadership was not unaware of the changes likely to take place in world power balances as more and more nations acquired nuclear capabilities. In May 1958 General Liu Ya-lou, Commander of the PLA Air Force, predicted that "China's working class and scientists" would be able to produce atomic bombs and rockets "in the not-distant future." By that time *another new turning point* would probably have been reached in the international situation with the socialist campaign growing stronger and the imperialist campaign weaker.[34]

THE QUEMOY-MATSU CRISIS AND EARLY PUBLIC EXCHANGES
IN THE SINO-SOVIET CONTROVERSY

The Quemoy-Matsu crisis of August–October, 1958, may have represented a relatively low-risk Chinese Communist attempt to test United States intentions in the Taiwan Straits area. More specifically, Peking hoped to demonstrate, perhaps, that the new Soviet capability would be sufficient to deter the United States from the use of, or from serious consideration of using, tactical nuclear weapons—with a consequent inhibition of cold-war effectiveness. In the course of the conflict it became evident, however, that without active Soviet collaboration the Chinese could not achieve even their more limited objectives in the Taiwan Straits.[35]

---

[31] Alice Langley Hsieh, *op. cit.*, pp. 110–16; "Many Major Improvements Introduced in Army Training Work," *Chieh-fang-chün Pao*, Peking, August 8, 1957, in *SCMP*, No. 1692 (January 16, 1958), pp. 5–6; "New Training Program Promulgated by General Department of Supervision of Training," *Chieh-fang-chün Pao*, Peking, January 16, 1958, in *SCMP*, No. 1786 (June 6, 1958), pp. 6–9.

[32] Liu Ya-lou, "Seriously Study Mao Tse-tung's Military Thinking," *Chieh-fang-chün Pao*, Peking, May 23, 1958, in *SCMP*, No. 1900 (November 24, 1958), pp. 5–10.

[33] "Resolute Carrying Out of Party's Military Line," editorial in *Chieh-fang-chün Pao*, Peking, August 1, 1958, *SCMP*, No. 1881 (October 24, 1958), p. 2.

[34] Liu Ya-lou, "Seriously Study Mao Tse-tung's Military Thinking," *Chieh-fang-chün Pao*, May 23, 1958, in *SCMP*, No. 1900 (November 24, 1958), pp. 5–10.

[35] For somewhat differing analyses and interpretations of the crisis see Alice Langley Hsieh, *op. cit.*, pp. 119–30; Tang Tsou, *The Embroilment over Quemoy:*

In the course of the crisis Khrushchev announced in a letter of September 7 to President Eisenhower that Moscow would interpret "an attack on the People's Republic of China" as "an attack on the Soviet Union."[36] It must not have escaped the attention of Chinese Communist leaders, however, that Khrushchev's threat of deterrence had not come until *after* Peking had announced its willingness to resume ambassadorial talks with the United States.[37]

On October 12, 1958, Su Yü—having urged a military establishment after the Soviet model—was replaced as Chief of Staff by Huang K'o-cheng, who, as a member of the secretariat of the Central Committee, provided an important tie between the party and the armed forces.[38]

In less than a year there were further changes. In September 1959 Marshal P'eng Teh-huai was replaced as Minister of Defense by Marshal Lin Piao. At the same time General Lo Jui-ch'ing, who had been serving as Minister of Public Security, succeeded General Huang K'o-cheng as Chief of Staff. Lo was known more as a policeman than a soldier. It was reported that P'eng had questioned the validity of Mao's theories of partisan warfare in a nuclear age and had resisted continuing party control over the Army.[39] P'eng is asserted also to have written a letter to the Communist party of the Soviet Union criticizing the communes and the Great Leap Forward.[40] Under such circumstances—a Chinese military officer seemingly appealing to Moscow over the heads of his own government and party superiors—the personal relationship between Khrushchev and Mao could have suffered further strain. At the same time two Vice-Ministers of Foreign Affairs, Wang Chia-hsiang and Chang Wen-t'ien, failed reappointment, and Ch'en Yün, a vice-chairman of the CCP, fell from grace. All three officials—and many men in lesser positions—were believed to have been associated with Marshal P'eng in criticizing basic policies.

Mao, Chiang and Dulles (University of Utah: Institute of International Studies, 1959); Donald S. Zagoria, *The Sino-Soviet Conflict, op. cit.,* pp. 200–221; and Charles A. McClelland, "Decisional Opportunity and Political Controversy: The Quemoy Case," *Conflict Resolution,* Vol. VI, No. 3 (September 1962), pp. 201–13.

[36] *New York Times,* September 9, 1958, p. 1.

[37] Chou En-lai's statement on Taiwan Straits as reported by *NCNA,* Peking, September 6, 1958, in *SCMP,* No. 1851 (September 11, 1958), pp. 1–2.

[38] Alice Langley Hsieh, *op. cit.,* p. 117; also in Chinese Hellschreiber, *NCNA, Peking,* October 12, 1958.

[39] For differing analyses of P'eng's dismissal compare David A. Charles, "The Dismissal of Marshal P'eng Teh-huai," *The China Quarterly,* No. 8, October–December, 1961, pp. 63–76, with Alice Langley Hsieh, "Communist China and Nuclear Warfare," *ibid.,* No. 2, April–June, 1960, pp. 1–15; and also Alice Langley Hsieh, *Communist China's Strategy in the Nuclear Era, op. cit.,* pp. 173–81.

[40] David A. Charles, op. cit., p. 64.

It is worth noting that Marshal P'eng's major policy attacks coincided with Khrushchev's announcement of his forthcoming visit to the United States. Over succeeding weeks the closer the rapport which seemed to be developing — from the Peking viewpoint — between Khrushchev and his capitalist hosts, the more bitter the Chinese Communist denunciations of revisionism and of those comrades "seeking to drive a stake into the heart" of the Communist bloc. Under these circumstances, any revelations concerning P'eng's alleged complaints to Moscow—and any further evidence of Soviet interference in Chinese domestic affairs—would have been particularly galling.

It was against this background of conflicting national viewpoints and interests that doctrinal debates between the Russians and Communist Chinese tended increasingly to emerge.

EMERGENCE OF THE CONTROVERSY INTO PUBLIC VIEW

The first public broadside in the Sino-Soviet controversy was opened by *Tass* on September 4, 1959, with a virtual disavowal of Peking's position in the Sino-Indian border dispute. In fact, as we have seen, the dispute dated back to the first assessments of Soviet ICBM achievements of 1957—and before that, to the Twentieth Congress of the Communist Party of the Soviet Union in February 1956.

Events of the Hundred Flowers period had been sufficient to smash any illusions Mao Tse-tung and his colleagues may have cherished about the popularity of their regime and the unity of party and nonparty elements. It seems reasonable to assume that this disillusionment—along with domestic economic difficulties—strengthened left-wing tendencies within the leadership at the expense of those who would have preferred to move somewhat more cautiously.[41]

After the Twentieth Congress the Sino-Soviet controversy came to embrace such crucial issues as how a communist party should achieve power in an advanced industrial state and in an economically retarded nation; how the transition to socialism should be accomplished; whether the peaceful coexistence of states with differing social systems was relatively feasible or infeasible; what the probabilities were of avoiding both local and large-scale wars; and how the likely consequences of a nuclear war ought to be estimated.

The chief doctrinal differences between Moscow and Peking

[41] See Roderick MacFarquhar, "Communist China's Intra Party Dispute," *Pacific Affairs*, December 1958, pp. 323–35; and also his "The Leadership in China," *The World Today*, August 1959, pp. 310–323. MacFarquhar identifies Chou En-lai, Ch'en Yi, Li Fu-ch'un, Li Hsien-nien, and Po I-po as supporting the more gradual approach, and Liu Shao-ch'i and Teng Hsiao-p'ing as preferring "speed and balance."

emerged from their separate evaluations of characteristics and implications of "the new epoch." The Chinese Communists made clear that they stood "against war and in favor of peace." They recognized, also, the possibility that large-scale war might be avoided and that, in special circumstances, a Communist-led movement might achieve power without major violence. Peking insisted, on the other hand, that Lenin's theory of imperialism was not obsolete, and that "none of the new techniques like atomic energy, rocketry, and so on" had altered the basic characteristics of world imperialism and its epoch or the revolutionary principles put forward by Lenin.[42]

"The capitalist-imperialist system absolutely will not crumble of itself," *Hung Ch'i* [Red Flag] declared on the anniversary of Lenin's birth. "It will be overthrown by the proletarian revolution within the imperialist country concerned, and the national revolution in the colonies and semi-colonies."[43] Mao Tse-tung and his colleagues conceded the *desirability* of achieving proletarian power and the transition to socialism by peaceful means. Such possibilities should be seized whenever they became apparent—as Lenin himself had long before pointed out. "However, this sort of opportunity is always, in Lenin's words, an extraordinarily rare opportunity in the history of revolutions."[44]

THE ACHIEVEMENT OF POWER AND THE ROLE
OF THE BOURGEOISIE

With respect to achievement of power the Chinese Communists tended to perceive domestic revolutionary conditions within a given country as crucial, whereas the Russians saw the "essence, content, and nature of the decisive tasks of the present epoch" as overriding. The Chinese Communists, not unlike M. N. Roy at the Second Congress and thereafter, emphasized "revolution from below"; that is, they tended to discount the revolutionary role of the national bourgeoisie and to depend more heavily than the Russians upon development of the revolution, from the very first, under the hegemony of the proletariat. This meant that they were inclined to distrust, as compared with the Soviet Russians, too great a dependency upon collaboration with non-Communist leaders such as Jawaharlal Nehru and Gamal Abdel Nasser. On the other hand, the Russians—as compared with the Chinese Communists—saw more possibilities for the achievement of power through relatively "peaceful" approaches.

[42] See "Long Live Leninism," *Hung Ch'i* [Red Flag], No. 8, April 22, 1960, as translated in *Peking Review*, No. 17 (April 26, 1960), p. 12.
[43] *Ibid.*
[44] *Ibid.*, p. 18.

In their attitudes toward the underdeveloped countries Soviet Russian theoreticians placed heavy emphasis upon "revolution from above" by advocating support for "national bourgeois" leaders, even without "proletarian hegemony," and by advocating large-scale technical assistance to emerging nations.

In an article on the bourgeoisie of the new nations, *Pravda* declared:

The working class is the most consistent enemy of imperialism. Nevertheless Lenin considered it natural that *at the beginning* of any national movement the bourgeoisie play the role of its hegemonic force (leader) and urged that in the struggle for the self-determination of nations support be given to the most revolutionary elements of the bourgeois-democratic national-liberation movements.[45]

Pravda took sharp issue with the "leftists" and "doctrinaires" who were criticizing national liberation movements which did not fit into the expected pattern. In several Asian countries, and especially in Africa, the vast majorities were peasant. In these environments "the central task in freeing themselves from the yoke of imperialism" would remain for a considerable time a matter of "struggle not against capital but against survivals of the Middle Ages." Consequently, the local workers, peasants, and intelligentsia must frequently cooperate with "that part of the national bourgeoisie which is interested in independent political and economic development of its country and is ready to defend its independence against any encroachments by the imperialist powers."[46]

At the 21st Congress of the CPSU in February 1959 Khrushchev pointed out that many "bourgeois nationalist" leaders in the emerging nations were on record as favoring socialism. True, it was frequently difficult for them "to utter the word 'communism,' " and it was not always clear what they meant by socialism. Yet there could be no doubt that several of these leaders were benevolently oriented toward the socialist countries and did not regard them as antagonists. On the contrary, they knew that their desire to build a new life without colonial oppression or imperialist interference would not be frustrated by the Soviet bloc. This recognition was sufficient for the establishment of friendly relations and strong economic ties with these states.[47]

Soviet foreign policy had always emphasized "mutual assistance"

[45] "*Pravda* on Supporting the 'Bourgeoisie' in New Nations," *Current Digest of the Soviet Press*, XII, No. 34, September 21, 1960, p. 18.

[46] *Ibid.*

[47] Leo Gruliow (ed.), "The Documentary Record of the Extraordinary 21st Communist Party Congress" (Khrushchev's concluding remarks, February 5, 1959), *Current Soviet Policies*, III (New York: Columbia University Press, 1960), p. 201.

and cooperation in building socialism and communism. But in the new epoch, Kuusinen declared on Lenin's anniversary: ". . . we have a broader understanding of the international duty of our socialist country—we understand it as rendering assistance to those liberated peoples, too, who are not included in the world system of socialism."[48]

From the Peking viewpoint these arguments were highly erroneous. The bourgeoisie, according to Chinese Communist theoreticians, "can not," "dare not," and "will not" lead the "true peasants' revolution" prerequisite to a "democratic revolution."[49] According to Vice-Chairman Tung Pi-wu, there was no country in the epoch of imperialism that could achieve victory under the bourgeoisie. The key to victory, Liu Shao-ch'i made clear, depended upon a firm seizure of hegemony by the proletariat through the Communist party. Without specific reference to the Russians he recalled how "right opportunists" in China during the 1920's had made the crucial error of "capitulation" toward the bourgeoisie. It was Mao Tse-tung, he reminded fellow Communists, who had corrected this mistake in China.[50]

PEACEFUL ROADS TO POWER AND THE TRANSITION
TO SOCIALISM

The feasibility of "peaceful" roads to power was not a wholly new concept in Marxist-Leninist theory. As far back as April 1924 Stalin had declared in a lecture at Sverdlov University:

. . . in the remote future, if the proletariat is victorious in the most important capitalist countries, and if the present capitalist encirclement is replaced by Socialist encirclement, a "peaceful" path of development is quite possible for certain capitalist countries, whose capitalists, in view of the "unfavorable" international situation, will consider it expedient "voluntarily" to make substantial concessions to the proletariat.[51]

In the aftermath of World War I Lenin and his colleagues had perceived the imperialist powers caught irrevocably in Olympian struggles against each other and also predisposed, by their very nature, toward aggression against the Soviet Union and Communist movements elsewhere. It was out of these massive upheavals that world communism would eventually emerge.

[48] Otto Kuusinen, "Lenin Anniversary Meeting at Moscow Sports Palace," *Soviet News* (London: Soviet Embassy, 1960), No. 4255, p. 63.

[49] Wang Chia-hsiang, "The International Significance of the Chinese People's Victory," *Ten Glorious Years* (Peking: Foreign Languages Press, 1960), p. 275.

[50] Liu Shao-ch'i, "The Victory of Marxism-Leninism in China," *Peking Review*, No. 30 (October 1, 1959), p. 7.

[51] Joseph Stalin, *Problems of Leninism* (Moscow: Foreign Languages Publishing House, 1947), p. 45.

Since those days the situation in the world had undergone significant changes, Khrushchev told the 20th Congress of the CPSU in February 1956. In less than four decades the forces of "socialism and democracy" had increased beyond measurement, whereas capitalism had lost much of its former strength. More and more, throughout the world, socialist encirclement of capitalism was replacing the former capitalist encirclement of socialism. People in various countries, comparing the two systems, were becoming aware of the "decisive advantages" of socialism over capitalism. Undeniably socialism possessed a great power of attraction for the workers, peasants, and intellectuals of all countries. "The ideas of socialism," he declared subsequently, "are indeed coming to dominate the minds of all working mankind."[52]

The socialist world system, then, was becoming "the decisive factor in the development of human society," and this phenomenon must be recognized, according to Khrushchev, as "the main distinguishing feature of the epoch." With this crucial readjustment in the world balance of forces, more and more possibilities would emerge for revolutions by peaceful means. "The transition to socialism in countries with developed parliamentary traditions," he asserted, "may be effected by utilizing parliament, and in other countries by utilizing institutions conforming to their national traditions."[53]

The working classes in a number of capitalist countries were now achieving a real opportunity for uniting the overwhelming majority of the people under their leadership and for securing the transfer of the basic means of production "into the hands of the people."[54] Under these circumstances the proletariat should be able to capture a stable majority in parliament and transform the whole institution from an organ of bourgeois democracy into a genuine "instrument of the people's will"—a new, proletarian "people's state" in parliamentary form.[55]

Khrushchev and his colleagues foresaw possibilities of a transitional "democracy of a new type" in certain highly developed capitalist countries—a "democracy that would be neutral, opposed to war, and pre-disposed toward the nationalization of monopolies." The transition to socialism in these states would be greatly facilitated.[56]

[52] N. S. Khrushchev, *Report of the Central Committee, 20th Congress* Soviet News Booklet No. 4 (London: Soviet Embassy, 1956), p. 30.

[53] N. S. Khrushchev, "For New Victories for the World Communist Movement" (Results of the meeting of representatives of the Communist and Workers' Parties), *World Marxist Review*, Vol. 4, No. 1 (January 1961), p. 22.

[54] N. S. Khrushchev, *Report of the Central Committee, 20th Congress, op. cit.*, p. 30.

[55] *Ibid.*, p. 30.

[56] *Fundamentals of Marxism-Leninism* (Moscow: Foreign Languages Publishing House [1960?]), pp. 591 ff.

Along these same lines the December 6, 1960, Moscow Declaration of the Conference of Representatives of the 81 Communist Parties advanced the concept of "national democracy"—a transitional form of government between bourgeois nationalism and "socialism," but without the heavy emphasis on proletarian hegemony which had been so characteristic of Mao Tse-tung's New Democracy. The proposition was that a national democracy would oppose imperialism, reject Western aid in favor of Soviet aid, undertake agrarian reform, and ensure Communists a prominent—though not a leading—role in policy making. These "national democracies" would represent a transitional stage prior to the Communist achievement of power.[57]

Wherever capitalism was still powerful and had control of a huge police and military establishment, of course, the "reactionaries" would present serious resistance. In those countries the transition to socialism would emerge from sharp revolutionary struggle.[58]

The Chinese Communists asserted, on the other hand, that it was unrealistic—and diametrically opposed to Marxism-Leninism—to hold that capitalism could "peacefully grow into socialism."[59] The capitalists would not give in so easily. Undoubtedly the proletariat would have to seize power and smash the old state machine first. Later, *having achieved political power,* it might be entirely feasible to proceed with the socialist transformation "peacefully."[60] Whether this transition in a given country would be carried out through armed uprising or relatively peacefully would be determined by the relation of classes in the local situation.

CURRENTS OF THE CONTROVERSY IN SOUTH ASIA

In late 1958 or early 1959 Sino-Soviet interests in Southeast Asia seem to have reached a level of reciprocally acknowledged conflict. From that point forward the Soviet Union sought control over Communist movements and increased penetration of nationalist parties and governments—both at the expense of the Chinese Communists. Particularly, the Soviet Union attempted to strengthen its relations with India—at a time when conflicts were admittedly increasing along the Sino-Indian frontier.[61] Both Moscow and Peking wanted

[57] "Text of the Statement by Leaders of 81 Communist Parties after Meeting in Moscow," *New York Times,* December 7, 1960, p. 15.

[58] N. S. Khrushchev, *Report of the Central Committee, 20th Congress, op. cit.,* p. 30; also *World Marxist Review, op. cit.,* p. 22.

[59] "Long Live Leninism," *Hung Ch'i,* No. 8 (April 22, 1960), as translated in *Peking Review,* No. 17 (April 26, 1960), p. 16.

[60] *Ibid.,* p. 22.

[61] For an interpretation of these developments by a defector from the Soviet Diplomatic Corps in Burma, see Aleksandr Kaznacheev, *Experiences of a Russian*

to hasten the expulsion of Western economic, political, and military influence from South and Southeast Asia, but neither capital was able to collaborate effectively on a joint policy for the region—or willing to modify its own interests in favor of the aspirations of the other.

Refractions of the distinct Soviet Russian and Chinese Communist approaches had long been evident in India. Indeed, during the first decade and a half after World War II both the Maoist model of revolution in the countryside and revolution by ballot, as frequently advocated by the Russians, were tested there.

In the early days of India's independence Indian Communists established in the Telengana region of Hyderabad and neighboring states a rural border region government close to the Maoist model. The attempt was to organize the peasants into a Red Army and to establish in the countryside the basic institutions of government. Momentarily, the border region regime embraced a territory as large as many European states, but the undertaking was short-lived, since Nehru did not hesitate to use Indian army units against the Communist guerrillas.

Subsequently, during the mid-1950's, the Communists of Kerala State achieved by ballot a plurality which entitled them to power in the local parliament. This victory was also short-lived, however, inasmuch as Communist power was dissolved by act of the central government and new elections called.

With the emergence into public view of the Sino-Soviet controversy, it became evident that the Indian Communist party was divided into what amounted to pro-Peking and pro-Moscow wings.[62] During the late 1950's and early 1960's, moreover, Soviet technical assistance to India came to rival Soviet assistance to China. Even more remarkable was Moscow's scarcely disguised support of India in its military activities along the Chinese border.

Meanwhile, the implications of the Chinese Communist and Soviet Russian models for revolution and development were being examined and debated by Communist leadership not only in Asia but also in Africa and Latin America.

IMPLICATIONS OF NUCLEAR WARFARE AND POSSIBILITIES FOR PEACEFUL COEXISTENCE

The Russians perceived other crucial characteristics in "the new epoch." The development of nuclear weaponry, for example, had

---

Diplomat in Burma (Philadelphia and New York: J. B. Lippincott Company, 1962), especially chap. 11.

[62] See, for example, Sareak Katrak, "India's Communist Party Split," *The China Quarterly*, No. 7 (July-September, 1961), pp. 138–47.

made large-scale warfare unfeasible.[63] In view of the destructive capabilities inherent in modern warheads and missiles, only "madmen and maniacs" could favor another world war.[64] The overwhelming requirement now was for the "peaceful coexistence" of states with different social systems.

As a consequence of Marxism-Leninism's "mighty material force," however, and as a consequence of its growing attraction for people everywhere, there was not—in all the world—a power capable of barring the road to socialism.[65] Under these circumstances large-scale war was not "fatalistically inevitable." Local wars—such as "the aggression of Britain, France and Israel against Egypt"—might break out, but even this possibility was diminishing.[66]

Soviet leaders admitted the probability that "wars of liberation" would have to be fought in certain countries dominated by the "imperialists," but in this sphere, also, various new and relatively peaceful alternatives were becoming available.

Speaking before the CPSU Presidium in April 1960 Otto Kuusinen asserted:

. . . in order to be loyal to Marxism-Leninism today it is not sufficient to repeat the old truth that imperialism is aggressive. The task is to make full use of the new factors operating for peace in order to save humanity from the catastrophe of another war.[67]

The prevention of large-scale war had become, for the Russians, "the question of questions."[68]

The Chinese Communists took a different view: the imperialists would not retire from the struggle voluntarily, and a major war was therefore not an improbability. But only capitalism would be destroyed by a nuclear holocaust, not communism. In his essay entitled *On the Correct Handling of Contradictions Among the People* Mao Tse-tung had recalled in 1957:

The First World War was followed by the birth of the Soviet Union with a population of 200 million. The Second World War was followed by the emergence of the Socialist camp with a combined population of 900 million.

---

[63] N. S. Khrushchev, "On Peaceful Coexistence," *Foreign Affairs*, XXXVIII, No. 1 (October 1959), pp. 1–18.

[64] "Nikita Khrushchev's Speech at the Third Congress of the Rumanian Workers Party," *Soviet News*, No. 4292 (June 22, 1960), p. 240.

[65] N. S. Khrushchev, "For New Victories for the World Communist Movement," *op. cit.*, p. 3.

[66] *Ibid.*, p. 13.

[67] Otto Kuusinen, "Lenin Anniversary Meeting at Moscow Sports Palace," *op. cit.*, p. 64.

[68] Khrushchev's report on the Moscow Conference, *World Marxist Review*, Vol. 4, No. 1 (January 1961), pp. 11–12.

If the imperialists should insist on launching a third world war, it is certain that several hundred million more will turn to socialism. Then there will not be much room left in the world for the imperialists, while it is quite likely that the whole structure of imperialism will utterly collapse.[69]

Not weaponry, nor even nuclear weaponry, but the leadership of the proletariat—that was the crucial factor for the future just as it had been in the past.

The Chinese Communists did not hesitate to recall how it had been Mao Tse-tung—and, by implication, not the Russians—who had overthrown Chiang Kai-shek and driven out the imperialists. "Things turned out exactly as Comrade Mao Tse-tung predicted."[70]

IMPLICATIONS FOR THE FUTURE

How did the Sino-Soviet differences seem to balance out? Were the conflictual elements in the relationship sufficient to disrupt their common bonds, or were the interests of the two leaderships—as Communists—stronger than their divergencies as Russians and Chinese?

With the whole world moving rapidly into a new era—an era of exploding populations, automation, and possibilities for cybernetic control of industries and perhaps even populations; of space exploration; and of undreamed potentials for harnessing nuclear energy to shape the world or destroy it—prediction was hazardous. It seemed reasonable to suppose, however, that in the long run these basic factors —population, automation, space, and nuclear energy—would do more to shape the course of Sino-Soviet relations, and even, indeed, the whole course of human events, than many of the day-to-day problems that plagued Soviet and Chinese Communist leaderships, as well as statesmen elsewhere.

A few moments of sober thought might have raised grave doubts, for example, whether the People's Republic of China had yet focused adequate attention on the absolutely fundamental problem of population, or whether the Soviet Union—or any other nation, in the long run—could evade the crucial challenge of the race between technology and production on the one hand and population on the other, not only in China but also around the globe. To be fit for human habitation a large part of the earth's surface demanded engineering and reorganization on a massive scale—the restoration of worn-out soil, the

[69] Mao Tse-tung, *On the Correct Handling of Contradictions Among the People* (New York: New Century Publishers, 1957), p. 29.

[70] "A Basic Summing Up of Experience Gained in the Victory of the Chinese People's Revolution," *Hung Ch'i* [Red Flag], November 2, 1960, as translated in *Survey of China Mainland Press,* No. 2375 (November 9, 1960), p. 9.

transportation of water, the building of roads, the reorganization of social systems, the education of the people, and so forth. A major question was who should do it—the Communists or some other dictatorship or tyranny, or the people themselves in an atmosphere of relative freedom—and by what means. It was inescapable, however, that in many areas the slightest improvement in production or housing or health facilities was followed soon by a rise in population. Entirely too little systematic thought was being given to the problem of how to keep populations in balance with productivity—or how people were to be fed and governed, with some preservation of individuality, in the huge belt cities which almost certainly would erupt (if mankind avoided self-destruction) over wide stretches of the earth.

Similarly, the gnawing question might have been raised whether Peking or Moscow or Washington or any other capital had yet paid sufficiently sober and responsible attention to the meaning of a world-wide competition in nuclear weaponry, or the speed with which a "brush-fire" conflict might reach missile proportions, or the implication of new methods of warfare possibly spreading into space.

Here and there some cynic might have speculated whether the development of nuclear weaponry and other means of wholesale annihilation were not part of a huge Darwinian process of selection, regulation, and limitation—evolution's relentless control over a species that could split the atom but had not mastered the secret of how to restrain its powers of production, or how to settle its conflicts peacefully.

How much time was left for Man to decide his fate?

The future was indeed in grave doubt. Meanwhile the Soviet Russians and the Communist Chinese were plunging forward like a pair of ill-mated bullocks, horns locked—yanking, hauling, heaving, and crowding their way along a tight path through the swamps of destiny.

A SELECTED BIBLIOGRAPHY

COMINTERN AND SOVIET SOURCES

"Appeal of the Provisional Soviet Government of China and the Revolutionary War Council of the Chinese Red Workers' and Peasants' Army to the Chinese People," *International Press Correspondence*, January 26, 1933.

"The CC of the CP of China on the Coup de Main in Fukien," *International Press Correspondence*, February 23, 1934.

CHEN KWANG. "The Forthcoming First Chinese Soviet Congress," *International Press Correspondence*, July 12, 1930.

CHEN PAN-TSU (Ch'en T'an-ch'iu). "Reminiscences of the First Congress of the Communist Party of China," *Communist International*, October 1936.

CH'EN SHAO-YÜ (Wang Ming). "The Only Road for the Salvation of the Chinese People," *Bolshevik*, April 15, 1937.

"Declaration of the Chinese Communist Party and the Present Political Situation in China," *Novyi Vostok*, No. 2, 1922. This declaration was translated from Chinese into Russian by A. E. Khodorov. From the Russian version Olga Gankin has made an English translation, which is on file in the Hoover Institute and Library. The Chinese text is not available.

EHRENBURG, G. B. *Sovetskii Kitai.* Moscow, 1933.

GRIGORIEV, B. "China in Its Eighth Year of the War," *Bolshevik*, Nos. 17–18, 1944.

IVIN, A. "The Partisan Movement in China," *International Press Correspondence*, May 22, 1930.

KARA-MURZA, G. (comp.), and MIF, P. (ed.). *Strategiia i taktika Kominterna v natsional'no-kolonial'noi revoliutsii na primere Kitaia.* Moscow, 1934.

KUO. "On the First Congress of the Chinese Soviets," *International Press Correspondence*, July 12, 1930.

LENIN, V. I. *Imperialism, the Highest Stage of Capitalism.* Moscow: Foreign Lang. Publ. House, 1947. First published 1916.

——. *"Left-Wing" Communism, an Infantile Disorder.* Moscow: Foreign Lang. Publ. House, 1947. First published 1920.

LI. "Der 1 Kongress der Vertreter der Sowjetgebiete Chinas," *Die Kommunistische Internationale*, April 9, 1930.

MAGYAR, L. "Japanese Imperialism in Manchuria," *International Press Correspondence*, October 1, 1931.

MAO TSE-TUNG. "On the Dictatorship of the People's Democracy," *Pravda*, July 6, 1949.

MIF, P. *Heroic China.* New York: Workers' Library Publishers, 1937.

MOLOTOV, V. M. "The Carrying Out of the Five Year Plan," Report

Delivered at the II Session of the Central Executive Committee of the Soviet Union, *International Press Correspondence*, January 7, 1932.

Pervyi Kongress Kominterna, Mart, 1919. Moscow, 1933.

Pervyi S'ezd Narodov Vostoka, Baku. Stenograficheskie otchety. Petrograd, 1920. A manuscript translation by Xenia Eudin is available in the Hoover Institute and Library, Stanford, California.

Protokoll, 10 Plenum des Exekutivkomitees der Kommunistischen Internationale, 3 Juli 1929 bis 19 Juli 1929. Hamburg-Berlin: Verlag Carl Hoym, n.d.

Räte China. Dokumente der Chinesischen Revolution. Moscow-Leningrad, 1934.

Report of the Fifteenth Congress of the Communist Party of the Soviet Union. London, 1928.

"Report of Mao Tse-tung to the Second Congress of Chinese Soviets," *International Press Correspondence*, June 29, 1934.

"Report to the XVI Party Congress, July 5, 1930," *International Press Correspondence*, July 17, 1930.

"Resolution of the Chinese Question," *International Press Correspondence*, June 16, 1927.

"Resolution of the ECCI on the Present Situation of the Chinese Revolution," *International Press Correspondence*, July 28, 1927.

"Resolution on the International Situation," Joint Plenum of the Central Committee and the Central Control Commission, *International Press Correspondence*, August 18, 1927.

ROGOV, V. "On the Eve of the Third Anniversary of the War in China," *Mirovoe Khoziaistvo i Mirovaia Politika*, No. 4/5 (Moscow, 1940).

The Second Congress of the Communist International, Proceedings of the Petrograd Session of July 17th and of the Moscow Sessions of July 19th–August 7th, 1920. Moscow, 1920.

Soviety v Kitae (Soviets in China), translated from German. Moscow: Partiinoe Izdatel'stvo, 1934.

STALIN, J. "The Political Report of the Central Committee of the XVI Party Congress of the CPSU, June 27, 1930," *International Press Correspondence*.

———. *Problems of Leninism.* Moscow: Foreign Languages Publishing house, 1940. First published 19—.

TANG SHIN SHE. "The Canton Government and the Revolutionary Movement in China," *International Press Correspondence*, April 8, 1926.

"Theses of Comrade Stalin for Propagandists, Approved by the CC of the CPSU," *International Press Correspondence*, April 28, 1927.

VIII S'ezd, Rossüskoi Kommunisticheskoi Partii (Bolshevikov). Moscow, 1919.

VKP (b), 18th Congress, Moscow, 1939. *Land of Socialism Today and Tomorrow: Reports and Speeches.* Moscow: Foreign Languages Publishing House, 1939.

VOITINSKY, G. "The Situation in China and the Plans of the Imperialists," *International Press Correspondence*, May 6, 1926.

"The War in the Far East and the Tasks of the Communists in the Struggle Against the Imperialist War and the Military Intervention Against the USSR," *International Press Correspondence*, October 20, 1932.

XVI S'ezd Vsesoiuznoi Kommunisticheskoi Partii (b); Stenograficheskii Otchet. Moscow, 1931.

CHINESE COMMUNIST SOURCES

"An Examination of the Practical Struggle for Consolidation and Strengthening of the Proletarian Leadership," *Tou-cheng*, February 4, 1933.

CH'EN PO-TA. "The October Socialist Revolution and the Chinese Revolution," transmitted in English Morse to North America by the New China News Agency, November 7, 1949.

CH-EN LU-HSIU. *Kao ch'üan-tang tung-chih shu* (Letter to the Comrades). December 10, 1929. Shanghai, 1929.

CH'IEN TUAN-SHENG, "How the People's Government Works," *China Reconstructs*, No. 4 (Peking, July/August 1952).

China (People's Republic of China, 1949) Laws, Statutes, etc. Peking: Foreign Languages Press, 1949.

Chung-kuo hsien-tai ko-ming yün-tung shih (A History of the Contemporary Revolutionary Movement in China). 4th ed., n.p., 1938.

"Conditions for Preparing the Victory of a Regime in One or Several Provinces," *Hung Ch'i*, April 5, 1930.

"Declaration of the People's Political Consultative Conference," *China Digest*, Supplement VII, Nos. 1, 2 (Hong Kong, 1949).

"The First Letter of Ch'en Tu-hsiu Concerning the Problem of the Chinese Eastern Railway," *China's Revolution and Opportunism* (Chung-kuo ko-ming yü chi-hui chu-i). Min-chih Book Store, 1929.

"For the Bolshevik Offensive Line of the Party," *Tou-cheng* (Struggle), February 23, 1933.

Jen-min shou-tse, 1950 (People's Handbook, 1950). Shanghai, 1950.

JEN PI-SHIH. "Agrarian Reform in Communist China," *New China News Agency*, transmitted to the United States in English Morse, April 13, 14, 15, 16, 17, and 19, 1948.

"A Letter to All Party Members Concerning the Development of Party Organization," *Hung Ch'i*, March 26, 1930.

"A Letter to the Central Committee of the Chinese Communist Party by the ECCI, Received November 16, 1930," *Shih-hua*, December 14, 1930.

"A Letter to the Chinese Communist Party from the Executive Committee of the Comintern, February 8, 1929," *Erh chung-ch'uan-hui chüeh-i an* (Resolutions of the Second Central Congress of the Chinese Communist Party), June 1929.

Li Ang. *Hung-se wu-t'ai* (The Red Stage). Chungking, 1942.

Li Li-san. "Ready to Establish the Revolutionary Regime," *Hung Ch'i,* March 26, 1930.

"Li Li-san's Conclusions," *Pu-erh-sai-wei-k'o,* May 10, 1931.

Mao Tse-tung. *Concerning Practise.* Bombay: New Age Printing House, 1951.

———. *On Coalition Government, Report to the Seventh Congress of the Chinese Communist Party.* Yenan, 1945.

"The Problem of the Proletarian Hegemony," *Hung Ch'i,* May 24, 1930.

"The Report of the Far Eastern Commission of the Comintern in Regard to the Third Plenum of the Chinese Party and the Errors of Comrade Li Li-san," *Pu-erh-sai-wei-k'o,* May 10, 1931.

"Resolutions for Acceptance of the Directive Letter of the Comintern Dated October 26, 1929 Concerning the Nationalist Reorganization-alists and the Task of the Chinese Communist Party, Passed by the Central Politburo on January 11, 1930," *Hung Ch'i,* February 1930.

"A Summary of the Declaration of the All-China Conference of Delegates from the Soviet Areas," *Hung Ch'i,* June 21, 1930.

"Ti erh-tz'ü ch'üan-kuo tai-piao ta-hui hsüan-yen" (Manifesto of the Second Congress), quoted in Chu Hsin-fan, *Chung-kuo ko-ming yü Chung-kuo she-hui ko chieh-chi* (The Chinese Revolution and China's Social Classes). Shanghai, 1930.

BOOKS, PAMPHLETS, ARTICLES, AND SPEECHES

The Autobiography of Mao Tse-tung, as told to Edgar Snow. Hong Kong: Truth Book Company, 1949.

Barnett, A. Doak. *Communist China and Asia.* New York: Harper and Brothers, 1960.

———. *Communist Economic Strategy: The Rise of Mainland China.* Washington: National Planning Association, 1959.

Boukharine, N. *Les Problèmes de la Révolution Chinoise.* Paris: Bureau d'éditions de diffusion et de publicité, 192–?.

Brandt, Conrad. *Stalin's Failure in China, 1924–1927.* Cambridge: Harvard University Press, 1958.

Brandt, Conrad, Schwartz, Benjamin, and Fairbank, John K. *A Documentary History of Chinese Communism.* Cambridge: Harvard University Press, 1952.

Brière, O. "Twenty-five Years of the Chinese Communist Party, 1921–1946," Aurora University *Bulletin,* VII, No. 3 (1946).

Burnham, James. *First Act in China.* New York: Viking, 1938.

Chang Kuo-t'ao. "Mao—A New Portrait by an Old Colleague," *New York Times Magazine,* August 2, 1953.

Chow, Tse-tsung. *The May Fourth Movement.* Cambridge: Harvard University Press, 1960.

The Communist Manifesto of Karl Marx and Friedrich Engels. International Publishers Edition, with an introduction and explanatory notes by D. Ryazanoff. New York, 1930.

COMPTON, BOYD. *Mao's China: Party Reform Documents, 1942–44.* Seattle: University of Washington Press, 1952.

CONSIDINE, LEONARD. "Communist China," *The Manchester Guardian,* Vol. 63, No. 15, through Vol. 64, No. 5 (1950–51).

DILLON, E. J. *The Eclipse of Russia.* New York: George H. Doran Company, 1918.

ENGELS, FRIEDRICH. *Herr Eugen Duhring's Revolution in Science (Anti-Duhring).* New York: International Publishers, 1935.

FAIRBANK, JOHN K., and TENG, S. Y. "On the Ch'ing Tributary System," *Harvard Journal of Asiatic Studies,* June 1941.

FISCHER, LOUIS. *The Soviets in World Affairs.* London: J. Cape, 1930,

GLUCKSTEIN, YGAEL. *Mao's China: Economic and Political Survey.* Boston: Beacon Press, 1957.

HATANO, KEN'ICHI. "History of the Chinese Communist Party," *Ajia Mondai Koza.* Tokyo, 1939. Vol. II, pp. 23–46.

HERSHEY, AMOS S., and HERSHEY, SUSANNE W. *Modern Japan.* Indianapolis: The Bobbs-Merrill Co., 1919.

HSIAO, TSO-LIANG. *Power Relations within the Chinese Communist Movement, 1930–1934.* Seattle: University of Washington Press, 1961.

HSÜ, LEONARD SHIH-LIEN. *Sun Yet-sen, His Political and Social Ideals.* Los Angeles: University of Southern California Press, 1933.

HUDSON, G. F., LOWENTHAL, RICHARD, and MACFARQUHAR, RODERICK. *The Sino-Soviet Dispute.* New York: Frederick A. Praeger, 1961.

ISAACS, HAROLD R. *The Tragedy of the Chinese Revolution.* 2d Rev. ed. Stanford: Stanford University Press, 1961. (First edition 1938.)

KIANG, WAN-HAN. *The Chinese Student Movement.* New York: King's Crown Press, 1948.

LIFTON, ROBERT JAY. *Thought Reform and the Psychology of Totalism.* New York: W. W. Norton, 1961.

LOBANOV-ROSTOVSKY, PRINCE A. *Russia and Asia.* New York: The Macmillan Company, 1933.

LONDON, KURT (ed.). *Unity and Contradiction.* New York: Frederick A. Praeger, 1962.

MACFARQUHAR, RODERICK. *The Hundred Flowers Campaign and the Chinese Intellectuals.* New York: Frederick A. Praeger, 1960.

McLANE, CHARLES. *Soviet Policy and the Chinese Communists, 1931–1946.* New York: Columbia University Press, 1958.

MACNAIR, H. F. *China in Revolution.* Chicago: University of Chicago Press, 1931.

"Manifesto on the Seizure of Chiang Kai-shek (1936)," in Lawrence K. Rosinger, *China's Wartime Politics, 1937–1944.* Princeton: Princeton University Press, 1944.

MARX, KARL. *Capital,* translated from the third German edition by Samuel Moore and Edward Aveling. London: Swan Sonnenschein, 1889.

MITAREVSKY, N. *World Wide Soviet Plots.* Tientsin: The Tientsin Press, n.d.

MORAES, FRANK. *Report on Mao's China.* New York: The Macmillan Company, 1953.

MURPHY, J. T. *New Horizons.* London: John Lane, 1941.

NEUBERG, A. (Heinz Neumann). *L'Insurrection Armée.* Paris: Bureau d'Éditions, 1931.

NORTH, ROBERT C. "M. N. Roy and the Fifth Congress of the Chinese Communist Party," *The China Quarterly,* No. 8, October–December, 1961.

NORTH, ROBERT C., and EUDIN, XENIA J. *M. N. Roy's Mission to China: The Communist-Kuomintang Split of 1927.* Berkeley: University of California Press, 1962.

ROY, M. N. *Revolution and Counter-Revolution in China.* Calcutta: Renaissance Publishers, 1946.

SCHWARTZ, BENJAMIN. "Biographical Sketch, Ch'en Tu-hsiu, Pre-Communist Phase," *Papers on China,* Vol. 11. Harvard University, 1948.

———. *Chinese Communism and the Rise of Mao.* Cambridge: Harvard University Press, 1951.

SOKOLSKY, GEORGE E. "The Kuomintang," *The China Year Book,* 1928.

———. *Tinder Box of Asia.* New York: Doubleday, Doran & Company, Inc., 1933.

STALIN, J. "The Prospects of the Revolution in China," *International Press Correspondence,* December 23, 1926.

TANG, PETER S. H. *Communist China Today.* Vols. I and II. New York: Frederick A. Praeger, 1957 and 1958.

TROTSKY, LEON. *Problems of the Chinese Revolution.* With appendices by Zinoviev, Vuyovitch, Nassunov, and others. New York: Pioneer Publishers, 1932.

———. *The Stalin School of Falsification.* New York: Pioneer Publishers, 1937.

WALKER, RICHARD L. *China Under Communism, The First Five Years.* New Haven: Yale University Press, 1955.

———. "The Working Class in Communist China," *Problems of China* (1953), Vols. III–IV.

WHITE, JOHN ALBERT. *The Siberian Intervention.* Princeton: Princeton University Press, 1950.

WHITING, ALLEN S. *Soviet Policies in China, 1917–1924.* New York: Columbia University Press, 1954.

WILBUR, C. MARTIN (ed.). *The Communist Movement in China,* An Essay Written in 1924 by Ch'en Kung-po, Reproduced for Private Distribution by the East Asian Institute of Columbia University, 1960.

WILBUR, C. MARTIN, and HOW, JULIE LIEN-YING. *Documents on Com-*

munism, Nationalism, and Soviet Advisers in China, 1918–1927. New York: Columbia University Press, 1956.

WILLOUGHBY, W. W., and FENWICK, C. G. *Types of Restricted Sovereignty and of Colonial Autonomy.* Washington: Government Printing Office, 1919.

WOO, T. C. *The Kuomintang and the Future of the Chinese Revolution.* London: G. Allen & Unwin, 1928.

WU, YUAN-LI. *An Economic Survey of Communist China.* New York: Bookman Associates, 1956.

YARMOLINSKY, ABRAHAM (trans. and ed.). *The Memoirs of Count Witte.* New York: Doubleday Page & Co., 1921.

ZAGORIA, DONALD S. *The Sino-Soviet Conflict, 1956–1961.* Princeton: Princeton University Press, 1962.

DOCUMENTARY COLLECTIONS AND OTHER SOURCES

Accounts and Papers, State Papers, CXXX (1902), Dispatch to His Majesty's Minister at Tokyo, January 30, 1902.

BOCK, BENJAMIN. "The Origins of the Inter-Allied Intervention in Eastern Asia 1918–1920." An unpublished doctoral dissertation in the Hoover Library, Stanford University, 1940.

BRANDT, CONRAD, SCHWARTZ, BENJAMIN, AND FAIRBANK, JOHN K. *A Documentary History of Chinese Communism.* Cambridge: Harvard University Press, 1952.

"A Brief History of the Chinese Communist Party," translated by the East Asia Institute, Columbia University, from *Su-lien yin-mou wen-cheng hui-pien* (Collections of Documents on the Soviet Conspiracy). Peking, 1928.

BUNYAN, JAMES, AND FISHER, H. H. *The Bolshevik Revolution, 1917–1918.* Hoover Library Publications, No. 3. Stanford: Stanford University Press, 1934.

CARPENTER, FRANCIS ROSS. "The Peasant Policy of the Chinese Communists with Special Reference to the Post-World War II Era." Master's thesis, Stanford University, 1950.

China Handbook, 1937–1943.

China Handbook, 1937–1945. New York, 1947.

The China Year Book, 1921–1922.

The China Year Book, 1923–1924.

The China Year Book, 1924–1925.

The China Year Book, 1928.

The China Year Book, 1931.

"The Chinese Communist Movement." Washington, D.C.: Military Intelligence Division, War Department, 1945, as reproduced in the United States Senate, Committee on the Judiciary, *Institute of Pacific Relations, Hearings Before the Sub-committee to Investigate the Administration of the Internal Security Act and Other Security Laws,*

Part 7A, Appendix II. Washington: United States Government Printing Office, 1952.

CHINESE MINISTRY OF INFORMATION. *Collected Wartime Messages of Generalissimo Chiang Kai-shek, 1937–1945.* New York: The John Day Company, 1946.

"The Chinese Renaissance and Its Relation to Soviet Policy in the Far East," from J. C. Huston, Consul, American Consulate General, Tientsin, China, File 800, October 8, 1923.

COMPTON, BOYD. *Mao's China: Party Reform Documents, 1942–44.* Seattle: University of Washington Press, 1952.

"Conference of Hsien Magistrates in North China, September, 1951," *Current Background,* No. 148, January 4, 1952.

DEGRAS, JANE (ed.). *Soviet Documents on Foreign Policy, 1917–1924.* Issued under the auspices of the Royal Institute of International Affairs. London: Oxford University Press, 1951.

Documents Illustrating the Hostile Activities of the Soviet Government and the Third International Against Great Britain. Great Britain Foreign Office. London, 1927.

GOOCH, G. P., AND TEMPERLY, H. W. V. (eds.). *British Documents on the Origins of the World War, 1898–1914.* London: Foreign Office, 1926–38.

HATANO, KEN'ICHI. *Saikin Shina Nenkan* (New China Year Book). Tokyo, 1935.

HUSTON, JAY CALVIN. "Sun Yat-sen, the Kuomintang and the Chinese-Russian Political Economic Alliance," unpublished manuscript now on file in the Hoover Institute and Library; prepared by an American consular official in China at the time.

JAPAN, MINISTRY OF FOREIGN AFFAIRS, Intelligence Division (Joho-bu). *Shina Kyôsantô Shi* (A History of the Chinese Communist Party). Ken'ichi Hatano, ed. Tokyo (?), 1932.

LA FARGUE, THOMAS EDWARD. *China and the World War.* Hoover War Library Publications No. 12. Stanford: Stanford University Press, 1937.

MACMURRAY, J. V. A. (ed.). *Treaties and Agreements With and Concerning China.* New York: Oxford University Press, 1921.

MAO TSE-TUNG. *China's New Democracy.* Sharaf Athar Ali translation as reproduced in U.S. Congress, House Committee on Foreign Affairs, *The Strategy and Tactics of World Communism,* Supplement III, "Communism in China." Washington: Government Printing Office, 1949.

Memorandum of the Special Delegation of the Far Eastern Republic. Released by the Special Delegation of the Far Eastern Republic to the United States. Washington, 1921.

OTSUKA, REIZO. "Red Influence in China," *Institute of Pacific Relations,* Japanese Council Papers, No. 17. Tokyo: Nihon Kikusai Kyokai, 1936.

Papers Relating to the Foreign Policy of the United States, Russia (1918). Publication of the Department of State. Washington.

PRICE, ERNEST BATSON. *The Russo-Japanese Treaties of 1907–1916 Concerning Manchuria and Mongolia*. Baltimore: The Johns Hopkins Press, 1933.

"Records of the 18th Ordinary Session of the Assembly," *League of Nations Official Journal*, Special Supplement No. 169. Geneva, 1937.

"Regulations Governing the Organization of People's Tribunals," passed by the Government Administrative Council July 14, 1950, and ratified by Mao Tse-tung as chairman of the Central People's government on July 19, and promulgated on July 20, 1950, *Current Background*, No. 150 (January 10, 1952).

Report of the International Commission of Judges Appointed to Inquire into the Causes of the Disturbance at Shanghai May 30, 1925. Shanghai, 1925.

ROCKHILL, WILLIAM WOODVILLE. *Treaties or Conventions with or Concerning China and Korea, 1894–1904*. Washington: Government Printing Office, 1904.

A Short Outline History of the Far Eastern Republic. The Special Delegation of the Far Eastern Republic to the United States was responsible for publication. Washington, 1922.

SHU-CHIN TSUI, "The Influence of the Canton-Moscow, Entente," *The Chinese Social and Political Science Review*, quarterly publication of the Chinese Social and Political Science Association, XVIII (Peiping, 1934).

"Sino-Japanese Conflict," *League of Nations Official Journal*, Special Supplement, No. 169. Geneva, 1937.

TANG CHUNG-HSA (Teng Chung-hsia). "The Communist Labourers' Movement in China," a document seized by authorities in a raid on the Soviet consulate in Canton, December 1927, and translated for the *South China Morning Post*, February 6, 1928.

T'IEN LIU. "The Development of a Collective Farm," *Jen Min Jih Pao*, March 24–25, as translated and reproduced in *Current Background*, No. 176, May 2, 1952.

To the Washington Conference on the Limitation of Armaments. Released by the Special Delegation of the Far Eastern Republic. Washington, 1922.

The Treaties of Peace, 1919–1923. New York: Carnegie Endowment for International Peace, 1924.

United States Relations with China (White Paper), Department of State Publication 3573, Far Eastern Series 30, released August 1949.

VARNECK, ELENA, AND FISHER, H. H. (eds.). *The Testimony of Kolchak and Other Siberian Materials*. Stanford: Stanford University Press, 1935.

"Washington Conference on the Limitation of Armaments," *International Conciliation*, No. 172.

SPECIAL COLLECTIONS

"Draft Survey of Materials Relating to Communism in China, 1927–34."
Collected by Harold R. Isaacs. Hoover Institute and Library, Stanford University.

The Jay Calvin Huston Collection. Hoover Institute and Library, Stanford University.

INDEX

Africa, 8, 284
Agrarian program of CCP, 102–3, 116, 121, 127, 153–56, 171–72, 179–80; put into effect, 243–46, 248, 252, 253–55. *See also* Peasantry
Agrarian Reform Law, 245–46
Anfu clique, 44, 47, 54, 68
Anglo-Japanese Alliance (1902), 38
Army, Chinese (Kuomintang), 81, 88, 89–90, 92, 104–5; "Ironsides" (2d Army Group), 113, 119; in W.W. II, 189, 191, 204–5, 206; and Red Army, 191, 223f, 235–40 *passim*. *See also* Red Army
Asia, 10, 56, 60–61, 69, 201; former Chinese empire in, 31–32, 77, 260n; China's role in, 258–60
Asiaticus (Hans Mueller), 188
August 7 Conference, 110–11, 115f, 128, 172
Autumn Crop Uprising (1927), 112f, 115–16, 128, 172

Baku Conference (1920), 42
Bandung Conference (1954), 262, 273
Barnett, Doak, 272
Barr, Major General David, 239–40
Bolshevism, *see* Tactics and strategy; Theory
Border regions, govt. of, 126, 181, 189ff, 191–93, 255
Borodin, Mikhail, 66, 79, 82, 91, 100–101; activities in China, 72–76, 85–89 *passim*, 105–8 *passim*
Boxer rebellion, 66; indemnities of, 45f, 48f, 51
Brest-Litovsk, Treaty of, 15, 23
Bubnov, A. S., 90
Bukharin, N. I., 91, 97, 104–5, 128, 258; a Right deviationist, 121, 136, 156, 194; mentioned, 90, 120
Bulganin, N. A., 271
Bulgaria, 2, 17
Burma, 32, 260n, 261–62
Byrnes, James, 221, 227

Cadres, training of, 197–98, 251–53
Cairo Declaration (1943), 207, 214, 229
Canton province: Sun Yat-sen's govt., 55, 68, 70, 84–85; Borodin in, 72–76, 85–89 *passim*; insurrections in, 112f, 114–15, 117–20

CCP, *see* Communist party, Chinese
Chanchung (South Manchurian) Railway, 37f, 147, 215, 218f, 266–69 *passim*
Chang Fa-k'uei, 114, 118–20, 131
Chang Hsüeh-liang, 123, 131, 162, 177
Chang Hsün, 68
Chang Kuo-t'ao: career of, 55, 59, 111, 128, 157, 167, 180; on events of 1931–34, 158–59, 164, 166; the Long March, 174–75; on united front policy, 176f, 180; mentioned, 56n, 64, 143, 161, 169f, 173, 199
Chang T'ei-lei, 114f
Chang Tso-lin, 47ff, 52, 68, 89; and coup of 1925, 94, 95–96; and Chinese Eastern Ry., 122
Chang Tsung-ch'ang, 94f
Chang Wen-t'ien (Lo Fu), 140, 164, 281
Changsha, 102f, 126, 162f, 169; Red Army attack on, 138, 139–40
Ch'en, Eugen, 107f, 114, 161
Ch'en Ch'iung-ming, 55, 68, 70
Ch'en Kuo-fu, 205
Ch'en Li-fu, 205
Ch'en Po-ta, 12
Ch'en Shao-yü, *see* Wang Ming
Ch'en T'an-chiu, 56n, 57
Ch'en Tu-hsiu: career of, 53–60 *passim*, 110–11, 124; and the Kuomintang, 64, 77; and Mao, 169, 172; mentioned, 69, 91, 96, 140, 194
Ch'en Yün, 247, 281
Ch'eng Ch'ien, 97
Cheng Feng movement, the, 181, 196–200
Chennault, Claire Lee, 237n
Chiang Kai-shek, 160f, 175, 185–86, 202, 240; rise to power, 72, 76, 86–90, 92–97, 125, 138, 181; at war with CCP, 151–52, 163–64, 223–26, 235–40 *passim*; kidnaping of, 177; leadership of Kuomintang, 181, 202–3, 235; and U.S. officials, 207–8, 209–10, 212, 215, 221; U.S. aid to, 207, 223, 226, 237, 273; mentioned, 2, 5, 71, 81, 91, 98, 100, 108, 138, 147, 191, 218. *See also* Nationalist China
Chicherin, G. V., 45, 47, 52, 69
Chieh Hua, 140
Ch'in Pang-hsien, *see* Po Ku
China, 6, 16, 25, 31–34; Comintern agents